Forgotten Horrors 4
Dreams That Money Can Buy

For Emily —
Always great to
meet another B-horror
Fan —

[signature]

14 Nov. '09

Forgotten Horrors 4

Dreams That Money Can Buy

by Michael H. Price
and
John Wooley
Authors of a Great Many Things

[signature]

Midnight Marquee Press, Inc.
Baltimore, Maryland, USA

Also by Price & Wooley
The Big Book of Biker Flicks
Forgotten Horrors 3: Dr. Turner's House of Horrors
Southern-Fried Homicide (et Seq.)

Also by Michael H. Price
Daynce of the Peckerwoods: The Badlands of Texas Music
Mantan the Funnyman: The Life & Times of Mantan Moreland
The Ancient Southwest & Other Dispatches from a Cruel Frontier
Spawn of Skull Island: The Making of King Kong (Text and Audiobook Editions)
The Forgotten Horrors Collection (1929–Onward)
Human Monsters: The Definitive Edition
The Cinema of Adventure, Romance & Terror
Carnival of Souls
R. Crumb—The Musical!
Michael H. Price's Hollywood Horrors

Also by John Wooley
Ghost Band
From the Blue Devils to Red Dirt: The Colors of Oklahoma Music
Awash in the Blood
Dark Within
Tor Johnson: Hollywood Star
Plan 9 from Outer Space: The Graphic Novel (et Seq.)
The Twilight Avenger
The Miracle Squad
Hot Schlock Horror!

Cover and Interior Design by: Susan Svehla
Copyright © 2007 by Michael H. Price & John Wooley

ISBN 9781887664738
Library of Congress Catalog Card Number 2007921886
Manufactured in the United States of America
Printed by Odyssey Press
First Printing by Midnight Marquee Press, Inc., February 2007

Dedication

To
the Memory of Kate Worley,
and to Our Friend Jim Vance,
Who Carries On

Contents

1946-1947

1948

Prologue

File this one under "Say *what?*"

There is absolutely no social criticism, of even the most implicit kind, in science-fiction films. No criticism, for example, of the conditions of our society which create the impersonality and dehumanization which science-fiction fantasies displace onto the influence of an alien *It.*—Susan Söntag

Give this one an "Amen!"

I should know from experience—knowing myself, especially—that the most effectively vicious movies tend to come from ordinarily decent, well-socialized people struggling to understand the violence that helps to define this state of being we call the Human Condition... Star power and big-studio pedigree and fat budgets be damned—the real factor that announces a picture's significance is its attitude."—Martin Scorsese to M.H. Price, 1996

And for your further tormented consideration:

If everybody doesn't want it, nobody gets it.—Roger Price

One Author's Preface
by Michael H. Price

I was lurking at the threshold of birth in 1947 when there occurred a strange, uhm, occurrence that sent my father rushing off to a rural outpost not far from the city where our family was beginning to take shape. Government business, it was. And although John Andrew Price was not exactly in the business of government, still he had spent the recent outcropping of war as an industrial rationing warden.

Postwar, my father had become senior purchasing agent with a Texas-based oilfield, construction and ranching supplier whose branch offices reached as far westward as the federally hypersensitive town of Roswell, New Mexico. Dad knew metals, and the powers of military-industrial complexity knew to summon him when the occasion suited.

Whatever it was that had come to ground near Roswell, the object left traces. Any flesh-and-cartilage casualties had been dispatched to Parts Unknown, or at least Parts Off Limits. But some of the more casually retrieved fragments of a—a *what*? a vessel?—wound up at the Roswell plant of Clowe & Cowan, Inc. My father examined these in the hope of identifying some source of manufacture. He concluded only that they were akin to no metal he had encountered. And he pocketed a few shards to bring home, whether for further comparative analysis or merely as a memento. Dad would recall in later years that the substance embodied certain contradictory traits—such as rigidity seeming to co-exist with malleability—along with a symbolically engraved surface and a luminous aspect in dimmed lighting.

Dad would sketch out memorized approximations of such symbols—runic-looking, with recurring triangular and swastika-like shapes—when bored or impatient, when trapped on the telephone with a tedious caller or waiting for service in a restaurant. When asked for a real-stuff demonstration, he would insist, "Oh, I don't know what might ever've become of all that." And at length, he would cease talking about it altogether, clamming up or changing the subject whenever the matter might surface.

Perhaps my father felt leery of the more threatening factions of an Establishment of which his company was patently a part—and military threats are known to have been lodged against others who had exhibited too keen an interest in Roswell. And perhaps Dad feared public ridicule, which is the military-scientific system's more common method of marginalizing people who veer close to a guarded truth. That tactic certainly proved workable during the 1960s for Dr. Edward U. Condon, whose Air Force–sponsored (and purportedly empirical) investigation into the U.F.O. question proved early on to be an Emperor's New Clothes mission of debunking and denial: Any colleague who dared to challenge Condon's ain't-no-saucers stance risked branding as a nutcase.

And goodness knows, the saucer craze has generated more than its share of identifiably real kooks, acting on the one hand as free-agent crackpots and shilling on the other for the sake of orchestrated disinformation. It is probably not so much that any Truth Is Out There—Chris Carter notwithstanding—as it is that there are people at large and

The *Roswell Daily Record*, July 8, 1947

in charge who fear that some higher truth, once disclosed, could only inform them that Everything They Know Is Wrong.

The point of this household memoir is but to wonder (and *wonder*, whether verb or noun, is the operative term) whether I might have been exposed *in utero* to whatever strange radiance that controversial crash site might have yielded. According to Dad, the substance was in our house for some length of time. And then suddenly it was *not* in our house. And then my father, who loved a mystery in theory or in fiction but had no use for actual intrigues and treacheries, at length placed a favorite topic out-of-bounds—even to himself.

I often have pondered whether Dad might have disposed of those scraps in our town's Thompson Park Lake, which during the 1950s began coughing up the damnedest variety of deformed fish and pallid mutant-looking amphibians I ever have encountered—multicolored creatures, some as long as your arm or mine, with thin skins and thinner blood and the occasional third eye, like impossible descendants of a certain three-eyed fossil that had long been a prized display at the nearby Panhandle-Plains Historical Museum. For all the rest of his life, Dad would read exhaustively about U.F.O.-ology and the like (but would never discuss such issues), and he developed a taste for the more intelligent movies about visits from space, favoring *The Day the Earth Stood Still* and *Invaders from Mars* and Great Britain's *Quatermass* pictures—despite a professed dislike for weird fiction as a class. (He also enjoyed Alfred Hitchcock's *The Man Who Knew Too Much*, in either version, whether for its dramatic content or merely on account of its title.)

But about that radiant glow my Dad had described: Suspicion of any effects is beside the point. The belief, if not the outright knowledge, of the stuff's *having been there* is unnerving enough. Probably impulsive speculation, but all the same—my first consciously articulated thought, uttered with a vocabulary and a sense of place that a child shouldn't have developed before the age of two, was this: "What in hell am I doing here?" Precisely the words.

An onslaught of Romper Room Existentialism, maybe—or what else? No telling. My immediate household was a nurturing place, sure enough, and my parents were keen on cultural interests and education beyond any routine schoolhouse curriculum, so I really had no cause to consider what, in or out of hell, I might be doing there. My mother, Thelma Adeline Price, saw to it that I was reading at a grammar-school level and studying music theory by age four. My uncle on the less populous maternal side, Grady L. Wilson, was likewise attuned, with a show-business management career and a circle of friends and colleagues whose very presence defined the concepts of integration and multiculturalism long before Texas had begun to get shed of its segregationalist heritage. On Dad's side, our hell-bent-for-procreation extended family leaned more toward Southern Redneck Honyockery, in whose company I felt about as right as Haile Selassie at a Klan rally. All due respect, y'know.

I also developed, early on, an appetite for offbeat forms of literature and entertainment. No—*affinity* is more like it, for even the many specimens that I don't particularly enjoy still exert a certain fascination and command a certain respect, grudging or not. I haven't the vaguest notion of what it is that I might be looking for (although just the searching has yielded some tolerable by-products, including these books), but that question of "What in hell am I doing here?" has proved itself chronic, usually in synch with the abiding attraction to topics that most folks will dismiss as bizarre. Normalcy, of course, is nothing more nor less than where one feels most agreeably at home, and even Franz Kafka had his homing instinct of bemused disorientation upon which to fall back when everything else failed.

What it is that I am doing, right here and right now, is working alongside my old-time pal John Wooley to put the 'way-the-hell-past-due wraps on this fourth volume of *Forgotten Horrors*—speaking of the bizarre—whose specific contents date from precisely the year of my arrival and my earliest attempts at settling into something resembling Polite Society. The movies thus considered reflect, in turn, the obsessions of a world gone nuclear and maybe even alien, or at least alienated. The paranoid-or-maybe-not speculations of *Let's Live Again,* for example, and the atom-spy shenanigans of *Sofia,* and the tormented Afrocentrism of *The Betrayal (film noir,* literalized along ethnic lines) have more in common than their origins or their immediate agendas might suggest.

The postwar 1940s saw a gathering surge in science-fictional entertainment (and yes, the origins are duly pinpointed in *Forgotten Horrors 3*), which by 1947 was well along toward a reassertion as a prolific genre, intellectualized somewhat beyond the roughhouse fantasies of the Saturday-matinee cliffhanger serials. The serials, whose S-F sector had proved itself more science-farce than science-fantasy, were ripe for extinction by this time, their reasons-for-being gradually usurped by feature filmmakers whose least efforts were more earnest than most of the serials. That darker strain of S-F can only have been a pop-cultural outcropping of the State of Doubt, more so than any State of Peace, in which World War II had left a supposedly triumphant America.

Having fought long and hard to liberate humankind from the genocidal specter of Nazism, the United States found itself torn by its internal heritage of festering class-and-culture hatreds, by epidemic fears of the A-bomb, and by a steadily worsening Ugly American image among even its more cordial global allies (not to mention any Cold War mentality). The Roosevelt Administration's Good Neighbor Policy, directed toward the Latinate nations as a means of fostering Western Hemisphere solidarity in wartime, had withered under the Truman White House to a state of condescension at best—international statesmanship, reduced to the blithering boosterism of some provincial Chamber of Commerce—as the European Communist Bloc began exerting an appeal to the prevailing dictatorial tendencies of political interests south of the U.S. borders. And the idealistic new United Nations, barely into its second year and planning a beacon-of-enlightenment headquarters in Manhattan, already had developed disagreeable tendencies among its would-be saviors of humanity from its warlike self.

1947 *Time* magazine features the forthcoming marriage of Britain's Princess Elizabeth.

The noisier cultural-and-political happenings of 1947 included the scandalous first showings of high-fashion designs by Christian Dior; the marriage of Great Britain's Princess Elizabeth to the Duke of Edinburgh; the Brooklyn Dodgers' signing of Jackie Robinson as the first black player in major-league baseball, and a year's suspension for that team's defiant manager Leo Durocher (without whom the Dodgers won the pennant, anyhow); Congress' passage of the Taft-Hartley Labor Act in defiance of the Truman White House; and a spreading concern over Communist influences allegedly holding forth in Hollywood, amongst other precincts.

Such high-profile events and chronic occurrences tended to overshadow the year's more influential and lasting breakthroughs, including the creation of a full-fledged Central Intelligence Agency, as an offshoot of the transformation of the U.S. Army Air Corps into the self-contained U.S. Air Force; and the French government's imperialistic refusal to acknowledge an indigenous government in the Indo-Chinese principality of Vietnam. To say nothing of the emergence of a powerful new collective voice in the American mass media: Television began to evolve in earnest from a limited-range indulgence to a department-store staple with programming calculated to serve Mass Man by Mass Means, as the Twentieth Century's answer to Voltaire, my cousin Roger Price, would put it. (On a lesser scale of mass-communications, the dreaded fax machine was introduced as a commercially attainable product, however costly.) Together or separately, such developments would prove scarier over the long haul than any number of Commies in Hollywood, Dior and/or Durocher, or the film industry's entire output of horror pictures for the postwar era.

The horror pictures—and the recurring, related outcroppings of *film noir*, and a prevailing tendency toward weirdness in even comedies and horse operas—were, for that matter, scarcely more than an artistic and commercial response to the encroaching creepiness of the postwar Real World.

Thus do John Wooley and I find the stage set for the concentration of kinema that follows, herewith if not hitherto. Or perhaps the movies fare just fine on their own merits or lackings, without any baggage of knowing what was going on in the world outside the (mostly) off-Hollywood studios thus involved. *You* be the one to figure that one out, okay?

Jungle Sam Katzman, Jeanne Dean and Spencer G. Bennett take a break on the set of *Voodoo Tiger*.

As usual, we have combed the general output of the lower-rent filmmaking companies—with some salient exceptions, typically accounting for such Poverty Row alumni as Sam Katzman and Dore Schary, who had infiltrated the major studios but remembered their origins. We have turned up the customary playbill of pure-bred genre items, unclassifiable oddities, and nearer-the-mainstream fare infused with a certain dark peculiarity. Sheer volume of titles, 130 and change, narrows the immediate chronological orbit to 1947–1948.

Our standard agreement with H.P. Lovecraft's common-sense theory of weird fiction (in a nutshell: Horror Is Where You Find It) bears hammering, of course.

And so does this line from Conan Doyle, as uttered through his most famous mouthpiece, Sherlock Holmes: "To the man who loves art for its own sake, it is frequently in its least important and lowliest manifestations that the keenest pleasure is to be derived."
—Michael H. Price
Fort Worth & Points Beyond
www.fortworthbusinesspress.com

The Other Author's Preface by John Wooley

Dreams That Money Can Buy is not only the subtitle of this particular entry in the *Forgotten Horrors* canon; it also is the name of an exceptionally *different* theatrical feature from 1948, conceived and directed by a noted group of *avant garde* artists and brought to the screen with little if any sense of commercial potential. For that reason, it would seem to be the antithesis of the pictures covered here, most of which were brought to the screen by small-time entrepreneurs with no more noble intentions than turning a quick buck.

In fact, though, the consciously artistic *Dreams* and, say, the consciously *in*artistic *Campus Sleuth*—which immediately precedes *Dreams That Money Can Buy* in the chronology of this book—have more in common than you might think, especially if you decline to see one representing art and one representing commerce, but instead see both as fantasies—as dreams, if you will. For audiences of the late 1940s, after all, *Campus Sleuth* was a little dream that a bit of money could buy.

By laying down a dime or 15 cents at the box office, a gawky, socially awkward kid could live for a few hours in a world of jitterbugs and bobbysoxers, running right alongside June Preisser and Freddie Stewart through an idealized teenage life—spiced, in the case of *Campus Sleuth*, with a disappearing corpse. This is not quite the same thing as the wild imagery and experimental-theater techniques on display in *Dreams That Money Can Buy*, but *Campus Sleuth* is a dream, nonetheless, and a pretty good one, if you happen to be in the right mood.

And that is what most of the pictures in this volume are: little dreams, made all the more dreamlike by their obscurity. The pictures that Michael H. Price and the late George E. Turner chose to cover, in the earliest *Forgotten Horrors* volumes, are not big-studio productions full of high-wattage star power. Likewise for the films that I have been privileged to help uncover as the series continues.

As early as 1975–1980, Michael and George had turned away from the road more traveled by their movie-book-author cohorts and focused instead on the tawdry (but no less magical) Hollywood backstreet known as Poverty Row. From their Poverty Row vantage, actors gazed out at the Golden City just beyond their grasp and, between shots on cheap sets in quickie productions for directors far beneath the station of DeMille, imagined life as Gregory Peck or Loretta Young.

Seen today, these small-studio pictures carry quirky, almost heartwarming nobility. They know what they are, and the people involved—allowing for factors ranging from disillusionment to cynicism to John Barleycorn—seem to be doing the best they can. They know it's not MGM or Paramount, but, anyway, they are working. And as the dedicated thespian Clu Gulager once told us, during a conversation about the horror movies he tended to make in the latter part of his long career, "Actors *act*."

Without the bankable stars that all America knew, the people who made these films had to have Something Else going for them. And that Something Else was almost always an exploitable angle, something the theater owners could sell in lieu of marquee names. In the pictures examined between these covers, that Something Else was a horrific or bizarre element of one sort or another, ranging from simple murder to terrors far more fiendish. In the Westerns and the comedies, the horror element often came as a *lagniappe*, giving an extra thrill to the folks who probably would have shown up anyway.

That's the kind of thing we celebrate here. As Michael notes in his own preface: Horror Is Where You Find It. And while that element is easier to find in the genre-fied movies we all know about, we figure it is at least as rewarding to discover it in forgotten or overlooked places. This is why we revel in sharing the joy of discovery in these pages,

Dreams That Money Can Buy

knowing that those of us drawn to these pictures are, after all, archaeologists in our way, lowering ourselves into ancient darknesses, shining our lights into a cavern of dreams.

And now, if you'll allow me, a few words about Michael H. Price.

Michael and I first met at one or another of entrepreneur Larry Lankford's great Dallas Fantasy Fair comics-and-movies conventions during the 1980s, finding ourselves increasingly thrown together on panels that offered, as someone dubbed it, "alternative programming"—an alternative, that is, to whatever speech by whatever hot comic-book artist might be going on at the same time. Michael's day job then was as arts editor and film critic for the Fort Worth *Star-Telegram*, which made his work available to newspapers worldwide by the New York Times News Service. Like Michael, I was working as a news columnist while making time for outside projects, so it didn't take us long to notice that we had quite a bit in common—especially, the oddball interests and off-trail *oeuvres* that led the convention chairmen to use us for their "alternative programming" needs.

By the time I met Michael, I was already a big fan of *Forgotten Horrors: Early Talkie Chillers from Poverty Row*, the 1979 edition of that seminal volume Mike had done in collaboration with George Turner. And the thing I think I liked most about *Forgotten Horrors*—beyond the fact that it delved into movies I'd hardly even heard of, offering the skin-tingling thrill of discovery I had gotten as a kid with the likes of *Famous Monsters* and *Castle of Frankenstein*—was that it was remarkably free of pomposity, attitude and snarkiness. Those qualities had become the norm with tomes like *The Fifty Worst Films of All Time* and *The Golden Turkey Awards*, whose authors had proved themselves incapable of unearthing a sarcophagus without taking few pokes at the corpse inside. There was no sense of wonder in those books, only a sense of condescending smartassedness, of laughing at the kid in the raggedy clothes.

But *Forgotten Horrors* was something else. And the reason, I think, was that *its* authors weren't just critics, but also creators. They worked both sides of the street, and they knew and could feel for the people who'd made the pictures. Turner and Price were not averse to calling a dud a dud, but it was always with an understanding and a degree of sensitivity unknown to most Film Critics—then, and most certainly today.

Simple enough: Michael not only loves these old pictures; he also has an empathy with everyone who ever stood on one of the sets, banged out a script on a manual typewriter, tried valiantly to come up with fresh promotional material for a six-day wonder featuring the boss' spectacularly untalented girlfriend. And Michael has been writing about these people and the movies they made since he was a kid, keeping copious notes on virtually every film he has seen for the past 50 years or so—a fact that goes a long way toward explaining why there are so many detailed film-by-film evaluations in each *Forgotten Horrors*. Those overwhelmingly belong to Michael, as does the other material in each of these volumes.

Starting with *Forgotten Horrors 3*, following George Turner's passing, Michael invited me to contribute my own little filigrees here and there, and for that I will be eternally grateful. So thanks, Michael.

And thanks, too, to you folks who buy these books and share our sense of wonder and discovery. As Minnie Pearl used to say, I'm just so proud to be here.

—John Wooley
Foyil, Oklahoma
www.johnwooley.com

Acknowledgments

Our thanks in particular to Bob Kolba, movie buff *extraordinaire*, for a wealth of encouragement, insights and assistance. And a grateful nod to these helpful presences— whether past, posthumous or present-and-accounted-for:

Bud Abbott; Rogélio Agrasánchez; Ben & Buck Altman; Don & Jim Ameche; Christine Bayly; Ron & Margaret Borst; Larry Buchanan; Sumter Bruton; Bill Buckner; Yakima Canutt; Jim & Susan Colegrove; Richard L. Connor; Ray "Crash" Corrigan; Robert Crumb; Guillermo del Toro; William K. Everson; David F. Friedman; Josh Alan Friedman; Kerry Gammill; Tina Gorski; Jan Alan Henderson; Charlton Heston and Fraser Clarke Heston; Sam Katzman; Dennis King; Julie King; Larry L. King; Fuzzy Knight; Mark Martin; Don Myers; Darcy O'Brien; John E. Parnum; Robin Pen; Nat Pendleton; Gary Don Rhodes; Nathan Rich; Paul T. Riddell; Roy & Dale Evans Rogers; Angelo Rossitto; Ben Sargent; Martin Scorsese; Harry Semels; Larry D. Springer; Conrad Sprout; Frank Stack; Gary & Susan Svehla; D. Lee Thomas, Jr.; Bill Thompson; James Vance; Mark Evan Walker; John Wayne & Pilar Wayne Upchurch; Rich Wannen; Johnny Weissmuller; Michael Weldon; Chill Wills; Grady L. Wilson; Don Young; Marcella Moreland Young and Tana Young; and Terry Zwigoff

And on the Institutional Front: The Academy of Motion Picture Arts & Sciences; the Agrasánchez Film Archive; The American Film Institute; The American Society of Cinematographers; The American Society of Composers, Authors & Publishers; the Amon Carter Museum; ArtHouse, Inc., Film Exchange of New York; the Billy Barty Foundation and Little People of America, Inc.; the British Film Institute; *Fangoria* magazine; the Hoblitzelle Theatre Arts Library, University of Texas Humanities Research Center; the Library of Congress; Life Is a Movie (Dot-Com); Midnight Marquee Press, Inc.; the Modern Art Museum of Fort Worth; the National Association of Theatre Owners; the Screen Directors, Screen Producers, and Screen Writers Guilds; the Southwest Film & Video Archive, Southern Methodist University; and the U.S. Postal Service and its movie-star stamp ceremonial programs

Marginalia and Addenda
to Prior Volumes

Elzie C. Segar's Popeye the Sailor enjoyed no triumph more so than challenging Official Authority and proving himself correct in the process. One of Popeye's biggest kicks of his Depression-era heyday was that of identifying a mistake in the almighty Dictionary—seems Mr. Webster had mis-defined (in Popeye's perception, at least) one of the Sailor Man's favorite terms. The word was *yam*. You can figure out the resulting gag from there.

Yes, and if it was good enough for Popeye, then it's good enough for the accommodating readers of *Forgotten Horrors*, who have come through like troupers in pointing out the occasional lapses and holidays of judgment in our prior volumes.

It helps if the alert enthusiast calls a hiccup to our attention. Hence this prefatory section, which we also reserve as a place to trot out fresh insights and nuggets that we've unearthed with no coaching from the audience. Sort of a low-tech interactive thing, and it also spares us the trouble of overhauling entire books to accommodate a bushel or a peck of factoids. Herewith, some diggings from the strata of *errata*:

1935-1937

The New Adventures of Tarzan (Burroughs-Tarzan Pictures)— The reference to star player Herman Brix (see page 242 of *Forgotten Horrors: The Definitive Edition*) as an Olympian decathlon champion is a gaffe that went sailing clean over our heads, and over the heads of several fact-checking editors, through three editions spanning 1979-99. Brix was in fact a silver medalist, as a shot-putter. Chalk up this notable tweak to Don Myers, a helpful and communicative reader.

Source-author George E. Turner's original reference to Brix' Olympian background seems to have come from one or another of the *New Adventures of Tarzan* pressbooks, which of course dealt more in hype than in wool-dyed fact. We'd check back—but there is no telling where the main body of the merged Price & Turner files landed following George's death in 1999. More than 60 years of purposeful collecting, eBayed into oblivion by overanxious heirs more concerned with liquidation than with preservation. Jeeze Louise.

Island Captives (Falcon Film/Wm. Steiner)—We have continually excluded this lesser attraction, if only because it is, in essence, merely a Western-movie land-grab story transplanted to a Tahitian locale. Nothing particularly horrific, here, nor even remotely strange, except perhaps a generic conspiracy to murder a well-liked planter (John Beck) in the name of corporate progress. Come to think of it, corporate progress *is* a pretty ghastly phenomenon, considering all the hard-working souls who get ground into hamburger as the machinery advances. Eddie Nugent and Joan Barclay supply the element of romance, Carmen La Roux cranks the tensions as a tribal temptress, and dependable Forrest Taylor provides the right elements of malice and menace—just as he would do in many a frontier shoot-'em-up.

Round-Up Time in Texas (Republic Pictures Corp.)—Hiding in plain sight behind an innocuous title and a cowboy-crooner stereotype, this Gene Autry-starrer takes place not in Texas, but rather in South Africa, with a diamond strike as the provocation to mayhem. Autry and Lester "Smiley" Burnette square off against jungle terrors better suited to Frank Buck or Clyde Beatty. Burnette's musical interludes with the Cabin Kids—a Deep Southern harmonizing ensemble beloved to admirers of the *Our Gang* comedies—are implausible and delightful. Far and away off the beaten path. Hence the term *offbeat*.

1945-1946

An Angel Comes to Brooklyn (Republic)—In likening this benevolent fantasy to the 1947 *Miracle on 34th Street*, we had mentioned a not-until-1967 publishing status for Valentine Davies' source-story for *Miracle*. Correct that year to a timelier 1947, thanks to the California-based book dealer and collector Don Myers, who has the Harcourt Brace edition to back up the assertion. And while you're at it—if you're in possession of *The American Film Institute Catalogue of Motion Pictures Produced in the United States: Feature Films, 1941-50*—mark that same correction there. In either place, it's our error. Nice catch.

The Catman of Paris (Republic)—Don Myers questions whether that photo on page 183 of *Forgotten Horrors 3* depicts title player Douglass Dumbrille or his double, Robert "Bob" Wilke, adding: "Can't say that it really looks likes Dumbrille to me." Actually, it looks like the Catman of Paris to us—being as how we tend to forget who's playing whom while losing ourselves in the story at hand. But Myers' cordial challenge has a ring of truth about it. Anyhow, this official still from Republic Pictures may well be a makeup test that proved good enough to sock into the press kit.

Jungle Terror (Favorite Films)—Constant Reader Rich Wannen pegs this ill-documented entry as a featurized version of the Weiss Bros.' 1937 serial *Jungle Menace*, as acquired for release by Columbia Pictures. (Yes, and could the Weisses have used a *WB* logo and gotten away with it?) Wannen's deductions reconcile the two titles quite neatly. "Thanks for the mystery," he adds. And thanks right back atcha.
—M.H.P.
Back in the Saddle Again

1946–1947

A FIG LEAF FOR EVE

a.k.a.: Desirable Lady; Strips and Blondes; Hollywood Nights; Flaming Girls;
Not Enough Clothes; Reckless Youth; Room for Love
(Carry Westen Corp.)

The striptease racket and refined polite society provide the clash-of-cultures setting essential to *A Fig Leaf for Eve*. The ruthless scam that straddles these worlds is to present a voluptuous dancer as an heir to immense wealth. The scenarist is Harry O. Hoyt, a cornerstone figure in early-day picture-show fantasy but by now just another struggling survivor of the silent-screen era.

Hoyt (1891–1961) had directed the live-action business for the 1925 *The Lost World*, that feature-length proving ground for Willis O'Brien's creature-animation processes. Hoyt also had contributed to the script of a watershed mad-scientist melodrama of 1927 called *The Wizard*—something of an elaboration upon the similarly conceived *Go and Get It*, from 1920. Hoyt fell upon hard times during the 1930s with the collapse of his intended dinosaur epic *Creation*, which was absorbed into *King Kong*—without further need of Hoyt's involvement. Subsequent frustrations became a textbook example of the Law of Diminishing Returns as Hoyt attempted to retool the *Creation* scenario into a false-start production called *The Lost Atlantis*.

He had directed and written prolifically from 1919 on through the 1920s, but Hoyt's resume turned spotty as the Jazz Age gave way to the Great Depression. A majority of authoritative references will show Hoyt's career to have ended with a smattering of assignments during 1930–1933. But no, Hoyt carried on as a scenarist and story adapter, specializing in low-budget Westerns and oddball mysteries including two *Forgotten Horrors* entries from 1944–1945, *Lady in the Death House* and *The Missing Corpse*.

Hoyt had flirted with plagiarism in appropriating elements of Conan Doyle's *The Lost World* and James Barrie's *The Admirable Crichton* as templates for *Creation*. Hoyt's less obvious springboard for *A Fig Leaf for Eve* was the history-become-legend of Anastasia, as retold in Samuel Ornitz' novel *The Lost Empress*. Ornitz' version had fueled the superior 1932 thriller *Secrets of the French Police*, which was in production at RKO-Radio Pictures while Hoyt was hanging on at the same studio with the foredoomed money pit of *Creation*.

Proxy title card for one of the various reissues of *A Fig Leaf for Eve*

The little-seen and absorbingly shabby *A Fig Leaf for Eve* is a guttersnipe variant on the Anastasia fable, with Jan Wiley as stripper Eve Lorraine and Phil Warren as talent agent Mac McGrath, who attempts to advance Eve's career via notoriety in lieu of artistry. No sooner has Mac arranged to have Eve busted for indecent exposure, than bail bondsman Gus Hoffman (Eddie Dunn) becomes curious about Eve's lack of early memories. She knows she was orphaned as an infant, and she seems to remember something about her parents' having died in the collapse of a theater building.

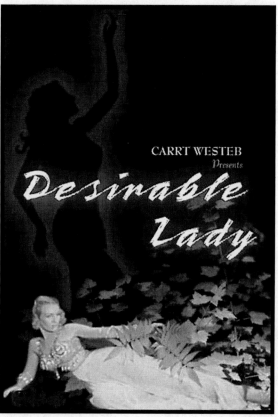

CARRT WESTEB
Presents

Desirable Lady

Hoffman finds a dormant notice of a reward for information involving a young woman whose parents had died 23 years ago in such a disaster. This woman stands to inherit the estate of a hair-tonic tycoon.

Miss Wiley, a busy but ill-recognized actress since 1941, plays Eve with a scatterbrained but self-serious zeal, toeing a fine line between sleaziness and innocence as Eddie Dunn's conniving Hoffman steers her toward a strange and perilous foray into the borderlands of class discrimination. *Fig Leaf* presents itself as a comedy, but Miss Wiley's portrayal is more that of a likeably vulnerable sort who buys into a treacherous ploy that might leave her wealthy but indebted—or might leave somebody dead. Eve suspects she has a cultured lineage, even though she wouldn't know culture if it should bite her.

Hoffman presses an introduction to wealthy Horace Sardam (Edward Keane), who accepts Eve as a long-lost niece. Horace's snobbish wife, Lavinia (Betty Blythe), denounces Eve after Mac offhandedly mentions the public-lewdness pinch. A purported great-aunt, Sarah Burch (Janet Scott), warms to Eve, however, and the question of kinship is admitted into court. A haughty might-be cousin, Millicent (Marilyn McConnell), preys upon Eve's desire for acceptance and tricks the girl into a humiliating attempt to recite Shakespeare during a high-society benefit. Shamed but game, Eve rallies with a crowd-pleasing coochie dance.

Hoffman baits Mac into a confrontation over the pending inheritance. A struggle for a gun leaves Hoffman dead, Mac on the lam and Eve charged with murder. Mac regains his wits, 'fesses up to what proves to have been an accidental shooting, and attends to Eve's release. A lawyer (Emmett Vogan) establishes Hoffman's deceit, but Horace concludes that Eve must really be the lost heiress. She has half a mind to withdraw her claim, but Mac persuades her otherwise with an impulsive marriage proposal.

This one-and-only production of the Carry Westen Corp. boasts raggedy production values; stream-of-consciousness writing that sometimes rings true and sometimes does not; and portrayals ranging from the dreadful to the sublime. Marcel LePicard's photography is a distinct plus, inasmuch as the veteran Poverty Row camera chief knew just how to draw attention from the threadbare settings and find the soul of Eve's predicament. The out-of-nowhere finale assures the heroine, a lowbrow Candide, of a life of luxury that might or might not be her birthright, but Phil Warren's manipulative agent-turned-suitor would seem to promise further such exploitation. Eve's obliviousness might be a case of good acting on Miss Wiley's part—or maybe not. In any event, Eve emerges as just the type to make every guy in the audience want to step forward as her protector.

Low-billed and ill-utilized Chester Conklin was a pioneering comedian of silent-era Hollywood, an early colleague of Charles Chaplin, and a dependable but increasingly obscure character player through the 1940s. Conklin had retrenched by the middle 1950s as a department store Santa Claus, but he made sporadic returns to the screen into the '60s. Conklin died at 83 in 1971.

The supporting players are more caricatures than characters, although Janet Scott conveys well the generosity and loneliness of the great-aunt and Edward Keane seems genuinely helpful as the uncle. Betty Blythe, once a top-drawer leading lady in the likes of 1921's *Queen of Sheba* and the 1925 *She*, conveys a memorable coldness as Keane's Social Register wife. Director Donald Brodie (who figured oftener as a small-parts actor) leaves it to the players to convey any urgency, and the climactic struggle is poorly blocked and staged. Though patently not one of those disgraceful adults-only pictures, *A Fig Leaf for Eve* seems most comfortable with itself during Miss Wiley's discreet striptease routines.

A Fig Leaf for Eve appears to have been filmed during 1944–1945—such is the (unregistered) copyright date on a print we turned up in 1975, bearing the proxy title of *Hollywood Nights*—and then given a formal, if sporadic, release during 1946–1947. Carry Westen, the sole-operator corporation behind the film, changed the title to *Strips and Blondes* for delivery to the New York State Board of Censors in 1947. Other re-christenings followed during the early-to-middle 1950s. *Strips and Blondes* was restored during 1954–1955, when the film recirculated under at least two other titles. By whatever name, *A Fig Leaf for Eve* is an endearing mess of concentrated weirdness, ineptitude and artistry-by-default.

CREDITS: Presented by: Carry Westen; Producer: J. Richard Westen; Associate Producer: Raymond Fridgen; Director: Donald Brodie; Assistant Director: Alan Kadden; Scenario: Harry O. Hoyt; Adapted Screenplay: Elizabeth Hayter; Photographed by: Marcel LePicard; Art Director: Frank Dexter; Editor: Richard Carver; Decor: Earl Wooden; Music: Frank Sanucci; Sound: Lyle E. Willey; Makeup: William C. Oakley, Jr.; Hair Stylist: Marjorie Lund; Production Manager: Dick L'Estrange; Running Time: 69 Minutes; Released: During 1946-1955 on a State-by-State Basis

CAST: Jan Wiley (Eve Lorraine); Phil Warren (Dan "Mac" McGrath); Eddie Dunn (Gus Hoffman); Janet Scott (Sarah Burch); Emmett Vogan (Thomas W. Campbell); Betty Blythe (Lavinia Sardam); Edward Keane (Horace Sardam); Marilyn McConnell (Millicent Sardam); Selika Pettiford (Organist); and Dick Rush, Cheerio Meredith, Herbert Evans, Chester Conklin, Jack Cheatham

CURSE OF THE UBANGI

a.k.a.: 9 Girls in Hell

(Esper Roadshow Attractions)

The historical record varies as to the nature of this elusive entry from the notorious exploitation-picture producer Dwain Esper. The most vivid description of *Curse of the Ubangi* is contained in a narrative continuity submitted in 1947 to the New York State Board of Censors.

A narrator explains that the picture will examine religious beliefs outside Western civilization. Various Third World ceremonies, along with a Penitente crucifixion ritual from the American Southwest, provide illustrations.

The text veers to an indictment of hunters who capture wild animals for exhibition. The trapping of the African lion and the Bengal tiger is described. An expedition saves a group of monkeys from a snake attack, only to capture one monkey for a circus. A boy is shown destroying the eggs of alligators—then being attacked and presumably devoured. The leaders of an expedition bribe African guides to help capture a Ubangi woman. A tribal chieftain socks a curse on the safari.

Cut to a circus setting: A fall claims the life of an aerialist. A mass poisoning fells hundreds of carnies. An elephant stomps a clown. A panther mauls its trainer. A big top is destroyed by fire. The narrator asks: "Are these unforeseen manifestations of the supernatural at work?"

The ill-matched proxy title, *9 Girls in Hell*, comes from the New York State Archives and might just as easily be a case of bureaucratic mis-attribution. The American Film Institute suggests a feature-length running time of approximately 70 minutes. One text on exploitation films, *Forbidden Fruit* by Felicia Feaster and Bret Wood, cites *Curse of the Ubangi* as a short subject dating from 1934 and names the safari film *Ubangi* (1931)—photographed during a Belgian medical expedition of 1924—as the key source of (pirated) footage. The Feaster-Wood book also contains a fascinating anecdote from Esper's daughter, Millicent Esper Wratten, describing how she had been traumatized as a child upon witnessing the

"IT'S COOLER INSIDE"

Interstate Circuit's

CAPITOL Theatre

JUNGLE TERRORS

AT LARGE IN CIVILAZATION

AS HOODOO MAGIC STALKS THE CIRCUS!

MORE TERRIFYING THAN KING KONG AND INGAGGI!!

WEDS-FRI

CURSE OF THE UBANGI

Exclusive Hi Plains Engagement · Adults Only!

THE POWER OF SUPERSTITION UNLEASHED!
LUST GREED MYSTERY
THE CURSE OF THE UBANGI

filming of a hog-slaughtering sequence for *Curse of the Ubangi*. Dwain Esper, a resourceful hand at re-using his own and other artists' footage, could easily have cobbled and stretched a 1934 short into this presumed 1947 feature-length entry; certainly, the typewritten continuity sheets suggest a patchwork job.

The accompanying illustration, photographed in 1978 from an undated handbill in the Interstate Theatres collection at the University of Texas, demonstrates that *Curse of the Ubangi* played at least one of the West Texas Interstates—the Capitol, in downtown Amarillo—that were managed by Mike Price's uncle, Grady L. Wilson. The city of this particular Capitol Theatre is not specified, but the "Hi Plains" reference is a dead giveaway. The handbill's portrait of an ape-man, rampant, proves to have been lifted from the advertising materials for a much earlier (and more highly pedigreed) movie, Marshall Neilan's *Go and Get It* (1920). The actor thus depicted is Bull Montana, also of 1925's *The Lost World*—and assuredly *not* among the cast of *Curse of the Ubangi*. Are these unforeseen manifestations of Old School carnival ballyhoo at work?

CREDITS: Producer and Director: Dwain Esper; Written for the Screen by Hildegarde Stadie Esper [given elsewhere as Hildagarde]; Running Time: 70 (Est.) Minutes; Submitted during 1947 to the New York State Board of Censors

CAST: Thurston Nudson (Narrator)

GOING TO GLORY, COME TO JESUS
(Royal Gospel Productions/Toddy Pictures)

Royal Gospel Productions of New York was a throwback to the Harlem Renaissance, that upheaval in the Afrocentric arts that had come to flourish since around 1915, in likely response to the death of the more nearly complacent and compliant black leader Booker T. Washington. The movement saw a creative outpouring that included the maturation of jazz as America's own distinctive classical music, influencing such Dominant Culture artists as George Gershwin and Paul Whiteman; the rise of such poet-philosophers as Langston Hughes and Zora Neale Hurston; and the emergence of painters, including Laura Wheeler Waring and William H. Johnson, who made manifest a society hitherto invisible within the Art Establishment. All concerned held fast to Aaron Douglas' open challenge to "establish an *art era*... not white art painted black," but rather artistry torn from "the souls of our people."

Cinema is the medium least influenced by the Harlem Renaissance, despite the strivings of such revolutionary filmmakers as Noble Johnson and Oscar Micheaux and the

ROYAL GOSPEL PRODUCTIONS PRESENTS
The Spiritual Masterpiece
"Going to Glory" "Come to Jesus"

occasional showcase for black artistry from within the mainstream Hollywood studios. Genuinely black-independent filmmaking suffered from a lack of production-and-distribution resources. White-financed filmmaking by black talents, on the other hand, leaned toward broadly comedic forms that, although more endearing than the self-serious films of Micheaux, prove lacking in the social assertiveness of the Renaissance artists.

The truest of the Harlem Renaissance filmmakers, Spencer Williams, Jr., had been a part of the movement during the 1920s and '30s, when he had attempted to lend a cultural integrity to the Negro stories-in-cinema of the Jewish humorist Octavus Roy Cohen. But Williams did not break out as a moviemaker in his own right until the early '40s, when he delivered a rough-hewn epic of backwater spiritual folklife called *The Blood of Jesus*. This watershed film came along well after the acknowledged end of the Harlem Renaissance—and yet if ever there were a film wrested from the communal soul of a people, it is *The Blood of Jesus*.

Spencer Williams had continued in that vein through 1946, when he began pursuing larger opportunities. By 1947, Royal Gospel's *Going to Glory, Come to Jesus* looked decidedly imitative by comparison with the trails that Williams had blazed with *The Blood of Jesus* in 1941 and *Go Down, Death!* in 1946.

Going to Glory, Come to Jesus was filmed during 1946, then given a sporadic release in 1947. Ted Toddy's distribution company, which more often handled rambunctious black-ensemble comedies with an exploitation-market bias, could not have taken particular heart in what is essentially a religious parable, but the film contained enough in the way of supernatural shock value and jazzy music to suit Toddy Pictures' agenda.

The film may well be lost, for no print surfaced during exhaustive searches of the 1980s and '90s on behalf of the American Film Institute and the Dallas-based Southwest

Dreams That Money Can Buy

Film & Video Archive. Records on file with the New York State Archive are conspicuously lacking in overall filmmaker credits but provide a cast roster and a list of musical selections. The Motion Picture Academy's Production Code files contain accounts of censorship problems involving two risqué songs.

Irene Harper plays Lillie-Mae Scott, a preacher's daughter who finds herself courted by Satan (John Watts). The ordeal ends with her transformation into a crone. Although the experience proves to have been a dream, it is enough to drive Lillie-Mae straightaway back to the Amen Corner.

Royal Gospel Productions announced two additional features that appear not to have been issued, if completed at all. No further screen credits have turned up for any of the listed players. Vocalist Irene Wilson and the song-and-dance team of Miss Coot Grant & Kid Sox Wilson were significant players on the Harlem jazz scene, with careers dating from two decades earlier.

CREDITS: Director: T. Meyer; Story and Screenplay: Harry Tarr and Wesley Wilson; Based Upon: the Play *Going to Glory, Come to Jesus*, by Wesley Wilson and Leola Grant; Spirituals: "To Take My Troubles To," "I Don't Want a Body without a Soul," "Keep Your Trust in the Lord," "Come to Jesus," "Where He Leads Me, I Will Follow," "Take Me to the Water," "I Want To Go to Heaven" and "Down by the Riverside"; Sacred Composition: "Old Hundredth Doxology (Praise God from Whom All Blessings Flow)," from Psalm 134 (*Geneva Psaltery*), Music by Louis Bourgeois; Blues Songs: "I Was Glad," "You'd Better Watch Out" and "Regardless," Composer(s) Unacknowledged; Running Time: Approx. 80-90 Minutes; Released: During 1947 on a State-by-State Basis

CAST: Irene Harper (Lillie-Mae Scott); Lloyd Howlett (Rev. Mr. Scott); Eddie L. Fluker (Doctor); Anne H. Francis (Azaline); Charles A. Freeman (Prophet); Josephine Gertrude (Ethel); Wallace Harris (Walter); Marilyn Lawrence (Bessie); Thelma Lynch (Mrs. Sharpe); Thomas Quick (Joe); Dorothy Thomas (Hannah Jackson); Stella Van Derzee (Mrs. Scott); James Watts (Fred); John Watts (Satan); and the Royal Gospel Choir, Miss Coot Grant & Kid Sox Wilson, Irene Williams

LADY CHASER
(PRC Pictures, Inc./Producers Releasing Corp.)

Ann Savage, a defining lethal-lady presence of *film noir*, serves this slight entry more civilly than one might expect on the evidence of her fierce contribution to 1945's *Detour*. Savage seems downright helpful, in fact, during the opening frames of *Lady Chaser*, until a gesture of courtesy on her part proves fatal to an innocent character.

The point is kindness, plain and simple, when Inez Marie Polk (Miss Savage) offers an aspirin to a chance acquaintance, Dorian Westmore (Inez Cooper), who complains of a headache while visiting a Los Angeles department store. Dorian accepts the pill but tucks it away for future reference.

The tablet proves fatal to Dorian's wealthy uncle. Inez, reading a newspaper account of the death, realizes the dose had been meant for her—a token of appreciation from one of the people whom she has been blackmailing. Dorian's inability to name the source of the tablet leads to her arrest as a poisoner. Her fiancé, logger David Kane (Robert Lowery), undertakes to locate the mystery woman. A department-store maid (Marie Martino) seems only too willing to point Kane toward Inez Polk. A sneak attack leaves Kane unconscious and the maid dead.

The trail leads Kane and a news-reporter friend (Paul Bryar) to a hunting lodge, where Kane trounces two thugs who had been sent to kill him by Dorian's lawyer, Oliver Vickers (Frank Ferguson). Vickers is among Inez' blackmail victims; he is captured while confronting her. Inez, finally cornered, clears Dorian.

Director Sam Newfield is one of the leading lights of the *Forgotten Horrors* tradition, although he oftener shone less brightly than he should have as a consequence of spreading his talents too thin. *Lady Chaser* occupies a middle ground between competent hackwork and sharper craftsmanship—a film destined for obscurity even in its day, but distinguished by a cold-hearted show of passive villainy from Ann Savage; a bravura job of heroism from Robert Lowery; and a fine performance from Frank Ferguson as a menace camouflaged by social respectability.

Source-author G.T. Fleming-Roberts was a prolific pulpwood scribe best known for Captain Zero, last of the pulp magazines' costumed heroes (1949–1950). Fleming-Roberts' *Lady Chaser* scenario includes a credulity-stretching sequence where William Haade, as Inez' boyfriend, happens to choose not only the same big-city park but also *the same park bench* as Lowery's heroic David Kane, setting up a revelation for later on.

Screenwriter Fred Myton should shoulder a little blame, too, for some clunky patches of dialogue, often a foregone conclusion on Poverty Row. The film gets rolling in the evocative setting of a department store's writing room, the now-archaic predecessor of the Internet cafe—only warmer, and a great deal more elegant.

Newfield's unsubtle style proves right for the short running time. He uses one of his trademark fistfights, between Lowery and secondary heavy Haade, as more than punctuation: The slugfest, as well-staged as anything in Newfield's many Westerns, serves also to attract the police at a crucial moment. The horrific qualities derive largely from the old theme of a killer hiding behind a veneer of upstanding citizenship. Particularly memorable is one depiction of a remote murder, in which the screen fills with the torso of a gunman, advancing upon a screaming victim.

CREDITS: Producer: Sigmund Neufeld; Director: Sam Newfield; Assistant Director: Stanley Neufeld; Screenplay: Fred Myton; Scenarist: G.T. Fleming-Roberts; Photographed by: Jack Greenhalgh; Special Effects: Ray Mercer; Art Director: Frank Sylos; Editor: Holbrook N. Todd; Settings: Elias H. Reif; Properties: Eugene C. Stone; Music: Walter Greene; Sound: Charles Kenworthy; Makeup: Tom McDonald; Production Manager: Bert Sternbach; Running Time: 60 Minutes; Released: During 1947 on a State-by-State Basis

CAST: Robert Lowery (David Kane); Ann Savage (Inez Marie Polk); Inez Cooper (Dorian Westmore); Frank Ferguson (Oliver T. Vickers); William Haade (Bill Redding); Ralph Dunn (Inspector Brady); Paul Bryar (Garry); Charles Williams (Landlord); Garry Owen (Herman); Marie Martino (Anna Nelson)

THE RETURN OF
MANDY'S HUSBAND
(Lucky Star Production Co./Toddy Pictures Co.)

A feeble echo of Negro Vaudeville, *The Return of Mandy's Husband* served to reunite the lapsed comedy team of Mantan Moreland and Flournoy E. Miller, who are responsible for such WWII-era essentials of the *Forgotten Horrors* canon as *Lucky Ghost* and *Professor Creeps*. The placement in 1947 is but an educated guess: *The Return of Mandy's Husband* was never copyrighted as a motion picture, but chief backer Ted Toddy placed an unofficial 1947 copyright notice upon a sheaf of typewritten dialogue pages, and the New York State Board of Censors accepted the film for consideration on May 13 of that year. A search through *Variety* and other trade publications, along with scattered black-neighborhood publications, has turned up no contemporary reviews or news items.

Moreland (playing himself as a huckster with an outspoken dread of matters supernatural) and Miller (playing himself despite a fictional character name) establish a company called the Ghost Association, calculated to bilk customers who will pay to communicate with deceased loved ones. Moreland poses as a medium, Prince Alabastar Amsterdam.

Meanwhile, a henpecked husband named Henry Coffee fakes his death as a refuge from his wife, Mandy. He hides in an abandoned barn, where gangsters take him hostage. This would be the very place that Moreland and Miller have chosen for their debut séance. Moreland mistakes the hoodlums for ghosts; after their capture by the police, Miller presents Moreland as the hero responsible for routing the crooks. Henry Coffee remains hidden in the loft.

The pageant of absurdities ends abruptly with a session in which Mandy begs Moreland to conjure her husband's spirit. She swears she would never again mistreat him if only he would come back to life. Henry, overhearing, yells out, "*You wins, honey!*" Whereupon the ceiling caves in. Henry is plunged, as if from the heavens, into the arms of his wife. The Ghost Association's reputation is thus saved, although one can only wonder how the bogus spiritualists could ever follow such an act.

Mantan Moreland was nearing the end of a distinguished Hollywood career, busy but ill acknowledged for its brilliance, as his brand of humor became anathema to the policies of Race Uplift of the ever more influential National Association for the Advancement of Colored People. The NAACP's damnably well-intentioned objective here was to commit censorship—not so much upon Art, as upon functioning artists. Those who did not conform would be targeted for removal. The tactic calls to mind nothing so much as the Nazis' book-burnings and ethnic cleansing purges of so few years earlier.

Monogram Pictures' *Charlie Chan* series, in which Moreland played a recurring chauffeur-turned-sleuth role of mixed hilarity and heroism, had just two years more to run. Flournoy Miller, who was more interested in writing, had less to lose than Moreland in terms of professional momentum. By 1950, the N.A.A.C.P. had succeeded in a campaign to discourage the mainstream Hollywood studios from indulging such rambunctious displays of ethnicity lest caricature ensue, and Moreland retrenched into network radio and the nightclub scene. Chronic comeback attempts, right on into the 1970s, found Moreland's brisk timing and subversive good humor undiminished by advancing age, failing health or the dismissive punishments visited upon him by the forces of Political Correctness.

CREDITS: Executive Producer: Ted Toddy; Running Time: 49 Minutes; Released: During 1947 on a State-by-State Basis

CAST: Mantan Moreland (Mantan); Flournoy E. Miller (Alex); and John D. Lee, Jr., E. Hensley, McKinley Reeves, Terry Knight

QUEEN OF THE AMAZONS

(Screen Art Pictures Corp./Screen Guild Productions, Inc.)

Old-fashioned in the extreme and as burdened with ill-matched stock footage and superfluous narration as any of the *Ingagi* knockoffs of the 1930s, *Queen of the Amazons* also succeeds at inspiring the woodenest of performances from such ordinarily lively players as Robert Lowery, Patricia Morison, John Miljan, and J. Edward Bromberg. The story is of the Lost Safari variety, with one Jean Preston (Miss Morison) commissioning a search to locate her long-missing fiancé, Gregg Jones (Bruce Edwards), and at length finding herself mistaken for a fabled she-devil type.

A more genuinely wild woman proves to be a militant jungle-dweller known as Zeeda (Amira Moustafa), who has claimed Gregg as her consort and will stop at nothing to keep him captive. Explorer Gary Lambert (Lowery) seems every bit the He-Man Woman Hater/Great White Hunter until he is won over by Jean's shooting skills. A surprisingly cold twist transforms comic-relief player Bromberg into a loose-cannon sort, who finally requires killing lest he lapse further out of control. An ivory-rustling subplot proves more interesting than the central erotic tensions, which are resolved in an impossibly nice manner—with a double wedding for Jean to Gary and Zeeda to Gregg.

CREDITS: Presented by: Robert L. Lippert; Producer and Director: Edward Finney; Assistant to Mr. Finney: John Forster; Assistant Director: Wesley Barry; Story and Screenplay: Roger Merton; Photographed by: Robert Pittack; Art Supervisor: James Reimer; Art Director: Sandy Dexter; Editor: John Link; Music: Lee Zahler; Production Advisor:

A spot of wild woman captivity—that is, not to say Captive Wild Woman—from *Queen of the Amazons.*

Sherman Sanders; Studio Head: Dr. Ferenz H. Fodor; Running Time: 62 Minutes; Released: January 15, 1947

CAST: Robert Lowery (Gary Lambert); Patricia Morison (Jean Preston); J. Edward Bromberg (Gabby); Bruce Edwards (Gregg Jones); John Miljan (Col. Jones; Narrator); Amira Moustafa (Zeeda); and Keith Richards, Vida Aldana, Wilson Benge, Cay Forrester, Jack George, Hassan Khayyam

THE RED HOUSE
(Thalia Productions, Inc./United Artists Corp.)

All during the Depression years, while he established himself as a prototype for the Hollywood-style underworld boss, Edward G. Robinson sought a higher actorly ground as an all-'round character lead. If a law-abiding Orthodox Jew could masquerade with ticket-selling persuasiveness as an Italianate gangster, then what could he *not* play? Though popularly typecast as a consequence of his memorably ferocious work in *Little Caesar* (1931), Robinson managed a resounding self-parody by handling two distinct roles in *The Whole Town's Talking* (1935); brought a convincingly Asian dignity-under-duress to the role of a Westernized Tong executioner in *The Hatchet Man* (1932); and appeared quite like his natural self as a respected Broadway player-turned-avenger in *The Man with Two Faces* (1934). By 1940, Robinson was poised to weigh in as one of the screen's leading biographical interpreters: *Dr. Ehrlich's Magic Bullet* and *A Dispatch from Reuters* found the Broadway veteran holding forth with an epic historical resonance as, respectively, the scientist who discovered a remedy for venereal disease and the journalist who brought news reportage into the realm of higher technology.

SOL LESSER presents

EDWARD G. ROBINSON
LON McCALLISTER

"The RED HOUSE"

with JUDITH ANDERSON · RORY CALHOUN   ALLENE ROBERTS · JULIE LONDON
ONA MUNSON · HARRY SHANNON

Written for the screen
and Directed by
DELMER DAVES   From the novel "THE RED HOUSE"
by GEORGE AGNEW CHAMBERLAIN   Copyright by Thalia Productions, Inc.
Released thru United Artists

But the 1940s also cinched Robinson's credentials as one of the finer handlers of intimate psychological drama, as adept at understated villainy as at playing various identifiably ordinary chaps to whom fall extraordinary misfortunes. *Flesh and Fantasy* (1943), *Double Indemnity* and *The Woman in the Window* (both from 1944), *Scarlet Street* (1945), *The Stranger* (1946) and *Night Has a Thousand Eyes* (1948) all tapped in Robinson a gift for conveying desperate obsession and an air of torment with a rare economy of emotion.

The most unconventional of that small handful — and the most personally absorbing, for the actor — is *The Red House*, the result of a short-lived producing partnership between Robinson and the old-line Poverty Row impresario Sol Lesser.

Such a teaming would have been beyond Lesser's reach during the 1930s, for while Robinson was coming to the fore as a star player at Warner Bros., Lesser, a former theater operator, was asserting himself with such rough-and-ready fare as 1932's *Tarzan the Fearless* (see *Forgotten Horrors: The Definitive Edition*) and three opportunistic patchwork pieces: the feature-lengther *Thunder over Mexico* and the short subjects "Death Day" and "Eisenstein in Mexico." These entries from 1933–1934 were built of footage salvaged without authorization from Sergei Eisenstein's abandoned epic of 1931–1932, *¡Que Viva México!*

Lesser's ambitions ran quite beyond Poverty Row, and the occasional breakthrough — placing his indie production of *The Mine with the Iron Door*, for example, with Columbia Pictures — pointed the way to his arrival in 1941 as chief of production at RKO-Radio Pictures. Lesser would alternate from here on out between major-league security and the maverick-producer imperative. The partnership with Robinson was one of Lesser's bigger independent ventures.

The Red House is a nightmare-inducing study of a deteriorating mind, rendered with a subtle poignancy via Robinson's gift for seeming a lovable and nurturing sort, however brusque. He plays Pete Morgan, a recluse by preference, whose devotion to his adopted daughter, Meg (Allene Roberts), proves to hinge entirely upon her obedience. Meg, now approaching adulthood, innocently compromises the guarded security of the Morgan farm when she arranges for a classmate, Nath Storm (Lon McCallister), to sign on as Pete's handyman.

Pete, who has become such a hermit that he doesn't even realize the townspeople regard him as a hermit, proves a benevolent employer until one stormy night, when Nath announces his plan to take a short-cut home through the nearby Oxhead Woods. Pete begins raving about screams from a shunned house in that region, so unnerving the boy that he becomes lost and circles back to Pete's farmhouse.

Summoning his gumption in the days ahead, Nath determines to find the ominous Red House. Meg follows along, forgetting Pete's long-standing orders to steer clear of the woods. So does Nath's possessive girlfriend, Tibby Rinton (Julie London). A shadowy figure lurks along the backwoods trails, attacking Nath at one point. When Nath lets it slip that he and the girls have been searching for the Red House, Pete's dread of the wooded area lapses from the chronic to the acute. The prowler proves to be a local lout named Teller (Rory Calhoun), who takes rather too seriously Pete's orders to discourage people from entering the woods. Teller fires a warning shot at Meg, causing her to take a crippling fall, and the assaults can only escalate from here.

Pete, in his distraction, calls Meg by the name of Jeanie. Pete's long-suffering sister, Ellen (Dame Judith Anderson), sensing Pete's return to bad habits of many years previous, cautions him to remember how he had lost the affections of Meg's mother—Jeanie. Teller guns down Ellen when she rushes into the woods, intending to torch the Red House. Pete refuses to help his sister as she lies dying, cold-heartedly informing Meg that she and Ellen are suffering a just punishment for "defying the Red House."

Teller, who has meanwhile lured Tibby away from Nath, persuades her to skip town with him. Nath rushes in pursuit of Teller, only to find the police well ahead of the game. Finally at the breaking point, Pete confesses to Meg that he had murdered her parents and left their bodies in a reservoir underlying the grounds of the Red House. As Nath and the local sheriff (Arthur Space) approach, Meg screams for help. Pete begins to re-enact his crime-of-passion slaying of Jennie. Nath rescues Meg, and the sheriff pursues Pete to a plunge into the waters of the Red House. As Pete sinks, a wheel from Meg's parents' carriage floats to the surface.

True to the players' reminiscences excerpted below, E.G. Robinson proved as good a silent-partner boss on *The Red House* as he was a star player. There is a collaborative feel about the picture, a lifelike sense of entangled destinies in the face of gathering doom, that lends *The Red House* a resemblance to such weightier rustics-in-crisis fare as Lewis Milestone's 1939 *Of Mice and Men* and Robert Mulligan's *To Kill a Mockingbird* (1962). *House*'s Delmer Daves, though still fairly green as a director at this time, packed a wealth of experience in acting and screenwriting and overall filmmaking, dating as far back as a prop-boy hitch on James Cruze's epic *The Covered Wagon* (1923). Daves' screenplay for *The Red House* indulges Robinson with dialogue bordering on the florid, but Daves the director demands the restraint necessary to make Pete Morgan seem a man perpetually on the edge of a breakdown. Thus does Pete's account of "screams in the night" serve a dual function at a crucially early stage: Robinson on one level enjoys spooking the schoolboy thus regaled—but he also believes every word of the outlandish rant. (A magnificently designed tangle of underbrush completes the suggestion of a haunting; the place looks forbidding even by daylight.)

Lon McCallister, whose promising career would be stalled prematurely by his boyish aspect, serves ideally here as the high school kid who cracks a 15-year-old murder case through a combination of dumb luck and courage. Allene Roberts juggles virtue with a dawning stubborn streak as the endangered daughter.

Dame Judith Anderson, Australian by birth, had been one of the greatest of the legitimate stage's Lady Macbeths, and her film work since 1933 had typecast her almost thoroughly as a villainous sort. *The Red House* affords Lady Anderson a welcome change of pace, as a self-sacrificing householder who may be the only force holding her brother back from the abyss.

Julie London, whose greater fortunes lay ahead as the sultriest torch singer of the 1950s, does indeed recall Susan Hayward's mastery at portraying small-town tarts, bringing to the role considerably more than is written. Miss London told us this in a late-in-life interview:

> Mr. Robinson was an awfully kind man to work for, and to work with, too. He assured me that the kind of role I was handling [in *The Red House*] could establish me as an actress of Susan Hayward's style and caliber. I don't know that I actually believed him—I don't think I was anywhere near as good as Susan Hayward—but the thing was, he didn't lord it over us unproved talents, big-time star though he was. It might have been his company, but he made it plain that it was our movie, all of us, there, together.

Rory Calhoun reads the secondary menace as an overconfident lunkhead who performs most of the mayhem through carelessness. This was his first assignment as Rory Calhoun; born Francis Timothy Durgin, he had gone but little seen since 1944 as a Fox contract player, billed as Frank McCown. In a 1980 visit, Calhoun reflected on the experience of filming *The Red House*:

> Everybody ought to have 'em what they call a valedictory film, and I reckon this 'un [the 1980 production of *Motel Hell*] might as well be mine, raggedy though it be. I suppose you could say this'd be my way of coming full-circle back to my very first picture under the name of Rory Calhoun, a thing I did with Edward G. Robinson called *The Red House*.
>
> Now, Mr. E.G., he was the star of that picture—playing this deadly recluse of a farmer, nursing some grisly old secrets—and I was strictly there for support, although Mr. Robinson had the say-so to have 'em beef up my part to where I was pert' near as dangerous as he was. That was the picture that gave me the confidence to carry on, and even though it led to some bigger things, I've never forgotten the kindnesses shown me while we were makin' *The Red House*.
>
> So I guess you could say that by playin' this menacing ol' farmer character now, I'm givin' a salute to Mr. Edward G. Robinson and the

breaks he gave me when I was a youngster. Not that *The Red House* and *Motel Hell* should be even mentioned together in the same breath of air—but... well, you know what I mean.

The ideal complement to the fine ensemble playing of *The Red House* is Miklos Rozsa's evocative musical score, also known as *Suite in Four Movements*. The accompaniment stood alone nicely as an album from Capitol Records.

Robinson and Lesser called their company Thalia Productions; it dissolved after *The Red House* despite an announcement of additional projects. Lesser continued under the banner of Sol Lesser Productions, Inc., cranking out *Tarzan* pictures on through the 1950s. He died in 1980.

Robinson's lot became tougher during those postwar years, despite steady work all along. Though well known as a patriotic sort, he found his name linked with Communist-front agencies during the early 1950s but cleared himself with an impassioned appearance before the House Committee on Un-American Activities. Following a triumphant return to Broadway in 1956, with Paddy Chayefsky's *Middle of the Night*, Robinson retrenched in Hollywood as primarily a supporting character man. His autobiography, *All My Yesterdays*, appeared in 1973—the year of his death—and he was awarded a posthumous Oscar recognizing his body of work over the long haul.

CREDITS: Producers: Sol Lesser and Edward G. Robinson (as Silent Partner); Director and Screenwriter: Delmer Daves; Assistant Director: Robert Stillman; Based Upon: Elsie Jerusalem's 1932 Novel, *The Red House*; Photographed by: Bert Glennon; Second Cameraman: Ed Fitzgerald; Transparency Projection Photography: Warren Lynch; Art Director: McClure Capps; Editor: Merrill White; Decor: Dorcy Howard; Costumer: Frank Beetson; Music: Miklos Rozsa; Sound: Frank McWhorter; Re-Recording and Sound Effects Mixers: Joseph I. Kane, Eddie J. Nelson and Jack Noyes; Music Mixer: William H. Wilmarth; Makeup: Irving Berns; Production Manager: Clem Beauchamp; Running Time: 100 Minutes; Released: February 7, 1947

CAST: Edward G. Robinson (Pete Morgan); Lon McCallister (Nath Storm); Dame Judith Anderson (Ellen Morgan); Rory Calhoun (Teller); Allene Roberts (Meg Morgan); Julie London (Tibby Rinton); Ona Munson (Mrs. Storm); Harry Shannon (Dr. Byrne); Arthur Space (Sheriff); Walter Sande (Don Brent)

APACHE ROSE
(Republic Pictures Corp.)

Roy Rogers and Dale Evans may have made a more effective movie-star team before they became (in 1947) the most famous married couple in Hollywood's Western sector. *Apache Rose*, Rogers' first starring picture in color finds the artists as playful near-antagonists: He is a border patrolman in conflict with the customary land-grabbing and cattle-rustling conspiracies. Rogers also must contend with a murderous casino boss, impersonated by that great should-have-been star George Meeker. Miss Evans, playing a sexier variant on a Tugboat Annie-type, has a sweetheart (not Roy) who finds himself awash in gambling debts even as his ranch becomes the center of a covetous scam. An ee-

rie network of caverns (said to be haunted, naturally) and an ominous seagoing mob hideout complete the film's credential as an item ripe for rediscovery by the chills-are-where-you-find-'em audience.

The Rogers-Evans relationship seems a study in playful one-upsmanship from the outset, when Roy (playing himself, as usual) shoves Billie Colby (Miss Evans) into a river during a dispute involving the cargo aboard her tugboat. Helped out of the drink by her suitor, Carlos Vega (Russ Vincent), Billie turns hostile when Carlos proposes marriage. She will not even consider the prospect until he gives up gambling, which has put him nearly $150,000 in hock.

Roy and his sidekick Alkali Elkins (Olin Howlin) go prowling through the caves underlying Vega's hacienda and learn that a local criminal ring has good reason to nurture a ghostly legend surrounding the property. The caverns are ideal for hiding stolen livestock.

Reed Calhoun (Meeker), who runs the gambling ship S.S. *Casino*, presses Vega to sign over his ranch, which surrounds the caves, as a debt settlement. Vega holds out, for his cousin, Rosa (Donna Martell, a.k.a. DeMario), is co-owner of the property—and besides, they have just discovered signs of an oil strike.

After a sniper opens fire (unsuccessfully) on Rosa, Billie proposes to impersonate the near-victim to smoke out the racketeers. A kidnapper is gunned down by his accomplices during a failed attempt to abduct the disguised Billie, and Roy finds on the body a poker chip. Calhoun readily admits to ownership of the token, agreeing to conduct Roy on a tour of the *Casino*. Roy barely escapes after he overhears Calhoun and a henchman (John Laurenz) plotting another attack on Rosa. Calhoun escalates the campaign, scarcely caring whether he kills his intended victims, his pursuers or his fellow hoodlums. Roy finally gets the goods, and the drop, on Calhoun. Amid the turmoil, Billie steals aboard the betting ship and destroys Carlos' documents of indebtedness.

Roy Rogers was such a generous player as to allow his supporting cohorts—including his magnificent Palomino, Trigger—to upstage him, and even in his color process debut Rogers yields to a superb show of villainy from the handsome and athletic George Meeker.

Meeker (1889–1958) rewards the opportunity with a flamboyant show of backshooting malice—hardly in a league, prestige-wise, with his unforgettable moments in *Casablanca* (1942) and *The Ox-Bow Incident* (1943), but more liberal with the screen time. Later on in 1947, Meeker would register impressively as a fortune hunter lusting after heiress Dorothy Lamour in *Road to Rio*. Meeker had been an important leading man during the silent-screen years. He was, on the side, a championship polo player; this talent served him well in his many outdoor-action assignments, although his horsemanship was more English-style than Western. (And while we're about the subject of frontier villainy: *Apache Rose* set dresser Perry Murdock had served 1935's *Big Calibre*, an early-day linchpin of the *Forgotten Horrors* canon, as both screenwriter and mad-bomber bad guy.)

Former jazz–pop singer Dale Evans had handled a similarly feisty supporting role in Rogers' better-remembered 1946 starrer *Home in Oklahoma*. Many fans who know only her matronly heroic presence of the 1950s are surprised to find such a tomboyish zest in the Queen-to-be of the West. Olin Howlin makes a likable sidekick in the Fuzzy St. John–Gabby Hayes mold, and Russ Vincent is convincing as an irresponsible Latin-lover type whose sinful habits have finally caught up with him. Donna DeMario is appropriately tragic as one whose doom is sealed merely by her kinship to Vincent's Carlos. Bob Nolan & the Sons of the Pioneers, not to mention both Rogers and Miss Evans, justify *Variety*'s description of the film as "an oatuner" (show-biz shorthand describing a *tune*ful *oat* opera) with the usual nifty array of pop-Western harmonies.

The Trucolor process was a less expensive alternative to top-of-the-line Technicolor, which in any case had been refined to a more affordable state several years before *Apache Rose*. We have not seen a surviving print in pristine Trucolor, for by the time our households had first begun catching the Republic Rogerses on television during the 1950s, the black-and-white picture tube had become the Great Equalizer of all movies thus deployed. A much later bootleg-video copy, though taken from a color print, serves chiefly to illustrate the deterioration of the Trucolor dyes. *Forgotten Horrors'* co-founder, the late George E. Turner, once cited Trucolor as "a postcard-looking process—not quite *real*, but okay for big skies and vast landscapes." Which pretty well covers its worth to a Roy Rogers shoot-'em-up.

CREDITS: Associate Producer: Edward J. White; Director: William Witney; Assistant Director: Leonard Kunody; Screenplay: Gerald Geraghty; Photographed by: Jack Marta; Special Effects: Howard Lydecker and Theodore Lydecker; Art Director: Gano Chittenden; Editor: Les Orlebeck; Decor: John McCarthy, Jr., and Perry Murdock; Costumer: Adele Palmer; Music: Morton Scott; Songs: "Apache Rose," "Wishing Well" and "Ride, Vaquero!" by Jack Elliott, "There's Nothin' Like Coffee in the Mornin'," by Tim Spencer and Glenn Spencer, and "José," Composer Unacknowledged; Sound: Richard E. Tyler; Makeup: Bob Mark; Running Time: 75 Minutes; Released: February 15, 1947

CAST: Roy Rogers and Trigger, the Smartest Horse in the Movies (Themselves, More or Less); Dale Evans (Billie Colby); Olin Howlin (Alkalai Elkins); George Meeker (Reed Calhoun); John Laurenz (Pete); Russ Vincent (Carlos Vega); Minerva Urecal (Felicia); LeRoy Mason (Hilliard); Donna DeMario [Martell] (Rosa Vega); Terry Frost (Sheriff Jim Mason); Conchita Lemus and 'Strellita Baca (Dancers); Tex Terry (Likens); Bob Nolan & the Sons of the Pioneers (Themselves); Martin Garralaga (Proprietor); Fernando Alvarado and José Alvarado (Boys); James Linn (Driver)

THE BEGINNING OR THE END
(Metro-Goldwyn-Mayer Corp./Loew's, Inc./Paramount Pictures, Inc.)

New, clear proliferation: Although its major-league pedigree and a multi million-dollar investment place it well beyond the precincts of Poverty Row, Norman Taurog's *The Beginning or the End* is a crucial piece in the puzzle of atomic-devastation films that had begun falling into place toward the end of World War II—a piebald subgenre that would draw its greatest vitality from the mongrelized independent studios. The documentary-like tone of many of the B-movies' nuclear hair-raisers of the 1950s would derive explicitly from *The Beginning or the End*, which in that light must belong right here in its truer context. (Bert I. Gordon, a monster-movie impresario who presented several such pictures, seems to have drawn upon the big film's very title as an exploitative device, altering it but slightly to come up with 1957's *Beginning of the End*, in which gigantic grasshoppers invade Chicago. This titular resemblance caused a great deal of confusion when both films came into television syndication at approximately the same time.)

MGM made plenty of noise in pretending, during the waning months of 1945, that *The Beginning or the End* was to be the first of its kind, created in a race against similarly conceived projects at Twentieth Century-Fox and Paramount Pictures. Fox beat MGM to the box-office, of course, with its May 1946 release of the atom-spy thriller *Rendezvous 24*, even though MGM would pack a greater earnestness plus a sense of newsreel immediacy into *The Beginning or the End*. (The MGM entry was technically ready for release by autumn of 1946, but studio chief Louis B. Mayer delayed matters by demanding the addition of actual Hiroshima footage.)

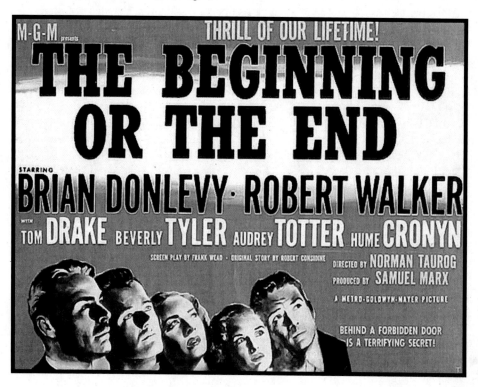

MGM also derailed a Paramount project called *Top Secret*, then absorbed it into *The Beginning or the End*. Paramount played right along with the ambush, turning over its story-and-script properties and hiring out producer Hal Wallis to MGM as a consultant—in exchange for an up-front fee and a long-term percentage of gross revenues. Wallis lunched out for years thereafter on the assertion that he had been not only the trailblazer in the fission-flicks phenomenon, but also gentleman enough to cede the match to come-lately MGM. MGM's Samuel Marx assigned himself prior claim, of course. Fox's Solomon "Sol" Wurtzel flattered himself likewise.

These old-line major players are perfectly welcome to their vain conceits, but in fact half a dozen movies—from studios large and small, and with varying degrees of atom-splitting interest—had gotten the drop on both *Rendezvous 24* and *The Beginning or the End* during 1945–1946:

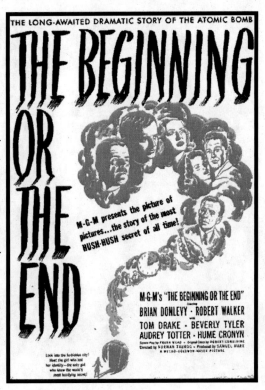

THE LONG-AWAITED DRAMATIC STORY OF THE ATOMIC BOMB

THE BEGINNING OR THE END

M-G-M presents the picture of pictures...the story of the most HUSH-HUSH secret of all time!

M-G-M's "THE BEGINNING OR THE END"
BRIAN DONLEVY · ROBERT WALKER
with
TOM DRAKE · BEVERLY TYLER
AUDREY TOTTER · HUME CRONYN
Screen Play by FRANK WEAD · Original Story by ROBERT CONSIDINE
Directed by NORMAN TAUROG · Produced by SAMUEL MARX
A METRO-GOLDWYN-MAYER PICTURE

Look into the forbidden city! Meet the girl who told her identity—the only girl who knew the world's most terrifying secret!

• *China's Little Devils*, from Monogram Pictures, predicted a generically conceived bombing raid on Tokyo, helped along by supernatural powers—months before the A-Bombing of Hiroshima and Nagasaki. (See *Forgotten Horrors 3*.)
• *Shadow of Terror*, from Producers Releasing Corp., became the first Hollywood film to remark on the war's emphatic climax. PRC simply tacked nuclear-test footage onto its already-completed melodrama about an imaginary super-explosive. (See *Forgotten Horrors 3*.)
• While *Shadow of Terror* awaited a late-fall general release, RKO-Radio Pictures and Twentieth Century-Fox jumped the gun in September with, respectively, *First Yank into Tokyo* and *The House on 92nd Street*.
• The U.S. government teamed with Warner Bros. to deliver *Appointment in Tokyo* in December of 1945.
• And between Fox's release of *Rendezvous 24* and MGM's early-1947 splash with *The Beginning or the End*, Universal entered the nuclear-scare sweeps with *Danger Woman* (1946).

All of which add up to reduce the issue of Who Got There First? to a so-what-the-hell academic parlor game at best. Seems to us, anyhow, that the first horrors-of-the-atom picture—if anybody actually wants to get so all-fired obsessive-compulsive about Absolutes—might even be something so prescient as *The Invisible Ray* or *Death from*

The vigil before the bombing.

a Distance or *The Phantom Creeps*, from Back in the Day when one World War had seemed more than enough.

Suffice that there is a pattern emerging, here, and that *The Beginning or the End* is strategically positioned to fix a template for any number of lower-rent films to follow. By 1948, the oddly matched likes of *Sofia*, *Design for Death*, *Women in the Night*, *Walk a Crooked Mile* and *Who Killed Doc Robbin* would be dipping wholeheartedly into the mysteries of nuclear fission. After a lull during 1949, the subgenre would come into its own in 1950 with an agenda ranging from the dry factuality of *Farewell to Yesterday* and *Fifty Years before Your Eyes* to the more picaresque likes of *Rocketship X-M*, *Destination Moon*, *The Flying Saucer* and *Radar Secret Service*.

The Beginning or the End opens with cautionary praise for the unleashed atom from Dr. J. Robert Oppenheimer (Hume Cronyn), who proceeds to discuss the phenomenon in terms of parallel research campaigns in Germany and America. Matt Cochran (Tom Drake), a U.S. scientist, is more keenly concerned with the atom as a source of productive energy. Key participants here are Enrico Fermi (Joseph Calleia) and Albert Einstein (Ludwig Stossel, who would become more famous in years to come as the Little Old Winemaker in a run of television commercials). President Roosevelt (Godfrey Tearle) encourages a broadening of purely peaceable research, but following the country's entry into the war in 1941 he authorizes a two-billion-dollar bomb-development project.

Cochran, newly married and concerned for the very soul of his country, challenges the ethics of the project, which to his mind reduces the United States to the level of Germany's warlike interests in fission. In 1945, new President Truman (Art Baker) vows to carry on the bomb venture, and Oppenheimer's laboratory at Los Alamos, New Mexico, accepts the first payload of U–235, an essential component. As the research builds toward a showdown, Cochran and a military observer, Col. Jeff Nixon (Robert Walker), find themselves drawn ever deeper into the intrigues. On August 5, 1945, Cochran dies from radiation poisoning. The next day, the bomb is loosed upon Hiroshima.

The narrative tone is more gung-ho than apologetic or questioning, but the film makes a valiant attempt to cover both sides of what has become a perpetual controversy. The matter-of-fact attitude precludes much in the way of conventional screen acting—although Tom Drake takes a passionate Everyman stance as the martyred conscience of the piece, and Beverly Tyler matches Drake's intensity as his widow-in-waiting. *The Beginning or the End* nails its now-it-can-be-told attitude with a prologue designed to look like a separate short subject: In a mock-newsreel segment, Hume Cronyn (in character as Oppenheimer), Brian Donlevy (as the bomb-project overseer, Maj. Gen. Leslie R. Groves) and other players entomb a time capsule marking the discovery of atomic devastation. These portrayals were by design authorized, inasmuch as MGM had consulted with Harry S Truman, Groves and Dr. Oppenheimer during pre-production. Maj. Charles Sweeney, pilot on the Hiroshima run, became a technical adviser, and MGM sought advice from Francis J. Spellman, Archbishop of New York, who had conducted a God-on-our-Side High Mass for American servicemen assigned to the bombings of Hiroshima and Nagasaki. Strategic location filming took place at Los Alamos, at Oak Ridge, Tennessee, and at Carswell Air Force Base (known among the more waggish locals as "Crashwell") in Fort Worth, Texas.

MGM had announced prematurely that Clark Gable, Van Johnson and Lionel Barrymore would handle leading roles. Eleanor Roosevelt involved herself during the spring of 1946, protesting Barrymore's scheduled portrayal of Franklin D. Roosevelt on grounds that the actor had made disparaging comments about the late Chief of State. Although production had begun by now, MGM delayed the filming of Barrymore's segments until he could explain himself to the former First Lady. Barrymore insisted that his remarks had been misinterpreted, but the Roosevelt family was so adamant that MGM replaced Barrymore with Godfrey Tearle.

Even without Johnson, Gable and Barrymore, the massive cast roster (the formidable block of type just below) is a veritable *Who's Who*—not only of top-shelf major-league character players, but also of B-movie standbys including the *Superman* serials' Kirk Alyn; *Invaders from Mars'* Jimmy Hunt; *Strangler of the Swamp* thesp and director-in-waiting Blake Edwards; and veteran second-stringer bad guy Martin Kosleck. Brian Donlevy's brusque impersonation of Leslie Groves foreshadows his portrayal of a (fictional) space-race scientist in two Hammer Films productions of the 1950s, *The Quatermass Experiment* (a.k.a. *The Creeping Unknown*) and *Quatermass II* (a.k.a. *Enemy from Space*).

CREDITS: Producer: Samuel Marx; Director: Norman Taurog; Assistant Directors: Stanley Goldsmith and Frank Myers; Screenplay: Frank Wead; Story: Robert Considine; Photographed by: Ray June; Special Effects: Warren Newcombe and A. Arnold Gillespie; Associate Effects Artist: Donald Jahraus; Montage Effects: Peter Ballbusch; Art Directors: Cedric Gibbons and Hans Peters; Editor: George Boemler; Decor: Edwin B. Willis; Associate Set Dresser: Keogh Gleason; Costumer: Irene; Musical Score: Daniele Amfitheatrof; Sound: Douglas Shearer; Makeup: Jack Dawn; Technical and Military Advisers: Dr. H.T. Wensel, Dr. Edward R. Tompkins, Dr. David Hawkins, W. Bradford

Shank, Col. William A. Consodine, Lt. Col. Charles W. Sweeney, Maj. Glen Landreth and Paul Van Sloun; Special Consultant: Archbishop Francis J. Spellman; Unit Manager: Sergei Petschnikoff; Advisor: Hal B. Wallis; Casting: Bobby Webb; Running Time: 112 Minutes; Released: Following Washington, D.C., Premiere on February 19, 1947

CAST: Brian Donlevy (Maj. Gen. Leslie R. Groves); Robert Walker (Col. Jeff Nixon); Tom Drake (Matt Cochran); Beverly Tyler (Anne Cochran); Audrey Totter (Jean O'Leary); Hume Cronyn (Dr. J. Robert Oppenhemer); Hurd Hatfield (Dr. John Wyatt); Joseph Calleia (Dr. Enrico Fermi); Godfrey Tearle (Franklin D. Roosevelt); Victor Francen (Dr. Marré); Richard Hayden (Dr. Chisholm); Jonathan Hale (Dr. Vannevar Bush); John Litel (K.T. Keller); Henry O'Neill (Gen. Thomas F. Farrell); Warner Anderson (Capt. William S. Parsons); Barry Nelson (Col. Paul Tibbets); Art Baker (Harry S Truman); Ludwig Stossel (Albert Einstein); John Hamilton (Dr. Harold C. Urey); Frank Ferguson (Dr. James B. Conant); Tom Stevenson (Dr. E.P. Wigner); John Gallaudet (Dr. Leo Szilard); Nella Walker (Grace Tully); Edward Earle (Charles G. Ross); Moroni Olsen (Dr. Arthur H. Compton); Norman Lloyd (Dr. Troyanski); Jim Davis (Pilot); Charles Trowbridge (Walter S. Carpenter, Jr.); Frank Wilcox (Dr. W.H. Zinn); Henry Hall (Gen. Brehon Somervell); Paul Harvey (Lt. Gen. W.D. Styer); Larry Johns, John Albright and Douglas Carter (Quaker Scientists); Robert Emmett Keane (Dr. Rand); James Bush (Dr. Ernest O. Lawrence); Trevor Bardette (Doctor); William Wright (Col. John Lansdale); Damian O'Flynn (C.D. Howe); Martin Kosleck (Dr. O.R. Frisch); Rudolph Anders (Prof. Schmidt); Torben Meyer (Milkman); William Forrest (Brigadier General); Erville Alderson (Secretary of War Henry Stimson); Clarke Hardwicke (Enola Gay Co-Pilot); Guy Williams [Screen Debut] (Enola Gay Bombardier); Greg Barton (Enola Gay Navigator); William Bishop (Enola Gay Electronics Officer); William Leicester (Enola Gay Flight Engineer); William Roberts (Enola Gay Radio Operator); Jack Sterling (Enola Gay Tailgunner); Bob Gilbert (Enola Gay Lieutenant); Brad Slaven (Enola Gay Assistant Gunner); Richard Terry (Enola Gay Radar Operator); Emmett Vogan (Medical Officer); Forbes Murray (Briefing Officer); John B. Kennedy (Narrator, Newsreel Segment); Charles Bradstreet (Guard); Michael McGrath (Dr. Kistiakonsky); Frank Leigh (British General); Frank Baker (Canadian Officer); John Banner (German Laboratory Assistant); Otto Reichow, Jack Worth, Frederick Giermann, Fred Nurney and Jerry Schumacher (Nazi Officers); Arno Frey (Nazi Official); Hans von Mohrhart (Danish Customs Agent); Hans Schumm (Nazi Police Officer); Don E. Lewis (Secret Service Agent); David Thursby (English Policeman); Leslie Vincent (English Scientist); Ann Howard (English Laboratory Assistant); Patricia Medina (Mrs. Wyatt); Stanley Blystone (Civilian Guard); Connie Weiler and Jon Gilbreath (Attendants); Frank Erickson and Ray Paige (Metermen); Larry Blake (Military Policeman); Dorothy Scott (Laboratory Assistant); Earl Hodgins (Gateman); George Peters (Nurse); Harry Denny (Officer); Eddie Parks (Bystander); Sybil Merritt (Guide); Ed Cassidy (Rafferty); Robert Malcolm (Keith); Frank Scannell (Winne); Harry T. Wensel (Wensel); Paul Bryar (Army Officer); Walter Baldwin and Louis Mason (Laborers); Ralph Dunn (Guard); Tom Pilkington (Man with Counter); Charles Peck (Courier); King Lockwood (Col. Nichols); Selmer Jackson and Mike Kilian (Senior Engineers); Tom Dillon (Gregor); John James (Engineer); Frank Dae, Boyd Davis and George Carleton (Senators); Carlyle Blackwell (Armed Officer); Richard Abbott (Danish Resistance Leader); Philip Ahlm and Bert Davidson (Armed Guards); John Gannon and Bobby Jordan (Orderlies)

LAW OF THE LASH

(PRC Pictures, Inc./Producers Releasing Corp.)

*…the injection of corny psychological overtones fails
to come off.*—From the *Variety* review

Larry Buchanan, a towering presence among the Poverty Row filmmakers, will figure mightily in the *Forgotten Horrors* collection when inevitably we go tearing into the 1960s. No time like the Here-and-Now to give the artist a premature due, for Buchanan's take on Alfred "Lash" LaRue (1917–96), star player of *Law of the Lash*, is a gemlike crystallization of the sharp decline and slight resurgence of one of the great oddball-Western heroes.

Law of the Lash is, for the record, more a curiosity than an outright thriller. Its inclusion here serves chiefly to represent LaRue's *Cheyenne Kid* series, which would continue with *Border Feud*, *The Fighting Vigilantes*, *Ghost Town Renegades*, *Return of the Lash* and *Stage to Mesa City*, all during 1947–1948. As though LaRue's weapon of preference, a 20-foot bullwhip, were not a sufficiently peculiar attention-grabber in a genre where the six-shooter held sway, *Law of the Lash* calls upon LaRue and comical sidekick Al "Fuzzy" St. John to undermine a criminal gang by inflicting an acute case of derangement upon one of its members.

St. John's mush-mouthed geezer act had made him a favorite cohort of several shoot-'em-up stars; he was outdone in popularity only by George "Gabby" Hayes and Lester "Smiley" Burnette. St. John had long since established his credential for severity and vengeance, as well. In 1943's *Death Rides the Plains*, the actor takes dire affront at a serial-killing ranch-theft conspiracy, being a surviving relative of one victim. And in 1945's *His Brother's Ghost*, St. John essays the figurative title character, bent upon avenging his twin's murder via a spectral impersonation.

St. John's tactics in *Law of the Lash* are more of the torture-by-annoyance variety, but they serve well to drive henchman Lefty (Lee Roberts) to the ragged edge. Undercover Marshal Cheyenne (LaRue), being the gentlemanly sort who'd rather capture than kill, takes Lefty

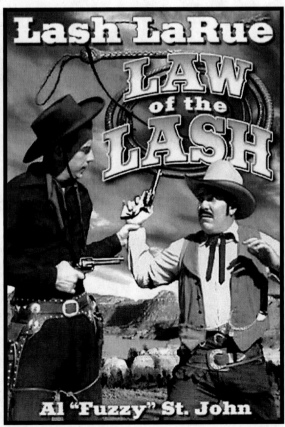

hostage early on, the better to smoke out a gang run by an oily no-account named Decker (Jack O'Shea). Lefty's ordeal drags on for days while Cheyenne scouts out the territory, finally using Lefty's horse to beat a trail to the hideout while releasing Lefty afoot—thus manipulating Decker into wondering whether Lefty might be in cahoots with Cheyenne. The psychological torments, though merely a superficial plot device, serve to render *Law of the Lash* distinctive, and Roberts plays the crack-up well.

The resolution is nonviolent by Gothic Western standards. Bob Steele or Ken Maynard, among LaRue's artistic forebears, would have established a grand body count en route to imposing Law and Order upon such a crooked outpost. But at least LaRue plays it out with the classic-manner gritted teeth and implacable attitude. His bullwhip maneuvers are astonishing—and genuine, a case of athletic precision approaching the realm of special effects—and especially so in the climactic disarming of Jack O'Shea.

Four decades later, Lash LaRue still had the chops. Larry Buchanan, who had once sought in vain to enlist LaRue for a proposed teleseries, met the actor during the late 1980s at a convention in Hollywood. "All in black, with the leather hat string flapping under his chin, he snapped the bullwhip so that the tip just missed the microphone," wrote Buchanan in a reminiscence for the catalogue-*cum*-magazine of McFarland & Co., Inc., Publishers. "The amplified crack of the leather was thunderous."

"Lash gained a modest but respectable following in early television," said Buchanan. "Thereafter, the story… followed the old Hollywood cowboy tradition: booze, old-time religion and rootless wanderings." Buchanan's many letters seeking LaRue had gone unanswered.

All those years later, upon approaching LaRue in person, Buchanan handed the lapsed star a business card.

"I got some of your letters and phone messages, podner…," as Buchanan quotes LaRue. "But somp'n' happened to me when I went on the bum… Since I got off the rotgut and made a deal with the Man Upstairs, I'm one happy *hombre*, havin' one hell of a time."

LaRue ran in circles uncommon for a Western-movie star, his friendships including the Beat Era philosopher-comedian and monologue artist Richard "Lord" Buckley (1906-1960). John Wooley once asked LaRue about that connection, "and a kind of hipster's smile came over his face." John's 1992 account of the interview included these observations:

> You won't often hear a B-Western star quoting the late hipster Lord Buckley, but LaRue can, and does: "'The bad jazz a man blows lives long after he's cut out—and the good things he might do are forgotten with his face.'
>
> "They'll forget your face in a hurry, too," he added.
>
> "Buckley was an entertainer's entertainer," said LaRue. "I met him down in Miami. When I came into the place he was playing, he did a double-take."

Larry Buchanan has noted that "some wise-acre called [LaRue] the poor man's Humphrey Bogart." It is beside the point to ponder whether LaRue brought any acting ability to the screen, for his short-lived Hollywood career and his follow-through endeavors in carnival exhibitions and Deep Southern hellfire evangelism depended entirely upon a flamboyant presence. Suffice that LaRue's command of the bullwhip and his confidence in addressing the camera justified every foot of, *uhm*, footage that PRC Pictures expended on him.

Fuzzy St. John, Richard Cramer and Lash LaRue in *Law of the Lash*. LaRue's resemblance to Humphrey Bogart is unmistakable in this image.

CREDITS: Producer: Jerry Thomas; Director: Ray Taylor; Assistant Director: F.O. Collings; Screenwriter and Production Manager: William Nolte; Photographed by: Robert Cline; Special Effects: Ray Mercer; Editor: Hugh Winn; Supervising Editor: Norman A. Cerf; Decor: Louis Diage; Music: Albert Glasser; Music Supervisor: Dick Carruth; Sound: Glen Glenn; Makeup: Austin Bedell; Running Time: 53 Minutes; Released: February 28, 1947

CAST: Al "Lash" LaRue (Cheyenne Kid [Davis]); Al "Fuzzy" St. John (Fuzzy Q. Jones); Lee Roberts (Lefty); Mary Scott (Jane Hilton); Jack O'Shea (Decker); Charles King (Sheriff); Carl Matthews (Blackie); Matty Roubert (Pee Wee); John Elliott (Dad Hilton); Charles Whitaker (Bart); Ted French (Smitty); Richard Cramer (Bartender); Brad Slavin (Sam)

THE GHOST GOES WILD

(Republic Pictures Corp.)

The ghost of the title can be accepted literally, without fear of any debunker cop-outs. *The Ghost Goes Wild*, is, all the same, more a screwball-slapstick bedroom farce than a hair-raiser—dually centered upon an eccentric artist's romantic complications and legal woes and a campaign of humiliating revenge by the departed spirit of a henpecked squire. An indebtedness to Thorne Smith's celebrated *Topper* yarns is patent, but of course *The Ghost Goes Wild* is scarcely a patch on the *Topper* comedies that Hal Roach had produced during 1937–1941.

Painter Monty Crandall (James Ellison) incurs the wrath of a snooty widow, Susan Beecher (Ruth Donnelly), when his unflattering likeness of her sees print. It helps matters none at all that Monty's fiancée, Phyllis Beecher (Anne Gwynne), is Susan's niece. Dogged by the threat of a lawsuit, Monty retreats to his farmhouse in Connecticut, a historic site called Haunted Hill—no relation to Vincent Price's digs in a more famous movie. The very name of Monty's home bespeaks an old superstition, and in fact Monty has purchased the place because it is reputed to harbor the ghost of Benedict Arnold. (Sounds like a kindred property to Boris Karloff's house in 1942's *The Boogie Man Will Get You*—a site presumed haunted by Uncas, Last of the Mohicans.)

A séance staged by Monty and Phyllis is interrupted by the arrival of Irene Winters (Stephanie Bachelor), a wayward wife who considers Phyllis her rival for Monty's affections. Irene's husband, Bill Winters (Grant Withers), barges in—brandishing a gun.

Monty, who is innocent of any such canoodlery, retreats outside, only to become lost in a thunderstorm. He stays missing for days. A premature report of Monty's death prompts his boss, Max Atterbury (Jonathan Hale), to propose a séance at Haunted Hill. Monty has sneaked back home and is taking a snooze beneath a sheet in this same room.

The participants in the séance scram in terror after they hear Monty yawn and see the stirring of his bed sheet. Monty's butler, Eric (that delightful scene-stealer, Edward Everett Horton), recovers his wits sufficiently to suggest that Monty remain hidden until the troubles with Susan Beecher and Bill Winters can be sorted out.

Among all the ghost-gawkers on parade here, only Eric succeeds—without half trying—at summoning a wraith. This spook would be one Timothy Beecher (Lloyd Corrigan), Susan's late husband. Timothy declares his intention to get back at his wife for the humiliations she had visited upon him in life; he also seems to know some information that could prove damaging to Bill Winters.

Timothy seems incapable of materializing except at short range. So Eric and Monty masquerade as ghosts to throw a scare into Susan—who seems convinced of a haunting at first but soon wises up and escalates her grudge campaign. Things are looking bad for Monty until Timothy throws his voice into the courtroom, revealing old embarrassments that cause Susan to drop her lawsuit. Bill is likewise moved to stop threatening Monty, who is last seen locked in an embrace with Phyllis.

At just an hour-and-change running time, *The Ghost Goes Wild* takes an inordinately long stretch to get to its point, which is the materialization of Lloyd Corrigan's pudgy little fussbudget of a ghost. Corrigan and Edward Everett Horton make a winning comedy team, overshadowing James Ellison and the exotically lovely Anne Gwynne at every turn. Director George Blair seems undecided throughout as to how the yarn wants playing—Grant Withers' gun-packing hothead seems to belong in some other movie entirely—but Horton and Corrigan exert a helpful control. (Corrigan was a former director of solid skill but modest output, with the 1937 Karloff-starrer *Night Key* among his niftier work.) Horton comes best equipped of all the players at coping with the scatter-shot absurdities of the screenplay; the role prefigures his many contributions to the television cartoons of Jay Ward, half a generation later. Ruth Donnelly is a hoot

as an indignant grouch on a collision course with a supernatural comeuppance. Jonathan Hale shines briefly as a conniver whose reasons for seeking to commune with Ellison's (presumed) ghost are less than well intentioned.

CREDITS: Associate Producer: Armand Schaefer; Director: George Blair; Assistant Director: Johnny Grubbs; Screenplay: Randall Faye, from His Collaborative Story with Taylor Caven; Photographed by: John Alton; Special Effects: Howard Lydecker and Theodore Lydecker; Art Director: Hilyard Brown; Editor: Fred Allen; Decor: John McCarthy, Jr., and George Milo; Costumer: Adele Palmer; Musical Director: Morton Scott; Music: Joseph Dubin; Sound: Victor Appel; Makeup: Bob Mark; Running Time: 66 Minutes; Released: March 8, 1947

CAST: James Ellison (Monty Crandall); Anne Gwynne (Phyllis Beecher); Edward Everett Horton (Eric); Ruth Donnelly (Susan Beecher); Stephanie Bachelor (Irene Winters); Grant Withers (Bill Winters); Lloyd Corrigan (Timothy Beecher); Emil Rameau (Prof. Jacques Dubonnet); Jonathan Hale (Max Atterbury); Charles Halton (T. O'Connor Scott); Holmes Herbert (Judge); Edward Gargan (Magazine Vendor); Gene Garrick and Michael Hughes (Reporters); William Austin (Chauffeur); Pierre Watkin (Murgatroyd); Frances Morris (Secretary); Olaf Hytten (Valet); Ralph Dunn (Bailiff); Bob Wilke (Hobo); Jack O'Shea (Trucker)

FALL GUY

(Monogram Productions, Inc./Monogram Distributing Corp.)

Cornell Woolrich's cocaine-binge yarn "C-Jag," from that quintessentially hard-boiled pulp magazine *Black Mask*, is the sturdy basis of *Fall Guy*—itself a tough egg of a movie that announces its cruel intentions early on as star player Clifford Penn collapses in a drug-induced stupor while clutching a bloodied knife.

Hospitalized and identified as former soldier Tom Cochrane, the cokehead appears incoherent but soon rallies and steals away undetected. Cochrane's brother-in-law, police detective Mac McClane (Robert Armstrong), shelters Cochrane and summons Lois Walters (Teala Loring), Tom's fiancée. Lois evades her over-protective guardian, Uncle Jim Grossett (Charles Arnt), and arrives just in time to overhear Cochrane mutter something about killing a woman while under the influence. Lois pledges her loyalty to Cochrane, who now struggles to remember his misadventure.

A flashback finds Cochrane attending a party where he drinks to excess and keels over in a stupor. He wakes alone in an unfamiliar apartment, where a closet yields a woman's corpse. He picks up a knife and a key, then steps outside to a telephone booth, where his collapse and discovery by a beat patrolman bring the film full-circle to its beginning.

McClane wants to take Cochrane to headquarters, but Lois persuades the detective to investigate solo. There follows an eerie cityscape search for the murder scene, through all-night grindhouse movie theaters and neon-ghostly concrete corridors—dogged at every turn by McLane's distrustful commanding officer (Douglas Fowley) and shadowed by a mysterious chap. Cochrane finally realizes that the murder scene is a suite upstairs from the wild party.

The hunt also turns up an ostensibly helpful fellow called Joe (Elisha Cook, Jr.) and a nightclub vocalist named Marie (Virginia Dale). Marie admits to her sweetheart, Mike (Jack Overman), that she had been hired—by a stranger who ordered her to skip town after paying off Joe as an accomplice—to ply Cochrane with booze and dope. While Mike keeps Cochrane from confronting Marie, the singer goes home, only to find Lois' Uncle Jim—her mysterious employer, and also the lurking observer—who strangles her. A rooftop struggle between Jim and Cochrane ends when Mike guns down the pillar-of-society bad uncle. Turns out that the closeted murder victim was Jim's blackmailing and dope-pushing mistress. Jim had killed her with the intention of setting up Cochrane, well known as an unemployed boozer, as the fall guy.

Woolrich's tacit condemnation of intoxication as a will-destroying agent—he was no stranger to the sauce—assured Monogram Pictures of no censorship problems with Hollywood's Production Code. The telling is perfectly loyal to the spirit and the letter of Woolrich, but for the appropriate veneer of postwar social malaise. The visual style is adequate for Woolrich, but all wrong for the *film noir* style that *Fall Guy* otherwise captures. Camera chief Mack Stengler re-creates the numbing gray throb of Monogram's wartime mad-doctor films more so than he advances the Germanic-influenced light-and-shadowplay of classic *noir*. (Edward J. Kay's musical score, too, recalls his early-'40s work for Monogram, although Kay spices the mix with a jazzy incidental song.) Director Reginald LeBorg, however, comes well equipped to convey the panicked desperation of a vintage Woolrich protagonist—here, the likable but weak-chinned Clifford Penn—and the worried attempts at helping or harming him from a faithful circle of friends and a narrowing field of tormentors. The hidden villain is not really all that well hidden, for Charles Arnt seems from the outset altogether too protective of leading lady Teala Loring and inordinately hateful toward Penn. Even so, Arnt's forced unmasking is played with a bracing ferocity.

Robert Armstrong plays the determined cop-in-the-family with all the plainspoken efficiency he had displayed in *King Kong*, 'way back in 1933. Miss Loring is the supportive sweetheart every shell-shocked returning G.I. should have had waiting for him, and Virginia Dale gives the doomed Marie a longing air that renders her treacheries at least explicable. Low-billed Jack Overman is a standout as the resentful boyfriend who arrives too late to save Dale but still gets in the last word with her killer. Elisha Cook, Jr., has too small a part to justify his world-class presence, but by just standing there looking half-weasly and half-apologetic he nails the film's authority as a modest definition of the *noir* style.

If the story has a familiar ring, that can only be because Woolrich used the same essential situation in the more famous "And So to Death," which *Argosy* magazine published in 1941, the year following the appearance of "C-Jag" in *Black Mask*. Woolrich sold "And So to Death" to Paramount Pictures' Pine-Thomas unit, which adapted it as *Fear in the Night*—the same year that Monogram issued *Fall Guy*. Partner-producers William H. Pine and William C. Thomas remade *Fear in the Night as Nightmare* in 1956, for release by United Artists.

CREDITS: Producer: Walter Mirisch; Director: Reginald LeBorg; Assistant Director: Frank Fox; Screenplay: Jerry Warner; Additional Dialogue: John O'Dea; Based Upon: Cornell Woolrich's Story, "C-Jag," (October 1940, *Black Mask;* Reprinted as "Cocaine" in the January 1947 *Black Mask*); Photographed by: Mack Stengler; Stills: Don MacKenzie; Special Effects: Augie Lohman; Technical Director: Dave Milton; Editors: William Austin and Edward Mann; Decor: Vin Taylor; Music: Edward J. Kay; Song: "Tootin' My Own Horn," by Edward J. Kay and Eddie Cherkose; Sound: Tom Lambert; Production Manager: William Calihan, Jr.; Running Time: 64 Minutes; Released: March 15, 1947

CAST: Clifford Penn (Tom Cochrane); Robert Armstrong (Mac McClane); Teala Loring (Lois Walters); Elisha Cook, Jr. (Joe); Douglas Fowley (Shannon); Charles Arnt (Jim Grossett); Virginia Dale (Marie); Iris Adrian (Mrs. Sindell); Jack Overman (Mike); John Harmon (Ed Sindell); Christian Rub (Janitor); Harry Strang (Taylor); John Bleifer (Clerk); Lou Lubin (Benny); George Backus (Police Physician); Theodore Gottlieb (Inmate); Bob Carleton (Pianist); and Franklin Dix, Monty Ford, Wally Walker, Katherine Marlowe, Marlyn Gladstone, Edna Harris

THE GUILTY

(Jack Wrather Productions, Inc./Monogram Productions, Inc./ Monogram Distributing Corp.)

Cornell Woolrich was on a roll in Hollywood during the 1940s—although the cinematic revival of his pulp stories did little to draw the author out of a self-damning pattern of reclusiveness and chronic alcoholism. Woolrich seems to have felt a deeper affinity with his typewriter than with any human acquaintances; this alienation informs his every glum utterance upon the printed page, even when he resorts to the reassuring device of a happy (or more accurately, forlornly hopeful) ending. Monogram followed through promptly on *Fall Guy* with *The Guilty*, from a Woolrich piece in *Detective Fiction Weekly*. Both films had been produced during November-December 1946.

Texas oilman-industrialist Jack Wrather weighed in here as a movie producer, with sufficiently agreeable results to keep him in the business for another six pictures over the next 11 years. Wrather's peak accomplishment in show business, however, came with his acquisition of the long-running CBS-TV franchise *Lassie*. Which makes rather a peculiar companion-piece to any of Cornell Woolrich's tales of doom and desperation.

Former child star Bonita Granville (who married Wrather in 1947 and assumed executive responsibilities with the diversified Wrather Corp.) toplines *The Guilty* as twins Linda and Estelle Mitchell, one a murder victim and the other a nymphomaniac who figures somehow in the case. An extended flashback establishes the horrific circumstances.

Mike Carr (Don Castle), while awaiting Estelle's arrival at a tavern, regales the barman (Thomas Jackson) with the grisly tale: Johnny Dixon (Wally Cassell), Mike's war buddy and roommate, is a shell-shocked binge drinker who loves Linda but cannot rid himself of man-hungry Estelle. Estelle has also forced her lustful attentions upon Mike. His first encounter with Linda assures Mike that she is the virtuous opposite of Estelle. Mike manages to lure Estelle away from a confrontation with Johnny and Linda. Linda is later reported missing. Johnny becomes the key suspect after Linda turns up dead and entombed atop his apartment building. Mike helps him elude arrest.

Police detective Heller (Regis Toomey), attempting to persuade Mike to betray Johnny, offers a cringe-inducing account of the murder. Choked almost to death, Linda Mitchell had been shoved into the narrow chute of an incinerator. The killer had broken her neck in the process—then changed his mind about burning her body, wrenched her free and stowed her away in a barrel on the rooftop.

Mike, certain of Johnny's innocence, lures his pal out of hiding. Heller arrests a Mitchell-household boarder named Alex Tremholt (John Litel). Tremholt renews the accusation against Johnny, who flees again despite the apparent case against Tremholt. Mike thwarts a suicide attempt by Johnny.

Back in the present day, Mike establishes that the meeting with Estelle is no nostalgic reunion. He forces her to revisit the apartment building, all but accusing her of her sister's murder. Heller is waiting—but not to arrest Estelle. A janitor has discovered an object lodged in the incinerator chute, bearing Mike's fingerprints. Mike had mistaken Linda for Estelle, the intended victim.

"So that's the whole story," as Mike sums things up. "Linda's dead, and Estelle is alive because of my blind murderous jealousy. Anyway, who'd want to look at a girl for the rest of his life and always be reminded of murder?"

The kinship between *Fall Guy* and *The Guilty* runs scarcely deeper than the Woolrich origins and the Monogram pedigree, for *The Guilty* is altogether a more richly *noir*-ified production, especially in Henry Sharp's crisp-and-cold camerawork. Rudy Schrager's orchestral score is more progressive than Edward J. Kay's old-fashioned, business-as-usual cues for *Fall Guy*. Trade publications of the day reported that Jack Wrather was so pleased with the early progress that he boosted the budget, assuring the little picture of a finer texture even though its shooting schedule remained as tight as that for *Fall Guy*.

The use of two typically Woolrich protagonists — Wally Cassell's hapless, blackout-prone loser and Don Castle's glad-handing Best Chum incarnate — cranks the tension a few notches. Neither actor is particularly spellbinding, but director John Reinhardt plays them well off one another and together they convey the conflicts-of-self that can only represent Woolrich's fantasy-realm alter egos. Few other authors have managed to transform such inner pity and low esteem into results so satisfying. Bonita Granville is convincing enough as both the good sister and the predatory sister, although her work here is no match for the twinned portrayals that Olivia de Havilland had given the year previous in *The Dark Mirror*. Regis Toomey (who, like his *Fall Guy* counterpart Robert Armstrong, had seen better days during the 1930s) is quite good as the relentless sleuth.

CREDITS: Producer: Jack Wrather; Associate Producer: James C. Jordan; Director: John Reinhardt; Assistant Director: William Forsyth; Screenplay: Robert Presnell, Sr.; Based Upon: Cornell Woolrich's Story, "He Looked like Murder," from the February 8, 1941, *Detective Fiction Weekly* (Published Elsewhere as "Two Men in a Furnished Room"); Photographed by: Henry Sharp; Special Effects: Howard Anderson; Art Director: Oscar Yerge; Supervising Editor: William Zeigler; Editor: Jodie Caplan; Decor: Harry Reif; Wardrobe: Jack Masters; Music Director: David Chudnow; Musical Score: Rudy Schrager;

Sound: J.T. Corrigan; Makeup: James Barker; Production Manager: Ben Berk; Running Time: 71 Minutes; Released: March 22, 1947

CAST: Bonita Granville (Linda Mitchell and Estelle Mitchell); Don Castle (Mike Carr); Wally Cassell (Johnny Dixon); Regis Toomey (Heller); John Litel (Alex Tremholt); Thomas Jackson (Tim McGinniss); Netta Packer (Mrs. Mitchell); Oliver Blake (Jake); Caroline Andrews (Woman Hailing Taxicab)

UNTAMED FURY
a.k.a.: Swamp Virgins
(Danches Bros. Productions/Producers Releasing Corp.)

Leigh Whipper, a severely dignified black actor, ranged all over the narrow landscape afforded Old Hollywood's players of color, prowling every corner in search of—not merely work, but work that would allow him to radiate some class. Whipper was as likely to be seen balefully tormenting Mantan Moreland in *King of the Zombies* as he was to be found lending a sad commentary on the pleasures of solitude to *Of Mice and Men* or volunteering himself as the conscience, ill-heeded, of a lynch mob in *The Ox-Bow Incident*.

Whipper serves impressively as the swamp-dwelling narrator, and the nearest thing to a box-office name, in Ewing Scott's *Untamed Fury*—regaling a visiting journalist (Norman MacKay) with a tale of a violent clash between sons of Florida's Okeefenokee Swamp region.

Mikel Conrad plays 'Gator Bait Blair, so named because his father, Nubie Blair (Jack Rutherford), had used him as a child to lure alligators into traps. Steve (a.k.a. Gaylord) Pendleton plays Jeff Owens, whose father (Charles Keane) also calls the swampland home but intends for his boy to get himself a decent citified education. The youths have grown up as daredevil antagonists, but Jeff's departure for college sets the rivalry onto a grimmer course.

Years later, Jeff returns to the Okeefenokee as a civil engineer, dead-set upon improving the lot of the locals through newfangled technology and all-purpose social enlightenment. Even Jeff's father resents the intrusion, and the Blairs turn downright hostile. Only 'Gator Bait's sister, Judie (Mary Conwell), now a comely young woman, seems to appreciate Jeff's efforts. A romantic triangle threatens to develop among Jeff, 'Gator and Patricia Wayburn (Althea Murphy), owner of a tour-guide service where 'Gator works. Judie corners the market on Jeff's affections when she salvages his surveying equipment from an act of vandalism by 'Gator.

Threatened with police intervention, Old Man Blair reads 'Gator the riot act. 'Gator pretends to develop a sympathy with Jeff's cause, only to attack Jeff with a strangling vine while guiding him through a desolate patch of swampland. Jeff responds by saving 'Gator from an alligator attack, but the ingrate in turn leads an armed raid on Jeff's construction crew. A later attempt on Jeff's life lands 'Gator in a quicksand bog—from which Jeff unaccountably rescues the murderous backwoodser. Finally 'Gator sees the error of his ways, and the tale ends with an uplifting handshake of reconciliation.

Producer/director Ewing Scott's source-story, a literary-prize medalist published as "'Gator Bait," started out meaner but was softened and broadened considerably in the translation to a shooting script. Any traces of horrific impact remaining must lie in the oppressive green hell of the (authentic) shooting locations; in the (staged) alligator hunts and attacks; in the sister's putting aside her fear of the reptiles in order to retrieve the engineer's wrecked equipment from a river bottom; and in the savagery, however petulant, of Mikel Conrad's performance. Although the original story resonates with a folkloric purity, its adaptation comes off more as a watered-down imitation of Henry Hathaway's famous *The Trail of the Lonesome Pine* (1936), with Steve Pendleton approximating the Fred MacMurray role of the intrusive Voice of Progress and Conrad taking a superficially menacing approach to the Henry Fonda character, a distrustful yokel. Its tear-jerking sentimental hokum aside, *Lonesome Pine* remains a gutsy picture with the gumption to take pride in its brutal essence. *Untamed Fury*'s make-nice resolution defeats the pulp-like essence of the yarn, stranding it somewhere nearer *Reader's Digest* territory. Alexander Laszlo's musical score is suitably

unnerving, anticipating his finer-than-the-material compositions for 1959's similarly swampbound *Attack of the Giant Leeches*.

Pendleton was a busy talent in those days, with nearly 50 feature-film credits spanning the period from 1941 through 1950, but stardom eluded him. Mikel (known later as Mike) Conrad was an aggressive newcomer to film in 1947, and he would remain busy for the balance of the decade—but *Untamed Fury* was in its day hardly the type of picture to assure any player's prospects. E.G. Marshall, though a familiar name (and especially so as an Emmy-winning television star) in years to come, served this picture as a low-billed nobody. More screen time, even a meatier role, for Leigh Whipper would have improved things considerably; his framing segment holds the promise of a naturalistic tragedy left unfulfilled.

Ewing Scott, who had been an assistant director to Jean Renoir on Fox's 1941 production of *Swamp Water*, spent much of the decade attempting to peddle "'Gator Bait" as a screen property. His breakthrough with Danches Bros. Productions served merely to connect Scott with a family of movie-struck dilettantes: Abe, Ralph and George Danches were wholesale grocers from Cleveland who had made a fortune during World War II with a process for dehydrating eggs. The Danches hung on in Hollywood, and in association with Scott, for another picture, 1948's *Harpoon*, but then returned to doing what they did best. Scott bowed out after *Arctic Manhunt* (1949) for Universal-International, another starring picture for Mike Conrad. (Conrad's turn as a writer-producer-director and star player on 1950's *The Flying Saucer* appears to have been inspired by occurrences—whether real or imagined—during the Alaskan location shooting for *Arctic Manhunt* during the winter of 1947.)

George Danches, however, retained a resentful interest in the film industry. More than four years after *Untamed Fury* had proved itself anything but a moneymaker, Danches filed suit against Eagle–Lion Pictures, the somewhat more upscale reincarnation of Producers Releasing Corp., and its parent company, Pathé Industries, charging breach of contract, improper accounting tactics and failure to promote the film to fullest advantage. The picture, of course, had been its own worst enemy at the box office, with zero marquee value and the industry's assurance of a niche that the tradepaper *Variety* had pegged early on as "the lower half of the duals," meaning supporting status in double-bill engagements. Danches had sought $250,000 in reparations, but the absence of adjudication records suggests that Eagle–Lion likelier paid him an out-of-court settlement just to shut up and go away.

The film and its source-materials bear no kinship (beyond a swampland setting) to an exploitation film of 1976 called *Gator Bait*.

CREDITS: Producer and Director: Ewing Scott; Assistant Director: Daniel D. Doran; Screenplay: Taylor Caven and Paul Gerard Smith; Based Upon: Ewing Scott's 1943 Story, "'Gator Bait"; Photographed by: Ernest Miller; Editor: Robert Crandall; Musical Score Composed and Conducted by: Alexander Laszlo; Recording: Cuyler Tuthill; Production Supervisor: George Danches; Alligator Sequences Staged by: Ross Allen; Running Time: 65 Minutes; Released: March 22, 1947

CAST: Steve Pendleton (Jeff Owens); Mikel Conrad ('Gator Bait Blair); Leigh Whipper (Uncle Gabe); Mary Conwell (Judie Blair); Althea Murphy (Patricia Wayburn); Jack Rutherford (Nubie Blair); Charles Keane (Rufe Owens); Rodman Bruce (Lige); Paul Savage (Swamper); E.G. Marshall (Pompano); Norman MacKay (John Bradbury)

YANKEE FAKIR

(Republic Pictures Corp.)

W. Lee Wilder's career as a producer had started off promisingly during the middle 1940s, but he soon made plain his shortcomings by presenting himself as a director, as well. While his brother, Billy Wilder, soared to ever greater prominence as a major-league screen director, W. Lee remained part of the lesser ranks, delivering films that, though redeemingly bizarre and lurid, might most charitably be described as interesting failures.

Yankee Fakir is just such a film, although it is further distinguished by Wilder's ineptitude at comedy. A marginally weird element, involving an iridescent glow surrounding certain citizens of an Arizona border town, proves merely a plot device calculated to appeal to a popular fascination with radioactive substances.

Douglas Fowley stars as a traveling peddler who stumbles into a tangle of small-time political corruption and murder. Joan Woodbury, still as luscious as she had appeared in 1936's *The Rogues Tavern*, plays the daughter of a border patrolman. Clem Bevans plays a crusty prospector who disguises himself as a wealthy out-of-towner in an awkward ruse to smoke out the culprits. Tommy Bernard, a high-spirited kid actor, cracks the case without half trying. The villainy quotient is unremarkable.

CREDITS: Producer and Director: W. Lee Wilder; Assistant Director: Mack V. Wright; Screenplay: Richard S. Conway; Scenario: Mindret Lord; Photographed by: Robert W. Pittack; Supervising Editor: John F. Link; Editor: Joseph B. Caplan; Decor: Vincent A. Taylor; Costumer: Voyle Hazen; Music: Alexander Laszlo; Sound: Ferol Redd; Makeup: Jack Casey; Production Manager: Bartlett A. Carre; Running Time: 71 Minutes; Released: April 1, 1947

CAST: Douglas Fowley (Murgatroid Bartholomew "Yankee" Davis); Joan Woodbury (Mary Mason); Clem Bevans (Shaggy Hartley); Ransom Sherman (Prof. Newton); Frank Reicher (H.W. Randall); Marc Lawrence (Duke); Walter Soderling (Sheriff); Eula Guy (Mrs. Tetley); Forrest Taylor (Mason); Elinor Appleton (Jenny); Peter Michael (Walker); Elspeth Dudgeon (Scrubwoman); Ernie [as Ernest] Adams (Charlie); Tommy Bernard (Tommy Mason)

VIOLENCE
(B&B Pictures Corp./Monogram Distributing Corp.)

Just as the Nazi menace didn't really go away upon the collapse of the Third Reich, neither did Hollywood's fascination with Fascism as an exploitable (melo)dramatic concept. *Violence* (like the slightly later *The Burning Cross*) concerns itself with the postwar rise in new and resurgent hate-mongering organizations. The life-models in this instance included the Atlanta-based Columbians, Inc., whose agenda called for the deportation of black citizens to Africa and the forced assimilation or banishment of Jews.

The hate group here is called United Defenders, whose ploy is to recruit alienated returning soldiers under the guise of patriotism. The thugs' opening act is to kill war veteran Joe Donahue (Jimmy Clark) before he can follow through on his plan to quit the organization. The Defenders' Los Angeles secretary, Ann Mason (Nancy Coleman), is an undercover journalist gathering material for an expose.

En route to a meeting with her editor (Pierre Watkin) in Chicago, Ann is involved in a traffic accident and develops amnesia as a consequence. A Defenders agent, Steve Fuller (Michael O'Shea), who has been following Ann, introduces himself to her as her fiancé and brings her back into the fold as a zealous activist.

The organization seems secure until Sally Donahue (Cay Forrester) comes looking for Joe—her missing husband. Ann offers her help, but Defenders chief True Dawson (Emory Parnell) informs Ann that Joe had vanished following a theft from the treasury.

Ethnic hatreds fuel the storyline of *Violence*.

Steve develops misgivings after new facts come to light, and Ann becomes torn between loyalties. Her memory gets a nudge when her editor contacts her, and a slap-in-the-face from high-strung Defenders lieutenant Fred Stalk (Sheldon Leonard) clears Ann's mind entirely. She and Steve find themselves held captive, but they manage to manipulate Dawson and Stalk into killing one another.

Violence had gone into production during December of 1946, while riot-incitement charges were pending in Georgia against the Columbians, Inc. The screenwriters revised the script amidships to make its story even more topical. In mid-February of 1947, two months before *Violence* reached the screen, two officials of the Columbians were convicted of beating a black man, and of usurping police authority and stockpiling dynamite with antisocial intentions.

Nancy Coleman is effective as the amnesiac crusader, and her transformation into a proselytizing tool of the Fascist group comes about by persuasive degrees. Emory Parnell and Sheldon Leonard make a fine team of heavies, conveying that attitude of humorless glee that characterizes many a political extremist. Michael O'Shea does well as the insider who comes to see the error of his ways. Edward J. Kay's music conveys an appropriate sense of suffocating desperation.

CREDITS: Co-Producer and Director: Jack Bernhard; Co-Producer: Bernard Brandt; Assistant Director: Eddie Davis; Dialogue Director: Escha Bledsoe; Story and Screenplay: Stanley Rubin and Louis Lantz; Photographed by Henry Sharp; Special Effects: Augie Lohman; Editor: Jason Bernie; Set Designers: Oscar Yerge and Richard Streit; Set Dresser: Otto Siegel; Hair Stylist: Lorraine MacLean; Music: Edward J. Kay; Sound: Earl Sitar; Makeup: Charles Huber; Production Supervisor: Glenn Cook; Production Manager: William Calihan; Running Time: 72 Minutes; Released: April 12, 1947

CAST: Nancy Coleman (Ann Mason); Michael O'Shea (Steve Fuller); Sheldon Leonard (Fred Stalk); Peter Whitney (Joker Robinson); Emory Parnell (True Dawson); Pierre Wartkin (Ralph Borden); Frank Reicher (Pop); Cay Forrester (Sally Donahue); John Hamilton (Dr. Chalmers); Richard Irving (Latimer); Carol Donne (Bess Taffel); Jimmy Clark (Joe Donahue); Drew Demarest (Quincy); William Ruhl (Taxi Driver); Dick Rich (White); Frank Cady (Jepson); Harry Depp (Martin); Helen Servis (Martha Van Ives); Mary Donovan (Girl in Window); Bob Faust (Man in Window); Barbara Bettinger (Nurse)

SPOILERS OF THE NORTH
(Republic Pictures Corp.)

If there is a harpoon on deck in the first act, then by the finale it must have been put thoroughly well to use as a murder weapon—a fundamental rule of this peculiar strain of melodrama. "A mixture of sex and salmon," as the *Variety* reviewer pegged it, Richard Sale's *Spoilers of the North* takes a lurid low road through the Alaskan high country, seasoning Republic Pictures' specialty of outdoor action with the essential *film noir* equation of erotic tensions and violence. The mayhem issues from the dirty deeds of a fishery owner, played by top-billed Paul Kelly, who not only exploits the native resources to near-depletion but also abuses the loyalties of his brother and a temperamental part-Indian woman.

The *femme fatale* role is the splendid work of Adrian Booth, who had only recently begun using that name. The former big-band vocalist had spent the first half of the 1940s as Lorna Gray, starring in a run of low-budgeters at Monogram, Republic and Columbia and gracing the occasional big-time entry as a supporting player. Her most striking work in the wartime/postwar realm of *Forgotten Horrors* had occurred in *The Girl Who Dared*, *Fashion Model*, *Valley of the Zombies* and the *Captain America* serial, during 1944–1946. The re-christening was a ploy aimed at a sharper prominence, but apart from earning Miss Booth a cast billing a notch above Evelyn Ankers in *Spoilers of the North*, the strategy fizzled.

Adrian Booth deserved better—and received it, however briefly, in *Spoilers*. As the half-caste Jane Koster, she steals the show handily away from Kelly, who plays cannery operator Matt Garraway as a shameless rotter. Miss Ankers, in one of those departures from the endangered-heroine horror-movie stereotype that had become her lot at Universal Pictures, plays a corporate secretary who is so swayed by Matt's arrogant charm that she helps him bamboozle her company out of a large cash advance. James A. Millican is the straight-arrow kid brother, who grows to resent Matt's neglect of their fishery's day-to-day business.

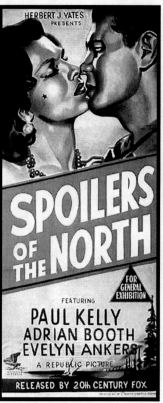

Booth handily commandeers these intrigues after Laura Reed (played by Miss Ankers) arrives at the cannery, innocently completing a romantic triangle than can only collapse into treachery and mayhem. Having promised a greater payload than he is prepared to deliver, Matt uses Jane to tap into fishing privileges granted only to the local Indians. Jane's ostensible boyfriend (Ted Hecht) barges in on Matt's crooked scheme—so Jane kills the youth. Even as the slaying provokes an investigation, Matt escalates his racket, plotting a huge catch in blatant defiance of the fish-and-game wardens. Jane, finally wising up to Matt's greater fondness for Laura, skewers him with a harpoon.

This bravura show of ferocity should have led upward, but Miss Gray-become-Booth "still found herself competing with horses for the affections of cowboy stars of B Westerns," as the historian Ephraim Katz has put it. By 1949, she had married the actor David Brian and retired from the screen. Yet another identity awaited her, however, as an ordained evangelical minister.

Richard Sale was due for bigger breaks, though sporadic, as a citizen of Hollywood. Before he had cracked the movie racket, the former newspaperman was probably best known as the creator and writer of the *Daffy Dill* series in *Detective Fiction Weekly*, a popular pulp magazine that had run a decade's worth of *Dill* yarns beginning in 1934. Sale was one of those penny-a-word fictioneers who could convey wild mayhem with a light touch—a talent on display not only in the newsroom-based *Dill* tales, but also in such breezy novels as *Benefit Performance* (1946) and the Hollywood-set *Lazarus #7* (a.k.a. *Lazarus Murder Seven*; 1942).

Sale's work as a director following *Spoilers of the North* includes the intriguing likes of 1951's *Let's Make It Legal*, featuring a mature Claudette Colbert and an up-and-coming Marilyn Monroe, and the comedic quasi-fantasy *My Wife's Best Friend* (1952). Sale also wrote a number of pictures, including the extremely weird allegorical Western *The White Buffalo* (1977), from his novel. Sale left his most emphatic mark with one picture, 1955's *Gentlemen Marry Brunettes*. He co-scripted, co-produced, directed and even wrote songs for that sequel to the 1953 blockbuster *Gentlemen Prefer Blondes*.

CREDITS: Associate Producer: Donald H. Brown; Director: Richard Sale; Assistant Director: Jack Lacey; Screenplay: Milton M. Raison; Photographed by: Alfred Keller; Special Effects: Howard Lydecker and Theodore Lydecker; Art Director: Paul Youngblood; Editor: William Thompson; Decor: John McCarthy, Jr., and Perry Murdock; Musical Director: Mort Glickman; Sound: Richard Tyler; Makeup: Bob Mark; Running Time: 66 Minutes; Released: April 24, 1947

CAST: Paul Kelly (Matt Garraway); Adrian Booth (Jane Koster); Evelyn Ankers (Laura Reed); James A. Millican (Bill Garraway); Roy Barcroft (Moose McGovern); Louis Jean Heydt (Inspector Cal Winters); Ted Hecht (Joe Taku); Harlan Briggs (Salty); Francis McDonald (Pete Koster); Maurice Cass (Doctor); Neyle Morrow (Johnny); Bobby Barber (Steward); Charles Morton (Slim); and Ethan Laidlaw, Marshall Reed and Tex Terry (Fishermen)

WHISPERING CITY
Canadian Title: La Fortresse
(Quebec Productions Corp./The J. Arthur Rank Organization/
Eagle–Lion Films, Inc./Pathé Industries, Inc.)

Canada, despite its geographical immensity and robust economy, was so passively dependent upon Hollywood and the British film industry during most of the Twentieth Century that its own picture-making community long remained under-developed. The occasional feature-film breakthrough—most notably 1914's *Evangeline* and 1931's *The Viking*—meant only sporadic bursts of productivity in an industry that historically had concerned itself with patriotic documentary films.

That nonfiction sector thrived especially during the wartime 1940s, a period distinguished by the Scots-born John Grierson's tenure as chief of the Film Board of Canada, but the distinctively Canadian narrative feature remained a rare commodity. Grierson, a critic-turned-filmmaker, appears to have coined the very term *documentary*, as applied to a film devoted to factual realism. His departure for America in 1945 left the Canadian documentary form amply prepared to carry on, but Canada's apathy toward its native feature-filmmakers continued apace, with Quebec the only province making any such gains as the '40s wore on into the '50s.

Most such pacesetting entries from Quebec went unseen outside the French-speaking locales, but Fedor Ozep packed such international appeal into *Whispering City* as to make it a contender. The $600,000 budget bespoke a tremendous confidence in the film's chances outside its native territory. For once, Great Britain's powerful J. Arthur Rank Organization bought into a Canadian production in a turnabout from imposing its output upon Canada, and Hollywood's ambitious Eagle–Lion Films followed suit. It helped considerably that Helmut Dantine and Paul Lukas brought big-time credentials to the project, including the still-fresh popular memory of Lukas' 1943 Oscar for *Watch on the Rhine*.

The story is a pleasing snarl of murderous intrigues, centering upon an overconfident young journalist (Mary Anderson) who has obtained information that could prove damaging to one Albert Frederic (Lukas), a prominent lawyer and patron of the arts. Intent upon disposing of the reporter before she can publish a story, Frederic turns to his protégé, a high-strung composer named Michel Lacosta (Dantine). Lacosta is susceptible to Frederic's manipulations, what with a history of alcoholic blackouts and a suicidal wife (Joy Lafleur). There follows a trail of crosses and double-crosses, with an unlikely romance to complicate matters.

Lukas, a former matinee idol of the Budapest stage, had long since established himself as the American film capital's most dependable Continental European type. Here, he trades strikingly upon the image of suave villainy that he had perfected during the '40s. Dantine, a Vienna-born fugitive from the Third Reich, plays the ill-balanced *artiste* with all the right mannerisms of agitation and near-madness, neatly diverting the viewer's attention from the possibility that he might turn out to be a square shooter after all. Mary Anderson delivers a pert and courageous interpretation of the gal-reporter character, and her air of determination is accurate to the profession. The crucial newsroom setting is especially true to life. The photography, by former Cecil B. DeMille associate Guy Roe, captures well the contrasts between the realm of the fine arts and the coarser world of the newspaper business.

Whispering City proved to be the final effort from director Ozep. He had become an influential contributor to the Russian cinema as early as 1916 but exiled himself to Germany following the completion in Berlin of a Soviet–German production of Tolstoy's *Der Lebende Leichnam* (*The Living Corpse*) in 1929. Fleeing the rise of Nazism, Ozep re-established himself as a filmmaker in France but neglected to secure citizenship. This oversight branded him a Displaced Person upon the outbreak of World War II, and the French placed him in an internment camp—from which he was freed only after the fall of Paris to the Nazis. Ozep fled again to Morocco and then to Canada, where he delivered one of the country's rare feature-film entries, a Chopin biography called *The Music Master* (1943). A brief sojourn in America found him co-directing the anti-Axis drama *Three Russian Girls* (1944), as remade from a Soviet film of 1941. Ozep died in 1949.

CREDITS: Producers: George Marton and Paul L'Anglais; Director: Fedor Ozep; Screenplay: Rian James and Leonard Lee; Scenario: George Zuckerman and Michael Lennox; Photographed by: Guy Roe; Editor: Douglas Bagler; Music: Jean Deslauriers; Running Time: 95 Minutes; Released: Following Previews in Toronto during May of 1947; U.S. Release: November 15, 1947

CAST: Helmut Dantine (Michel Lacoste); Mary Anderson (Mary Roberts); Paul Lukas (Albert Frederic); John Pratt (Durant); Joy Lafleur (Blanche Lacoste); George Alexander (Police Inspector); Mimi d'Estee (Renée Brancourt); Henri Poltras (Assistant Police Inspector)

SCARED TO DEATH
(Golden Gate Productions, Inc./Screen Guild Productions, Inc.)

Christy Cabanne had been a top-shelf screen artist of the silent age, an actor from 1910 with the D.W. Griffith company who also assisted the Master and then graduated by 1913 to fully fledged directing assignments, often devising his own scenarios. Cabanne's perceived brilliance is generally held to have faded after 1926, when he had handled

casting and second-unit direction on *Ben-Hur*, but amid his mounting regimen of low-budget programmers during the early-talkie years can be found the 1934 *Jane Eyre*. That entry is at least the *meisterwerk* of Poverty Row, or so we declared it in the original *Forgotten Horrors*—and it is handily the equal or better of many major-studio period romances of the Depression era.

Nothing else in Cabanne's extensive (quantity-over-quality) resume of the 1930s and earlier '40s

GOLDEN GATE PICTURES, Presents

SCARED TO DEATH

staring

BELA **LUGOSI** · GEORGE **ZUCCO**
NAT **PENDLETON** · MOLLY **LAMONT**

PHOTOGRAPHED IN **Full NATURAL COLOR**

DISTRIBUTED BY SCREEN GUILD PRODUCTIONS

comes near the tongue-in-cheek surrealism of *Scared to Death*, which occurred in the midst of a run of late-in-life assignments that also included the thoroughly conventional likes of *Dixie Jamboree*, *The Man Who Walked Alone*, *Sensation Hunters*, *Robin Hood of Monterey*, *King of the Bandits*, *Black Trails* and *Silver Trail* (1944–1948). Cabanne was the last artist one would associate with any movements smacking of Dadaism or avant-garde-ness, but one would have to look to the calculated weirdness of Luis Buñuel and Salvador Dali or Jean Cocteau to find a film any more bizarre than *Scared to Death*.

Compounding the interest is *Scared to Death*'s station as a transitional piece for Bela Lugosi, a rickety bridge from a stretch of stardom at Monogram Pictures to Lugosi's more pitiable assignments of the 1950s. (Lugosi's apparent resurgence with *Abbott & Costello Meet Frankenstein*, in 1948, would prove him well prepared for better prospects that failed to materialize.)

Now, *Scared to Death* is an easy mark for those who enjoy ridiculing low-budget spookers—the same people who'd go about razzing the maimed and the crippled among humankind, if only such acts weren't so inconvenient and socially unacceptable—but the film's facile incoherence and air of otherworldly detachment exercise a dream-state fascination for the absorbed viewer. Compounding the sense of Dadaism-by-default is the photography in Cinecolor, that vivid but unnatural-looking process whose developers had intended it as a cheaper alternative to Technicolor. Lugosi's one star turn in color *would* have to come in such an acquired-taste oddity, but then the actor can only have felt fortunate to have landed here at this stage of a declining career.

Decline or not, Lugosi is in forbidding if self-caricatured form as a magician named Leonide, the cousin of a strange professor, Dr. Van Ee (George Zucco). The Van Ee household is in turmoil, thanks to the doctor's high-strung daughter-in-law, Laura (Molly

Lamont), who on the one hand suspects her husband (Roland Varno) and his father of trying to wreck her mind—but on the other refuses to pack up and scram. Leonide remembers the house from its days as an asylum, where he had been an inmate.

Dr. Van Ee seeks the help of Leonide and his dwarf assistant, Indigo (Angelo Rossitto), in sorting out a mystery. Laura is obsessed with guilt over having betrayed her former husband and show-business partner to the Nazis in occupied France. It develops that the presumed-dead spouse (Lee Bennett) is alive and in league with Leonide. Laura lives up to her title role when she drops dead from fear of a lurking assailant.

That frank synopsis accounts only for the flashback. The framing segment occurs in a morgue, where two surgeons (Stanley Andrews and Stanley Price) regard the corpse of Laura Van Ee and wonder aloud what could have croaked her. Molly Lamont also serves as the narrator, a voice-from-the-slab gimmick anticipating the device that Billy Wilder *nearly* used in his celebrated *Sunset Blvd.*, only three years later. *Scared to Death* also harks back to a couple of Depression-period gems, RKO-Radio Pictures' *The Phantom of Crestwood* and Paramount's *Murder by the Clock*, in its use of a ghostly mask as a device to terrorize the victim of a stalking.

Any concept of immersion-in-character acting is irrelevant. Likewise for the concept of linear narrative, although W.J. Abbott's original scenario trades on pulp-fiction literary conventions and Nazi atrocities of the all-too-recent war years. But then, neither is anyone merely going through the motions or groping for a story worth the telling. The portrayals all seem as calculatedly unreal as an act of ritual pageantry: None of them—not even Nat Pendleton's indignant cop character, a peculiar carryover from his recurring work as a cartoonish Nemesis for the team of Bud Abbott & Lou Costello—ever quite intersects with any recognizable reality. For these very reasons, and certainly not in spite of them, the film has become a treasure to cherish, even if its reason for being is incomprehensible.

CREDITS: Producer: William B. David; Director: Christy Cabanne; Assistant Director: Robert Farfan; Story and Screenplay: W.J. Abbott; Photographed by: Marcel LePicard; Art Director: Harry Reif; Editor: George McGuire; Decor: Frank Dexter, Sr.; Wardrobe: Albert Deano; Music: Carl Hoefle; Sound: Glen Glenn; Makeup: Roland Ray; Hairdresser: Evelyn Bennett; Production Manager: Walt Mattox; Running Time: 68 Minutes; Released: May 3, 1947

CAST: Bela Lugosi (Leonide); George Zucco (Dr. Van Ee); Nat Pendleton (Bill Raymond); Molly Lamont (Laura Van Ee); Joyce Compton (Jane); Gladys Blake (Lilybeth); Roland Varno (Ward Van Ee); Douglas Fowley (Terry Lee); Stanley Andrews and Stanley Price (Surgeons); Angelo Rossitto (Indigo); Lee Bennett (René)

THE ROAD TO HOLLYWOOD

(Astor Pictures Corp./Mack Sennett Productions/
Educational Films Corp. of America)

A sort of backhanded starring vehicle for Bing Crosby, *The Road to Hollywood* is not any new-for-1947 production, but rather an opportunistic scam calculated to ride the backdraft of the singer-actor's famous *Road* series of mystery-adventure spoofs, co-starring Bob Hope. Paramount's *Road to Morocco*, *Road to Zanzibar*, *Road to Utopia* and so forth had proved a ticket-selling sensation since the early 1940s, and *The Road to Hollywood* can only have been so christened in a coattail ploy by its default-producer, Bud Pollard. This patchwork effort beat the Crosby-Hope starrer *Road to Rio* to the box office with a six-month headstart in 1947.

The feature draws its substance from a cobbled-together string of early-1930s short musical-adventure-romance pieces in which the up-and-coming Crosby had starred for veteran comedy producer Mack Sennett at Educational Films, an old-line Poverty Row outfit. Only marginally thrilling but possessed of an overall surreal weirdness, the pageant does include a scary series of encounters with a rampant lion, which is depicted at one point with a crudely animated special-effects leap—probably the earliest cinematic ances-

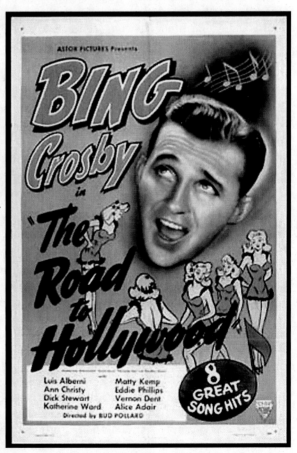

tor of the pixel-perfect big cat that proved such a show-stopper in Ridley Scott's *Gladiator* (2000).

The greater relevance here of *The Road to Hollywood* lies in the involvement of Pollard, whose 1933 production of *The Horror* is a linchpin in the *Forgotten Horrors* canon. Although he never proved himself any great shakes as a filmmaking artist, Pollard was a highly visible and well-liked member of the Directors Guild—serving as its president at the time of *The Road to Hollywood*.

The short subjects providing fodder for *The Road to Hollywood* are "I Surrender, Dear," "One More Chance," "Billboard Girl" and "Dream House," all from 1931–1932. The compilation serves chiefly to illustrate how much more adventurous a singer Crosby had been in the early days—and to point up how much more confident a screen player he had become over the long haul. Bob Hope told us in 1981 that Crosby had found *The Road to Hollywood* "kind of an embarrassment—he was afraid people might think he had okayed it as a vanity thing. I think it probably just heightened the folks' interest in our legitimate *Road* pictures, though."

Of course, neither Crosby nor anyone else involved with the original productions had okayed *The Road to Hollywood*, which came together as a found-object production. A more inventive use of such Sennett footage would occur with 1949's *Down Memory Lane*, without the over-emphasis upon Bing Crosby and *with* the approval and participation of Mack Sennett.

The studio behind the assembly of *The Road to Hollywood* was not even a studio in the strict sense. Founded during the Depression years by Robert M. Savini, Astor Pictures Corp. dealt principally in the distribution and reissuing of films from other sources. The company had its occasional big-picture experiences—including an ambitious re-edit of William S. Hart's 1925 epic, *Tumbleweeds*, in 1939, and scattered art-picture coups including the domestic U.S. distribution of *Peeping Tom* and *La Dolce Vita* during the 1960s. But Astor's chief distinction was its longevity in a sector of the industry known chiefly for its impermanence.

CREDITS: Executive Producer: Robert M. Savini; Producer and Re-Editor: Bud Pollard; Original Directors: Mack Sennett, Leslic Pearce and Del Lord; Sound Engineers: Paul Guerin and Arthur Blinn; Running Time: 55 Minutes; Released: Following New York Opening on May 7, 1947

CAST: Bud Pollard (Narrator); Bing Crosby (Himself); Luis Alberni (Marquis); Patsy O'Leary (Ethel Bangs); Arthur Stone (Arthur and Uncle Joe); Eddie Phillips (Reginald Duncan); Julia Griffith (Mother); Vernon Dent (Director); Ann Christy (Betty Brooks); Katherine Ward (Mrs. Brooks); Matty Kemp (Percy Howard); Marion Sayers (Peggy); George Gray (George Dobbs); Alice Adair (Mrs. Dobbs); and Marjorie "Babe" Kane, George Pearce, Dick Stewart, Jimmy Eagles, Lincoln Steadman

HARD BOILED MAHONEY
(Jan Grippo Productions/Monogram Productions, Inc./
Monogram Distributing Corp.)

The Bowery Boys, that team of childlike hooligans descended from Monogram's *East Side Kids* series and Universal's *Little Tough Guys* franchise, never forgot their larger origins in Sidney Kingsley's Depression-era tenement drama *Dead End*. Slapstick though their leanings became, Leo Gorcey, Huntz Hall *et al.* kept the faith with the spirit of Skid Row desperation so that when an opportunity presented itself for a meatier story, they were prepared to do it justice. Or a semblance thereof.

Lest we over-dignify *Hard Boiled Mahoney*, it bears remembering that the *Bowery Boys* pictures invariably put the lowbrow laugh-getting imperative first. But like many of Elvis Presley's later prefabricated-hit records—where the singer would deliver the pop-schlock commercial goods on the plug side and then use the seldom-played flip to transmit secret signals of his thwarted bluesman ambitions—the *Bowery Boys* films usually contain a grimmer sub-texture that ripples toward the surface with diverting results.

That texture becomes all but dominant in William Beaudine's *Hard Boiled Mahoney*, which finds Leo Gorcey's fast-talking Slip Mahoney impersonating a vacationing private detective with results altogether deadlier than the easy-money game that he and his pals had envisioned. Two intertwined missing-persons cases lead to a syndicate that controls a crooked fortune-telling racket. The slaying of a purported psychic (sneaky-looking Pierre Watkin) is traced to a mob chief (the mountainous Dan Seymour, handling what would have been the Sydney Greenstreet role in a bigger and more dead-earnest picture). At stake is a cache of blackmail-fodder love letters.

Gorcey and Hall, upstaging their fellow team players even more so than usual, handle the wisecracking, language-mangling heroics as ably as Bob Hope would do in his various big-studio parodies of the *film noir* idiom. The chums seem convincingly in mortal peril, and Betty Compson—that faded but still game silent-screen star—helps out with a resourceful portrayal of a client-turned-rescuer. The imposing Noble Johnson, best remembered for the 1932–1933 combo of *The Most Dangerous Game* and *King Kong*, has a thankless bit role. (Johnson, a mulatto who could pass on film or in real life for practically any ethnicity, was bound for bigger things in the real-estate investment industry.) The predictable upshot, apart from the inevitable capture and humiliation of Dan Seymour, is that this irresponsible flirtation with danger has netted the Bowery Boys absolutely nothing in the way of financial gain. More surprising is that director Beaudine actually wrests a measure of suspense from the fellows' extended predicament.

New York-born Beaudine (1892–1970) had directed such big-timers as Mary Pickford and W.C. Fields during his early span of near-greatness. His notoriously low-rent pictures of comparatively more recent times have, of course, obscured Beaudine's importance as something close to a founding father of the industry.

Following an early tour of duty with D.W. Griffith, Beaudine had begun directing in 1915, coming into his own as an acclaimed feature-film artist in 1922. A Depression-era

sojourn in England proved a breakthrough in its own right, but it also rendered him obscure upon his return to America.

As a mainstay-by-default of Monogram Pictures, Beaudine hacked 'em out prolifically but with little artistic flair. One anecdote from the 1940s has Beaudine replying thusly to a front-office order to hurry up with a current assignment: "You mean that somebody out there is actually waiting to see this?" The account is possibly apocryphal but nonetheless has the ring of truth.

CREDITS: Producer: Jan Grippo; Production Supervisor: Glenn Cook; Director: William Beaudine; Assistant Director: Frank Fox; Screenplay: Cyril Enfield; Additional Dialogue: Edmond Seward and Tim Ryan; Photographed by: James Brown; Special Effects: Augie Lohman; Art Director: Dave Milton; Decor: George Milo; Supervising Editor: Otho Lovering; Editor: William Austin; Music: Edward J. Kay; Sound: Elden Ruberg; Sound Technician: John Carter; Production Manager: William Calihan, Jr.; Running Time: 63 Minutes; Released: May 10, 1947

CAST: Leo Gorcey (Slip Mahoney); Huntz Hall (Sach); Bobby Jordan (Bobby); Gabriel Dell (Gabe); Betty Compson (Selena Webster); Billy Benedict (Whitey); David Gorcey (Chuck); Teala Loring (Eleanor Williams); Dan Seymour (Dr. Armand); Byron Foulger (Prof. Quizard); Patti Brill (Alice); Pierre Watkin (Dr. Rolfe Carter); Danny Beck (Lennie the Meatball); Bernard Gorcey (Louie); Carmen D'Antonio (Receptionist); Noble Johnson (Hasson); William Ruhl (McGregor); Bob Faust (Tom Williams); Teddy Pavelec (Thug); Pat O'Malley (Police Lieutenant); Charles Phillips (Customer); Jack Cheatham (Police Sergeant)

BELLS OF SAN ANGELO
(Republic Pictures Corp.)

If the kids overlook the satirical implications, they should take this one to their sadistic little hearts… [W]ith the aid of the pic's Trucolor tinting, the gore literally runs red. The kids will especially like that.—From the *Variety* review

Roy Rogers, that happy-cowboy Role Model who is perhaps the unlikeliest recurring presence in the mottled tapestry of *Forgotten Horrors*, takes a grouchier and less dashing stance in *Bells of San Angelo*. This fierce entry pivots on lethal mayhem aplenty and forensic procedural investigation to match, with an odd play-within-a-play entrapment ruse; an emissary from Scotland Yard; a funny-guy sheriff with a secretive past; and a teasing hint of gender confusion involving co-star Dale Evans.

ROY ROGERS *KING OF THE COWBOYS* / TRIGGER *THE SMARTEST HORSE IN THE MOVIES* — **BELLS OF SAN ANGELO** *in TRUCOLOR* / A REPUBLIC PRODUCTION

Roy, more hard-bitten and frustrated than usual, is a border agent assigned to halt a serial-murder case centering upon a silver mine. Approaching the property, Roy witnesses a slaying on the spot—perpetrated by guards working for mine operators Rex Gridley (John McGuire) and Gus Ulrich (David Sharpe). Roy finds on the corpse a chunk of pure ore—whether stolen or planted, he cannot determine. Sheriff Cookie Bullfincher (reedy-voiced Andy Devine) wants to arrest Ulrich but learns that Gridley has issued a standing order, perfectly legal within the law-unto-itself company, to shoot on sight anyone suspected of thievery.

Roy, already impatient with a confounding assignment, is infuriated to learn that a writer of sensationalized Western novels is due to visit the nearby village of Rancho San Angelo. Roy sends his deputies to discourage the new arrival, but they are expecting author Lee Madison (Miss Evans) to be a man. Lee overhears the lawmen muttering about how Roy doesn't want some thrill-mongering pulp-hack snooping about, so she introduces herself by a phony name and they give her a chivalrous lift into town. The masquerade is short-lived, and Lee soon enough proves her mettle. She suggests that Roy read one of her novels, *Murder on the Border*—which might lend some insight into his investigation—but he scoffs. Later, Roy figures even a fictional clue might be better than his prevailing state of cluelessness and gives the book a skim.

Another murder finds Roy searching in vain for evidence, but his Palomino steed, Trigger, turns up pay-dirt with a piece of ore embedded in a hoof. Meanwhile, an English lawyer named Lionel Bates (Olaf Hytten) shows up looking for one George Wallingford Lancaster on orders from Scotland Yard. Sheriff Bullfincher is unnerved to learn of the Englishman's mission.

Roy finds the silver from Trigger's hoof to be of low grade as compared with the chunk found on the slain man's body. He and Bullfincher and Lee go prowling about the

Dreams That Money Can Buy

69

mine, which proves to be no workable lode but instead a holding pen for smuggled Mexican silver. Gridley's mob escalates its terroristic acts, subjecting Bates to a sadistic bullyragging and abducting Lee. Roy himself comes in for one of the most violent multiple-assailant beatings seen in *any* Western (and not just the generally tamer such pictures of the '40s).

Roy rallies the neighboring ranchers, who storm the mine, and then he pursues Gridley to a mountainside showdown—only to halt when the madman threatens to kill Lee. Calling out to Roy in cryptic terms, Lee suggests a re-enactment of a death scene from her novel. This stunt convinces Gridley that Roy has been shot, and the overconfident killer ventures within grabbing range. Roy is of course too much the gentleman to do more than knock Gridley unconscious. Yes, and how the Western-hero ethic has changed by now from the vengeful Depression-era heyday of Hopalong Cassidy and the angry young John Wayne!

The mystery of Sheriff Bullfincher is almost left a raveled thread, but an epilogue reveals that he is the missing reluctant aristocrat Lancaster—heir to the entire San Angelo Territory land grant. Lee announces that the adventure has given her the inspiration for a new novel.

Though very much an advancement of the singing-cowboy phenomenon, *Bells of San Angelo* also takes the palm for meanness and a willingness to make Roy Rogers less of an idealized Westerner. Comedy relief is parceled about equally between Andy Devine, as a lawman who behaves more like a sidekick, and Olaf Hytten as the veddy British visitor. Hytten's staging of an English-style fox hunt—with a possum pinch-hitting for a fox—serves a humorous function but also dovetails with one of the more vicious episodes. Divine's husky voice was no gimmick, but rather a manifestation of a damaged larynx from a misfortune suffered in childhood; he parlayed the disability into a lasting career as a beloved character actor.

The location shooting around Las Vegas is a distinct plus, with arid scenic values quite different from the familiar Hollywood-area sites. Principal photography ran for nearly two months during late 1946 and early 1947, delayed in mid-course beyond Republic's usual quick-and-cheap pace by a heavy snowfall. The generous running time allows the musical selections (by the Sons of the Pioneers, plus Rogers and Miss Evans) to breathe without detracting from the action. That action, incidentally, includes one of the more breathtaking fistfights in the genre, pitting Rogers against stuntman/actor David Sharpe.

CREDITS: Associate Producer: Edward J. White; Director: William Witney; Assistant Director: Jack Lacey; Screenplay: Sloan Nibley; Story: Paul Gangelin; Photographed by: Jack Marta; Special Effects: Howard Lydecker and Theodore Lydecker; Art Directors: Gano Chittenden and Frank Arrigo; Supervising Art Director: Russell Kimball; Editor: Les

Orlebeck; Set Designers: John McCarthy, Jr., and Helen Hansard; Music: Morton Scott; Orchestrations: Mort Glickman; Songs: "Hot Lead" and "Lazy Days," by Tim Spencer; and "Cowboy's Dream of Heaven," "I Love the West," "I Like To Get Up Early in the Morning" and "The Bells of San Angelo," by Jack Elliott; Sound: Fred Stahl; Makeup: Bob Mark; Running Time: 78 Minutes; Released: May 22, 1947

CAST: Roy Rogers and Trigger, the Smartest Horse in the Movies (Themselves); Dale Evans (Lee Madison); Andy Devine (Sheriff Cookie Bullfincher); John McGuire (Rex Gridley); Olaf Hytten (Lionel Bates); David Sharpe (Gus Ulrich); Fritz Leiber (Padre); Hank Patterson (Old-Timer); Fred "Snowflake" Toomes [as Toones]: (Cook); Eddie Acuff (Bus Driver); Bob Nolan & The Sons of the Pioneers (Themselves); James Linn, Ray "Doc" Adams and Whitey Christy (Guards); Charles Sullivan (Roberts); Ray Turner (Mailman); Eddie Parker and Fred Graham (Henchmen); Luana Walters (Clerk); Keefe Brasselle (Sentry); Rex Rossi (Ramón)

REPEAT PERFORMANCE
(Eagle–Lion Films, Inc./Bryan Foy Productions/Pathé Industries, Inc.)

Warner Bros.' loss became Eagle–Lion Films' gain when Joan Leslie, one of the 1940s' most famous girl-next-door ingénues, ended an ugly patch of salary-and-type-casting litigation with the big studio and abandoned corporate security for the chancier realm of free-agent stardom. Miss Leslie's first break outside the Warners lot came with a demanding role in *Repeat Performance*, as a sym-pathetic murderess granted a second chance to do things up right. The ploy did not work out well over the longer haul—although her decline was gradual, reaching a premature retirement in 1956—but Miss Leslie's work is excellent here, in a well-mounted production representing an unusually hefty outlay for Eagle–Lion.

Repeat Performance also marks a first for Rich-ard Basehart, as a recruit to the screen following his acclaimed work in *The Hasty Heart* on Broadway. *Repeat*'s world premiere took place in Basehart's hometown of Zanesville, Ohio, where once he had seemed likely to succeed his father as editor of the lo-cal newspaper. Although *Repeat Performance* faced Basehart with the risk of typecasting as a madman who figures surprisingly in the climax, he embraced the challenge with a wholehearted portrayal—and then followed through upon it with a career-making impersonation of another sort of maniac in 1948's *He Walked by Night*. These proved to be strategic choices in a grander scheme, which Basehart sustained on through the 1970s with the simple tactic of confront-ing and defying popular expectations.

Richard Basehart—warming up for stardom in *He Walked by Night*—and Joan Leslie at the jarring climax of *Repeat Performance*.

Sheila Page (Miss Leslie) is a Broadway actress burdened with a disloyal, alcoholic husband, Barney Page (Louis Hayward), whom she guns down on December 31, 1946. Sheila confesses the deed to an eccentric friend, a poet named William Williams (Basehart), and he suggests that they seek the counsel of her producer, John Friday (Tom Conway). Sheila wishes aloud that she could start the past year over from scratch—knowing then what she knows now.

Sheila inexplicably finds herself alone while approaching John's address. The date has reverted to January 1, 1946. She rushes home, where to her relief she finds Barney alive, well and sober. Complications pile up dauntingly, however, and Sheila finds that even her knowledge of events yet to come cannot prevent them from happening all over again—perhaps with even more ruinous results than she remembers. The restoration of her marriage is, as before, compromised by a homewrecker named Paula Costello (Virginia Field). A predatory patron of the arts (Natalie Schafer) attaches herself to Williams, only to have him committed to an asylum for the insane on no greater grounds than his bohemian mannerisms. Barney's affair with Paula turns ever more demeaning to Sheila, but when he is paralyzed following a drunken fall she stalls her career in order to nurse him back to health.

By Christmastime, Barney has recovered sufficiently to become a threatening figure, ungrateful and abusive. Sheila visits Williams at the asylum, finding him genuinely maddened by the ordeal. Williams seems philosophical about the year's strange events and is obviously more worried about Sheila's safety than he is about his own plight. On New Year's Eve, Barney attacks Sheila, who draws a gun in self-defense. Williams, who has escaped from custody, arrives in time to kill Barney. As he is led away by the police, Williams muses that the Fates care little about any patterns of events, "as long as the result is the same."

Forgotten Horrors 4

The Basehart character's apparent cosmic awareness, left tantalizingly unexplained except for one terse exchange with Miss Leslie, is the crowning touch of weirdness in a tale that gracefully treads a fine line between time-paradox fantasy and cruel naturalism. Director Alfred L. Werker, a veteran B-movie workhorse capable of the occasional outburst of inspired brilliance (including 1939's *The Adventures of Sherlock Holmes*), tackled *Repeat Performance* as a replacement for the up-and-coming Jules Dassin. Werker allows no forcibly eerie contrivances to intrude upon the telling, which unfolds like some dream of which the dreamer is helplessly aware. *Repeat Performance* derives from a popular novel that RKO-Radio Pictures' Val Lewton had once considered as a property worth filming, and indeed Werker and camera chief L.W. O'Connell bring to the tale a dire matter-of-factness reminiscent of the Lewton films. The presence of Tom Conway, who had played a recurring character in the Lewton productions of *Cat People* and *The Seventh Victim* (1942–1943), renders this resemblance all the more striking.

Repeat Performance serves notice primarily that Joan Leslie was both ready and able to break free of the too-wholesome typecasting with which Jack L. Warner had saddled her. The industry was neither ready nor able to follow through on her commitment to a greater versatility. Basehart proves himself both a capable scene-stealer and a generous ensemble player, conveying a poignant tenderness, if not a tender poignancy, in his shared moments with Miss Leslie. Louis Hayward, who accepted the top-billed bad-husband role as a replacement for Franchot Tone, overplays his character's every vile utterance but proves more convincing in the scenes of short-lived domestic tranquility. Virginia Field, borrowed from Paramount Pictures, is precisely right for the Other Woman part. The casting of name-brand players of Broadway and Hollywood pedigrees underscores Eagle–Lion's ambitions to cinch itself as a pretender to major-studio status; the budget, though undeclared publicly, has been estimated near the million-dollar mark.

Joan Leslie re-established herself later on during the 1950s as a high-fashion designer and philanthropist. She returned briefly to the screen in 1989 for a clever inside-joke cameo in *Turn Back the Clock*, a remake-for-television of *Repeat Performance*.

CREDITS: Producer: Aubrey Schenck; Director: Alfred L. Werker; Assistant Director: Robert Stillman; Screenplay: Walter Bullock; Based Upon: William O'Farrell's 1942 Novel, *Repeat Performance*; Photographed by L.W. O'Connell; Photographic Effects: George J. Teague; Special Process Art: Jack R. Rabin; Art Director: Edward C. Jewell; Supervising Editor: Alfred De Gaetano; Editor: Louis H. Sackin; Decor: Armor Marlowe; Costumer: Oleg Cassini; Musical Score: George Anthiel; Musical Director: Irving Friedman; Sound: J.N.A. Hawkins; Special Sound Supervision: Leon Becker; Sound Mixer: W.C. Smith; Makeup: Bud Westmore; Hair Stylist: Eunice; Running Time: 92 Minutes; Released: May 30, 1947

CAST: Louis Hayward (Barney Page); Joan Leslie (Sheila Page); Virginia Field (Paula Costello); Tom Conway (John Friday); Richard Basehart (William Williams); Natalie Schafer (Eloise Shaw); Benay Venuta (Bess Michaels); Ilka Gruning (Mattie); Abe Dinovich (Vendor); Jean Dutriz (Ricardo); Tim Murdock (Actor); Lory Leeman and Mildred Sellers (Actresses); Mike Lally, Dick Gordon, Bud Townsend, Gale Ronn, Ann Roberts and Valerie Traxler (Guests); Patrick Hurst (Virgil); Raymond Largay (Hillgardner); Jean Del Val (Waiter); Mack Williams (Doctor); Alf Haugan (Attendant); Michael Markham (Stage Manager); Leland Hodgson (Steward); Phillip Morris (Cop)

KILLER AT LARGE
(The New PRC Pictures, Inc./Producers Releasing Corp./Pathé Industries, Inc.)

As though America's returned soldiers hadn't enough psychological baggage trailing them from World War II, they found their prospects compromised by racketeers ready and willing to bilk them of their hard-earned G.I. compensation, especially in the crucial housing market. A tentatively reorganized PRC Pictures, still struggling to sustain an identity in the face of its parent company's transformation to Eagle–Lion Films, sought to shed light upon such swindlers in *Killer at Large*. The film's shallow populism and lurid presentation hark back more strikingly to the same old PRC, which knew that cheap thrills were more attractive than social messages to its essentially Joe Average audience of *schlubs*, rubes and honyocks.

Likely few housing-scam entrepreneurs ever resorted to serial murder as readily as do the perpetrators in *Killer at Large*. The tale hangs on a newspaper reporter, Paul Kimberly (dependable Robert Lowery), who quits his job in disgust after editor Edward Denton (Frank Ferguson) declares him a crackpot for covering an apparent suicide as though it were a murder. Paul knows that the victim, a disgraced big shot with the Veterans Administration, had reason enough to stay alive, what with a crack at getting off the hook by turning fink in a real-estate scandal.

Denton begins to sense the truth of Paul's claims, however, and lures Paul back into the fold by the ruse of assigning the story to a greenhorn reporter, Anne Arnold (Anabel Shaw), daughter of publisher Vincent Arnold (Charles Evans). Neither Paul nor Anne has an inkling that Arnold is the brains behind the racket.

Arnold's wronged mistress, Margo (Ann Staunton), threatens the publisher with blackmail. At a meeting with housing official and nightclub operator Brent Maddux (Leonard Penn), Paul persuades Anne that they should pool their investigations, and soon the journalists become romantically involved. Henchmen Chips Rand and Bull Callahan (George Lynn and Dick Rich) murder Maddux in full view of Paul, who alerts the law before breaking the scoop. Anne reports this development to her pillar-of-society daddy, who berates his thugs for such sloppy work. They redeem themselves by doing away with Margo, then take out after Paul, who escapes.

Paul uncovers documents incriminating Arnold and confronts him at gunpoint. Arnold has the drop on Paul, however—but the antagonists are distracted by the arrival of Rand, who guns down the publisher and starts to make off with a fortune in misappropriated G.I. loan money. Rand is about to open fire on Paul, but the dying Arnold kills Rand. Anne, though shattered to learn the dirty lowdown about her father, still manages to write the story of his unmasking. Which sounds to us like a conflict of interest that no respectable metro daily would allow.

But like a newspaper that won't allow the facts to get in the way of a good story, *Killer at Large* is hardly the type of picture to ground its events in a practical reality—and never mind its pretensions to postwar social relevance. (The plot is basically a citified variant upon the old cowboy-movie situation involving the bad banker and the deed to the ranch.) And besides, the tearful spectacle of Anabel Shaw, banging out a combination of hot story and personal tragedy on deadline, is about as emotional a moment as director William Beaudine ever allowed himself during a long encampment on Poverty Row. This indulgence is enough in itself to render the film dear to the hearts of us low-budgeter enthusiasts.

CREDITS: Producer: Buck Gottlieb; Director: William Beaudine; Assistant Director: Barton Adams; Screenplay: Fenton Earnshaw and Tom Blackburn; Photographed by: James Brown; Settings: Glenn Thompson; Supervising Editor: Alfred DeGaetano; Editor: Harry Reynolds; Music: Albert Glasser (Mis-Attributed to Alvin Levin in Published Reviews); Music Supervisor: Dick Carruth; Sound: John Carter; Makeup: Bob Cowan; Production Manager: Bert Sternbach; Running Time: 63 Minutes; Released: May 31, 1947

CAST: Robert Lowery (Paul Kimberly); Anabel Shaw (Anne Arnold); Charles Evans (Vincent Arnold); Frank Ferguson (Edward Denton); George Lynn (Chips Rand); Leonard Penn (Brent Maddux); Ann Staunton (Margo); Dick Rich (Bull Callahan); Eddie Parks (Clerk); Stanley Blystone (Capt. McManus); Howard Mitchell (Whiteman); Jack Cheatham (Brandon); Hazel Keener (Miss Riley); Hildegarde Ackerman (Hat-Check Girl); Charles King (Barkeep); Brooks Benedict (Croupier); Phil Arnold (Cabbie).

WEB OF DANGER
(Republic Pictures Corp.)

The lovely Adele Mara, oftener cast to type as a lethal seductress in low-rent *film noir* productions, takes a well-deserved leading role in *Web of Danger*. She is a wonder to behold as a plucky waitress who becomes the *femme* side of a romantic triangle along with two roughnecks from a construction crew. *Web of Danger* is, among other things, a prototypical near-disaster movie, trading on a threat of floodtide devastation and certain-death falls from daunting heights in a way that points toward the Great Disaster Movie Scare of the 1970s. (We emphasize that phrase *points toward*, so don't get your hopes up too high.)

The real stars of the film, in that actionful respect, are the special-effects masters Howard

A REPUBLIC PICTURE

WEB OF DANGER

and Theodore Lydecker, who gave Republic's principal output of chapter-a-week serials a visual edge over the bigger studios' cliffhangers and still made the time to distinguish many of Republic's feature-length attractions with dazzling miniatures and life-size properties. Their falling-dummy sequences are still the best in the business, photographed in real time with a respect for gravity and perspective that eludes many modern-day artists in the more easily controlled realm of digital-image fakery. Underneath its chronic pretensions to mainstream appeal and occasional finery, Republic was as lowborn and scrappy a studio as Monogram and PRC—but only Republic had the Lydecker brothers.

Web of Danger comes right to the point with a boisterous blue-collar opening sequence, establishing a rivalry between construction foreman Ernie Reardon (Bill Kennedy) and his superintendent, William O'Hara (Damian O'Flynn) for the affections of Peg Mallory (Miss Mara). Unnerved by a tense encounter, Peg boards a bus supposedly bound out of town but falls asleep en route and finds herself arrived—and temporarily stranded—at O'Hara's bridge-construction site.

Alerted to an approaching storm, O'Hara orders double-time on the project to allow the evacuation of a nearby village. Peg pitches right in to help keep the overtaxed crewmen appropriately caffeinated. She misses a step while aloft on a scaffold, and Ernie catches her. O'Hara, enraged at seeing Peg in Ernie's arms, orders her off the site. As Peg makes ready to depart, the crew learns that the surrounding roads have been washed out.

It is during the frantic building of a temporary bridge that the film finds its own higher ground: A crewman named Slim (William Hall) snags himself between high beams, and O'Hara attempts a precarious rescue. Slim falls to his death. A massed evacuation conveys the urgency of the floods to come, but the film contents itself with getting the people to safety *before* any epic destruction can take place. The running time is under an hour, after all.

The storm comes and goes courtesy of the stock-footage bins. Television syndication of the past 30 years has shown two distinct cuts—one, utilizing snippets from the 1933 *Deluge* plus commonplace newsreel-type flooding; the other, minus the *Deluge* clips.

The yarn climaxes *after* the flooding, with a slugfest between Reardon and O'Hara while Peg awaits a taxi. Reardon loses the fight, but O'Hara concedes the rivalry—and tosses Reardon, unconscious, into the cab with Peg.

CREDITS: Associate Producer: Donald Brown; Director: Philip Ford; Assistant Director: Don Verk; Screenplay: David Lang and Milton M. Raison; Photographed by: Alfred S. Keller; Special Effects: Howard Lydecker and Theodore Lydecker; Art Director: Gano Chittenden; Editor: William Thompson; Decor: John McCarthy, Jr., and George Suhr; Music: Mort Glickman; Sound: Fred Stahl; Makeup: Bob Mark; Running Time: 58 Minutes; Released: June 10, 1947

CAST: Adele Mara (Peg Mallory); Bill Kennedy (Ernie Reardon); Damian O'Flynn (William O'Hara); Richard Loo (Wing); Victor Sen Yung (Sam); Roy Barcroft (Monks); William Hall (Slim); J. Farrell MacDonald (MacKronish); Michael Branden (Ramsey); Ed Gargan (Dolan); Chester Clute (Bellyaching Customer); Ralph Sanford (Peterson); Russell Hicks (Gallagher); Wade Crosby (Bixley); George Lewis (Masher); Edythe Elliott (Red Cross Volunteer); Tex Terry (Trucker); Bob Wilke (Wagon Driver); Diane Quillen (Clerk); and Nolan Leary, Marshall Reed

THE HAT-BOX MYSTERY

(Screen Art Pictures Corp./Screen Guild Productions, Inc.)

She tried to focus a camera and found she was aiming a gun!

with
TOM NEAL
PAMELA BLAKE
ALLEN JENKINS
VIRGINIA SALE
ITS EXCLUSIVE

And no, this one is not a head-in-a-box shocker, so relax. Anyone thus interested is directed straightaway to *Night Must Fall*, a big-time picture of 1937 that lies decidedly outside the precincts of this volume. Or to its British remake of 1964. Or to 1934's *The Man Who Reclaimed His Head* if not *its* remake, 1945's *Strange Confession*.

Lambert Hillyer's *The Hat-Box Mystery* is altogether more tame than any of those others, although it is in itself a somewhat off-the-path murder yarn. Distinguished by a neat private-eye portrayal from *Detour*'s Tom Neal, the film also sports an unusual device for introducing its principal players, avoiding scrolled billing. Neal walks right onto the screen, addresses the audience directly and then introduces himself, leading ladies Pamela Blake and Virginia Sale and sidekick Allen Jenkins. This is a memorable gimmick, but hardly the sort to launch any trends.

The story opens with a campaign by a blackmailer named Stevens (Leonard Penn) to make life miserable for Marie Moreland (Olga André), a high-society dame. She resists. At the office of absentee private eye Russ Ashton (Neal), secretary Susie Hart (Pamela Blake) impulsively accepts a case from a disguised Stevens. Pretending to require evidence for a divorce, Stevens gives Susie a hatbox that supposedly contains a camera with an external shutter-trigger.

She follows instructions—only to find herself (apparently) wounding Marie. The box contains a gun, not a camera. While Susie cools her heels in the lockup, Russ returns from a business trip and goes to search Marie's apartment. He is ambushed by Stevens and an accomplice (Zon Murray). Russ persuades the law to free Susie as bait for the real assailant. A policeman who had witnessed the attack could swear he heard two shots.

After the shooting proves fatal to Marie, Susie is re-arrested for murder and then re-released by arrangement with Russ, who orchestrates a phony news story about Marie's recovery. Thus drawn out of hiding, Stevens and his boss, Flint (William Ruhl), only prove all the more menacing—capturing Susie and forcing her to write a suicide note containing a confession. Russ and the police arrive just in time to save Susie from a defenestration. Turns out that the hatbox gun had contained blanks. Stevens, having entertained second thoughts about using the hapless secretary to perform the deed, had fired the fatal shot from hiding and let her serve merely as a patsy.

Streamlined in the extreme at only 45 minutes, The Hat-Box Mystery contains the right elements to put its not-entirely-baffling story across. The basis seems to have been a Real World subway assault that took place in New York in 1946, with a sawed-off shotgun hidden in a parcel.

Neal plays it breezy but determined as the manipulative private eye, who exerts such an inappropriate influence over the police that he must have some damaging goods on the district attorney's office. Jenkins provides the principal comic relief as a slow-witted assistant who answers to the unlikely name of Harvard, and Sale is winning as Jenkins' sweetheart and principal means of support. Miss Blake does well as the flighty secretary. Leonard Penn sounds the right notes of conniving menace, especially while sporting a sinister set of chin-whiskers as a disguise. The film seems to have been intended as the launcher of a series, for the principal cast and crew returned for the following month's The Case of the Baby Sitter—a more lighthearted and even briefer (at 41 minutes) private-eye yarn, involving dishonor among diamond thieves.

CREDITS: Presented by: Robert L. Lippert; Executive Producer: Maury Nunes; Producer: Carl K. Hittleman; Director: Lambert Hillyer; Assistant Director: Robert Farfan; Screenplay: Don Martin and Carl K. Hittleman; Story: Maury Nunes and Carl K. Hittleman; Photographed by: James Brown, Jr.; Special Effects: Ray Mercer; Art Director: William Glasgow; Editor: Arthur A. Brooks; Music Supervisor: David Chudnow; Musical Score: Darrell Calker; Sound: Roy Meadows; Makeup: Robert Cowan; Running Time: 45 Minutes; Released: June 12, 1947

CAST: Tom Neal (Russ Ashton); Pamela Blake (Susie Hart); Virginia Sale (Veronica Hooper); Allen Jenkins (Harvard); Leonard Penn (Stevens); Olga André (Marie Moreland); Ed Keane (District Attorney); Zon Murray (Joe); William Ruhl (Flint); and Tom Kennedy, Al Hill, Bob Nunes

KILLERS ALL
(Del Cal Theatres, Inc.)

After the lapse of a long-standing Production Code taboo that had prevented the making of any film related to the career of John Dillinger, Monogram Pictures delivered such a finely wrought biopic in *Dillinger* (1945) as to corner the market on popular interest in the defunct badman and forestall any imitations. Two documentary-like pictures also sought to exploit Dillinger and his no-account kind during this same period:

• Dwain Esper's *The March of Crime* (1946) is a lurid muddle of found-object footage and droning carney-spieler narration, as sanctimonious and sleazy as anything Esper ever patched together in the name of sanitary sex, dope avoidance or mental hygiene.

• Charles Henkel's more interesting *Killers All* takes a somewhat higher road in using archival film clips to remind the youth of America that Crime Does Not Pay. The thrill quotient and the coherent editing render tolerable the forcible moral lesson.

A discussion of such Depression-era cases as the Lindbergh abduction and the Barker Mob's rampages serves to explain laws that allow federal agents to shoot first and sort things out later — Zero Tolerance in a healthier prototype form, without the trendy nomenclature or the risk of criminalizing ordinary civilians. The brilliant careers thus surveyed include those of Dillinger, Bonnie Parker and Clyde Barrow, and Raymond Hamilton, a mouth-breather who became one of the youngest Americans confronted with the death penalty. The kidnapping and rescue of Oklahoma oilman Charles Urschel leads to the nabbing of a Who's Who of Depression-period hoodlums, including George "Machine Gun" Kelly and the family mob known as the Bloody Shannons. If memory serves — going all the way back to a grade-school assembly-hall screening of *Killers All* in 1955 — the film packs a respectable charge of grisly death-scene images. Haven't seen the film since; it might reasonably be considered missing if not lost outright.

CREDITS: Editor in Charge of Production: Charles Henkel; Running Time: 50-60 Minutes (Approx.); Copyrighted: June 26, 1947; Released: On a State-by-State Basis

CAST: Roy Rowan (Narrator)

HEARTACHES
(Producers Releasing Corp./Pathé Industries, Inc.)

Heartaches, now — where'd you dredge that'n up from? Hadn't thought of it in years! Little bitty ol' picture, it was, where they let me just kind of carry the story along by default — y'know? It was s'posed to be one of those crackerjack-crime buster things, with this smarty-pants hero tryin' to get to the bottom of some murders croppin' up around this glamour-boy Hollywood-star character, and I was in the right place at the right time to be the hidden murderer, which I just naturally played by bein' myself. Except that I never murdered anybody, outside of in the movies. The part needed kind of an ugly ol' boy — and nobody's ever accused me of bein' much to look at—who also had him this good singin' voice, and so it suited me jus' fine. Mostly of all, it let me remind people that I had been a fair to middlin' good ballad singer, back before I turned more to playin' movie characters.—Chill Wills; from a conversation during the middle 1970s

Chill Wills (1903–1978), a genial and boisterous character man who kept busy well into the 1970s, started out as a tent-show entertainer in rural Texas while still a child. Wills possessed one of the most lilting and melodic singing voices in Southwestern Vaudeville, and he retained that quality even after his voice had darkened to a rain barrel-deep basso-baritone—even, for that matter, after advancing age and a superhuman appetite for bourbon had rendered his delivery guttural and rasping. The sense of note-perfect melody and impeccable timing remained with him to the last.

That long-sidelined singing career comes ominously to the fore in Basil Wrangell's *Heartaches*, which Wills serves as an anything-but-handsome crooner—secretively providing the splendid singing voice of a matinee idol whose career depends upon the deception. *Heartaches*, which takes its title from a perennial hit song by John Klenner and Al Hoffman, is in fact an unattributed remake of *The Phantom Broadcast*, a linchpin film in the Depression-era span of *Forgotten Horrors*. This patent act of plagiarism, though reprehensible on the face of it, gilds the theft nicely with a fine show of versatility from Wills as a too-generous pal whose misguided loyalties and festering resentments can only drive him to the breaking point.

The loyalties are less than reciprocal: Arrogant Vic Morton (Ken Farrell), a former dance-band saxophonist, owes his newfound stardom in more or less equal measure to his profile and to the hidden singing voice of his business partner (Wills), a piano accompanist who bears the unlikely name of Boagey Mann. The secret is guarded by a privileged few, including Morton's publicist, Toni Wentworth (Sheila Ryan). Toni's engagement to a snoopy newspaperman, Jimmy McDonald (Edward Norris), threatens to flummox the situation just as Morton's next picture is going into production. Morton receives a series of menacing anti-fan letters by post, and a prop gun loaded with live ammunition almost does away with him.

McDonald learns the secret, all right, but promises Toni he will keep mum. Meanwhile, Morton nixes a broadcasting deal lest his ghost-voicing scam be found out. The repercussions lead to a matched pair of slayings.

A reciprocal confrontation from *Heartaches*

McDonald gains Boagey Mann's confidence and learns that Mann, not Morton, had been the star player of their small-time nightclub act. Hollywood had pegged Morton as a celebrity-in-waiting on grounds of looks alone, and Morton demanded that Mann supply the singing voice off-camera. Mann feels he owes Morton, who once had saved his life, but McDonald senses grimmer currents at work.

So the reporter arranges a trap, using himself and Morton as bait but hedging his bets by loading Mann's pistol with blanks. The reporter taunts Mann into a confession, then goads him beyond all good sense—unaware that Mann has reloaded with the genuine article. The dumb-luck intrusion of a police detective (James Seay) provides a last-minute rescue.

As Wills' dreadful pun of a character name would suggest—and yes, *Boagey Mann* ranks right up there with *Oliver Klozoff* and *I.P. Freely* as a low-denominator laugh-getter—*Heartaches* is as concerned with facile chuckles as with deadly intrigues. Edward Norris looks every bit the courageous newspaperman, but he plays it more in the vein of a Bob Hope or a Fred MacMurray, spreading on the nervous reactions and facetious banter a bit too thickly.

Third-billed Chill Wills makes the picture more properly his own with a measured performance of brooding, underplayed menace, prefaced by a lengthy stretch where he seems a

"Just call me a professional Sentimental Fool," Chill Wills wrote in a bit of correspondence to Mike Price, more years ago than anybody here cares to enumerate. If that self-description is accurate, then it means by extension that Wills also was one fine actor—for his portrayal in Basil Wrangell's *Heartaches* is a marvel of menacing, cynical ferocity, quite at odds with Wills' boisterous, generous and often overemotional nature.

genuinely okay sort, by turns garrulous and melancholy—just as Wills was in real life. But the screenplay denies Wills the showy final confrontation that all this hard work has earned him: Wills must make do with a garden-variety capture by a cop who hasn't even been paying particularly close attention. To compound the insult, Norris gets in a sappy last word with a gag calculated to show just how shaken the encounter with Wills has left him.

Ken Farrell is suitably unpleasant as the self-important mock-singer, who deserves every threat—including the red-herring device of intimidating mail—and then becomes a red herring himself. Farrell's Vic Morton is a broad-stroke replica of every vaguely gifted star-of-the-moment who has ever taken a tentative success too seriously. Sheila Ryan makes a spirited leading lady, torn between her professional vows of silence and misgivings over the mayhem to which she might be a party. PRC's emerging Western star, Lash LaRue, holds down a smaller part.

Chill Wills told us in 1975 that he regarded *Heartaches* as "a throwaway" in its day, "just somethin' to do during what was lookin' like a long lull between bigger pictures. Every time things'd slow down, I'd get to missin' the old music-makin' times with my

I first met Chill Wills when I was six years old, in 1954. The meeting seemed a magical chance encounter, but soon proved to be a benevolent prank orchestrated by my Uncle Grady Lee Wilson, a movie-theater operator who counted Mr. Wills among his show business chums.

My folks and I were dining out one Sunday at Sammy's Steak House in Amarillo, Texas, when I heard a familiar booming voice from an adjoining room.

"I hear Francis!" I announced.

"Francis who?" asked my father.

"Francis the Talking Mule!" I said. "He's right here in this restaurant!"

Without so much as a "May I, please?" I darted off in the direction of the voice—only to find my Uncle Grady and a rugged-looking guy, seated at a table in the company of two voluptuous usherettes from Grady's Paramount Theatre.

"You lookin' for somebody, son?" asked Chill Wills, whom I wouldn't have known from Adam's Off Ox at the time.

"Uhm," said I, somewhat at a loss, "just a mule. Who are *you*?"

"Well, me an' yo' uncle, here, we's the only two jackasses within spittin' range," said Mr. Wills, then: "Francis the Talkin' Mule—at yo' service, son."

Of course, the *Francis the Talking Mule* movies added up to one of Mr. Wills' steadier gigs during those years—a different variety of phantom-voice assignment. My fondness for the *Francis* pictures turned into a friendship with the Big Chill, and we stayed in touch over the long haul, what with Mr. Wills' frequent visits to Texas. He barged in on my newspaper office in Amarillo one afternoon in 1968, stewed to the nostrils but irresistibly friendly, and spent a good hour spinning Hollywood yarns and flirting with every secretary and lady-reporter type on the premises. Chill Wills, crocked, was more articulate and spellbinding than most people are when sober. He declared the visit incomplete until he had shaken hands with our chief editor, the impeccably well-mannered Wesley S. Izzard. "Cousin Wes," Mr. Wills called the boss on a moment's acquaintance, but then Chill Wills seldom met anyone he didn't address as "Cousin." Mr. Izzard proved a good sport and later wrote fondly of the meeting.

Then during the 1970s, Mr. Wills became an occasional sit-in vocalist with my supper-club jazz trio. His mournful rendition of the Jacques Prevert-Joseph Kosma-Johnny Mercer standard "Autumn Leaves," half-crooned and half-recited, haunts me to this day.

Avalon Boys, and this one let me make some music as well as play the kind of a role I seldom was offered. 'Course, that wasn't the first time I had dubbed in the singin' from off-camera for some other character, y'know: I supplied Stanley Laurel's singin' voice for that barroom scene in his and Babe Hardy's picture, *Way Out West* [1937], too."

Wills' show of menace in *Heartaches* is distinctive among his big-screen work—a rarity matched only by his ferocious turn in a memorable episode of *Rod Serling's Night Gallery* from the early '70s, "The Little Black Bag."

CREDITS: In Charge of Production: Ben Stoloff; Producer: Marvin D. Stahl; Director: Basil Wrangell; Dialogue Director: Benny Rubin; Assistant Director: Allen Wood; Screenplay: George Bricker; Story: Monte F. Collins and Julian I. Peyser; Based Upon: Tristram Tupper's Screenplay for the 1933 Monogram Pictures Production of *The Phantom Broadcast* (Unacknowledged); Photographed by: Jack Greenhalgh; Photographic Effects: George J. Teague; Art Director: Edward C. Jewell; Supervising Editor: Alfred DeGaetano; Editor: Charles Gross, Jr.; Decor: Armor Marlow; Costumer: Dorothy Drake; Musical Director: Irving Friedman; Incidental Music: Emil Cadkin; Songs: "Can't Get That Gal," "Never Knew I Could Sing" and "I'm So in Love," by Kim Gannon and Walter Kent, and "Heartaches," by John Klenner and Al Hoffman; Sound: J.N.A. Hawkins; Sound Mixer: Perce Townsend; Makeup: Ern Westmore; Hair Stylist: Eunice; Running Time: 71 Minutes; Released: June 28, 1947

CAST: Sheila Ryan (Toni Wentworth); Edward Norris (Jimmy McDonald); Chill Wills (Boagey Mann); Ken Farrell (Vic Morton); James Seay (Lt. Danny Armstrong); Frank Orth (Mike Connelly); Chili Williams (Sally); Charles Mitchell (Pete Schilling); Al "Lash" LaRue [as LaRue] (DeLong); Ann Staunton (Anne Connelly); Phyllis Planchard (Lila)

BLACKMAIL (1947)
(Republic Pictures Corp.)

Not to be confused with Alfred Hitchcock's breakthrough talking picture or the like-titled 1939 Edward G. Robinson vehicle from MGM—or with most other feature films, for that matter—this *Blackmail* is a bang-bang Republic programmer with *noirish* elements and a plot that calls for a soggy corpse to disappear from the bottom of a swimming pool. But it is mainly noteworthy for the screen debut of Dan Turner, Hollywood Detective with a capital *H.D.* The long-lived pulp-magazine character packs a transcendent wackiness that still attracts new fans today, a good half-century after he, and the pulps as a cultural linchpin, expired.

Veteran Republic scripter Royal K. Cole makes a fair stab at transferring that wackiness to the screen, crafting a scenario—based upon the *Dan Turner* pulp story "Stock Shot"—that finds smart-alecky P.I. Turner (William Marshall) hired by playboy Ziggy Cranston (Ricardo Cortez) to find out who's behind a shakedown. Cranston, a successful Broadway producer and radio-network owner, also has a Gambling Jones—as well as a momentary weakness for a casino thrush named Carla (Stephanie Bachelor). His blow-off drink with Carla turns out to be a Mickey Finn; when he awakens the next day,

Dreams That Money Can Buy

83

Cranston finds that certain compromising photos have been taken of him and the singer, which the unnamed photogs seem to believe are worth $50,000 to suppress. When Carla falls through a penthouse window to her death, the price is jacked up to 150 grand by a fringe gambling character named Blue Chip Winslow (George J. Lewis), who'll otherwise implicate Ziggy in the croaking.

Eventually, Blue Chip ends up at the bottom of the Cranston pool, apparently shot by Ziggy. But by the time Turner can drag in the L.A. law, represented here by that B-movie authority figure Grant Withers, the body goes missing, and neither Z. Cranston nor his platinum-haired protégé, Sylvia Duane (Adele Mara), seems to know anything about any killing. It falls to the garrulous gumshoe to make his way through a gambling den or two and unravel the whole thing, with the resolution dished up in classic *film noir* style.

The theorist Arthur Lyons, in his fine *Death on the Cheap: The Lost B Movies of Film Noir* (2000), puts *Blackmail* "in the running for the worst tough-guy private-eye movie ever made." Lyons adds that Marshall's way with the wisecracking lines makes him "come off as a buffoon." Well, the occasional line does hang out there on Marshall a bit, but Lyons' evaluation seems unduly harsh. *Blackmail* is at least consistently entertaining in a dopey sort of way—which is more than can be said for some of the bloated big-budget *policiers* that have come along in times much more recent.

Lyons also speculates that *Blackmail* represented Republic's attempt to do a B-picture version of what RKO-Radio Pictures had accomplished in 1944 with *Murder, My Sweet*—that is, to turn a singer into a movieland tough guy. (Marshall had been a vocalist with Fred Waring's Pennsylvanians and, later, fronted his own band; *Murder, My Sweet*'s Dick Powell was a singin' fool in his own right, more strikingly identified with musical extravaganzas than with any hard-boilers.) The theory rings true, especially when one considers that most of Marshall's other work for the studio came in vest-pocket musicals like *Earl Carroll Sketchbook* (1946) and *Calendar Girl* (1947). But whether *Blackmail* was a calculated move or just another day at the office for the actor, it ends up as a weird little spin on the typical Republic crime thriller, stuffed with such studio stock players as Lewis, Tristram Coffin (of *King of the Rocket Men*), Gregory Gay and the ubiquitous villain Roy Barcroft playing Spice Kellaway, proprietor of the Silver Swan nightspot. The exotic-looking Adele Mara seldom appears in anything less revealing than a swimsuit, which is to the good, and silents-into-talkies star Cortez and veteran Withers act and react like the old pros they are.

Dan Turner, as created and written by an ex-newspaperman named Robert Leslie Bellem, was one of the longest-running characters in the pulp magazines, beginning in 1934 and continuing for decades in such titles as *Hollywood Detective*, *Spicy Detective* and *Speed Detective*. Bellem knocked out hundreds of Turner stories, many of them short on logic but long on action, characterization and entertainment value. Narrated by Turner himself, the tales set forth a remarkably stylized language that both tweaks and sends up the lingo of the hard-boiled detective—that uniquely American spin on the detective-story hero that had itself been born in such pulp magazines as *Black Mask* and *Dime Detective* during the 1920s and early '30s.

The Turner pulps often contained comic strips as well, and it must be noted that Marshall, physically, makes a pretty good live-action approximation of his comic-panel counterpart, especially as drawn by illustrator (and later, comic-book editor) Adolphe Barreaux. Turner's nutty slang, however, does not transfer as well. Screenwriter Cole often substitutes less radical wisecracks for Bellem's unique linguistic forays, and director Lesley Selander seems inadequately committed to the detective's idiosyncratic essence. Also on the negative side is the inexplicable decision to paint Turner as a New York detective called to L.A. rather than as a Hollywood studio troubleshooter. Nothing is made of the fish-out-of-water angle, and the Movietown milieu, a big part of the pulp stories, goes by the boards, as does the long-running relationship between Turner and the L.A.P.D.'s Inspector Donaldson that was a strength of the pulp tales. ("Flag your didies down here, Dave—and bring a meat wagon," the pulps' Turner might bark into the telephone at Donaldson. "I've found your blackmailing quail, and she's dead as Vaudeville!")

Possibly intended as the catalyst for a series, *Blackmail* instead ended up as a stand-alone. Not until 1990, 43 years later, would Turner return to the screen. The occasion was a made-for-TV movie, *Dan Turner, Hollywood Detective*, starring Marc Singer (best known for *Beastmaster* and the teleseries *V*) and directed by Christopher Lewis. Lewis' mother, Loretta Young, had once been married to *Blackmail*'s Grant Withers. Intended to be the vanguard of a series of television features, the 1990 film, like *Blackmail*, spawned no sequels. It did, however, appear in the home-video market with a couple of seconds of partial nudity added and a re-christening to *The Raven Red Kiss-Off*. For more about that film, see the introduction to *Roscoes in the Night* (Adventure House; 2002), a collection of Dan Turner pulp stories as anthologized by John Wooley, who also scripted the 1990 movie. In the interest of B.F.D. (Belated Full Disclosure) and all that.

CREDITS: Associate Producer: William J. O'Sullivan; Director: Lesley Selander; Assistant Director: Allen K. Wood; Screenplay: Royal K. Cole; Additional Dialogue: Albert DeMond; Based Upon: Robert Leslie Bellem's Story, "Stock Shot"; Photographed by: Reggie Lanning; Editor: Tony Martinelli; Art Director: Frank Arrigo; Decor: John Mc-

Carthy, Jr., and James Redd; Sound by: Herbert Norsch; Music: Mort Glickman; Makeup: Bob Mark; Running Time: 67 Minutes; Released: July 24, 1947

CAST: William Marshall (Dan Turner); Adele Mara (Sylvia Duane); Ricardo Cortez (Ziggy Cranston); Grant Withers (Inspector Donaldson); Stephanie Bachelor (Carla); Richard Fraser (Antoine); Roy Barcroft (Spice Kellaway); George J. Lewis (Blue Chip Winslow); Gregory Gay [Gaye] (Jervis); Tristram Coffin (Pinky); Eva Novak (Mamie); Bud Wolfe (Gomez); and Joy Barlow, John P. Barrett, Tom London, Muni Seroff, Ben Welden, Robert J. Wilke

KILLER DILL
was comedy

(Nivel Pictures, Inc./Max M. King Productions/Screen Guild Productions, Inc.)

The old corpse-in-the-lingerie-trunk ploy comes into play in *Killer Dill*, a Prohibition-flashback comedy with deadly public-enemy overtones, starring career milquetoast Stuart Erwin as the owner of the lingerie.

Johnny Dill (Erwin) has perfectly wholesome reasons for keeping such dainties on hand, of course: He is a salesman of suchlike and a pretty good one, at that. Johnny is a washout, however, in the romance department, and so when his sweetheart, Judy Parker (Anne Gwynne), throws him over for his blowhard lawyer pal William T. Allen (Frank Albertson), Johnny figures that drastic measures are called for.

So he hauls off and takes his assistant, Millie Gardner (Dorothy Granger) out to the movies. This surreal film-within-the-film is something a whole lot like Warner Bros.' 1931 hit, *The Public Enemy*. Johnny is appalled by the antics of the villain, whom Millie finds just ever so charming.

So Johnny decides his nice-guy demeanor is getting him nowhere and starts behaving like a movie gangster. A visit to a low dive leads to an encounter with Big Nick Moronie (Ben Welden), the life-model for the gangster in the movie Johnny has just watched. Johnny demonstrates his toughness by giving the mobster a yank on the schnozzola. By one of those absurd coincidences that amount to business-as-usual with the Poverty Row studios, Big Nick turns out to be Johnny's across-the-hall neighbor in an apartment building.

But Nick won't be living there for long. Or anywhere, for that matter. A mob hit leaves Big Nick croaked and crammed into one of Johnny's lingerie chests. Johnny dis-

covers the stiff, but his panicky attempts to dispose of it lead to his branding as Nick's slayer. He even inherits Nick's spot on the FBI's Most Wanted list, as Public Enemy Number 21.

This reputation persists even after Johnny is cleared of the charge—despite the inept representation of lawyer Allen—but the usual round of crosses and double-crosses among the surviving gangsters keeps the suspense and the hilarity about equally cranked. Johnny gets the

Stuart Erwin attempts a tough guy stance in drop on Big Nick's killer, Little Joe (Mike
Killer Dill.

Mazurki), with a toy pistol, only to find himself in fresh peril, then rescued again by the timely arrival of rival thugs. Allen turns out to be in the employ of an ambitious gangster named Maboose (Milburn Stone), who had bribed Little Joe to kill Big Nick. Judy decides that Johnny is her more type, after all.

Killer Dill is set in 1931, and it plays out very like one of the groundbreaking Warners' gangster pictures from that very period—almost a prototype for one of Mel Brooks' savvy genre parodies of the 1970s. Frank Sylos' art direction and William A. Sickner's camerawork are big plus-factors, and the generous running time accommodates the deployment of a mock feature-film that gives milquetoast Erwin the inspiration to transform himself into a tough guy. (The famous grapefruit-in-the-face scene from *The Public Enemy* is spoofed to pleasing effect.)

At 73 minutes, *Killer Dill* was too long in its day to serve as a backup attraction for double-feature engagements—and not big enough in terms of star appeal to justify top-of-the-bill promotion. That length also finds director Lewis D. Collins ill-prepared to pace the misadventure with sufficient urgency, especially when the script's tangled mess of dishonor-among-thieves becomes too incoherent to contemplate.

The screenplay seems more concerned with facile ironies—assigning big Mike Mazurki the character name of Little Joe, for example, and christening Milburn Stone's scheming mobster with a sound-alike reference to the criminal mastermind of Fritz Lang's famous *Dr. Mabuse* films of the 1920s and '30s. Stuart Erwin is fine in the title role, but Anne Gwynne is too good for her merely scenic character. Mazurki, Stone, Ben Welden and Anthony Warde all do well by their wiseguy assignments, and Frank Albertson etches a love-to-hate-him portrait as the glad-handing weasel of a lawyer.

CREDITS: Producer: Max M. King; Director: Lewis D. Collins; Assistant Director: Ralph Slosser; Screenplay: John O'Dea; Story: Alan Friedman; Photographed by: William Sickner; Special Effects: Ray Mercer; Art Director: Frank Sylos; Editor: Marty Cohn; Decor: Harry Reif; Wardrobe: Isidore Berne; Music: Johnny Thompson; Sound: Glen Glenn; Production Manager: George Moskov; Running Time: 73 Minutes; Released: August 2, 1947

CAST: Stuart Erwin (Johnny "Killer" Dill); Anne Gwynne (Judy Parker); Frank Albertson (William T. Allen); Mike Mazurki (Little Joe); Milburn Stone (Maboose); Dorothy Granger (Millie Gardner); Anthony Warde (Louie Moroni); Ben Welden (Big Nick Moronie); Shirley Hunter (Gloria); Stanley Ross (Mushnose); Will Orlean (Movie Gangster); Charles Knight (Jack); Stanley Andrews (Jones); Julie Mitchum (Secretary); and Dewey Robinson, Julie Gibson, Lola Jensen, Margaret Zane

DRAGNET (1947)
(Fortune Film Corp./Screen Guild Productions, Inc.)

Just the facts, ma'am or sir: Jack Webb's famous *Dragnet* series came along quite a bit later than this like-titled production, which is irrelevant to the exploits of Officer Joe Friday and *vice versa*. Webb, in fact, would draw his inspirations from a 1948 film, *He Walked by Night*, in which he handled a small role. And we're still wading through 1947 with the present *Dragnet*.

Henry Wilcoxon stars as Inspector Geoffrey James of Scotland Yard, called in on an American case involving the beachfront discovery of a corpse packing a cache of the Crown's legal tender. The body is coated in a fluorescent dye commonly used in seagoing rescues, which might indicate a shipwreck—except for no evidence of a drowning. Identification of the victim requires a few tries to get it right.

The trail leads to a seaside shack, where James finds himself under attack from a maniacal beachcomber (Douglass Dumbrille), who also seems to have some relationship with a mystery woman (Virginia Dale) lurking about the premises. The motivating scam proves to have more to do with jewel thievery than with mayhem for its own sake, but the creepy atmosphere takes the film to that Next Level of interest. Wilcoxon carries things ably as the determined C.I.D. man, and Mary Brian lends both heroic and scenic

LUST...
for riches
LOVE...
of jewels
LURES
her to doom!

Bert M. Stearn presents

DRAGNET

Starring HENRY
WILCOXON
MARY BRIAN

with
DOUGLAS DUMBRILLE · VIRGINIA DALE
DOUGLAS BLACKLEY · TOM FADDEN

value as an airline hostess with an unusual interest in the case. Both players addressed the cameras only sporadically during the 1940s; their occasional appearances are more than welcome. Maxine Semon shines briefly as a bubble-headed blabbermouth waitress.

The running time feels overlong at 71 minutes, much of that wasted by superficial jabbering in the dialogue department and a dawdling pace from director Leslie Goodwins. A savvier low-budget house, such as PRC, could have cranked out the same yarn in a slick hour-or-less, with no essential narrative sacrificed and plenty of momentum gained.

CREDITS: Presented by: Bert M. Stearn; Producer and Original Scenarist: Maurice H. Conn; Director: Leslie Goodwins; Assistant Director: Cy Roth; Screenplay: Barbara Worth and

Harry Essex; Photographed by James S. Brown, Jr.; Art Directors: Seymour Roth and Frank Sylos; Editor: Paul Landres; Decor: Elias H. Reif and Fay C. Babcock; Musical Scoring and Direction: Irving Gertz and Edward Kay; Sound: John R. Carter; Running Time: 71 Minutes; Released: August 16, 1947

CAST: Henry Wilcoxon (Inspector Geoffrey James); Mary Brian (Anne Hogan); Douglass Dumbrille (Frank Farrington); Virginia Dale (Irene Trilling); Maxine Semon (Mabel Carter); Douglas Blackley and Ralph Dunn (Cops); and Tom Fadden, Edward Earle, Don Harvey, Bert Conway, Douglas Evans, Allan Nixon, Paul Newlan, Leonid Snegoff, Hugh Prosser

THE PRETENDER
(W.W. Productions, Inc./Republic Pictures Corp.)

The first crook to figure out that Professional Respectability makes a pretty good front should have taken out a patent on the idea, for it has not only served the white-collar criminal element over the long stretch—but also provided a lucrative springboard for any volume of tense storytelling. The corrupted endeavor in W. Lee Wilder's *The Pretender* is the stock market, transformed from profession to racket by Albert Dekker.

Now, brokerage manipulations, as crooked dealings go, are about as enthralling as a corporate balance sheet. As Dorothy L. Sayers, the literary realm's greatest compiler of crime-story anthologies, would have put it: Thievery by itself is of but little interest, except to the thief and the victim and the law. But if one should compound that thievery with sins more lurid and a confrontation with death—then, the world wants to watch. So leave it to Dekker to raise the ante on his money-grubbing schemes by resorting to ill-intentioned courtship and hired-gun murder, only to spend most of his own starring movie cowering in paranoid terror.

Cowering might seem a tall order for Dekker, whose massive frame and athletic bearing were only enhanced by a calculating intellectualism—suggesting, in just the narrow frame of reference of one genre, almost a merger of the brawn and rowdiness of Lon Chaney, Jr., and the brainy reserve of Boris Karloff. If the title role in *Dr. Cyclops* (1940) had not defined Dekker in such a light, then certainly his Louis XIII in *The Man in the Iron Mask* (1939) and his portrayal of twins—one a solid citizen, the other a homicidal idiot—in *Among the Living* (1941) would do the trick.

Wilder, who should have stuck with producing and left the directing to abler hands, imposes a stodgy pace quite at odds with Dekker's vigorous perfor-

mance and Don Martin's agile screenplay. Dekker plays Kenneth Holden, who has stayed afloat in a turbulent stock market by siphoning margin requirements from the account of a too-trusting client (Selmer Jackson). None of which would be catching up with Holden any time soon, if not for a sudden drop in the industrial averages, which prompt Holden to propose marriage to another client, wealthy Claire Worthington (Catherine Craig). She nixes the come-on, explaining that she is otherwise engaged but declining to name the lucky guy.

Claire changes her mind in favor of a sudden marriage to Holden—but only after Holden has hired gangster Victor Korrin (Alan Carney) to determine the identity of the fiancé and have him murdered. Which suddenly leaves Holden the target of his own scheme.

The designated hit man, a thug called Fingers (Tom Kennedy), is left to his own devices after Korrin is slain in a vaguely related incident before he can call off the contract. There follows an ordeal in which Holden becomes a nervous recluse, stockpiling food and attempting in vain to alter his appearance, and finally fleeing into the night—only to become a casualty of his own bad driving. Fingers at length approaches the widowed Mrs. Holden, handing to her an envelope of money from a business deal that he explains has fallen through.

The agonies read more grippingly than Wilder allows them to play, leaving Dekker to enthrall the viewer with a fine show of self-inflicted madness rather than drawing the viewer into any intimate identification with the madman. Serial champ Linda Stirling makes an impressively vengeful gang moll. Catherine Craig plays the bewildered heiress with a vulnerable haughtiness, and Charles Drake has some nice moments as the rejected fiancé who (being a doctor) comes up with some highfalutin theories about Dekker's strange behavior. Tom Kennedy and Alan Carney make a fine pair of heavies. Carney's work here is all the more impressive if placed in context with his comedy-team work at RKO-Radio Pictures. The pairing of Carney with Wally Brown would lead neither artist to prominence as a funnyman, but their few pictures as a duo include the memorable *Zombies on Broadway* (1945), in which Brown & Carney share top billing with Bela Lugosi.

In keeping with the tale's psychological concerns, Paul Dessau's original orchestral score bears mentioning as a real mood-builder, graced with some eerie proto-synthesizer Theremin passages by Dr. Samuel J. Hoffman.

CREDITS: Producer and Director: W. Lee Wilder; Assistant Directors: Mack Wright and Ralph Slosser; Screenplay: Don Martin; Additional Dialogue: Doris Miller; Photographed by: John Alton; Art Director: F. Paul Sylos; Supervising Editor: John F. Link; Editor: Asa Boyd Clark; Costumer: I.R. Berne; Music: Paul Dessau; Theremin Effects: Dr. Samuel J. Hoffman; Sound: Herbert Norsch; Makeup: Don Cash; Production Manager: George Moskov; Running Time: 70 Minutes; Released: August 16, 1947

CAST: Albert Dekker (Kenneth Holden); Catherine Craig (Claire Worthington); Charles Drake (Dr. Leonard Koster); Alan Carney (Victor Korrin); Linda Stirling (Flo Ronson); Tom Kennedy (Fingers); Selmer Jackson (Charles Lennox); Charles Middleton (William); Ernie Adams (Thomas); Ben Welden (Mickie); John Bagni (Hank Gordon); Stanley Ross (Stranger); Forrest Taylor (Dr. Stevens); Greta Clement (Margie); Peter Michael (Stephen); Peggy Wynne (Miss Chalmers); Eula Guy (Nurse); Cay Forrester (Evelyn Cossett); Michael Mark (Janitor); Dorothy Scott (Miss Michael)

Looks like a hopeful ending after all for the Gas House Kids—barring the taint of a sorry imitation of the Bowery Boys franchise.

THE GAS HOUSE KIDS
"IN HOLLYWOOD"

(PRC Pictures Inc./Eagle–Lion Films, Inc./Pathé Industries, Inc.)

What a bring down for Carl "Alfalfa" Switzer and Tommy "Butch" Bond—from major-league kid-stardom in the *Our Gang* comedies, to the shabby imitation-Bowery Boys indignities of PRC's *Gas House Kids* series.

The Gas House Kids "In Hollywood," complete with awkward punctuation, is the third-and-last of a misguided series. It qualifies as a horror picture by virtue of an off-kilter scientist (Milton Parsons) who intends to use the corpse of a deceased colleague as a conduit between "this world and the next," quote/unquote. Complicating matters are a purportedly haunted mansion; a crooked mob seeking a hidden fortune; a tough-guy movie star (Michael Whalen) who pretends to befriend the kids while conspiring with the gangsters; and a stale selection of vanishing corpses. The film marks a small transition for director Edward L. Cahn, who had been a workhorse on MGM's *Our Gang* shorts and would

become a specialist in drive-in-movie exploitation fare during the '50s.

Carl Switzer was the freckle-faced, google-eyed *Our Gang* member with the Perma-Press cowlick and the singing style that could strip the varnish off furniture. His fans have been known to voice dismay upon discovering the *Gas House* films and seeing how dissipated the kid was looking at only age 21. (Tommy Bond, who had played Alfalfa's own personal Nemesis in the *Our Gangs*, fared somewhat better.) Those who recoil from the forcible cuteness of Switzer's kid-star appearances will find the *Gas House*rs merely an added touch of unseemliness.

At any rate, Switzer had few enough prospects remaining in Hollywood that he moved along to shabbier endeavors yet, including gambling and a hunting-guide business. He was shot to death in 1959 during a dispute over money, and an inquest ruled the homicide justifiable. Switzer's slaying made for sensational headlines just as the *Our Gang* shorts were finding a new audience of television-addicted school kids.

The *Gas House* series had started out somewhat more promisingly in 1946 with Sam Newfield's *Gas House Kids*, a nice-try stab at recapturing some of the social-problem dramatic ballast of Sidney Kingsley's *Dead End*. Lowbrow comedy took over with *Gas House Kids Go West* and continued through the present selection—whose original work-in-progress title had been *It's Moider*.

CREDITS: Producer: Sam Baerwitz; Director: Edward L. Cahn; Assistant Director: Bert Glazer; Dialogue Director: Monte Collins; Screenplay: Robert E. Kent; Photographed by: James Brown; Art Director: F. Paul Sylos, Sr.; Supervising Editor: Alfred De Gaetano; Editor: W. Donn Hayes; Musical Supervisor: Dick Carruth; Music: Albert Glasser; Sound: Frank Webster; Makeup: Roland Ray; Production Manager: Buck Gottlieb; Running Time: 67 Minutes; Released: August 23, 1947

CAST: Carl "Alfalfa" Switzer (Alfalfa); Bennie Bartlett (Orvie); Rudy Wissler (Scat); Tommy Bond (Chimp); James Burke (Lt. Mack); Jan Bryant (Hazel Crawford); Michael Whalen (Lance Carter); Douglas Fowley (Mitch Gordon); Frank Orth (Police Captain); Lyle Latell (Henchman); Milton Parsons (Gately Crawford); Kenneth Farrell (Edwards); Gene Roth (Cop)

HAL ROACH'S
"CURLEY" COMEDIES
(Hal Roach Studios, Inc./United Artists Corp.)

Carl "Alfalfa" Switzer and Tommy Bond (see the *Gas House Kids* entry, above) were hardly the only *Our Gang* alumni to fall upon difficult times as age and the standard curse of childhood stardom caught up with them. *Our Gang*'s creator, Hal Roach, had sold that lucrative franchise to MGM in 1938, only to watch helplessly as the big studio transformed the rambunctious team once known as Roach's Rascals into a regimented phalanx of do-gooder busybodies and pathetic whiners. These abominations continued to surface into 1944.

"The *Our Gang* comedies turned grotesque under MGM's influence," Roach told us in 1992. "My old-time Rascals had been as close to natural kids as Hollywood ever got, with few enough exceptions, and the way MGM turned them into little plastic good-citizen zombies was ghastly to behold. And goodness knows, I'd never have hired that horrid little Mickey Gubitosi, not while *my* name was attached to the series." (Mickey Gubitosi eventually became Robert "Bobby" Blake, a notoriously eccentric—and later, just-plain notorious—leading man and character actor.)

In 1947, Roach sought to recapture the near-naturalistic appeal of his original *Our Gang*ers of the 1920s and '30s. No longer a major-league player except in the emerging realm of television production, Roach made *Curley*, also known as *The Adventures of Curley & His Gang*, on the cheap as part of the *Streamlined* series of big-screen short features that he had launched in 1941. He found a plucky youngster named Larry Olsen to play the neighborhood ringleader, William "Curley" Benson. Scenarist Dorothy Reid, better known for a string of anti-drug and rackets-buster melodramas dating from the 'twenties, took the low road to a shooting script by cribbing situations from the early-talkie *Our Gang* pictures. It comes as no surprise that the *Curley* pictures contain offbeat touches—especially the second entry, *Who Killed Doc Robbin*—for Roach had been a pioneer in genre-splicing of humor and weirdness to mutual advantage. Both films were shot in 1946, then released a year apart during 1947–1948.

Roach's good intentions were hardly enough. The *Curley* films stink like nobody's business, with or without comparison against their superior *Our Gang* models. Larry Olsen is not even up to the par of a Carl "Alfalfa" Switzer or a past-his-prime George "Spanky" McFarland—and never mind the all-'round natural-kid presence of, say, a Jackie Cooper or a Scotty Beckett that these situations demand. The Olsen child whines and blubbers

as wretchedly as the despised Mickey Gubitosi-become-Robert Blake, and he seems afflicted with self-consciousness throughout.

More winning are two black youngsters, Renée Beard and Donald King, whom Roach christened Dis & Dat in a condescendingly quaint attempt to recapture the warmth and resourcefulness of such *Our Gang* mainstays as "Sunshine Sammy" Morrison, Allen "Farina" Hoskins and Matthew "Stymie" Beard. Dis & Dat make a mischievous pair, stealing the show(s) without half trying.

The greater interest of the *Curleys* lies in a backstage controversy that the first film provoked—innocently so—with an influential Deep Southern censor named Lloyd T. Binford.

Binford, by this time in his 80s, had long been a tyrannical influence with the Memphis Board of Censors, often haranguing the Motion Picture Association with diatribes about the perceived lewdness or social irresponsibility of this film or that. The nasty-minded old curmudgeon's loudest grandstand play to date had been to orchestrate a provincial ban on MGM's *Dr. Jekyll & Mr. Hyde* (1941), on grounds that leading lady Ingrid Bergman was "an immoral woman"—an allusion to a media-orchestrated scandal involving her and the Italian filmmaker Roberto Rossellini. The society of censors, like those of the Puritans and the Roundheads, is distinguished by a tendency to stay awake nights worrying that somebody, somewhere, might be enjoying life.

Like many another honkified Southerner of his day, Lloyd Binford also was a devout segregationist who embraced the view that black citizens were perfectly tolerable as long as they stayed marginalized. A belief in the myth of race is all that is necessary to make anyone, whether white or black or plaid, a racist, and Binford and his kind carried that belief to its oppressive extreme.

Binford's Memphis Board of Censors took severe exception to *Curley*'s effortless show of integration (another carry-over, in fact, from the *Our Gang* short subjects). In announcing a regional ban, Binford wrote to United Artists that his agency "was unable to approve your *Curley* picture with the little Negroes… The South does not permit Negroes in white school [*sic*] nor recognize social equality between the races, even in children."

Hal Roach seized the opportunity to let Binford's complaint generate some publicity. In a formal press release, the producer fired back: "I started making *Our Gang* comedies many years ago, and they played all over the country, including the South. No serious objection was voiced to the showing of a colored youngster as a member… Young children of various races play together without friction until their elders inoculate them with the venom of race prejudice. The aged Mr. Binford is still fighting the Civil War, apparently forgetting that white and Negro servicemen in American uniforms fought and died together in two World Wars to defend and protect the basic rights Binford would destroy."

The Motion Picture Association threw in with Roach and United Artists in a lawsuit, attacking the Memphis Board of Censors for unconstitutional tampering with freedom of speech. The case dragged on for more than two years until the Supreme Court of Tennessee ruled in favor of Binford, and the U.S. Supreme Court rejected a bid for appeal in 1950. By which time, *Curley* and its ill-advised sequel had become forgotten films.

Those forgotten films are remembered herewith, with merciful brevity:

• *Curley*, a.k.a. *The Adventures of Curley and His Gang* and, elsewhere, as **Part No. 1 of *The Hal Roach Comedy Carnival*—**Curley (Larry Olsen) and his classmates await the arrival of a new schoolteacher, whom they expect to be a crabby old maid. The new arrival is, however, pretty young Mildred Johnson (Frances Rafferty). Curley meets Mildred without knowing of her mission and informs her of the unpleasant reception the kids have prepared for their new teacher. The pranks backfire, of course, and an implausibly powerful toy automobile veers out of control. A happy ending is a foregone conclusion, but not before Curley has inflicted upon the viewer an excruciating display of guilt-ridden remorse. The Cinecolor process lends an otherworldly aspect.

A reissue as *The Hal Roach Comedy Carnival* found *Curley* paired with *The Fabulous Joe* (1947), a domestic farce involving a talking dog.

CREDITS: Presented by: Hal Roach; Executive Producer: Hal Roach, Jr.; Producer: Robert F. McGowan; Director: Bernard Carr; Assistant Director: John H. Morse; Screenplay: Dorothy Reid; Based Upon: Robert F. McGowan's Original Scenarios; Additional Dialogue: Mary McCarthy; Photographed by: John W. Boyle; Special Effects: Roy Seawright; Art Director: Jerome Pycha, Jr.; Editor: Bert Jordan; Decor: William Stevens; Wardrobe: Harry Black; Music: Heinz Roemheld; Sound: William Randall; Makeup: Burris Grimwood; Running Time: Varies from 45 to 54 Minutes; Released: August 29, 1947

CAST: Larry Olsen (William "Curley" Benson); Frances Rafferty (Mildred Johnson); Eilene Janssen (Betty); Dale Belding (Speck); Gerald Perreau (Dud);

Ardda Lynwood (Ardda); Kathleen Howard (Aunt Martha); Edna Holland (Miss Payne); Renée Beard (Dis); Donald King (Dat); Eugene Holland (Hank); Billy Gray (Sandy); George Nokes (Chuck); George McDonald (Bozo); Billy Andrews (Biff); James Menzies (Jimmy); Tommie Menzies (Tommy); Helen Brown (Miss Evans); Bob Bentley (Lt. Col. Martin); Ferris Taylor (Peace Justice); Barbara Woodell (Mrs. Benson); Eddie Dunn and Jim Farley (Baggage Handlers); Guy L. Beach (Stationmaster); Syd Saylor (Cabbie); Fred Trowbridge (Conductor)

• *Who Killed Doc Robbin*, a.k.a. *Curley and His Gang in the Haunted House* and, elsewhere, as Part No. 2 of *Laff Time*— George Zucco, that *eminence grise* among Old Hollywood's brainier villains, serves a wastefully self-caricatured function here as the apparently deceased Dr. Hugo Robbin. Robbin's nurse (Virginia Grey) stands accused of his murder. Courtroom testimony by Curley (Larry Olsen) and his various neighborhood pals, who had gone snooping about Dr. Robbin's laboratory, establishes sinister doings afoot involving a coveted nuclear-fission gizmo.

A fresh tour of the property finds the kids menaced by a gorilla (Charles Gemora, whose long string of ape impersonations includes *Bear Shooters*, from the Depression-era heyday of *Our Gang*). The gorilla, once gunned down by the police, proves to be a disguised Dr. Robbin, who had faked his demise in order to incriminate the nurse and the true inventor (Whitford Kane) of the atomic-energy device.

A reissue as *Laff Time*, the last of Roach's *Streamlined* series, found *Doc Robbin* paired with *Here Comes Trouble* (1948), a gangster spoof. A much later television-syndicate presentation saw *Curley* and *Who Killed Doc Robbin* fused into a single episodic feature. The patchwork reconfigurations helped the material none at all.

CREDITS: Presented by: Hal Roach; Executive Producer: Hal Roach, Jr.; Producer: Robert F. McGowan; Director: Bernard Carr; Dialogue Director: John H. Morse; Assistant Directors: James Lane and Jack Temple; Screenplay: Maurice Geraghty and Dorothy Reid; Based Upon: Original Scenarios by Robert F. McGowan; Photographed by: John W. Boyle; Camera Operator: Ellis W. Carter; Associate Cameraman: William Anzer; Gaffer: Cliff Hutchinson; Stills: Eugene Hackley; Special Effects: Roy W. Seawright; Miniatures: Fred Knoth; Art Director: Jerome Pycha, Jr.; Editor: Arthur Seid; Decor: William Stevens; Properties: Charles Oelzel; Assistant Propmaster: Mitch Grimes; Wardrobe: Harry Black; Wardrobe Assistants: Earl Leas and Mary Barnard; Music: Heinz Roemheld; Sound: William Randall and Dick Burgess; Boom Operator: Omar Farrell; Cable Operator: Al Cram; Makeup: Burris Grimwood; Hair Stylist: Loretta Francell; Production Manager: Sidney Van Keuren; Script Supervisor: Charles Morton; Casting: Menifee Johnstone; Casting Assistant: Ann Purdy; Grip: Edward Comfort; Best Boy: Gordon Wells; Technician: Arthur Gerstle; Child Welfare Supervisor: Fern Carter; Chimp Trainer: Albert Antonucci; Dog Trainer: Sam Williamson; Running Time: 50 Minutes; Released: August 29, 1947

CAST: Larry Olsen (Curley); Eilene Janssen (Betty); Gerald Perreau (Dudley); Ardda Lynwood (Ardda); Dale Belding (Speck); Renée Beard (Dis); Donald King (Dat); Virginia Grey (Ann Loring); Don Castle (Lawyer); George Zucco (Dr. Hugo Robbin); Paul Hurst (Jailkeeper); Whitford Kane (Fix-It Dan); Wilton Graff (Prosecutor); Claire Dubrey (Housekeeper); Grant Mitchell (Judge); Charles Gemora (Gorilla); Marshall Ruth (Police Sergeant); Allen Matthews (Motorcycle Cop); John Canady (Bailiff); Frank O'Connor (Prowl Car Cop); Bill Ruhl (Homicide Inspector); William Forrest, Jr., and Steve Carruthers (Reporters); Rags (Dog)

ALONG THE OREGON TRAIL
(Republic Pictures Corp.)

An intimidating portrayal of megalomania from a less-than-likely bad-guy actor distinguishes this otherwise slight series-starrer for the singing-cowboy hero Monte Hale.

That villain would be Clayton Moore, who was almost two years away at the time from his career-making but talent-confining identification with the Lone Ranger. Moore plays Gregg Thurston, a would-be empire builder at large in the Missouri Territory around 1840—the right place at the right time for the right land-grabber to stake out a sovereign territory all his own.

The cavalry around Ft. Bridger finds itself endangered as a consequence, and trail guide Monte Hale (playing himself, or possibly an ancestor) is pressed into service despite his own need to track down vengeful badman Jake Stoner (Roy Barcroft, grandest of Republic's in-house villains) before Stoner can track him down. Monte's mentor, Kit Carson (Forrest Taylor), insists that they have a greater duty to the government.

Stoner is just as frustrated. His henchmen persuade him to drop the grudge hunt for Monte because their big boss, Thurston, has more urgent business. The paths of Monte and Thurston soon cross, and Monte determines that Thurston is running guns to the local Indians as a reward for their depredations against the more well intentioned settlers. Gaining the trust of a tribal chieftain (Noble Johnson), Monte disposes of Stoner in a fair-and-square duel ordered by the chief, then foils Thurston's scheme to attack the fort and confronts the madman in a wild running gunfight within a cavernous warehouse.

Clayton Moore steals the show with a severe, flamboyant portrayal quite at odds with his own nice-guy approach to heroism of years to come. Roy Barcroft supplies able backup villainy. Monte Hale would be no match for these villains if he did not have the advantage of series stardom. The script even allows Hale to steal Moore's sweetheart (Adrian Booth)—but only after Moore has mistreated her. The token presence of such historic personages as Jim Bridger and Kit Carson is mere fodder for name-dropping. The musical selections are few enough to keep from compromising the ferocious action, and they feature the pleasing backup work of Foy Willing & The Riders of the Purple Sage—anachronistic in light of the story's period setting, but so what of it?

CREDITS: Associate Producer: Melville Tucker; Director: R.G. Springsteen; Assistant Director: Herb Mendelson; Screenplay: Earle Snell; Additional Dialogue: Royal K. Cole; Photographed by: Alfred S. Keller; Special Effects: Howard Lydecker and Theodore Lydecker; Art Director: Fred Ritter; Editor: Arthur Roberts; Decor: John McCarthy, Jr., and Helen Hansard; Costumer: Adele Palmer; Music: Mort Glickman; Songs: "Oregon" and "Along the Wagon Trail" by Foy Willing, and the Traditional Ballads "Sweet Betsy from Pike" and "Pretty Little Pink"; Sound: Earl Crain, Sr.; Makeup: Bob Mark; Running Time: 64 Minutes; Released: August 30, 1947

CAST: Monte Hale (Himself); Adrian Booth (Sally Dunn); Clayton Moore (Gregg Thurston); Roy Barcroft (Jake Stoner); Max Terhune (Max); Will Wright (Jim Bridger); Wade Crosby (Tom); LeRoy Mason (John Fremont); Tom London (Driver); Forrest Taylor (Kit Carson); Foy Willing & The Riders of the Purple Sage (Themselves); Steve Rains (Steve); Noble Johnson (Chief); Kermit Maynard (Marshal); Frank O'Connor (Elderly Man); and Donia Busey

IN WHICH PHILO VANCE
SOJOURNS ON POVERTY ROW

(PRC Pictures, Inc./Eagle–Lion Films, Inc./Pathé Industries, Inc.)

The *Philo Vance* franchise really should have caught on better as a PRC venture. The studio's transformation to Eagle–Lion Films was proceeding apace, promising at last to rise above its seedier origins (which were perfectly respectable, in their way). *The Hollywood Reporter* predicted that the series would continue, but PRC yanked the plug

after only three entries.

The sleuth Philo Vance had evolved from the novels of S.S. Van Dine into a movie character as early as 1929, in Paramount's *The Canary Murder Case*, starring William Powell. Powell played Vance repeatedly, following through with *The Greene Murder Case* (1929), *The Benson Murder Case* (1930) and, in a move to Warner Bros., *The Kennel Murder Case* (1933). Subsequent Vances would include the likes of Basil Rathbone,

Warren William, Edmund Lowe, Grant Richards, James Stephenson, Paul Lukas and, in England, Wilfred Hyde-White.

PRC's first answer to such heavy-duty portrayals was Alan Curtis, a former fashion model who had broken into Hollywood a decade earlier and long since proved his worth at both Byronic romanticism and brooding villainy. His turn as a wrongfully accused murder suspect in Universal's *Phantom Lady* (1944) is one of the *film noir* tradition's finer portraits of bewildered alienation. Curtis died at 43 in 1953.

As Philo Vance, Curtis consistently hits the right notes of arrogance and impatient efficiency, with a sly conspiratorial air to rival that of Rathbone and a drollness reminiscent of Warren William. Curtis' successor, William Wright (who died at 38 in 1949), takes more of a hard-boiled approach, suited to the times, and is as effective. PRC's *Vances* were shot back-to-back, from September of 1946 through January of 1947. Their order was rearranged for release, and the first-produced became the last-issued. Van Dine receives no on-screen credit, the movie rights having been ceded to PRC by a freelance producer and trademark holder named James S. Burkett. Herewith:

• *Philo Vance's Secret Mission*—This entry is restored here to a truer chronology. *Philo Vance's Secret Mission* was produced as the series-launcher but wound up being shunted to the end in order of opening dates; the studio saved the best for last.

The series makes better sense if one starts watching with *Secret Mission*: Otherwise, there is a disorienting change from Alan Curtis to William Wright, and back again, in the leading role. Too, Vance and his partner-in-sleuthing, Ernie Clark (played here by Frank Jenks, one of the better Runyonesque character men), stand out here as a bantering team that could have evolved nicely; their grip on the nuances of character is stronger in *Philo Vance's Gamble*, which catches Curtis in the process of moving out of his predecessors' imposing shadows.

Pulp-horrors magazine publisher Martin Jamison (Paul Maxey) invites Vance to write a novel based on the unsolved slaying of Jamison's business partner, Haddon Phillips. Jamison turns up murdered, his body stashed in the trunk of Vance's automobile. Vance gets romantic with Mona Bannister (Sheila Ryan), Jamison's secretary—only to wind up accusing

HE'S OCCUPIED WITH MURDER . . . BUT PRE-OCCUPIED WITH LOVE!

Philo Vance is all wrapped up in his work . . . an old mystery to solve . . . and a new girl to date!

Philo Vance's SECRET MISSION

with
ALAN CURTIS · SHEILA RYAN · TALA BIRELL · FRANK JENKS

her of murder. It develops that Jamison had accused Phillips of embezzlement. Phillips turns up alive and dangerous but elusive; he had faked his own murder seven years ago in order to evade a criminal rap and collect an insurance settlement. Mona, relieved to learn that Vance's charge against her had been a ruse, pesters the detective to marry her, but Vance prefers bachelorhood.

Lawrence Edmund Taylor's original screenplay is a pleasing tangle of messy intrigues, with Phillips' presumed widow (the luscious Tala Birell) contemplating marriage only so that Phillips can kill her new husband and assume his identity. Reginald LeBorg directs the proceedings with a lurid pulp sensibility that is right for the story, but quite at odds with S.S. Van Dine's more mannerly approach to mayhem.

CREDITS: Producer: Howard Welsch; Director: Reginald LeBorg; Dialogue Director: James Flood; Screenplay: Lawrence Edmund Taylor; Based Upon: the Character Created by S.S. Van Dine (Unattributed); Photographed by: Jackson Rose; Photographic Effects: George Teague; Assistant Director: Howard W. Koch; Art Director: Perry Smith; Supervising Art Director: Edward Jewell; Editor: W. Donn Hayes; Supervising Editor: Alfred DeGaetano; Decor: Armor Marlowe and Clarence Steenson; Costumer: Dorothy Drake; Sound: J.N.A. Hawkins; Makeup: Bud Westmore; Hair Stylist: Eunice; Running Time: 58 Minutes; Released: August 30, 1947

CAST: Alan Curtis (Philo Vance); Sheila Ryan (Mona Bannister); Tala Birell (Mrs. Phillips); Frank Jenks (Ernie Clark); James Bell (Harry Madison); Frank Fenton (Paul Morgan); Paul Maxey (Martin Jamison); Kenneth Farrell (Joe); Toni Todd (Louise Roberts)

• *Philo Vance's Gamble*—This second entry in order of shooting was the first to reach the screen. It pivots on a serial-murder case motivated by a fabulous emerald. Terry Austin, second-billed as an actress-friend of Vance's, seems to have an inappropriately keen interest in the guarding of the gem. A midnight gathering of armed suspects keeps the tension well cranked to the end, but it is a child's toy gun with which Vance trumps the deal.

CREDITS: Producer: Howard Welsch; Director: Basil Wrangell; Assistant Director: Ivan Volkman; Dialogue Director: Stewart Stern; Screenplay: Eugene Conrad and Arthur St. Claire; Story: Lawrence Edmund Taylor; Photographed by: Jackson Rose; Photographic  Effects: George Teague; Art Director: Perry Smith; Supervising Editor: Alfred DeGaetano; Editor: W. Donn Hayes; Decor: Armor Marlowe and William Kiernan; Costumer: Dorothy Drake; Music: Irving Friedman; Western Electric Sound: J.N.A. Hawkins; Sound Mixer: W.C. Smith; Makeup: Bud Westmore; Hair Stylist: Eunice; Running Time: 62 Minutes; Released: April 13, 1947

CAST: Alan Curtis (Philo Vance); Terry Austin (Laurian March); Frank Jenks (Ernie Clark); Tara Birell (Tina Cromwell); Gavin Gordon (Oliver Tennant); Cliff Clark (Inspector Heath); James Burke (Lt. Burke); Toni Todd (Geegee Desmond); Francis Pierlot (Roberts); Joseph Crehan (District Attorney Ellis Mason); Garnett Marks (Charles O'Mara); Grady Sutton (Willetts); Charles Mitchell (Guy Harkness); Joanne Frank (Norma Harkness); Dan Seymour (Jeffrey Connor)

• *Philo Vance Returns*—This third-shot and second-released entry was in fact previewed simultaneously with *Philo Vance's Gamble*, though issued two months later.

Terry Austin returns, this time playing a likely suspect and/or victim among former wives and a jilted fiancée of playboy Larry Blendon (Damian O'Flynn). Blendon turns up slain immediately following the murder of his latest conquest (Ramsay Ames, seen all too briefly). Iris Adrian and Ann Staunton round out the roster, and grandmotherly Clara Blandick—still playing to type, a generation after such triumphs as *Tom Sawyer* and *Drums of Jeopardy*—hovers over the proceedings as the guardian of the Blendon fortune and reputation.

William Wright picks up the Vance role with a no-nonsense efficiency, and Leon Belasco contributes a helpful dose of comedy relief as a theatrical impresario who appoints himself Vance's assistant.

CREDITS: Producer: Howard Welsch; Director: William Beaudine; Assistant Director: Emmett Emerson; Dialogue Director: William Kernell; Screenplay: Robert E. Kent; Photographed by: Jackson Rose; Photographic Effects: George J. Teague; Art Director: Perry Smith; Supervising Editor: Alfred DeGaetano; Editor: Gene Fowler, Jr.; Decor: Armor Marlowe; Costumer: Dorothy Drake; Musical Director: Irving Friedman; Musical Score: Albert Glasser; RCA Sound: J.N.A. Hawkins; Sound Mixer: Percy Townsend; Makeup: Bud Westmore; Hair Stylist: Eunice; Running Time: 64 Minutes; Released: June 14, 1947

CAST: William Wright (Philo Vance); Terry Austin (Lorena Simms); Leon Belasco (Alexis Carnova); Clara Blandick (Stella Blendon); Ramsay Ames (Virginia Berneaux); Damian O'Flynn (Larry Blendon); Frank Wilcox (George Hullman); Iris Adrian (Choo-Choo Divine); Ann Staunton (Helen Varney); Tim Murdock (Cop); Mary Scott (Mary)

EXPOSED

(Republic Pictures Corp.)

Big ideas crammed into a tiny film give Adele Mara one of her more satisfying showcases, as a private detective who occupies a place in history somewhat larger than the picture itself. As the relentless Belinda Prentice in *Exposed*, tackling a case of corporate intrigues and serial murder, Miss Mara looks like nothing so much as a prototype for such breakthrough characters of the waning Twentieth Century as Max Alan Collins' comic-book sleuth, Ms. Michael Tree, and Sara Peretsky's V.I. Warshawski—the latter portrayed on film by Kathleen Turner in 1991.

Exposed is program-filler material of a finer texture, designed for no greater purpose than to be that Extra Added Attraction supporting some larger picture in the since-defunct double-feature tradition. The novelty of a *femme* crimebuster is enough to have made

ADELE MARA
ROBERT SCOTT
ADRIAN BOOTH
ROBERT ARMSTRONG
HARRY SHANNON

Directed by GEORGE BLAIR

A REPUBLIC PICTURE

the picture distinctive in its day, but a richly involved background story, an intricate knot of treacheries and a tense father-daughter relationship between Robert Armstrong and Miss Mara make the picture considerably more than it needed to be, at the time, to fulfill its bottom-of-the-bill imperative. The crowning touch is Bob Steele's snarling portrayal of a professional killer, a performance that crucially affirms the actor's commitment to outlast his fading stardom as a cowboy-movie hero.

Charles Moran's original story is a sustained baffler, beginning with an out-of-nowhere attempt to abduct Belinda Prentice, who is rescued by her tough-guy assistant, Iggy Broty (William Haade). Soon thereafter, Belinda is hired to investigate the irresponsible spending of one William Foresman III (Robert Scott), stepson of industrialist William K. Bentry (Russell Hicks). Bentry turns up dead in his own home, and Belinda finds a hypodermic syringe near the corpse. There follows a dodgy patch as Belinda's father, Police Inspector Prentice (Armstrong), demands to know what business she has in beating the law to the scene of a crime.

The stakes are the control of a corporate fortune and a potentially lucrative experimental cure for alcoholism; the latter accounts for more than a hint of bad-medicine quackery. The body count escalates in short order, along with likely suspect shenanigans from a daughter of the family (Adrian Booth) and a trusted lawyer (Charles Evans), and a nagging question of whether the next hypo to turn up will contain nutrients or poison. Director George Blair keeps the suspense and the mystery running about neck-and-neck, racing toward the fair-play revelation of a tenured household retainer (Harry Shannon) as the mastermind. Not to suggest that the butler did it all by himself.

If not for the splendid leading work of Adele Mara and William Haade, *Exposed* might belong by default to Bob Steele. The wiry sagebrush veteran surfaces very early as Miss Mara's would-be kidnapper and then crops up again as a lurking assistant to Jonathan Lowell, ordering Miss Mara to leave town immediately—or else. Likewise of a scene-stealing bent is Robert Armstrong, who as the gruff cop gets in the last word with a bit of unexpected praise for his daughter's sleuthery. Adrian Booth, like Miss Mara a former jazz-pop vocalist whose movie-star ambitions would take her no further than the B-picture realm, is very good as the conniving daughter who might or might not be a killer.

Miss Mara, better known as an irresistible seductress and all-'round Other Woman in numerous low-budgeters, seems more than merely grateful to have landed a sympathetic leading role in a picture all her own. Her drop-dead-beautiful Belinda Prentice is a resilient, resourceful and adventurous character of the sort around whom entire series have been built, with enough suggestions of back-story to make the present-day viewer wonder why additional adventures were not forthcoming.

The main backup player, William Haade, is likewise welcome in a rare semi-leading assignment. The Michigan-born Haade had since 1937 become a reliable presence as a burly menace—scary not merely because he looks tough, but because he is smart enough to use all that bulk to deadly advantage. Haade's droll sense of humor serves well the role of a big-lug assistant to Mara's street-smart detective-for-hire.

CREDITS: Producer: William J. O'Sullivan; Director: George Blair; Assistant Director: Bart Carré; Screenplay: Royal K. Cole and Charles Moran (from His Story); Photographed by: William Bradford; Art Director: James Sullivan; Editor: Irving M. Schoenberg; Decor: John McCarthy, Jr., and Charles Thompson; Costumer: Adele Palmer; Music: Ernest Gold; RCA Sound: Fred Stahl; Makeup: Bob Mark; Running Time: 60 Minutes; Released: September 8, 1947

CAST: Adele Mala (Belinda Prentice); Robert Scott (William Foresman III); Adrian Booth (Judith Bentry); Robert Armstrong (Prentice); William Haade (Iggy Broty); Bob Steele (Chicago); Harry Shannon (Severance); Charles Evans (Jonathan Lowell); Joyce Compton (Emmy); Russell Hicks (Col. William K. Bentry); Paul E. Burns (Prof. Ordson); Colin Campbell (Dr. Richard); Edward Gargan (Big Mac); Mary Gordon (Miss Keats); Patricia Knox (Waitress); George Davis (Arnold); Eddie Acuff (Cop); Larry Steers (Headwaiter)

MY FATHER'S HOUSE

(Kline-Levin Productions/The Jewish National Fund)

This Palestinian-American venture trades as strikingly upon the horrors of Nazism—after the war, but with the embittered memories yet fresh—as any Axis-buster propaganda piece from only several years earlier. *My Father's House* is at heart a cautionary indictment, related in pastoral tones. And yet the film delves with an undeniable sensationalism into the gathering madness of a Polish-Jewish youngster who, when smuggled into the (purportedly) Holy Land while the rest of his family is taken to a concentration camp, takes rather too earnestly his father's oath that they will meet again in Palestine.

Accepted by a kindly family that claims him as a nephew, David (Ronnie Cohen) soon realizes the kinship is false and runs away to carry on his search for that nebulous haven he calls "my father's house." At a communal farm, David meets Miriam (Irene Broza), whose loss of her husband and their child to the Nazis has rendered her withdrawn. The new friendship seems to restore Miriam. At length, however, David learns that his family had perished at Belgen. The realization drives him to revert to an infantile state, and he forgets even how to walk. Avram (Isaac Danziger), the leader of the collective, arranges for David to remain with Miriam, whose tender care gradually restores him.

This first feature-lengther from a slowly emerging Palestinian movie industry was mounted with a $200,000 grant supplied by America's Jewish National Fund, boosted by $50,000 out-of-pocket from director Herbert Kline and author Meyer Levin. Levin supplied a compassionately moving story, claiming in a scrolled foreword that the point was to concentrate on "the people of Palestine… not its politics." Propaganda insinuated itself backhandedly, however, in the artists' falsely naïve insistence upon portraying Palestinian life as agreeable beyond belief: In this fantasy-world take on that desert realm, the Palestinians and the Arabs get along famously with one another, everybody toils for the Common Good, and even the abiding specter of British colonialism can be ignored.

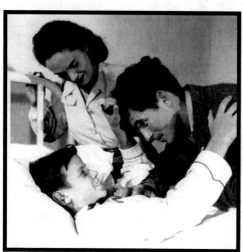

Perhaps Kline and Levin had hoped that wishing would make it so—but all these years and all the many coups and counter-coups later, that region remains a hotbed of intolerance and murderous indignation.

As to Palestinian-Arab relations, the very experience of attempting to perform post-production chores in that region undermined the film's peaceable arguments. As Levin told it in an article for *Theatre Arts* magazine, Palestine had no adequate film laboratories, and so the partners hired a lab in Cairo—where they lost their earliest footage in a raid by Egyptian authorities. They retrenched to Hollywood, but of course were unable to commute there regularly enough to

A hopeful connection is made in *My Father's House*.

view their own day-by-day results. All during the six-month shoot, the company was plagued with threats of violence and demonstrations of protest from the Arab League, which apparently was oblivious to the film's sympathetic treatment of that sector. At one point, the British colonial government demanded to examine the script; Levin supplied a proxy copy, omitting a scene in which refugees gain undocumented entrance to Palestine.

Filmed originally in Hebrew with a Palestinian ensemble cast (even though Kline could speak only English), *My Father's House* was dubbed into English during the editing process in Hollywood—the better to reach a U.S. audience. We have found no original-language version, in which the amateur actors would at least sound somewhat more natural. (A story in

A harrowing search for home and identity in *My Father's House*.

the Los Angeles *Times* held that the players gave phonetic readings in English, but Levin cited English-dubbing as a phase of post-production.)

Theatrical distribution, with Albert Margolies representing the Jewish National Fund as its booking agent, started out promisingly in New York but soon lapsed into a series of piecemeal engagements at synagogues, union halls and schoolhouses.

Levin simultaneously developed a like-titled novel from his screenplay. The Viking Press published the book to widespread critical acclaim during August-September of 1947, but the tie-in seems not to have helped the film's chances. Paramount Pictures' television subsidiary secured a remake option in 1970, but the project went only so far as an announcement to the press. Later pictures bearing the same title (from 1975 and 2002) derive from other sources altogether.

CREDITS: Producers: Herbert Kline and Meyer Levin; Director: Herbert Kline; Screenplay: Meyer Levin; Photographed by Floyd Crosby; Stills: P. Goldman; Assistant Camera Operator: Josef Saadia; Editor: Peter Elgar; Music: Henry Brandt, Utilizing Selections from *The Palestine Folk Symphony*; Song: "V'Ulay," Composer Unacknowledged; Sound: David Scott; Running Time: 85 Minutes; Released: on a State-by-State Basis Beginning September 25, 1947

CAST: Ronnie Cohen (David); Irene Broza (Miriam); Isaac Danziger (Avram); Herman Heuser (Abba); Joseph Pacovsky (Yehuda); Zalman Leiviush (Smulik); R. Klatchin (Waiter); Miriam Laserson (Nahama); Issasschar Finkelstein (Zev); Israela Epstein (Shulamich); Michael Cohen (Maccabee); Naomi Salzberger (Dvora); P. Goldman (Weisbrod); Y. Adaki (Jamal); Josef Saadia (Mustafa); and Herta Ohrbach, S. Leztvsh, H. Landesdorf, the Palestine Philharmonic Orchestra, the Hazamir Singers of Tel Aviv

RAILROADED!

(Eagle–Lion Films, Inc./Pathé Industries, Inc.)

The concept of gore as a box-office commodity in 1947 was quite different from that which would gerrymander the boundaries of horror during the early 1960s. Even by a quainter postwar definition, however, the term would apply to Anthony Mann's *Railroaded!* The tradepaper *Variety* meant business when it declared that John Ireland's portrayal "steeps this production in plenty of gore."

The film reminded more than one wide-awake critic of Hollywood's full-blooded mob-war shockers of the early Depression years. Of course, director Mann and his frequent collaborator, screenwriter John C. Higgins, felt a sharper influence from the hard-boiled pulp magazines of the day than from such tough-on-crime movies of the 1930s as *The Public Enemy*, *The Beast of the City* and *Let 'Em Have It.*

Top-billed Ireland plays career badman Duke Martin, whose opening deed—a robbery-turned-murder—is in fact a ruse to incriminate an innocent truck driver (Ed Kelly) as a cop-killing menace. Its title notwithstanding, *Railroaded!* proves to have less to do with Kelly's plight than with Ireland's show of psychopathic sadism in confrontation with a relentless lawman (Hugh Beaumont). Here we have precisely the sort of public enemy whom Chester Gould had in mind when populating the comic strip *Dick Tracy* with one grotesque menace-to-society after another. Particularly disturbing is Ireland's ritual of anointing his bullets in cologne and buffing his gun barrel before each new assault. This Freudian obsession, which could have played out ludicrously under a director less straightforward than Mann, ultimately will equip the law with a crucial clue.

The centerpiece is an extended bout of reciprocal treacheries between Ireland and Jane Randolph, who plays Clara Calhoun, a beautician doubling as Martin's moll and the custodian of a bookmaking operation. Martin does away with a beauty-shop assistant (Peggy Converse) whose honest testimony had threatened to compromise the frame job. Now suspecting Clara of a double-cross, Martin confronts her and then leaves peaceably enough—only to find her telephoning the law from a neighborhood drugstore. His retaliation remains shocking, even by the increasingly explicit standards of all those years since.

Ireland reaffirms that predatory madness with an attack on his boss (Roy Gordon), then takes out after the sister (Sheila Ryan) of the framed deliveryman. Only the intervention of Hugh Beaumont's steadfast Mickey Ferguson can put the *quietus* on Duke Martin's career. Mann paces the adventure with a sense of desperation that emerges, deceptively, from the vicarious thrills of a cops-and-robbers preamble—then draws the absorbed viewer inexorably into an identification with Ireland's rabid malice.

Hugh Beaumont, as the levelheaded investigator, dispenses retribution without flinching even though his character seems more the type who would prefer a clean capture. Jane Randolph makes an ideally cunning mate for Ireland, and Sheila Ryan serves well as both an innocent near-victim and a dawning romantic interest for Beaumont. Keefe Brasselle contributes his share of scene stealing as Ireland's disfigured accomplice.

Ireland, still a comparative newcomer at the time, was coming right up on such breakthrough assignments of 1948–1949 as *I Shot Jesse James* (as Bob Ford, who would appear to have shot Jesse James) and *All the King's Men*, in which his portrayal of a journalist embroiled in political corruption would land an Oscar nomination. (Ireland's work in 1948's *Open Secret* is curiously lacking by comparison.) Ireland spent the 1950s

Anthony Mann's *Railroaded!* combines the influences of Depression-era gangster films and hard-boiled pulp magazine fiction.

as a dependable character man, specializing in hard-case roles, but then—rather like the acclaimed star player of *All the King's Men*, Broderick Crawford—wasted his later years in a run of Italian-made low-budget actioners. Both Ireland and Crawford found it more agreeable to commit hackwork in Italy than to stay in Hollywood and face up to a mounting docket of drunken-driving charges. Still a commanding presence during his declining years, Ireland co-starred in 1979 in a Canadian-made takeoff on H.G. Wells called *The Shape of Things To Come*, for which *Forgotten Horrors* co-creator George E. Turner served as production designer and storyboard illustrator. Ireland died at 78 in 1992.

    Railroaded! has been falsely identified in times more recent as an adaptation of James P. McGuire's true-crime articles in the Chicago *Times*, a series whose account of a cop-killer frame-up informed the screenplay for Henry Hathaway's famous picture *Call Northside–777* (1948). Although the resemblance is distinct, *Railroaded!* boasts no formal connection with the McGuire pieces.

CREDITS: Producer: Charles D. Reisner; Director: Anthony Mann; Assistant Director: Ridgeway Callow; Dialogue Director: Stewart Stern; Screenplay: John C. Higgins; Based Upon a Story by: Gertrude Walker; Photographed by: Guy Roe; Special Photographic Effects: George J. Teague; Art Director: Perry Smith; Supervising Editor: Alfred DeGaetano; Editor: Louis H. Sackin; Decor: Armor Marlowe and Robert P. Fox; Costumer: Frances Ehren; Musical Director: Irving Friedman; Music: Alvin Levin; Sound: Leon Becker; Sound Mixer: John Carter; Makeup: Ern Westmore and Tom Tuttle; Hair Stylists: Eunice and Evelyn Bennett; Running Time: 72 Minutes; Released: September 25, 1947

CAST: John Ireland (Duke Martin); Sheila Ryan (Rosie Ryan); Hugh Beaumont (Mickey Ferguson); Jane Randolph (Clara Calhoun); Ed Kelly (Steve Ryan); Charles D. Brown (Capt. MacTaggart); Clancy Cooper (Jim Chubb); Peggy Converse (Marie Westin); Hermine Sterler (Mrs. Ryan); Keefe Brasselle (Kowalski); Roy Gordon (Jacklin Ainsworth); Ellen Corby (Mrs. Wills)

THE STORY OF MR. HOBBS
(Eastern Shore Studios/Mid-Century Pictures Corp.)

"You must have been reading Edgar Allan Poe."
"I never heard of 'im." —Exchange between Intended Victim and Aspiring Murderer in *The Story of Mr. Hobbs*

A provincial (though politically aware and environmentally savvy) Southern Gothic from a one-shot off-Hollywood company, the Nell Shipman–Lorenzo Alagia production of *The Story of Mr. Hobbs* makes for as fascinating a rediscovery as that of Marshall Neilan's Florida-made Voodoo romance, *Chloe* (1934), which long went unacknowledged in the larger scheme of Neilan's often brilliant career. The resurrection and restoration (insofar as possible) of *The Story of Mr. Hobbs* is a feat more nearly akin to the resurgence of Herk Harvey's Kansas-made *Carnival of Souls* (1962), whose rebuilding and return during 1989–1990 caused a popular sensation on the art-theater circuit.

But unlike *Carnival of Souls*, which at least had known extensive drive-in theater play as a brand-new release, *The Story of Mr. Hobbs* went largely unseen in its day. Likely a national-scale release was never even attempted, for no contemporary tradepaper reviews have surfaced. A retroactive premiere in 1996, with leading lady Frances Helm in attendance, provided a prestigious occasion for Cape Charles, Virginia, the out-of-the-way shooting site. But the film has gone largely unseen since then, except as a scholarly curiosity and a source of tourism-booster footage for Cape Charles' Chamber of Commerce. It is sometimes referenced by a work-in-progress title, *The Clam-Digger's Daughter*.

Director-of-record Alagia had dabbled in Hollywood under the name of Peter Varney, handling small roles in *Thirty Seconds over Tokyo*, *Till the End of Time* and *Song of Scheherazade* (1944–1947). He used a number of other names — including Grover Lee, Peter Locke, Arthur Varney and Baron Amerigo Serrano — as a less-than-prominent producer and director in England. John M. McCool, cited as producer, can only be a pseudonym for the pioneering Canadian-born filmmaker Nell Shipman, who kept abundant private memoirs but confounded history's attempts to chronicle her work by using a variety of masculine aliases. She was Alagia's wife and business partner — a genuinely maverick artist who during the 1920s had operated a backwoods movie studio, specializing in wildlife pictures, in Northern Idaho.

Six reels are known to survive of what appears to have been a seven-reel final cut of *Hobbs*. This is the story they tell:

Middle-aged clamdigger Crad Hobbs (Jack Hardwood) harbors a hatred-unto-death of a wealthy former neighbor named E.K. Lester. Lester's refusal years ago to underwrite Hobbs' attempt to build a breakwater around their coastal Virginia village has allowed the tides to diminish the shellfish beds. Lester's long-abandoned vacation home lies on nearby Hobbs Island, where Hobbs informs his daughter, Timmy (Helm), and her fiancé,

Bob Gilly (Robert Bolger), that he would kill Lester if given half a chance. Bob, an aspiring journalist, ridicules Hobbs' obsessions. Bob and Timmy elope—only to be drawn back into the circle when a local newspaper editor (Byron Halsted) assigns Bob to report on a diplomatic visit from E.K. Lester.

Lester (Alexander Campbell) has agreed to underwrite a military build-up in a Latin American nation that is under Communist threat. The transaction is to take place near Hobbs Island, and Hobbs is hired to pilot a boat bearing Lester. Learning his passenger's identity, Hobbs kidnaps Lester and imprisons him in the dilapidated summerhouse, where the rising tide will mean certain death. Lester appeals to Hobbs' patriotism and asks him to deliver the bankroll. Just as Hobbs ponders this entreaty, the film stops dead in its sprocket-tracks.

Nell Shipman

The mystery of the missing final reel may never be solved. The known remaining print had (apparently) long reposed undocumented in the private collection of the late Raymond Rohauer. Rohauer was a grasping and controversial archivist whose salvaging of such necessary American films as *The Old Dark House* (Universal; 1932) and the jinxed independent *Dementia* (more generally known in a diluted and dumbed-down cut called *Daughter of Horror*; 1955) can only be counted a mixed blessing. Rohauer seems to have prized possession over caretaking or accessibility, and the films' survival in such cases bespeak an amateurish approach to preservation and no discriminating taste as to print quality.

The print of *The Story of Mr. Hobbs* surfaced in 1988 during an inventory of the British National Film Archive by curator Luke McKernan. Records indicated that Rohauer had donated the movie to the British Film Institute in 1981. But the Rohauer Estate—which has done much to make the gems of the collection more widely available—shows no account of such a gift, or even of such a film's ever having fallen into the clutches of Raymond Rohauer. After four years' digging with precious few leads, McKernan traced *The Story of Mr. Hobbs* to Cape Charles and identified it as an intended release print of the project Cape Charles had known as *The Clam-Digger's Daughter*. Earlier preliminary titles were *Tides* and *A Tale of the Tidewater*.

Further light has been cast onto the film by surviving members of Nell Shipman's circle; by her correspondence and manuscripts in the archives of Boise State University, which establish *The Clamdigger's Daughter* as her final production; and by Cape Charles-area old-timers who have remembered that early autumn of 1947 when the movie company set up shop on a lonely beachfront. Perhaps the most nagging residue of mystery, apart from the absent climax, is a cryptic screen credit reading: "Recompiled for Release by Anthony A. Termini."

The photography is more scenic than dramatic, though technically crisp and rich in texture. The sound recording is quite vivid, even when measured by studio-production standards. The musical score, cued from library-stock sources, leans toward the melodramatic, hammering both the bucolic essence of the piece and its occasional outbursts of

Jack Hardwood as Crad Hobbs in *The Story of Mr. Hobbs.*

menace. The actors tend to overplay—the mark of inexperience—although Jack Hardwood conveys well the stubborn indignation of Crad Hobbs and his drawl matches the role.

The climactic exchange between Hardwood and Alexander Campbell, as the hated big-town moneybags, establishes not only that Hobbs' intended victim must be a decent and level-headed sort, after all, but also nails the barriers of class and culture that keep the men at odds. One choice bit of dialogue trades revealingly upon their incompatible definitions of the word *mad*. Campbell's Lester uses the term to mean that he considers his abductor *crazed*, but Hardwood's Hobbs interprets it as *angry*—and agrees wholeheartedly. The characters seem to find a common ground only when Lester challenges Hobbs' love-of-country, which is precisely where the film conks out to frustrating effect. It is tempting to imagine an upbeat resolution, but in the absence of a complete print or a shooting script one can concoct any sort of ending one fancies.

The only cast-roster name that crops up elsewhere in commercial cinema is that of Frances Helm, who made a tentative debut in *The Story of Mr. Hobbs* and then moved along to Broadway and Hollywood. Her later credits include *The Ugly American* (1963) and the made-for-television *Love and Betrayal: The Mia Farrow Story* (1995), in which Helm can be seen impersonating Maureen O'Sullivan.

Nell Shipman (1892–1974) left Vancouver for California as a teenager and established herself early on as a film player. She began writing for the screen in 1912 and turned director in 1914. Her first husband, Ernest Shipman, also was a filmmaker. Her occasional major-studio work in the post-silent era includes co-authorship of the scenario for Paramount's *Wings in the Dark* (1934), starring Myrna Loy and Cary Grant. Following her death, an autobiography-in-manuscript called *The Silent Screen and My Talking Heart* turned up; Tom Trusky, chief curator of the Idaho Film Collection at Boise State University, edited this work for publication. The site of the artist's 1920s filmmaking outpost, in Lionhead State Park at Priest Lake, Idaho, was christened Nell Shipman Point in 1977.

CREDITS: Presented by: Omar D. Crothers, Jr.; Executive Producer (Unattributed): Nell Shipman; Producer: John M. McCool; Director: Lorenzo Alagia; Assistant Director: Eddie Kelly; Screenplay: Rex Taylor; Camera Operator: Edward Hyland; Assistant Camera Operator: Timmy Fitzpatrick; Film Cutter: Patt Rooney; Sound: Duncan McLeod, Reeves Sound Studios, Inc.; Production Manager: Philip Rein; Recompiled for Release by: Anthony A. Termini; Running Time: 70 Minutes (Approx.), 60 Minutes in Surviving Print; Produced: During September-October of 1947; Release Date: Undocumented; Premiered as a Rediscovery at Cape Charles, Virginia: April 28, 1996

CAST: Jack Hardwood (Crad Hobbs); Frances Helm (Timmy Hobbs); Robert Bolger (Bob Gilly); Alexander Campbell (E.K. Lester); Jeraldine Dvorak (Glenda Lester); Frank

Richards (Spike); Al McGranary (Winnie Winston); Winifred Cushing (Marian Winston); Bertha Powell (Sis Abby); Sidney Easton (Ben); Byron Halstead (Sam Northrup)

HIGH TIDE
(Wrather Productions, Inc./Monogram Pictures Corp.)

Raoul Whitfield's 1932 *Black Mask* magazine story, "Inside Job," is a classic among the hard-boilers, mingling vicious deeds at every turn with just enough humanizing touches to make the reader feel a certain identification with the bad guy, if not necessarily a loss at his passing. This is the splendid basis of *High Tide*, director John Reinhardt's follow-through to the similarly hard-bitten *The Guilty*, from the ambitious new production company of movie-struck millionaire Jack Wrather.

L.A. newspaper editor Hugh Fresney (career tough guy Lee Tracy) and private eye Tim Slade (Don Castle), a former crime reporter, find themselves trapped in the wreckage of Fresney's automobile, which has veered off a high coastal highway and crashed onto the beach. Fresney muses on the events that have led him to this bad patch, which is as good an excuse as any for a flashback:

Fresney vows to halt a take-over plot by rackets kingpin Nick Dyke (Anthony Warde), who wants to buy Fresney's *Daily Dispatch* on the square but will resort to violence if all else fails. Dyke's bullying of Fresney's mild-mannered boss, Clinton Vaughn (Douglas Walton), creates tensions between the editors, and Fresney survives a stairwell attack that leaves Vaughn dead. Which leaves Slade on the spot, for Fresney had hired the investigator to help him dispense with any opponents.

Likely suspects apart from Dyke and Slade would include Vaughn's widow, Julie (Julie Bishop), who now inherits the

WHEN THEY START "DYNAMITING"...
A Tidal Wave of Mystery and Murder Thunders Across the Screen!

THE NEWS HAWK WHO LIKED TO SMASH PEOPLE!

THE "PRIVATE EYE" WHO WAS TOO QUICK ON THE DRAW!

MONOGRAM PICTURES presents

HIGH TIDE

A JACK WRATHER PRODUCTION
Starring
LEE TRACY · DON CASTLE · JULIE BISHOP · ANABEL SHAW
with REGIS TOOMEY · DOUGLAS WALTON

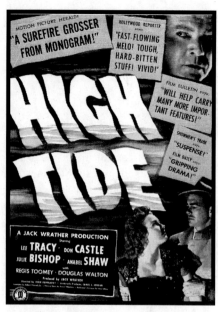

ownership of the *Dispatch*; and Vaughn's secretary, Dana Jones (Anabel Shaw), who proves to have been spying for Dyke. Slade has been fending off Mrs. Vaughn's advances while romancing Dana. The killings escalate as Slade finds himself in possession of an ominous briefcase. Hurrying to meet Fresney, Slade arrives in time to witness a fatal encounter between Dyke and Fresney. Dyke comes out the loser, and Fresney and Slade take off with the briefcase.

Along the coastal highway, Slade realizes that Fresney intends to kill him. He begins taunting Fresney with the knowledge that Fresney faked his own gunshot wounds in the stairwell hit on Vaughn—then adds that the briefcase does not contain the desired documents. In a rage, Fresney gives the steering wheel a violent yank, forcing the car over the cliff.

Back in the moment, Fresney is pinned in the wreckage. Slade maneuvers his way free. The tide is rolling in. Fresney summons his dying strength and takes aim on Slade—then has a change of heart. He asks Slade to see that the story of their misadventure be played on the front page, adding: "That'll be *my* high tide."

The Wrather coalition was a godsend for Monogram at a time when the little studio was trying to develop prestige on a competitive basis with the majors. *High Tide* comes across as more than a double-bill filler, with an every-dollar-on-screen texture and a bravura star turn that recalls Tracy's better days of the 1930s. Don Castle matches Tracy for intensity, and Julie Bishop and Anabel Shaw radiate star quality despite their comparatively small and unsympathetic roles. Regis Toomey makes a realistically down-to-earth police inspector, and Anthony Warde is persuasive as the scheming-weasel racketeer. Francis Ford—director John's brother, and a good-luck player for any film he happened to grace—stands out in a small tragic role as the guardian of the maguffin-like briefcase.

CREDITS: Producer: Jack Wrather; Associate Producer: James C. Jordan; Director: John Reinhardt; Assistant Director: William Forsyth; Screenplay: Robert Presnell, Sr.; Additional Dialogue: Peter Milne; Based Upon: Raoul Whitfield's Story, "Inside Job," from the February 1932 *Black Mask* Magazine; Photographed by: Henry Sharp; Camera Operator: William Clothier; Special Effects: Howard Anderson; Art Director: Lewis H. Creber; Supervising Editor: William Ziegler; Editor: Stuart S. Frye; Decor: Murray White and Theobold Holsopple; Wardrobe: Jack Masters; Musical Supervisor: David Chudnow; Musical Score: Rudy Schrager; Sound: Ferol Redd; Makeup: Paul Malcolm; Production Manager: Ben Berk; Running Time: 70 Minutes; Released: October 11, 1947

CAST: Lee Tracy (Hugh Fresney); Don Castle (Tim Slade); Julie Bishop (Julie Vaughn); Anabel Shaw (Dana Jones); Regis Toomey (Inspector O'Haffey); Douglas Walton (Clinton Vaughn); Francis Ford (Pop Garrow); Anthony Warde (Nick Dyke); Wilson Wood (Cleve Collins); Argentina Brunetti (Mrs. Cresser); George H. Ryland (Intern)

THE BURNING CROSS

(Somerset Pictures Corp./Screen Guild Productions, Inc.)

A social-agenda picture inspired by the U.S. military's progressive integration of its troops as a matter of practicality during World War II, *The Burning Cross* makes its bigot-buster arguments all the more arresting by couching them in a thrilling crime-melodrama context. The film sports a sad, knowing voice-over narration, *film noir*-style, from lead actor Hank Daniels in its extended-flashback account of a disappointed returning serviceman's susceptibility to the influence of a hate-mongering organization.

Aubrey Wisberg's original screenplay makes no bones about naming the Ku Klux Klan as the source of the troubles. Johnny Larrimer (Daniels), drifting aimlessly until drawn back to his hometown, learns in short order that his childhood sweetheart, Doris (Virginia Patton), has taken up with his pal, Tony (John Fostini), who had somehow ducked the draft. Johnny soon accepts employment as a strikebreaker, falling into the company of agitators determined to rid their community of blacks, Jews and foreign-born newcomers in general.

Tony notices Johnny's participation in an attack on a Swedish merchant but only warns his lapsed friend to steer clear of such bad company. Tony is abducted and slain in turn by the Klansmen, who have accepted Johnny as a recruit. Charlie West (Joel Fluellen), a black farmer who witnesses the slaying, confides in a trusted townsman who proves to be a Klansman. The thugs kill Charlie and torch his farmhouse.

Johnny, now suspected as an infiltrator, is marked for death. He confesses his involvement to his family but is abducted and taken away for a hanging before the local police can catch up with the hoodlums. Freed just in time, Johnny captures the ringleader (Dick Rich) and administers a beating while the law rounds up the other Klan klucks. Johnny's last-ditch show of heroism regains Doris' affections and wins him a promise of lenience.

Shortly before the opening of *The Burning Cross*, associate producer Selvyn Levinson told *Ebony* magazine that he had found an inspiration for the picture during a wartime hitch in China, where his entirely white aircraft battery was placed under supervision of a black sergeant. The soldiers developed such a camaraderie under this leadership that they became "the most proficient... on the field," according to Levinson, who added that his return to an ethnically divided America moved him to envision a film indicting the forces of bigotry.

Unable to secure bank financing or studio backing for the controversial project, Levinson raised $150,000 from sources he identified only as "individuals interested in tolerance." Levinson and Walter Colmes produced *The Burning Cross* independently, then arranged for its release through product-hungry Screen Guild. The project served to inaugurate the refurbished sound stages and laboratory at Hollywood's Motion Picture Center, formerly the headquarters of Metro Pictures Corp.

Colmes was singled out for a word of caution from the Production Code Administration: Chief censor Joseph I. Breen approved the script but warned that "the Negroes

Dreams That Money Can Buy

113

will at no time... be shown as too subservient, and... their dialogue... will be grammatical." Which was no challenge at all, for Levinson and Colmes wanted no part of reinforcing any stereotypes. Indeed, the tragic presence of Joel Fluellen, as a citizen who dooms himself by Doing the Right Thing, is one of the screen's more dignified portrayals.

The acting is otherwise adequate for the situations, with a sentimentally overwrought Virginia Patton serving as the love interest and a mean-looking Dick Rich calling the shots among the bad guys. Hank Daniels, in his last film of a brief career, is more convincing in Johnny Larrimer's more hateful moments than in his attempts to reconcile himself with Polite Society. His voice-over is nicely handled, proving at last to be a confession dictated to a police stenographer. Scripter Aubrey Wisberg would go on to write, and occasionally to produce, pictures more conventionally weird—including such inevitable *Forgotten Horrors* fodder as *The Man from Planet X* (1951), *Captive Women* (1952) and *Port Sinister* and *The Neanderthal Man* (both from 1953).

The Virginia Board of Censors banned *The Burning Cross* outright, citing it as a possible incitement to violence. Screen Guild responded with a lawsuit, but the picture's short span as a box-office commodity had run out before a slow-moving Southern justice system could address the complaint.

CREDITS: Producer and Director: Walter Colmes; Associate Producer: Selvyn Levinson; Assistant Director: George Moskov; Screenplay: Aubrey Wisberg; Photographed by: Walter Strenge; Special Effects: Ray Mercer; Art Director: Frank Sylos; Editor: Jason Bernie; Set Designer: Jacque Mapes; Properties: George Bahr; Wardrobe: James H. Wade; Music: Ralph Stanley; RCA Sound: Ferol Redd; Makeup: Ted Larsen; Running Time: 79 Minutes; Released: October 11, 1947

CAST: Hank Daniels (Johnny Larrimer); Virginia Patton (Doris Greene); Dick Rich (Lud Harris); Joel Fluellen (Charlie West); John Fostini (Tony Areni); Raymond Bond (Chester Larrimer); Walden Boyle (Walter Strickland); Alexander Pope (Howard Gibbons); Richard Bailey (Pelham); Matt Willis (Mort Dawson); John Doucette (Tobey Mason); Tom Kennedy (Police Sergeant); Ted Stanhope (Elkins); Glenn Allen (Bubby West); Maidie Norman (Kitty West); Jack Shutta (Hill); and Ross Elliott, Marjorie Manners, Helen Servis, Clinton Rosemond, Jamesson Shade

BURY ME DEAD

(Eagle–Lion Films, Inc./Pathé Industries, Inc.)

The problem with most soap-operatic melodramas is that they wallow in sin and self-sacrifice without giving fair due to the Wages of Sin—Death, that is, and the crueler the better. Bernard Vorhaus' *Bury Me Dead* is a refreshing exception—an unabashed sudser with the good gumption to place murder and its consequences atop a lurid agenda.

It all begins with June Lockhart's arrival as an onlooker at her own funeral, then escalates to a perilous search for the identities of the occupant of the coffin and *her* slayer. Along the way, *Bury Me Dead* turns up enough suspects—practically everyone on view—and lustful treacheries for almost twice the running time. A sophisticated use of flashback technique makes gripping use of a brisk 71 minutes. There is a wealth of deadly weaponry, fashioned from ordinary tool-shed implements. The telling is surprisingly frank for its day, with seething dialogue that gets directly to the point of a homewrecking campaign by Cathy O'Donnell, who plays Miss Lockhart's grasping sister.

Heiress Barbara Carlin (Miss Lockhart) is presumed dead after a fire at her estate. Once Barbara turns up alive and flabbergasted, her lawyer, Michael Dunn (Hugh Beaumont), advises her to proceed with caution. After all, Barbara's estranged husband, Rod Carlin (Mark Daniels), is still hovering about with an eye on an inheritance. Other likely suspects would be Rod's now-absent mistress, Helen Lawrence (Sonia Darrin); Helen's boss, prizefighter George Mandley (Greg McClure), who had been carrying on with Barbara; and Barbara's kid sister, Rusty (Miss O'Donnell), who as an adoptee stands to inherit zilch. Rusty, who is infatuated with Rod, also has been fooling around on the side with George. It turns out that the body at the funeral is that of Helen, who had tried to persuade Rod to kill Barbara. Or so Rod claims.

"HE WOULD STOP AT NOTHING TO GET ME OUT OF THE WAY... but WHO IS HE?"

BURY ME DEAD

with CATHY O'DONNELL · JUNE LOCKHART
HUGH BEAUMONT · MARK DANIELS
GREG McCLURE · MILTON PARSONS · VIRGINIA FARMER
Screenplay by KAREN deWOLF and DWIGHT V. BABCOCK · Based on a radio story by IRENE WINSTON
BEN STOLOFF in charge of production
PRODUCED BY CHARLES F. RIESNER · DIRECTED BY BERNARD VORHAUS
PRESENTED BY PRODUCERS RELEASING CORPORATION

Rod winds up on the losing end of a slugfest with George. Rusty shelters Rod and, while treating his injuries, confesses to her attempts to undermine the Carlins' marriage: "*You*'re the one that's locked deep down in my libido," Miss O'Donnell declares, purring the awkward line with enough conviction to make it work. (We have found no formal objections to such dialogue within the files of the Motion Picture Association's Production Code Administration—a curious lapse by an ordinarily vigilant institutional watchdog.) Anyhow, Rod will have no part of Rusty's come-on, and so she reports him as a murderer. Hell hath no fury, y'know.

While Rod makes his way back to Barbara to ask forgiveness, she finds herself attacked by an assailant wielding a tire iron. The attacker flees, unsuccessful. After Rod has arrived, only to be shanghaied by Rusty and the police, lawyer Dunn remains to comfort Barbara. He mentions offhandedly his knowledge that Helen had been beaten to death with a hammer—a detail yet unannounced by the police.

Meanwhile, Rod realizes that the party who would benefit most from Barbara's death is Dunn. He persuades the police to return with him to the mansion. Dunn corners Barbara in her boudoir, where he drenches the bed in kerosene. Rod, Rusty and the police arrive just in time. Barbara seizes the distraction, and also a pair of shears, to attack Dunn. The police finish off the shyster. It all ends with a promise of reconciliation for

Dreams That Money Can Buy

Rod and Barbara, although Rusty's closing vow to clean up her act rings somehow less than reassuring.

Bury Me Dead derives from a 1946 radio play so popularly well received that it was sold promptly for adaptation to the screen. Eagle–Lion Films announced the acquisition in February of 1947, intending to cast Una Merkel as the endangered heiress. June Lockhart was assigned the role, however, before filming began on April 7, 1947; she proved quite adept at conveying the character's domineering and reckless, self-centered nature. Cathy O'Donnell, top-billed despite a lesser role, provides a more fascinating presence as the sibling moved to deceit by an acute case of ants-in-the-pants. Hugh Beaumont, who alternated between heroism and malfeasance as a B-movie dependable, seems every bit the stabilizing presence until a late unmasking.

A fresh radio enactment of *Bury Me Dead* took place three months before the film's opening.

CREDITS: Producer: Charles F. Reisner; Director: Bernard Vorhaus; Dialogue Director: William Kernell; Assistant Director: Robert Stillman; Screenplay: Karen DeWolf and Dwight V. Babcock; Based Upon: Irene Winston's 1946 Radio Play, *Bury Me Dead*, as aired on *Molle Mystery Theatre* via the NBC Network; Photographed by: John Alton; Special Photographic Effects: George J. Teague; Art Director: Edward C. Jewell; Supervising Editor: Alfred DeGaetano; Editor: W. Donn Hayes; Decor: Armor Marlowe; Costumer: Henry West; Music: Emil Cadkin; Musical Director: Irving Friedman; Sound: Leon Becker; Sound Mixer: Richard DeWeese; Makeup: Ern Westmore and Tom Tuttle; Hair Stylists: Eunice and Lee McDougall; Running Time: 71 Minutes; Released: October 18, 1947

CAST: Cathy O'Donnell (Rusty); June Lockhart (Barbara Carlin); Hugh Beaumont (Michael Dunn); Mark Daniels (Rod Carlin); Greg McClure (George Mandley); Milton Parsons (Waters); Virginia Farmer (Mrs. Haskins); Sonia Darrin (Helen Lawrence); Cliff Clark (Archer)

JOE PALOOKA IN THE KNOCKOUT
(Monogram Productions, Inc./Monogram Distributing Corp.)

We had established over a generation ago, at the outset of this *Forgotten Horrors* exercise, that although murder *per se* might or might not be grounds for inclusion, murder with a Capital-*A* Attitude was pure-dee grist for the mill. And especially so, should unconventional means be employed. Murder by frozen-liquid missile (see 1936's *A Face in the Fog*), murder by toxic fumes (see 1935's *Rip Roaring Riley*, among others), murder by poison-saturated sweatrag (see 1936's *Prison Shadows*)—all have figured at one time or another in these volumes. Now comes *Joe Palooka in the Knockout* (based upon Ham Fisher's undeservedly popular comic strip), which posits the notion of a prizefight killing via a tainted mouth-protector. That the implement of death is one of the most trusted tools of the pugilist's trade, lends a black irony beyond the scope of the original comic-strip yarns.

This third of 10 Monogram *Palookas* stars dependable Leon Errol, one of Old Hollywood's great grouches and a favorite foil of W.C. Fields, as manager Knobby Walsh;

and Joe Kirkwood, Jr., as heroic pug Joe Palooka. Things start looking grim for Joe when opponent Jackie Mathews (Tom Garland) drops dead, apparently from a blow landed by Joe. In fact, Mathews had been overdosed with a sneak drugging that was supposed merely to have left him zonked out. Mathews' manager, Max Steele (Whitford Kane), had played along with the scam under threat of blackmail, but now he is furious to learn that things have turned lethal.

Whereupon Joe swears off fighting (a foreshadowing of John Wayne's withdrawal from the sport in *The Quiet Man*) and drifts about aimlessly—until an encounter with Mathews' fiancée (Trudy Marshall) leaves him convinced that Mathews had met with foul play. Another bearer of clues turns up defunct, and finally Joe finds himself marked for murder. Gambler John Mitchell (Marc Lawrence) and henchman Pusher Moore (Danny Morton) are caught tampering with Joe's gum-protector plate; they leave a locker-room attendant (Benny Baker) beaten nearly to death. Steele, fed up with it all, guns down Mitchell and Moore. Ringleader Howard Abbott (Morris Carnovsky) remains at large until confronted by the bereaved fiancée, who intends to shoot him. She is spared the trouble by Abbott's dog, whose ill-timed boisterous entrance causes the killer to shoot himself. Joe re-enters the ring and slugs his way to a championship.

Joe Palooka had come to the screen in 1934 as *Palooka*, a respectable one-punch job from the coalition of little Reliance Pictures and big United Artists Corp., starring Jimmy Durante as Knobby Walsh and the mild Stuart Erwin as the sweet-natured rube prizefighter Joe. *Palooka* is remembered fondly today, when remembered at all, as a showcase for Durante's signature song, "Inka Dinka Doo."

The Monogram series ran from 1946 into 1951. In addition to the viciousness at large in *Knockout*, the films would touch on such harrowing fare as sniper attacks (1946's *Joe*

Palooka, Champ); kidnapping and child exploitation (1948's *Joe Palooka in Winner Take All*); inflicted blindness (1948's *Joe Palooka in Fighting Mad*); and druggings and more druggings (1949's *Joe Palooka in the Big Fight* and 1950's *Joe Palooka in the Squared Circle*). In 1954, Joe Kirkwood, Jr., returned to the ring as producer-star of a low-rent television series called *The Joe Palooka Story*.

The character's origins and back-story ran deeper and darker: Cartoonist Ham Fisher had launched *Joe Palooka* in 1928 as a sentimentalized romance-adventure piece for the McNaught Syndicate, hackishly drawn and written for full measure of corn—except for a Depression-years stretch when the young Al Capp, as Fischer's anonymous assistant, took gradual charge of things with more intelligent results. Having raised *Palooka* to levels of sardonic wit beyond Fischer's lunkheaded grasp, Capp jumped ship and launched his own comic strip, the vividly satirical *Li'l Abner*.

Prevailing antagonisms kept Fischer and Capp at odds for years—a common scenario in which a supposed apprentice out-performs an oppressive boss. The *Joe Palooka* comic strip continued apace as a happy-sappy popular favorite, spawning movies and licensed toys and other such cultural detritus. (*Li'l Abner* found itself adapted sporadically to film during its earlier years—a 1940 grotesquerie that captured only the superficial attributes of Capp's brilliance, followed by a disappointing run of animated cartoons. The 1950s would see the Gene DePaul–Johnny Mercer musical *Li'l Abner* become a smash on Broadway, followed by a splendidly bombastic movie version.) The backstage hostilities culminated in Fischer's attempt to drum Capp out of the cartooning profession by calling their colleagues' attention to (forged) examples of hidden obscenities in *Li'l Abner*. His treachery exposed, Fischer dealt with the loss-of-face by committing suicide in 1955. *Joe Palooka* continued dispensing its pernicious brand of reactionary wholesomeness well beyond Fischer's lifetime, finally fading away in 1984. Capp, who nursed a grudge as relentlessly as Fischer but proved too honorable to resort to ambush defamation, told his side of the story in a bitterly hilarious essay called "I Remember Monster," never once mentioning his mentor-turned-tormentor by name. (The title, "I Remember Monster," is Al Capp's sarcastic evocation of John Van Druten's famous family-saga play, *I Remember Mama*, filmed in 1948.)

CREDITS: Producer: Hal E. Chester; Associate Producer: Bernard W. Burton; Director: Reginald LeBorg; Assistant Director: Wesley Barry; Screenplay: Nedrick Young; Based Upon: Ham Fischer's Comic Strip, *Joe Palooka*; Dialogue Director: G. Joseph Dell; Photographed by: William Sickner; Art Director: Dave Milton; Supervising Editor: Otho Lovering; Editor: Warren Adams; Decor: Raymond Boltz, Jr.; Hair: Lorraine MacLean; Music: Edward J. Kay; Songs: "You Don't Know What Love Is," by Gene DePaul & Don Raye, and "I Love You Much Too Much," by Chaim Towber & Don Raye; Sound: Tom Lambert; Makeup: Harry Ross; Production Supervisor: Glenn Cook; Prizefights Staged by: John Indrisano; Running Time: 72 Minutes; Released: October 18, 1947

CAST: Leon Errol (Knobby Walsh); Joe Kirkwood, Jr. (Joe Palooka); Morris Carnovsky (Howard Abbott); Elyse Knox (Anne Howe); Billy House (Sam Wheeler); Trudy Marshall (Nina Carroll); Marc Lawrence (John Mitchell); Whitford Kane (Max Steele); Benny Baker (Looie); Donald MacBride (Crockett); Danny Morton (Pusher Moore); Vince Barnett (Russell); Eddie Gribbon (Iggy); Sarah Padden (Mom Palooka); Clarence Muse (Smoky); Michael Mark (Pop Palooka); Jack Roper (Waldo); Tom Garland (Jackie Mathews); Cathy Carter (Nurse); Sam Hayes (Announcer); the Malone Sisters (Themselves); Wheaton Chambers (Doctor); Harry Strang, Stanley Blystone, Andy Andrews, Mike Gaddis and James Flavin (Policemen); John Indrisiano and Ralph Volkie (Referees); Steve Soldi (Peculiar Man); Dave Barrie (Eddie Steele); Jimmy Ames and Matt Willis (Detectives); Pat Goldin (Waiter); Jay Norris (Steve); David Hoffman (Ticket Taker); Ray Walker, Robert Conway, Ted Stanhope, Peter Virgo and Robert Earle (Reporters); Lew Hearn (Jim Nasium); Chester Clute (Desk Clerk); Paul Scardon (Railroad Counterman); Wally Roberts, Alan Foster, Phil Arnold, Harry Arnie and Mike Lally (Cabbies); Emmett Vogan, Jr. (Call Boy); George Hickman (Checker); Nolan Leary (Doorman); Darlene Morris (Girl); Robert Hale (Painter); Suni Chorre (Cardona); Howard Mitchell (Ringside Announcer); Meyer Grace (Boxer); Peter Cusanelli (Fat Man); and Teddy Pavelec

THE GANGSTER
(Allied Artists Productions, Inc./Monogram Pictures Corp./
Monogram Distributing Corp.)

Brothers Maurice and Franklin King did more than any other filmmaking artists over the long haul to elevate Monogram Pictures nearer major-studio caliber. (Perhaps *minimajor* is more like it, although that term would not come into vogue until the 1980s and the rise of New Line Cinema, New World Pictures and their upwardly mobile class of latter-day Poverty Row studios.)

Jack Wrather would accomplish similarly polished results for Monogram, but his independent studio was more a sideline than a principal endeavor—and King Bros. Productions had been longer at the game. The Kings were especially crucial in Monogram's gradual transformation to Allied Artists, which for a while, there, was a classier studio.

Maurice and Franklin favored hard-boiled crime yarns—much of their financial clout derived from an under-the-table communion with known mobsters—and their work proved nearly as innovative within this worthy genre as the productions of Darryl F. Zanuck and the Warners had been during the 1930s. The Kings were especially fond of baiting Joseph I. Breen, chief of H'wood's Production Code Administration, with temptations to com-

Barry Sullivan, the embodiment of madness and/or meanness, in *The Gangster*.

mit censorship. The waning months of 1946 found Breen still smarting over his failure to discourage the Kings from making *Dillinger* in 1945, and the resentful old watchdog leapt at the opportunity to catch them in some flagrant violation on *The Gangster*.

Breen, like any censor worth his shears, had a dirty mind and used it the way a bloodhound uses its nose. The Kings played directly to this talent in showing Breen's office a script-in-progress that established *The Gangster*'s title character as an entrepreneurial pimp. A Breen memo complained of an "unmistakable impression that [the character] is the operator of a chain of brothels." The Kings omitted all but a whiff of prostitution. In the parry-and-thrust ritual that followed, the Breen Office objected to an "inescapable inference of an illicit sex affair" between mobster and moll (and so what else is new?) and seemed appalled that an upstart hood and his henchmen were allowed to evade justice. The Kings retained the former element but ordered a rewrite on the latter.

Breen kept his spies watching the brothers during off-hours, as well. Early in March of 1947, while *The Gangster* was in full production, a Breen memo griped about "one recent occasion" on which Maurice and Franklin were overheard "making loud, unpleasant boasts that, because they had money, they could push things past the Breen Office and were making it known… that questionable material could have its way bought through the [Production Code Administration]."

Breen suggested later that the title be changed. The Kings replied that they had no A-list stars in their stable and thus required "sensational titles to interest the public."

That sensational title was, in the published opinion of *Variety*, the film's greatest strength as a box-office property. The review added: "Otherwise, [the] film fails to live up to [its] promise of violent action and proves a disappointment."

The Gangster cannot have been a disappointment to the King Bros., however, for the film fairly revels in its deliberately low-key mood of brooding unease. The screenplay, attributed to source-novelist Daniel Fuchs but containing the anonymous script doctoring of Dalton Trumbo, is a psychological study of a small-time hood named Shubunka (Barry Sullivan), who wants to better himself within the rackets but cannot subdue his abrasive personality. This is not the conventional rise-and-fall of *Little Caesar* or *The Public Enemy*, but rather the collapse of a thug who tries merely to hang on to his turf. Shubunka's enterprises extend well beyond his obvious ownership of a respectable soda shop, and early on a rival named Cornell (Sheldon Leonard) starts moving in on the works. Shubunka is such a rotter that he denies help to a desperate regular customer (John Ireland) but otherwise throws money away impulsively. Shubunka accuses his sweetheart, Nancy Starr (ice-skating athlete Belita), of complicity with Cornell. As his vicious nature leaves his few loyalists either dead or alienated, Shubunka finally gives up in despair. Trudging alone through a rainstorm, he shouts to Cornell, "You can have it all!"—just before he is gunned down.

Barry Sullivan and Belita (*née* Maria Belita Gladys Lyne Jepson-Turner) had co-starred in the King Bros.' first conspicuously extravagant production, *Suspense* (1946), she as an entertainer in danger and he as an opportunistic weasel. They play more caustically off one another in *The Gangster*, which allows Belita scarcely a trace of glamour except in a brief musical segment. The Kings had suspended Belita from the cast shortly before shooting began after she demanded billing over Sullivan. She retaliated by going to the press with complaints that she considered her costuming indecent and that the producers had barred her husband, Joel McGinnis, from the set. The differences were patched up in time for the start of principal photography in February, but the finished film finds Belita looking none to happy to be on deck. Which is precisely the correct attitude for the distrustful estrangements that the script forces upon her and Sullivan.

Sullivan works more amiably with Akim Tamiroff, who plays Shubunka's faithful-unto-death accomplice. Sheldon Leonard, Old Hollywood's most nearly perfect interpreter of Runyonesque mugs, seems more than a match for Sullivan in the takeover contest: Where Shubunka just wants to be loved on his own unlovable terms, Leonard's Cornell is a rotter entirely comfortable with his rottenness. Joan Lorring is a standout as the voice-in-the-wilderness conscience of the piece, an entirely decent clerk who isn't afraid to tell her boss where to get off. The most affecting portrayal belongs to John Ireland, most often cast as an embittered sort but quite poignant here as a born-loser simp whose financial anxieties drive him to crime.

The arch, almost poetic dialogue and prevailing Existential bleakness reflect the influence of Dalton Trumbo, a high-dollar screenwriter who was reduced to anonymous struggling in 1947 as a consequence of his involvement with the so-called Hollywood Ten—those movie-biz diehards who had squared off against contempt-of-Congress charges rather than testify about alleged ties to the Communist Party. Director Gordon Wiles prizes mood over pacing, but *The Gangster* justifies its 83 minutes with an unforgiving contemplation of a lost soul. The photography, by Universal's dependable Paul Ivano, is impeccably hard and cold, and Louis Gruenberg's music follows suit.

CREDITS: Producers: Maurice King and Franklin King; Director: Gordon Wiles; Assistant Director: Frank S. Heath; Screenplay: Daniel Fuchs (from His 1937 Novel, *Low Company*) and Dalton Trumbo (Unattributed); Photographed by: Paul Ivano; Special Effects: Roy W.

Seawright; Art Director: F. Paul Sylos; Editor: Walter Thompson; Decor: Sidney Moore; Costumer: Norma; Music: Louis Gruenberg; Orchestra Conducted by: Irvin Talbot; Song: "Paradise," by Gordon Clifford and Nacio Herb Brown; Sound: William Randall; Makeup: Ern Westmore; Assistant to Producers: Arthur Gardner; Dialogue Coach: Leon Charles; Technical Adviser: Herman King; Casting Assistant: Rose Alexander; Running Time: 83 Minutes; Released: Following New York Opening on October 30, 1947

CAST: Barry Sullivan (Shubunka); Belita (Nancy Starr); Joan Lorring (Dorothy); Akim Tamiroff (Nick Jammey); Henry Morgan (Shorty); John Ireland (Frank Karty); Sheldon Leonard (Cornell); Fifi D'Orsay (Mrs. Ostroleng); Virginia Christine (Mrs. Karty); Elisha Cook, Jr. (Oval); Ted Hecht (Swain); Leif Erickson (Beaumont); Charles McGraw (Dugas); John Kellogg (Sterling); Edwin Maxwell (Politico); Dewey Robinson (Billiards Player); Griff Barnett (Dorothy's Father); Murray Alper (Eddie); Shelley Winters (Hazel); Larry Steers (Headwaiter); Clancy Cooper, Jeff Corey and Peter Whitney (Mrs. Karty's Brothers); Bill Kennedy, Mike Conrad, Jack Reynolds and Larry Thompson (Thugs); Rex Downing (Messenger Boy); Ruth Allen (Singer); Billy Gray (Boy); Norma Jean Nilsson (Girl); Pat Emery (Miss Callister); Lennie Bremen and Alexander Pope (Loafers); Maxine Semon (Maid); Marie Blake (House Mistress); Anita Turner (Essie); Phyllis Ayres (Wife); Dolores Castle (Cigarette Girl); Sid Melton (Stage Manager); Delese Daudet and Jean Harrison (Dancers); Tommy Reilly (Pianist); Don Haggerty (Stranger); Michael Vallon (Man on Boardwalk); Jane Weeks (Girl in Hallway); Parker Gee (Man in Corridor); and Greta Granstedt, Marguerita Padula, Mike Lally, Sammy Shack, Jean Calhoun, Helen Alexander, Mike Gaddis, Jay Eaton, Zona King, Irene Brooks, Ralph Freeton, Gene Collins, Andy Andrews, Phil Arnold

LOVE FROM A STRANGER
(Eagle–Lion Films, Inc./Pathé Industries, Inc.)

Yes, and what better place to rediscover one of the grander forgotten horrors from outside the North American indie-studios province of *Forgotten Horrors*? The picture at hand is a remake from 1947—but what's the point of examining a remake without a familiarity with the source-film?

Lobby card from the original 1937 version.

And the basis? American director Rowland V. Lee's original *Love from a Stranger* (1937) is a British production mounted during a research trip for the made-in-Hollywood *Tower of London*. Here is perhaps the quintessential vehicle for Basil Rathbone's ability to project suave villainy. A composite adaptation of Frank Vosper's play, *Love from a Stranger*, and a tale by Agatha Christie, the film owes just as much to the Real World's Bluebeard and Brides-in-the-Bath murder cases.

More than a self-contained triumph, *Love from a Stranger* also cinched a working relationship between Rathbone and Lee that would carry over to *Son of Frankenstein*, *The Sun Never Sets* and *Tower of London*—all dating from that watershed year for Hollywood, 1939. *Stranger* finds Rathbone ideally in his element as a charming rogue who woos and weds a lottery winner (Ann Howard), only to reveal himself as a possessive tyrant who has made a habit of killing off his wives. His new intended victim turns the tables with a dose of poison and a bit of hair's-breadth psychological manipulation. Despite United Artists' show of confidence in acquiring *Love from a Stranger* for U.S. distribution, the film played only piecemeal Stateside during 1937–1938, plagued not by institutionalized censorship but by objections from various theater chains over its disturbing subject matter. It can only be reckoned curious that a British-

Sylvia Sidney and John Hodiak in Richard Whorf's American—though hardly Americanized—remake of *Love from a Stranger*.

made serial-killer shocker, issued only shortly before the enactment of a U.K.-European censors' ban on American horror movies, should have found such a hostile reception on these shores. (Another Rathbone-as-lady-killer picture, the American-made *The Mad Doctor*, would meet with comparable indifference at the box office in 1941.)

Flash forward to March-into-April of 1947: Here we find the ambitious upstart Eagle–Lion Films remaking *Love from a Stranger*, as supervised by former Warners executive James J. Geller and directed by Richard Whorf, better known as a specialist in lightweight fare. The finished result must wait six months for its trade-and-press previews in New York and Hollywood, where short-memoried critics will seize upon the stage-and-page connections but fail to spot the picture as a remake of any film. Apparently, the notoriety surrounding the death of playwright Vosper has overshadowed much else.

It is a wonder that Vosper's bad end inspired no lurid fiction, for the case still leaves much at which to guess. Vosper had starred as the villain in the 1936 London stage version, and he came to America with *Love from a Stranger* in September of that year, just as Rowland Lee was grooming Basil Rathbone for the movie version. The play tanked on Broadway. Vosper vanished from the ship bearing him back to England. His body eventually washed ashore in France. No cause of death could be determined.

In reviewing the 1947 version, the important trade publication *Variety* made almost as much of re-hashing the Vosper case as it did of dismissing the new film as "a fair thriller" that "never causes any spinal shivers." No mention was made of the 1937 film.

Dreams That Money Can Buy

In fairness, of course, Richard Whorf's *Love from a Stranger* does suffer by comparison with Rowland Lee's *Love from a Stranger*. Conspicuously missing this time out is a clear-cut sympathetic identification with the endangered new wife, who is capably enough played by Sylvia Sidney. Where Rathbone had served the Lee version as a playful rascal at first, revealing his obsessions only by degrees and never once challenging Ann Howard's ownership of the central role, Whorf allows new badman John Hodiak to commandeer the 1947 version by default. Hodiak's re-interpretation is over-obviously menacing, even at that stage of the story where the courtship should seem bright and alluring.

Hodiak is oddly cast as a South American fortune hunter named Pedro Ferrara. The new screenplay gives it away far too early that Ferrara has killed three wives for their money. In London, meanwhile, Cecile Harrington (Miss Sidney) wins £50,000 in a sweepstakes and prepares to sublet her apartment so that she and her roommate (Ann Richards) can go globetrotting. A disguised Ferrara appears, undermining Cecile's long-standing engagement to businessman Nigel Lawrence (John Howard) and sweeping her into marriage. Ferrara soon begins a campaign of psychological and financial manipulation, which Cecile discovers almost too late to save herself. She does manage to distract Ferrara with a threat of poisoning, but his undoing is the combination of a sound thrashing from Lawrence and a Scotland Yard man (Frederic Worlock) and a good trampling by a team of horses.

Few remakes could fall farther from their inspirations in terms of honoring the source. And yet Sidney seems properly in danger at the climactic moments, when finally the urgency of her situation catches up with the overcooked intensity of Hodiak's too-much, too-soon portrayal. Pleasant distractions along the way include John Howard, as the disappointed fiancé; Isobel Elsom, in a loopy impersonation of a hovering maiden aunt; and Ann Richards, as a levelheaded best pal. The turn-of-the century setting (19th-into-20th, that is) is adequately suggested. An over-emotive musical score, by Universal chillers veteran Hans J. Salter, telegraphs every gasp and shudder but meshes well with the noises of pounding surf and a big-finale thunderstorm.

CREDITS: Producer: James J. Geller; Director: Richard Whorf; Assistant Director: Emmett Emerson; Screenplay: Philip MacDonald; Based Upon: Frank Vosper's 1936 Play, *Love from a Stranger* and Agatha Christie's Story "Philomel Cottage" (from the 1934 Collection *The Listerdale Mystery & Other Stories*), as Also Adapted to the Screen for Trafalgar Films' 1937 *Love from a Stranger*; Photographed by: Tony Gaudio; Photographic Effects: George J. Teague; Art Director: Perry Smith; Supervising Editor: Alfred De Gaetano; Editor: Fred Allen; Decor: Armor Marlowe; Costumer: Michael Woulfe; Music: Hans J. Salter; Orchestrations: Emil Cadkin; Musical Director: Irving Friedman; Sound: J.N.A. Hawkins; Special Sound Supervisor: Leon Becker; Sound Mixer: Percy Townsend; Makeup: Ern Westmore and Del Armstrong; Hair Stylists: Eunice and Helen King; Production Illustrator: John Peacock; Running Time: 81 Minutes; Released: November 15, 1947

CAST: John Hodiak (Pedro Ferrara); Sylvia Sidney (Cecile Harrington); Ann Richards (Mavis Wilson); John Howard (Nigel Lawrence); Isobel Elsom (Auntie Loo-Loo); Ernest Crossart (Billings); Philip Tonge (Dr. Horace Gribble); Anita Sharp-Bolster (Ethel); Frederic Worlock (Inspector Hobday); Billy Bevan and Robert Cory (Cabmen); John Goldsworthy (Clerk); David Cavendish and Keith Hitchcock (Policemen); Phyllis Barry

(Waitress); Gerald Rogers (Postman); Colin Campbell (Teller); Clark Saunders (Sgt. White); Eugene Eberle (Bellboy); Charles Coleman (Doorman); Nolan Leary (Customer in Bar); and Donald Kerr, Abe Dinovich

BLONDE SAVAGE

(Ensign Productions of California/Producers Releasing Corp./Eagle–Lion Films, Inc.)

I was the villain in *Blonde Savage*, accused of doing away with my business partner and of course guilty as charged. Now, the villain is supposed to upstage everybody else, but one member of the company resented my hamming it up and didn't mind saying as much.

So here I am, just taking my mark for this one scene, when this excited little chap—he wasn't in the picture at all—barges in, grabs me by the arm, and says, very indignant: "Hey, fella! Step back, there! Can't you see you're blockin' my burro's face from the camera?"

Seems he was the little beast's owner, or its trainer, and he was sticking close by to make certain his creature got its proper turn in the spotlight!—Douglass Dumbrille; From a Conversation, ca. 1965

Ensign Productions' one-and-only foray into the feature-filmmaking sector promptly became absorbed into Eagle–Lion Films' relentless drive to establish itself as an aggressive contender in the postwar emergence of a number of new, or at least reconstituted, independent studios. The strategy proved futile in the larger scheme, for it was precisely

such a quantity-over-quality approach that had kept Eagle–Lion's springboard company, PRC, ghettoized within the industry during most of the decade.

Ensign's *Blonde Savage*, despite some exciting moments, is a none-too-special entry of the title-tells-all variety. The film stars burly Leif Erickson and wry Frank Jenks as aviators hired to explore a mysterious village along the African coastline. The Tarzan-styled title character, played with a voluptuous authority by the stage-trained Gale Sherwood, figures so matter-of-factly in the yarn that little interest is generated as to how she has come to be there. Her jungle-orphan back-story is such a blatant steal from Edgar Rice Burroughs that it is a wonder the author's trademark-wrangling goon squad did not unleash its lawyers.

Of course, *Blonde Savage* went largely unseen in its day, except as second-feature program padding. The title promises a caliber of excitement that is lacking in the desultory flashback construction—a framing segment discloses present-day murder raps against a prominent citizen and a semi-wild jungle empress, then proceeds to explain the circumstances—and Erickson's performance is more bluster than heroism. Frank Jenks tries too hard to keep the comedy relief perking along.

Miss Sherwood's tribal-ruler situation is laughably implausible, but she radiates confidence all the same and even receives a showcase for her talents as a light-opera singer. Her featured song is a haunting, percussion-driven piece called "Vaga," composed by Leo Erdody as an intermezzo to his overwrought dramatic underscoring. The lyric requires Miss Sherwood to approximate words drawn from the Swahili. Miss Sherwood, then 20, was in real life the wife of Howard Wayne McCoy, an Encino rancher and occasional small-parts actor.

Elsewhere on the plus side, Douglass Dumbrille accounts nicely for the element of villainy as a diamond-mine boss harboring some grim secret, and Matt Willis makes an effective secondary heavy. Dumbrille's overdue comeuppance plays out with a bracing abruptness. Veda Ann Borg, as Dumbrille's jungle-hating wife, seems as impatient to be done with the assignment as her character is fed up with the back-to-nature scene.

Extensive stock footage and (so producer Lionel J. Toll claimed) expressly commissioned expeditionary scenes are neatly matched with the made-in-America sequences, thanks largely to the use of a genuine Stateside jungle—not a backlot construction job—covering 100 acres of the Lucky Baldwin Ranch near Santa Anita. The massive landscaping project dated from late in the 19th century, an extravagant campaign that had collected botanical specimens from tropical regions around the world—and, in turn, had served as an inspiration to the design of the mansion grounds in Orson Welles' *Citizen Kane* (1941).

Blonde Savage's most memorable showpiece involves a spectacular fight-to-the-death between a maddened water buffalo and a gigantic python. Whether producer Toll underwrote or merely acquired this footage is open to question. The battle, though satisfactory on its own terms, is intercut with fearful reactions from the players.

CREDITS: Producer: Lionel J. Toll; Director: S.K. Seeley; Assistant Director: Bob Saunders; Story and Screenplay: Gordon Bache; Photographed by: William Sickner; Special Effects: Larry Chapman and Ray Mercer; Art Director: F. Paul Sylos; Editor: Paul Landres; Decor: Alfred E. Kegerris; Musical Score and Song, "Vaga," by: Leo Erdody; Sound: Sound Services, Inc; Production Manager: William A. Calihan; Running Time: 62 Minutes; Released: November 22, 1947

CAST: Leif Erickson (Steve Blake); Gale Sherwood (Meelah, *née* Lita Comstock); Veda Ann Borg (Connie Harper); Douglass Dumbrille (Mark Harper); Frank Jenks (Hoppy Owens); Matt Willis (Berger); Ernest Whitman (Tonga); Cay Forrester (Mary Comstock); John Dehner (Joe Comstock); Art Foster (Stone); Alex Fraser (George Bennett); Eve Whitney (Clarissa); James Logan (Inspector)

BANDITS OF DARK CANYON
(Republic Pictures Corp.)

A transitional picture in the Hollywood-cowboy tradition, *Bandits of Dark Canyon* is formally a star vehicle for Allan "Rocky" Lane and his mighty stallion, Black Jack, but the film draws greater momentum from a sympathetic fugitive portrayal by the veteran horse-opera hero Bob Steele. The film places itself squarely in the Frontier Gothic frame with a missing-corpse plot device and the presence of a phantom stalker with an appetite for goobers. (The matter of the peanuts bespeaks a kinship with the *film noir* idiom, which often assigns its miscreants some bit of idiosyncratic behavior that leads to identification if not necessarily capture. The *noir* tradition and the classic Hollywood Western of course, share the Gothic Expressionism of the German cinema as a springboard for style and attitude.)

Steele had been edging toward all-'round character-actor status since the early 1940s, when he graced *Of Mice and Men* as a bantamweight Nemesis for the burly Lon Chaney, Jr., and essayed the show-stopping role of a triple agent involved with the Nazi-as-necromancer activities of John Carradine in *Revenge of the Zombies*. Steele's role in *Bandits of Dark Canyon* mingles the expected derring-do with a valedictory air: Steele is by now a middle-aged *eminence grise*, demonstrating his abiding fondness for a genre that he has outgrown.

Steele, at 41, was slightly younger than Rocky Lane—both had cracked Hollywood during the 1920s—but Steele had better than a decade's head start in the cowboy-star department. He is ideally in his element as prison lifer Ed Archer, whose journey to a new hoosegow is interrupted by thugs who kill the driver and then search in vain for Archer. The prisoner has stolen another passenger's clothing and escaped incognito.

Texas Ranger Rocky Lane, riding in pursuit, finds a trail of peanut shells left by a sniper who had separated Archer from his horse. Archer emerges from hiding to steal Lane's mount and then rides to a reunion in his hometown—now, all but abandoned—with his friends Nugget (Eddy Waller), Joan Shaw (Linda Johnson) and Linda's Uncle Ben (John Hamilton). Linda has been looking after Archer's son, Billy (Gregory Marshall), concocting a white lie to let the

boy believe his father is a traveling lawman. Ben tells Archer, once a prosperous miner, that the local lode of gold has played out.

Ranger Lane hoofs it to town and demands the return of his horse. Billy intrudes, and Lane allows the boy to believe that Archer is a fellow enforcer. Later, Lane finds a cryptic note from somebody named Cromwell, summoning Archer to a rendezvous at midnight. Lane keeps the appointment, only to find Cromwell slain and, nearby, another load of peanut-shell rubbish.

As Lane prepares to escort Archer back into custody, another attack obliges the Ranger to use deadly force. Archer tells Lane about the murder case, which involved the death years ago of a business partner. Bogus lawmen arrive to complicate matters, and Nugget identifies a peanut-munching assailant (Roy Barcroft) as the colleague Arthur had supposedly killed. An exhumation finds the ex-partner's casket vacant.

Uncle Ben, meanwhile, gives himself away as the chief conspirator: He has been mining gold on the sly from Archer's property, allowing the town to wither as a convenient cover-up. Lane dispatches the mobsters with a cruel efficiency, leaving Archer a free and exonerated citizen.

A tense camaraderie informs this heroic collaboration, and Linda Johnson compounds the anxieties as a Steele loyalist who would rather see the convict free as a jailbreaker than attempt to clear his name through Due Process. Her conflicted character puts *Bandits of Dark Canyon* in the vanguard of the *noir*-styled Western trend that would blossom with such bigger pictures as *High Noon*, *Shane* and *Johnny Guitar* (1952–1954). The role of Steele's feisty, bewildered child is ably played by Gregory Marshall.

Bandits' bad-guy quotient is capably handled by Roy Barcroft, Republic Pictures' most dependable serial villain; and by the dignified John Hamilton, who seems a folksy friend-to-all until late in the game.

Neither Steele nor Lane enjoyed much in the way of continuing big-deal stardom as the 1940s yielded to the '50s, but then neither did either actor fade away. Their big-screen supporting appearances from here on out would grow to seem special occasions, and at length both found comfortable late-in-life berths in the realm of television comedy—Steele as the goofball Trooper Duffy on *F Troop* and Lane as the voice of a horse, of course, known as Mr. Ed.

CREDITS: Associate Producer: Gordon Kay; Director: Philip Ford; Assistant Director: Lee Luthaker; Screenplay: Bob Williams; Photographed by: Bob MacBurnie; Special Effects: Howard Lydecker and Theodore Lydecker; Art Director: Frank Arrigo; Editor: Les Orlebeck; Decor: John McCarthy, Jr., and George Milo; Music: Mort Glickman; RCA Sound: Earl Crain, Sr.; Makeup: Bob Mark; Running Time: 59 Minutes; Released: December 15, 1947

CAST: Allan "Rocky" Lane and Black Jack (Themselves); Bob Steele (Ed Archer); Eddy Waller (Nugget); Roy Barcroft (Jeff Conley); John Hamilton (Uncle Ben Shaw); Linda Johnson (Joan Shaw); Gregory Marshall (Billy Archer); Francis Ford (Horse Trader); Eddie Acuff (Farraday); LeRoy Mason and Bud Wolfe (Deputies); Jack Norman (Sheriff)

T–MEN
(Edward Small Productions, Inc./
Reliance Pictures/Eagle–Lion Films, Inc.)

The U.S. Treasury's enforcement arm tears into a kill-crazy counterfeiting ring in this essential *film noir* from producer Edward Small and director Anthony Mann. A big film by any standard, though brought in for a modest $450,000 on a rapid-fire, multi-city location-shooting schedule of less than two months, *T-Men* is a watershed in the art of portraying the naturalistic horrors of civilization in a cold, documentary-styled light.

The slaying of an informant prompts an infiltration strategy by agents Dennis O'Brien (Dennis O'Keefe) and Anthony Genaro (Alfred Ryder). In Detroit, where mob boss Carlo Vantucci (Anton Kosta) runs a produce market as a front, O'Brien and Genaro settle into a liquor-stamps counterfeiting shop. They peg a character known as the Schemer as Vanucci's Los Angeles connection. O'Brien tracks the once-powerful Schemer (Wallace Ford, working here under the nickname of Wally) to an L.A. bathhouse and engages him in a dice game, wagering with fake currency that prompts the Schemer to offer him a better grade of bogus greenbacks.

Genaro is accidentally betrayed in a chance meeting with a friend of his wife. A ranking mobster, Diana Simpson (Jane Randolph), orders Genaro's murder just as the agent has laid hands on the Schemer's notebooks. Genaro dies without implicating O'Brien, and the notebooks' code proves easily cracked. O'Brien's cover is rapidly eroding, and though wounded in a climactic chase, he decimates the gang with the help of a late-arriving swarm of policemen.

Dreams That Money Can Buy

Although many pictures beforehand—including *Secrets of the French Police* and *"G" Men* and Small's own production of *Let 'Em Have It* during the 1930s—had benefited from law-enforcement consultation, *T–Men* is the first such picture to derive directly from U.S. Treasury Department files. (Fox's similarly assisted *The Street with No Name* came along shortly thereafter, in 1948.) Extraordinary favors were granted for the making of *T–Men*, as exemplified by a title card: "The United States currency and the credentials of the Treasury Department... were photographed by special permission... Further reproduction... is strictly prohibited." The appearance of legal tender in U.S.-made pictures previously required foreign currency, usually of Mexican origin, as a stand-in. *T–Men* also boasts an introduction by Elmer Lincoln Irey, retired coordinator of what he calls "shock troops" for the Treasury Department. The associate producer, Turner B. Shelton, had been a Treasury Department aide.

Although the key performances are uniformly strong and the large backup cast is impressively deployed, *T–Men* is hardly a star-power movie. (Wallace Ford, of 1932's *Freaks* and many pictures over the long haul of the *Forgotten Horrors* canon, enacts the role of a faded mobster as though he were central to the story; Dennis O'Keefe defers to Ford's authority.) *T–Men* is without parallel in its matter-of-fact depiction of the post-WWII social malaise that allowed the underworld to assume a convincing façade of white-collar respectability. And the film boasts characterizing touches that belong as much to the artisans behind the cameras as to the ensemble cast. Camera chief John Alton depicts the slaying of a near-deaf character in purely visual terms, emphasizing the brutal fact that the killers have stolen their victim's hearing aid. Mann directs with a precipitous momentum that captures perfectly the government's promise of a nationwide crackdown on escalating crime as the war's end lapsed into a more insidious and divisive Cold War mentality.

T–Men received an Oscar nomination in the Sound Recording category. The story was adapted for broadcast while still in first-run theatrical release, with a *Lux Radio Theatre* presentation starring Dennis O'Keefe and Gail Patrick. *T–Men*, in turn, caused the larger studios to begin paying earnest attention to Mann and Alton.

CREDITS: Presented by: Edward Small; Producer: Aubrey Schenck; Associate Producer: Turner B. Shelton; Director: Anthony Mann; Dialogue Director: Stewart Stern; Screenwriter: John C. Higgins; Suggested by a Story by: Virginia Kellogg (Story Attributed Elsewhere to Henry Blankfort); Photographed by: John Alton; Photographic Effects: George J. Teague; Assistant Director: Howard W. Koch; Art Director: Edward C. Jewell; Special Art Effects: Jack R. Rabin; Supervising Editor: Alfred De Gaetano; Editor: Fred Allen; Decor: Armor Marlowe; Costumer: France Ehren; Musical Score: Paul Sawtell; Orchestrations: Emil Cadkin; Musical Director: Irving Friedman; Sound: Leon Becker; Sound Mixer: Frank McWhorter; Makeup: Ern Westmore and Joe Stinton; Hair Stylists: Joan St. Oegger and Alma Armstrong; Technical Adviser: Elmer Lincoln Irey; Running Time: 92 Minutes; Released: Following World Premiere in Los Angeles on December 25, 1947

CAST: Dennis O'Keefe (Dennis O'Brien); Mary Meade (Evangeline); Alfred Ryder (Anthony Genaro); Wallace Ford (Schemer); June Lockhart (Mary Genaro); Charles McGraw (Moxie); Jane Randolph (Diana Simpson); Art Smith (Gregg); Herbert Heyes (Chief Carson); Jack Overman (Brownie); John Wengraf (Shiv Triano); Jim Bannon

(Lindsay); William Malten (Paul Miller); Vivian Austin (Genevieve); James Seay (Hardy); John Newland (Jackson Lee); Tito Vuolo (Pasquale); John Parrish and Lyle Latell (Agents); Curt Conway (Shorty); Ricki Van Dusen (Passenger); Irmgard Dawson (Stewardess); Robert Williams (Captain of Detectives); Anton Kosta (Carlo Vanutcci); Paul Fierro (Chops); Louis Bacigalupi (Boxcar); Trevor Bardette (Rudy); William Yip (Merchant); Al Bridge (Agent in Phone Booth); Keefe Brasselle (Clerk); Jerry Jerome, Bernie Sell, Ralph Brooks and John Ardell (Dice Players); Cuca Martinez (Dancer); Salvadore Barroga (Houseboy); Frank Ferguson (Secret Service Agent); Cecil Weston (Proprietor); George Carleton (Morgue Attendant); Gayne Whitman (Narrator); and Les Sketchley, George M. Manning, Paul Hogan, Victor Cutler, Sandra Gould, Tom McGuire, Mira McKinney, Frank Hyers

1948

OUTRAGES OF THE ORIENT

a.k.a.: Atrocities of Manila; Atrocities of the Orient; Beast of the East
Source of Pirated Additional Footage: Nightmare in Red China
(Friedgen Enterprises/Social Service Pictures)

See women tortured with unspeakable barbarity!
—From the publicity campaign

Until a more-or-less consolidated and embellished re-cut version of *Beast of the East* and *Outrages of the Orient* surfaced during the waning 1950s under the title *Atrocities of the Orient*, these Filipino productions had circulated singly, as a double-bill attraction, and in various stages of re-edited incoherence since the '40s. Foreign by origin and none too dignified to begin with, naturalized through a filter of only-in-America sleazemongering, the titles as repackaged represent a resistant new strain of the U.S. exploitation-film virus.

Both principal source-pictures are anti-Japanese propaganda pieces, decrying war crimes while wallowing in brutality for no greater sake than vicarious thrills. Old-time exploitation impresarios Raymond and Lloyd Friedgen appear to have been the first to import these Third World epics to America, embellishing them awkwardly with musical

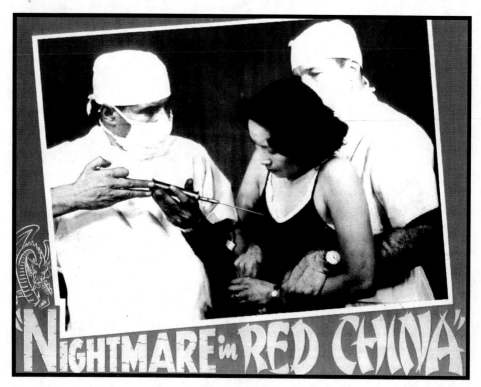

elements—Gershwin, no less!—and lurid advertising campaigns and making no pretense of social uplift. In essence, *Beast of the East* concerns a Filipino settlement that falls prey to the Japanese invaders while *Outrages of the Orient* deals with a brotherly estrangement during wartime. The deliberately fused version, *Atrocities of the Orient*, adds gratuitous scenes of ravishment from Rajaram Vankudre Shantaram's *Nightmare in Red China* (1955), an outcry against the Communist invasion of Tibet. Commercial video editions available nowadays range from a double-feature package of the principal source-films to the 1959 fusion-with-embellishments.

CREDITS: Producer: Don Jésus Cácho; Presented (in U.S.) by: Raymond Friedgen; Directors: William H. Jansen and Carlos Vander Tolosa; Assistant Director: Luis Galasanz; Written by: Carlos Vander Tolosa; English-Language Rewrite by: William H. Jansen; Photographed by: William H. Jansen and Carlos Vander Tolosa; Original Musical Score: Julio Esteban Anguita; Orchestrations: Bernardino F. Custodio; U.S. Re-Edits by: Lloyd Friedgen; Sound: Charles Gray; Released: Sporadically and in Varying Versions from 1948 into the 1970s

CAST: Linda Estrella; Alma Rosa Aguirre; Teddy Benavides; Bimbo Danao; Mona Lisa; Fernando Royo

WOMEN IN THE NIGHT
a.k.a.: Curse of a Teenage Nazi; When Men Are Beasts
(Southern California Pictures, S.A./Film Classics, Inc.)

[The film] tries to conceal its deficiencies behind a documentary beginning… as remote from a documentary as burlesque is from Shakespeare.—*The Los Angeles Daily News*

Yes, and never mind that there is a great deal of proto-burlesque *in* Shakespeare. There's no controlling these critics once the disease of arrogance takes hold.

But anyhow: Some of the immediate-postwar political thrillers cast as angered a gaze upon Nazi Germany as any of their wartime-propaganda counterparts had done. The German-made *Der Verlorene* (*The Lost One*), for example, found the self-exile Peter Lorre—long since become a leading citizen of Hollywood—returning in 1951 to the land of his earlier stardom to play an amnesiac Third Reicher driven to a homicidal madness by an onrush of memory. As an unwelcome reminder to a supposedly reformed Deutschland of its recent thuggish past, *Der Verlorene* met with such a backlash as to become virtually a lost film for many years. The hostile response also squelched any further writer-director ambitions that Lorre might have had.

The American-made *Women in the Night*, by contrast, entertained no such lofty intentions as those that would drive Lorre's film. It was meant as an exploitation picture, plain and simple, and in fact was financed by the St. Louis theaterman Louis K. Ansell as a sure-shot moneymaker for his own screens. The crew of artisans and technicians included the great German-born cinematographer, Dr. Eugen Schüfftan, along with a number of talents from Mexico's self-contained and culturally isolated film industry. *Women in the Night* proved to pack enough of an exploitable wallop—animalistic lust, a hefty mortality

It is a shocking, true story based on secret file case histories - hitherto only whispered - of crimes against women in Nazi and Japanese Officers' Clubs - those unsung heroines who, though forced to endure un-

Frame enlargement from the opening of the exploitation film *Women in the Night*.

rate, women-in-prison antagonisms and a trace of militaristic science fiction—that Film Classics, Inc., picked it up for a more generalized release. Ansell went back to running his grindhouses with fodder from other studios.

Women in the Night argues that the defeat of Nazi Germany hardly had put an end to the evils of the Third Reich. The tale begins in 1945, in a Shanghai hospital that serves as both a Nazi officers' club and a prison for women from various Allied nations. Sixteen-year-old Helen James (Kathy Frye) responds to the lustful attentions of a German officer by slashing him to death with a shattered goblet. Col. von Meyer (Gordon Richards) summons the prisoners for questioning, but none will name the killer. The women include an American journalist, Claire Adams (Virginia Christine); a French entertainer, Yvette Aubert (Tala Birell); and a Chinese heiress and political activist, Li Lung (Frances Chung).

Von Meyer intends to hand over to two callers from Japan, Col. Noyama (Richard Loo) and Prof. Kunioshi (Philip Ahn), a set of plans for a cosmic death-ray purported to make the A-bomb look like a popgun. Before Noyama and Kunioshi can arrive, however, the Allied bombings of Japan have altered the course of the war. Von Meyer decides to withhold the top-secret documents and use the women to distract the Japanese dignitaries. The prisoners are ordered to outfit themselves in evening gowns for a party.

Helen is reunited with her mother, Angela (Helen Brown), a servant confined to the hospital's laundry. Captivity has driven Angela insane.

The festive evening becomes an orgy of destruction in short order. Helen finds herself pursued by a would-be rapist. Angela's idea of protecting her daughter is to poison the girl in order to preserve her virtue. The mother is brought to von Meyer's quarters, where she defaces a portrait of Hitler. She is sentenced to die, whether for murder or for

Forgotten Horrors 4

the show of disrespect. Claire lures Kunioshi to his death at Li's hands. Claire's greater affections seem reserved for the Nazi officer von Arnheim (William Henry), who is in fact her husband, Philip Adams, of the U.S. Office of Strategic Services. Yvette takes a line of lesser resistance and bunks up with von Meyer.

Li's lover, Chang (Benson Fong), has infiltrated the hospital as a deliveryman, his cargo including enough dynamite to wreck the joint. The warden, Frau Thaler (Bernadene Hayes), falls to her death in a struggle with the women. The Germans open fire on the Japanese contingent, and the rebels ready a truck for a getaway. Yvette martyrs herself by touching off the dynamite, and the survivors observe the conflagration from a safe distance. Too bad the cosmic death-ray seems to have existed only on paper; a simple big boom suffices for a climax.

William Henry, creditable enough in an undercover heroic role, is overwhelmed as a dramatic presence by the women, who are uniformly capable. The lapsed big-time star Tala Birell has the richest part, as a secretly vengeful good-time floozy tormented by the memory of the German invaders' butchery of her family. Kathy Frye wears well the tragic intensity of a child who will kill rather than submit—only to be slain by her own deranged mother. Helen Brown, as the madwoman, nails the spirit of the picture with a tiny, gemlike scene that makes plain her contempt for the Reichsters.

Women in the Night did indeed present itself as a documentary-like account, offering a straightforward now-it-can-be-told prologue with an earnest declaration of hope that "an aroused public opinion will [assure] that this savagery to women will never be repeated." The film patently intended arousal of another sort, however.

The film's proxy name, *Curse of a Teenage Nazi*, makes no sense, in or out of context, except perhaps as a sucker-bait come-on. This re-christening appears to date from a roadshow engagement; a print bearing that lurid title also has turned up in small-market television syndication.

CREDITS: Producer: Louis K. Ansell; Associate Producer: Joseph K. Ansell; Director and Scenarist: William Rowland; Assistant Director: Jaime Luis Contreras; Story Adapted for the Screen by: Maude Emily Glass; Shooting Script: Ali M. Opar, Robert St. Clair and Edwing V. Westrate; Additional Dialogue: Arthur Jones and Louis K. Ansell; Photographed by: Eugen Schüfftan [as Shuftan] and José Ortiz Ramos; Stills: Francisco Urbina; Editor: Dan Milner; Music: Raul Lavista; Song: "Cherie" by Sid Robin; Sound: James T. Corrigan and W.M. Dalgleish; Makeup: Enrique Hutchinson; Hair Stylist: Angelina Mateos; Production Manager: Antonio Guerrero Tello; Assistant Production Manager: Roberto Figueroa Mateos; Script Supervisor: Carlos Villatoro; Grip: Jesús Diaz; Running Time: 90 minutes; Released: During January of 1948

CAST: Tala Birell (Yvette Aubert); William Henry (Philip Adams/Major Von Arnheim); Richard Loo (Col. Noyama); Virginia Christine (Claire Adams); Bernadene Hayes (Frau Thaler); Gordon Richards (Col. von Meyer); Frances Chung (Li Lung); Jean Brooks (Maya); Kathy Frye (Helen James); Helen Mowery (Sheila Hallett); Benson Fong (Chang); Helen Brown (Angela James); Frederick Giermann (Maj. Eisel); Philip Ahn (Prof. Kunioshi); Arno Frey (von Runzel); Beal Wong (Gen. Mitikoya); Iris Flores (Maria Gonzales); Frederick Brunn (Lt. Kraus); Harry Hays Morgan (Gen. Hundmann); Paula Allen (Nurse); Joy Gwynell (Suicidal Inmate); William Yetter, Sr. (German Officer); Noel Cravat (Japanese Officer); Paul Ander (German Physician)

SHADES OF GRAY

(U.S. Army Pictorial Service/U.S. Army Signal Corps)

Application [of military psychiatry] today should be…making good civilians out of the sufferers, rather than good combat soldiers. — From the *Variety* review

A recurring motif among the postwar entertainments we have gathered here is that of the alienated former G.I., driven to distraction if not criminality and/or madness by his return to a cold-shoulder anti-welcome from Polite Society. Uncle Sam's facile assumption that Everything's Going To Be All Right Now has served historically to plant trained killing agents back into ordinary civilian life, with the predictable consequence that many returning servicemen come ill equipped to cope with the social norms. In the Real World, such repatriated citizens seldom have committed any ghastly antisocial deeds: More commonly, they would fit back in as best they could and, from there, either adapted or suffered in tacit desperation. But we've known many a WWII combat veteran, of that dwindling generation that sired our own, who has suffered unbidden flashbacks of one degree or another — and who has wished that his return had been greeted with something warmer than a G.I. Loan and a hearty handshake. These guys had treated Hitler to an Axis-whipping, after all.

Shades of Gray, a government-financed dramatized documentary that proves significant in the present context, addresses no finer courtesies for the returned soldier, but it does offer insight into the psychological torments afflicting the conscripted warrior of the Twentieth Century. Its greater concern lies with the restoration of disturbed individuals to uniformed duty.

Narrator Harry Hennessy declares that as much as 70 percent of the populace suffers from some manner of personality disorder. This figure translates proportionately to the Armed Forces, which during World War II yielded 600,000 cases of neuropsychiatric illness in military hospitals. Re-enactments of case histories dwell more upon prevention and treatment than upon derangement, although there are bracing portrayals of (purported) cures brought about via drugs, hypnosis and electro-shock therapy.

The origin of *Shades of Gray* dates from 1946 and an internal-use Army film called *Let There Be Light*, which John Huston directed while on active duty. *Let There Be Light*, a purely documentary study of military psychiatry, earned sufficient acclaim that it could have been released to neighborhood theaters, but the Army withheld it lest the (actual) patients shown suffer an invasion of privacy. *Shades of Gray* was the result of this interest, with re-enactments of situations from *Let There Be Light* and other such personnel-only films — including one bearing the ominous title of *Combat Psychiatry*.

The acting, from both enlisted personnel and career actors, is generally good. The director, Joseph E. Henabery, was a silent-era veteran whose work from 1929 onward had consisted almost entirely of short subjects made for Warner Bros./Vitaphone's East Coast satellite studio. The shooting sites included the Army hospital at Northport, Long Island, and Astoria Studios, also on Long Island. Henabery's experienced command of short-form narrative — his most striking work occurs in a long-running series of one- and two-reelers, launched in 1937 with "The Attic of Terror" — proves an ideal credential for *Shades of Gray*.

Shades of Gray covers considerable ground in a brief running time but dwells rewardingly upon the necessary emotional nuances. The Signal Corps previewed the film in a 68-minute version, but the film was cut to 40 minutes for general distribution. *Shades of Gray* received an Oscar nomination in the documentary category, its dramatizations notwithstanding.

CREDITS: Producer: Frank J. Payne; Director: Joseph E. Henabery; Screenplay: John B. Davenport and Mortimer Offner; Photographed by: Gerald Hirschfeld; Editor: Eric Lawrence; Technical Advisors: Dr. George S. Goldman, Lt. Col. M.C. Res and Lt. Col. Frank Drake; Running Time: 40 minutes; Previewed at 68 minutes: During January of 1948

CAST: Harry Hennessy (Narrator); and Sandy Campbell, Ed Kreisler, Hal Vinson, John Leighton, Lewis Howard, Tom Nello, Bob Knight, Michael Higgins, Berton Tripp, Bill Hollandbeck, Ewing Mitchell, Neil McMahon, Hal Conklin, Ray Rahner

KILLER DILLER
(All American News, Inc.)

Herewith, a picture guaranteed to send the forces of bigotry into a dithering rage, even as it pretends to reinforce the jigaboo stereotypes that have long been employed as the mass-media definition of black citizens. The bourgeois Afrocentric-intellectual and black-separatism factions will cringe at the broad-stroke characterizations that predominate in *Killer Diller*—even as they

decry the film's unaffected and un-ironic usage of a dialect that has, in times more recent, been tagged with the pretentious name of Ebonics and thus granted a shallow measure of dignity. (More reassuring, perhaps, is the deployment of a few players who speak the King's English and hold responsible positions in society.)

The white-supremacist contingent and citizens more passively bigoted, on the other hand, will find *Killer Diller* all the more amusing for its convenient stereotyping value, even as the adherents of discrimination might rail at the freedom the film grants to black expression.

Any such extreme faction—and all have more in common than they might be willing to grant, in their shared belief in the myth of race—will let it go at that, missing the film's greater point altogether.

Dreams That Money Can Buy

Said greater point is the tacit and obviously un-calculated argument that the popular culture is better served by integration than by exclusion. *Killer Diller* was created, of course, to entertain those folks whom the Dominant Culture called colored patrons of colored theaters in colored neighborhoods. But behind the scenes, the film is pure integration. That fact is betrayed by the producer credit for a minor-league show-business impresario named E.M. Glucksman. Glucksman granted creative freedom in exchange for a bankable niche-market product.

The story finds entertainer Clinton "Dusty" Fletcher (playing himself, in a patented nightclub characterization) arriving to replace a theater's resident magician, the Great Voodoo, who has failed to return from a disappearing act. Dusty's first stunt is to cause the fiancée (Nellie Hill) of the boss, Mr. Dumdome (George Wiltshire), to vanish, along with a valuable necklace. Dusty does likewise with four inept cops—but they rematerialize promptly, having a distinct bearing upon what plot there is.

Meanwhile, Dusty woos Butterfly (Butterfly McQueen), Mr. Dumdome's secretary, while dodging the police and awaiting his turn on stage. Cut to the auditorium, where a grand procession of singers, dancers and instrumentalists supplies the film with a substance the story itself lacks. Nat "King" Cole, already a mass-audience name in the recording business but still some years away from a mainstream Hollywood breakthrough, leads his trio through a fine selection of tunes. Jackie "Moms" Mabley delivers her customary selection of folksy, mildly vulgarian stories and songs. The hoofer team of Patterson & Jackson, mountainous artists with extraordinary comic timing and fine singing voices, comes through with a medley of Tin Pan Alley gems—including "Ain't Misbehavin'," in which one dancer's tap shoes notate the melody—and manages a devastatingly accurate parody of the famous harmonizing quartet, the Ink Spots ("... only two of us, but we weigh as much as they do").

None of which pertains much to the backstage chase until the finale, when Dusty and the cops interrupt one of Moms Mabley's monologues. Dusty sends Moms to take his place in the pursuit—the policemen do not detect the switch—and begins to inspect the magical contraptions on stage. The Great Voodoo (Ken Renard) turns up, bearing the missing necklace, and is arrested. The tale ends with Dusty and Butterfly in a matrimonial clinch, which she reinforces with a pair of handcuffs.

The cross-cultural coalition that the journalist and songwriter Josh Alan Friedman defined in 1996 as a case of *Blacks 'n' Jews* (we recommend his album of that title) is responsible for most such purportedly all-black productions. This self-evident truth extends to the larger fact that history's great blues and jazz recordings, which led to the eruption of rock 'n' roll music halfway along through the Twentieth century, scarcely could have taken shape if not for a persistent synergy between black artistry and Jewish appreciation and marketplace savvy. For every pioneering black artist who struggled and died in cultural isolation, any number of others would benefit by connecting with white, usually Jewish, producers.

Killer Diller is thus hardly the only film of its kind, but it is the one most directly poised at the brink of the watershed 1950s, when finally a massed American population would fall under the spell of largely unadulterated black music in the guise of rock 'n' roll. The artists who would bring about the change included black players Chuck Berry, Little Richard Penniman, Ike Turner and veteran jazz singer Big Joe Turner—alongside such black-influenced white players as Gene Vincent, Carl Perkins, and Elvis Presley—but by and large the dealmakers and economic benefactors were Jewish.

Killer Diller and its companion film, *Boarding House Blues*, become, in this light, the most direct ancestors of the rock 'n' roll movies that would proliferate during the 1950s. The films document the ascent of the great storyteller-comedian Moms Mabley, a bit player in films since 1933's *The Emperor Jones*, who by the 1960s would become both a generally popular stand-up artist (a key influence upon Whoopi Goldberg) and a prevailing conscience of the Civil Rights movement. Here, too, is as true a barometer as can be found of the social climate that would allow the pianist-vocalist Nat "King" Cole to become a hitmaker for the mainstream recording industry and yet still confine his movie-star ambitions, for the time being, to Poverty Row. *Killer Diller* also showcases such terrific artists as bandleader Andy Kirk, blues singer Beverly White and Patterson & Jackson, who never quite made the leap to widespread acclaim.

Killer Diller is, of course, not a deliberately subversive film—nor did its obscure sector of the industry have any larger agenda than to sell tickets and maybe even "uplift the race," as the saying goes, in the process. The picture is only superficially weird, but its framing story contains some unsettling mock-mystical elements: Star player Dusty Fletcher materializes like a ghostly clown, popping up between George Wiltshire and Nellie Hill just as the couple is poised for a smooch. Just as abruptly, Fletcher vanishes, only to reappear behind Wiltshire. Fletcher's Vaudeville act consists of two *Caligari*-style closets, into which Hill and those bungling policemen disappear. Ken Renard comes on like some Negro Svengali.

Fletcher's romantic interest is played charmingly by the accomplished one-note actress Butterfly McQueen, who seems scarcely to have aged in the decade since her show-stopping performance in *Gone with the Wind* (1939). Miss McQueen has little more to do than giggle and wiggle at Fletcher's hints of a marriage proposal, but she takes charge of the relationship at the fade-out.

The law officers are played for laughs throughout, with little tough guy Freddie Robinson leading three big crybaby stumblebums. Beyond the Keystone Kops–style slapstick, they account for a surreal element of cinematic self-consciousness: While pursuing Fletcher, Robinson announces: "He went down there." The other cops ask how he knows, and Robinson replies, "'Cause I seen this picture befo'!" Augustus "Gus" Smith, the author and star of the historic stage play *Louisiana* and its 1934 film version *Drums o' Voodoo*, has an incomprehensibly small part as a stagehand.

Dusty Fletcher, a genial sort with real screen presence, was best known for a song called "Open the Door, Richard" and an accompanying monologue, in which he played a boozehound calling in vain for his pal to let him into their apartment. Fletcher and John "Spider Bruce" Mason had originated this routine in Chitlin' Circuit Vaudeville. As melodized by the saxophonist Jack McVea, the tune also would generate hit records for the Count Basie Orchestra and Louis Jordan's Tympani Five, among other jazz and R&B acts, and even crossed over to renditions by white-folks pop and hillbilly bands—inspiring along the way an answer-record, "Richard Ain't Gonna Open the Door," by a Texas-bred harmonizing ensemble called the Four Aces. In *Killer Diller*, Fletcher never gets around to performing "Open the Door, Richard," but he drops the occasional reference. He can be seen doing an extended version of "Richard" in a supplemental track of a 1987 video compilation called *The Nat "King" Cole Musical Story*, on the off-brand American Video label. Rudy Ray "Dolemite" Moore, a key heir to this tradition, has acknowledged Fletcher as an influence.

CREDITS: Producer: E.M. Glucksman; Director: John Binney; Story & Screenplay: Hal Seeger; Musical Arranger: Rene J. Hall; Dance Director: Charles Morrison; Assistant Director: Walter Sheridan; Photographed by: Lester Lang; Makeup: Rudolph G. "Doc" Liszt; Editor: L. Hesse; Costumers: Mme. Bertha & Eaves Costume Co.; Sound: Harold Vivian; Draperies: Frank W. Stevens; Art Director: Sam Corso; Running Time: 71 minutes; Produced: During 1947; Submitted for Copyright: 1948; Released: Region-by-Region, into the 1950s

CAST: Clinton "Dusty" Fletcher (Dusty); George Wiltshire (Mr. Dumdome); Butterfly McQueen (Butterfly); Nellie Hill (Lola); Freddie Robinson (Sarge); William Campbell, Edgar Martin and Sid Easton (Policemen); Augustus "Gus" Smith (Stagehand); Jackie "Moms" Mabley (Herself); Ken Renard (the Great Voodoo); Andy Kirk & His Orchestra; The Nat "King" Cole Trio; Ray Abrams & Shirley Green (Featured Saxophonists); Beverly White (Featured Vocalist); the Clark Bros. (Hoofers); the Four Congaroos (Dance Ensemble); Patterson & Jackson (Singers and Hoofers); and the Varietiettes Dancing Girls, from the Katherine Dunham School of Dancing

BOARDING HOUSE BLUES
(All American News, Inc.)

In this rambunctious companion piece to *Killer Diller* (above), Dusty Fletcher takes a similarly laconic star turn. *Boarding House Blues* trades more strikingly upon exaggerated terrors—comically rendered, of course—and the superstitions that prevail among show folk.

Dusty, a roomer in the boarding house of Moms Mabley (herself), infuriates the landlady by bringing a gorilla-suited chum named Steggy (John Riano) onto the premises. When another tenant, Boo Boo (Sid Easton), sneaks into Dusty's rooms in search of liquor, he is so shocked to see the mock ape that he scrams without catching up on his rent. Everybody is in arrears to Moms, who faces a deadline on the mortgage. So entertainers Marie Cooke and Marcellus Wilson propose to raise the money with a musical revue. Their producer (Augustus "Gus" Smith, more prominent here than in *Killer Diller*) balks, having become leery of show business thanks to a fortuneteller's warning of disaster. So Moms impersonates a psychic and pronounces the venture viable. Sure enough, the show is successful enough to save Moms' house—and to pad the negligible tale out to a generous feature-length running time. Secure once again, Moms resumes her favorite pastime of nagging Dusty.

The music is the greater point overall, with fine big-band R&B and eccentric hoofing by the likes of Lucky Millinder & His Orchestra, the team of Benjamin "Bullmoose" Jackson and Anisteen Allen, and "Crip" Heard, a one-legged, one-armed dancer.

CREDITS: Producer: E.M. Glucksman; Director: Josh Binney; Story: Hal Seeger; Photographed by: Sid Zucker; Camera Operators: Frank La Follette and George Stoetzel; Assistant Director: Salvatore Scappa, Jr.; Art Director: Sam Corso; Music: Henry B. Glover; Songs: "I Love You, Yes, I Do," by Sally Nix & Henry B. Glover, "You'll Never Know (If an Apple Is Ripe)" by Arthur Freed & Roger Edens, and "Throw It Outta Your Mind," "It Ain't Like That," "Let It Roll" and "I Will Hold You in My Arms Again Tonight," Composer(s) Uncredited; Sound: Harold Vivian; Makeup: Dr. Rudolph G. Liszt; Running Time: 87 minutes; Released: During 1948 on a State-by-State Basis

CAST: Dusty Fletcher (Himself); Jackie "Moms" Mabley (Herself); John Mason & Co. (Troupers); John D. Lee, Jr. (Stanley); Marcellus Wilson (Jerry Lewis); Marie Cooke (Lila Foster); Emory Richardson (Simon); Harold Cromer (Moofty); Sid Easton (Boo Boo); Freddie Robinson (Freddie); Augustus "Gus" Smith (Norman Norman); Edgar Martin (Joe); John Riano (Steggy); and Lucky Millinder & His Orchestra, Una Mae Carlisle, Benjamin "Bullmoose" Jackson, the Berry Bros., Lewis & White, Annisteen Allen [Given Elsewhere as Anistine], Paul Breckenridge, Stump & Stumpy, the Lee Norman Trio, "Crip" Heard, Vivian Harris

FOR YOU I DIE
(Arpi Productions, Inc./Film Classics, Inc.)

A severe concentration of prison-break vengeance, futile nymphomania *vs.* true love, alcoholism and family estrangements, John Reinhardt's *For You I Die* squanders such finer values on a heavy-handed soap-operatic treatment, with awkward and self-conscious dialogue and a finale as forcibly happy as it is clichéd.

Even so, the leading portrayals are winning—a death-do-us-part caliber of romantic attraction between Cathy Downs and Paul Langton—and low-billed Don Harvey registers well as a murderous jailbreaker who complicates matters, only to be denied the showy death scene he deserves. The presence of Roman Bohnen (beloved as a sentimental old duffer called Candy in 1939's *Of Mice and Men*) and Mischa Auer (back on Poverty Row after years in the big leagues) is incentive enough to sit tight and get a load of the picture.

Johnny Coulter (Langton) is poised for a formal release from prison when shanghaied into an escape plot by Matt Gruber (Harvey), who kills a guard just for the hell of it en route to a getaway. Gruber instructs Coulter to seek out Hope Novak (Miss Downs), Gruber's moll and onetime accomplice (or so he says), at the tourist lodge where Hope works. Coulter does so, except that he mistakes Hope's roommate, the antsy Georgie (Jane Weeks), for the genuine article and almost sabotages the rendezvous with Gruber. Even after the identities have been sorted out to satisfaction, Georgie keeps pestering

"Kiss me and Keep Kissing me..."

...KILLERS ARE CAUGHT WITH Brute Force ... By Getting the WOMEN Behind the GANGSTERS Behind the GUNS!

ARPI PRODUCTIONS

DEADLY...to expose!

DANGEROUS...to oppose!

DESTRUCTIVE...to defy!

FOR YOU I DIE

Cathy DOWNS • Paul LANGTON
with Mischa AUER • Roman BOHNEN
Marion KERBY • Jane WEEKS • Manuela CALLEJO
Released thru Film Classics, Inc.

Coulter for a tumble. (And how much greater an erotic charge the movies packed, back when the studios understood the power of suggestion!)

Hope wants nothing to do with Gruber, having been falsely accused (or so she says) of being his consort and accomplice. Gruber still has not arrived, and in the meantime Coulter begins settling in comfortably with the motor-court folks and even helps to thwart a holdup without tipping off the local cops to his fugitive status. But then, violent news reports show that Gruber is drawing nearer. His arrival triggers a brawl, during which the camp's well-liked alcoholic bum of a short-order cook (Bohnen) is gunned down. (It develops that Bohnen's Smitty is Hope's father, unbeknownst to her, but little is made of this revelation.)

A scoundrel's demise for Gruber would seen a foregone conclusion, but then maybe a fitting end for such a scoundrel is simply the opportunity to rot in prison. In any event, Coulter pulls off the capture in law-abiding fashion, turning himself in for good measure. Hope assures him that he will have a home with her once he has served out the remainder of his sentence.

Crime melodramas share much in common with soap operas—broken-heartedness being a principal ingredient of both—but *For You I Die* blurs the line to no particular advantage. There is a prevailing air of desolation and longing about the crucial motor-court setting that no amount of ferocity could overcome, anyhow, and even Mischa Auer's comedy-relief presence, as a touring entertainer, is of a decidedly morose timbre. Paul Langton's troubled hero is a solidly *noir*-inflected presence in a film that might have become a *bona fide noir* if shorn of its weepier qualities. Most viewers are content to remain ig*noir*ant of such distinctions, and are no better or worse off for the lapse. (Langton is best known to devotees of the monster-movie genre for his military-man portrayals in the likes of *It! The Terror from beyond Space*, *The Cosmic Man* and *Invisible Invaders*, from 1958–1959.)

The attitude of the film stems no doubt from the producers' ambition to get a top-of-the-line production, competitive in the mass-audience arena of crowd-pleasing sentimentality, out of a B-picture budget (which was a generous $300,000). Reinhardt, as director and co-producer, helped to stretch the resources by serving also as art director—a function well handled, with a persuasive air of isolation and spiritual desolation. Reinhardt, a prolific scenarist and former actor, had written for Fox's *Mr. Moto* series and turned out Spanish-language scripts for several ethnic-market U.S. productions. He also directed this same year's (in)tolerance drama, *Open Secret*. Robert Presnell and Reinhardt's Arpi Productions became one of the first independent studios to exploit the emerging medium of television—commissioning for *For You I Die* a special trailer for the broadcast arena.

CREDITS: Producers: Robert Presnell, Sr., and John Reinhardt; Director: John Reinhardt; Assistant Director: William Forsyth; Assistant to the Director: Peter Mayer; Screenplay: Robert Presnell, Sr.; Photographed by: William Clothier; Art Director: John Reinhardt; Editor; Jason Bernie; Decor: Murray Waite; Wardrobe: William Cogswell and Florence Hays; Musical Score Composed and Conducted by: Paul Sawtell; Sound: Frank Webster; Makeup: Ted Coodley; Hairdresser: Elaine Ramsay; Production Manager: Frank Parmenter; Production Aide: M. Pam Blumenthal; Gaffer: Roy Black; Assistant to the Producers: Mischa Auer; Running Time: 76 minutes; Released: January 2, 1948

CAST: Cathy Downs (Hope Novak); Paul Langton (Johnny Coulter); Mischa Auer (Alec Shaw); Roman Bohnen (Smitty); Jane Weeks (Georgie); Marion Kerby (Maggie Dillon); Manuela Callejo (Louisa Shaw); Don Harvey (Matt Gruber); Charles Waldron, Jr. (Jerry); Rory Mallinson (Mac)

HEADING FOR HEAVEN
(Ace Pictures, Inc./Producers Releasing Corp.)

Mantan Moreland used to tell the story of one Mr. Jones, whose dying words to his wife allowed as how he'd turn over in his casket if she should take another mate. Mrs. Jones died soon thereafter, and upon entering the celestial realm she inquired as to the whereabouts of Mr. Jones. There being so many Joneses in Heaven, St. Peter asked for a fuller description. Mrs. Jones related her husband's deathbed declaration, to which St. Peter replied: "Oh! You mean *Revolvin'* Jones!"

The film *Heading for Heaven* is unrelated to Mantan Moreland or his anecdote, but—yes, well, and don't let's spill everything at once.

Stuart Erwin stars as Henry Elkins, heir to a patch of undeveloped land outlying the town that bears his name. For generations, the Elkinses have ordered their heirs never to sell the property lest they be caught unprepared if and when Elkinsville spreads eastward. Henry honors this tradition despite the nagging of his wife, Nora (tough-talking Glenda Farrell), to sell out; his ambition is to build what he calls "a poor man's paradise" of affordable housing.

Stuart Erwin • Glenda Farrell • Irene Ryan

A crooked swami (Russ Vincent) enters the scheming, promising a prospective buyer that he will persuade Henry to come around and entrancing the gullible Nora in the process. Undaunted, Henry stretches his own resources to the limit by purchasing an adjoining tract. The plot (story, not land) takes a turn for the weirder when Henry visits a clinic for a physical exam and comes away with the mistaken impression that hc is about to die. He also mistakenly believes that Nora is about to leave him for the swami, and in a fit of dejection Henry writes a farewell letter and spends a night boozing it up at a riverside hobo encampment.

Evidence accumulates to make Henry seem a suicide. New information comes to light that would fulfill Henry's dream venture. So he crashes a séance, posing as his own ghost, and spooks the chiselers into coming clean about the scam. Henry remarks that his father and grandfather are probably so happy about the new deal that they are spinning in their graves. Cut to the graveyard, where we see the defunct Elkinses doing that very thing.

Stu Erwin is in top form as the mild-mannered populist real-estate heir, and Glenda Farrell matches Erwin for laugh-earning ability as the flighty social-climber wife. Milburn Stone stands out as a huckster in league with Russ Vincent's fake soothsayer. Irene Ryan proves a real scene-stealer as an outspoken servant.

CREDITS: Producer: George Moskov; Executive Producer: Jack Schwarz; Director: Lewis D. Collins; Assistant Director: Ralph Slosser; Screenplay: Lewis D. Collins and Oscar Mugge; Photographed by: George Robinson; Editor: Marty Cohn; Set Designer: Frank Sylos; Decor: Earl Wooden; Music: Hal Borne; Sound: Ferol Redd; Makeup: Bob Cowan; Production Manager: Leon Chooluck; Running Time: 65 minutes; Released: January 17, 1948

CAST: Stuart Erwin (Henry Elkins); Glenda Farrell (Nora Elkins); Russ Vincent (Swami); Irene Ryan (Molly); Milburn Stone (Harding); George O'Hanlon (Alvin); Janice Wilson (Janie Elkins); Ralph Hodges (Danny); Dick Elliott (Roger Wingate); Charles Williams (Eddie); Selmer Jackson (Doctor); Harry Tyler (Professor); Ben Welden (Sam); Betty Best (Lila); and Jack Del Rio

OPEN SECRET

(Marathon Pictures Corp./Harry Brandt Productions/
Eagle-Lion Films, Inc./Pathé Industries)

Director John Reinhardt took a beating upon the opening of *Open Secret*, which inspired this fugue from the *New York Times'* self-important Bosley Crowther: "It is cheap, amateurish, tactless, and incredibly poorly played."

Nor was Crowther hardly alone in his blowhard contempt toward Reinhardt's expose of violent bigotry as a linchpin of life in the Good Old U.S. of A. If many of the mainstream critics may merely have been parroting the influential Mr. Crowther in the hope that he might notice how smart they were, Archer Winsten of the *New York Post* weighed in with this more thoughtful appraisal:

> The filmmakers and the performers work hard and earnestly. It's not enough. This is thin ice. The point of a needle. It can make you feel actually uncomfortable as you realize that [the film's topic] is the big tragedy, this is the feeling that killed millions…, and it's being attacked here in a manner worthy of the battle to prove that crime does not pay or never bet on fights.

No doubt the critical brethren were waiting for something more along the high-minded lines of *Gentleman's Agreement* (1947–1948), or for another film with the tough-minded intelligence of *Crossfire* (1947). These had been the trailblazers in what *Variety* called

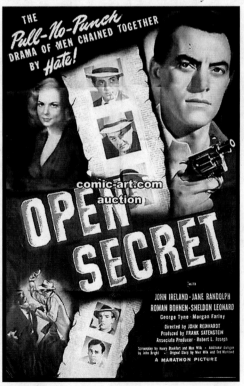

"an anti-Semitism cycle." But they can't all be Big & Important Motion Pictures, and sometimes a little movie can have just as much upon its mind—if not necessarily the resources or the sophistication to convey an idea to satisfaction. (*Open Secret* owes a greater debt of influence, actually, to 1937's *The Black Legion*. The backer, Harry Brandt, was a theaterman intent upon equipping his screens with a timely, exploitable product rather than a polite social-problem drama.)

Funny thing, though: *Open Secret*, with its gutsy, confrontational tone and its pull-no-punches indictment of the Real World horrors perpetrated by scared and intolerant citizens, holds up much better than Elia Kazan's naïve and overly mannered *Gentleman's Agreement*. The Kazan film lives or dies upon the questionable strength of a Jewish-by-convenience star turn from Gregory Peck, and upon the bourgeois-intellectual condescension of

Peck's standing up in defense of a culture not his own. *Open Secret* comes out slugging and flails its way unapologetically toward a slam-bang finale, suffering chiefly from John Ireland's dull leading performance but compensating within the supporting ranks. (Meanwhile, Edward Dmytryk's *Crossfire* proves the best of the lot as a taut thriller that also happens to be pursuing a social agenda.)

Open Secret concerns a mob that preys upon Jews and Italians. Its murderous activities have been documented in a set of candid photographs taken by an infiltrator, Ed Stevens (Charles Waldron, Jr.). When Stevens turns up slain and framed as the perpetrator of a recent murder, Stevens' friend Paul Lester (Ireland) sets out to hide the incriminating photos. The trail leads to a publisher (Morgan Farley), who uses a crime-busting magazine as a front for his top-dog status with the mob.

Ireland's stodgy underplaying aside, *Open Secret* nails a prevailing mood of unease, with strategic outbursts of shock value. Roman Bohnen registers formidably as a disappointed man who chooses to blame his failures upon immigrant citizens. Morgan Farley's unmasking comes at precisely the right moment, and his climactic confrontation with Sheldon Leonard—playing a cop of Italian ancestry—is a hair-raiser. George Tyne lends a helpful air of defiance as a camera-shop operator who, upon finding himself marked for persecution, outwits his tormentors. An undeveloped bit of suspense (probably a cutting-room sacrifice) lies in the suggestion that Ireland's landlady, played with a current of menace by Anne O'Neal, might be one of the terrorists. As Ireland's wife, Jane Randolph contributes little more than looks until the climactic struggle with Farley.

The original cut of *Open Secret* differs significantly from a mid-1950s reissue print, which is briefer by two minutes and deploys fewer ethnic slurs as a facile characterizing device for the wrongdoers. Producer Frank Satenstein had prevailed in a running argument with the Production Code Administration over the extensive use of such language, but this element is conspicuously less noticeable in the re-edit—which of course would have taken into account the film's suitability for television, which was a more civil medium in those days.

CREDITS: Producer: Frank Satenstein; Associate Producer: Robert L. Joseph; Assistant Producer: Leo Rose; Director: John Reinhardt; Assistant Directors: Leon Chooluck and Ralph Slosser; Photographed by: George Robinson; Screenplay: Henry Blankfort and Max Wilk; Based Upon a Story by: Max Wilk and Ted Murklund; Additional Dialogue: John Bright; Musical Score: Herschel Burke Gilbert; Editors: Jason Bernie and Stanley Frazen; Art Director: George Van Marter; Decor: Earl B. Wooden; Makeup: Ted Larsen; Production Manager: George Moskov; Props: George Bahr; Sound: Hugh McDowell; Assistant to Mr. Reinhardt: Peter A. Mayer; Running Time: 69 minutes; Released: February 14, 1948

CAST: John Ireland (Paul Lester); Jane Randolph (Nancy Lester); Roman Bohnen (Roy Locke); Sheldon Leonard (Sgt. Mike Frontelli); George Tyne (Harry Strauss); Morgan Farley (Phillips); Ellen Lowe (Betty Locke); Anne O'Neal (Miss Tristram); Arthur O'Connell (Carter); John Alvin (Ralph); Bert Conway (Mace); Rory Mallinson (Chuck Hill); Helena Dare (Mrs. Hill); Leo Kaye (Fatso); King Donovan (Gang Member); Tom Noonan (Bob); Charles Waldron, Jr. (Ed Stevens)

PERILOUS WATERS

(Norwalk Productions/Jack Wrather Productions/Monogram Distributing Corp.)

It was no small leap for Jack Wrather from the bloody-pulp origins of *High Tide* and *The Guilty* (which see, under 1947) to the pricier slick-magazine pedigree of *Perilous Waters*. But the Texas-based industrialist-turned-producer counted this one a strategic move in his bid for a stronger foothold in Hollywood. Capitalizing the independent production at a solid-but-unextravagant $250,000 and publicizing the popular source-story for a broadened appeal in the absence of star-power players, the Wrather company also used *Perilous Waters* to advance its build-up of Don Castle as a potential marquee name.

Castle, who had helped to carry *The Guilty* and *High Tide*, takes stronger charge of *Perilous Waters* as Willie Hunter, a jobless veteran of the war. Hopelessness drives Hunter to hire on to kill a crime-fighting publisher, Dana Ferris (the distinguished Samuel S. Hinds). Hunter's employer is a racketeer known as Boss Slade (Cy Kendall), who keeps members of his gang on watch to affirm the hit when Ferris' yacht sets out for Mexico.

Hunter's task grows ever more complicated: As the craft's resident electrician, he finds himself distracted by Ferris' man-hungry daughter (Peggy Knudsen); a stockbroker named Larkin (John Miljan), who has sidelines in bogus securities and blackmail; Ferris' secretary, Judy Gage (Audrey Long), who is under suspicion of carrying on an adulterous affair with Ferris and has something of a criminal record to boot; and Ferris' jealousy-ridden wife (Gloria Holden). Hunter and Judy fall in love and confide their grimmer secrets.

Hunter may have his murderous work cut out for him with all these meddling kin and business associates hovering about—but then again, he may not have to lift a finger toward the killing, for somebody else seems intent upon doing away with Ferris.

The infiltration begins to invert itself when an unrecognized assailant pitches Ferris overboard. Hunter rescues Ferris, who promotes him to bodyguard duties. Castle's grasp of the character, and of the crucial ensemble-acting job with Samuel S. Hinds, proves just right when Hunter reluctantly attempts to pull off the assassination but hesitates just long enough for Ferris to catch him at it. Hinds renders the big-shot near-victim more indignant than afraid,

and just credulous enough to let Hunter go. A dodgy last-ditch encounter with the nymphomaniacal daughter makes Hunter a fugitive after all. Slade's hoodlums show up to determine whether the hit on Ferris has been accomplished.

All ends well for all who deserve it, with Judy Gage finally tracking Hunter down to inform him that the law has caught up with Boss Slade. Hunter kills the vengeful thugs. In an out-of-nowhere too-happy ending, Ferris re-hires Hunter.

Leon Ware's novella *The Quest of William Hunter* is pulp-lit at heart, of course, but domesticated sufficiently to justify its serialization in so respectable a magazine as *Good Housekeeping*. Don Castle plays out his role with a greater disoriented desperation than the writing conveys, and Hunter seems ready enough at just the right times to commit murder. This is a case of Castle's making more of the part than is written—and overcoming Jack Bernhard's indifferent style of directing—to establish Willie Hunter as an easily manipulated bumbler who, having Served His Country obediently as a Navy man, comes home to less than a respectful welcome. The suspense owes itself almost entirely to Castle's savvy interaction with an assortment of antagonists, unlikely allies, victims and near-victims and annoyances as he struggles to find his place.

Audrey Long serves Willie Hunter's quest well as a friend in need, and Peggy Knudsen conveys a credible contempt for common decency as the antsy daughter. Cy Kendall registers memorably with a brief appearance as the criminal mastermind.

CREDITS: Producer: Jack Wrather; Associate Producer: James C. Jordan; Director: Jack Bernhard; Assistant Director: Milton Carter; Screenplay: Richard Wormser and Francis Rosenwald; Based Upon: Leon Ware's 1946 Novella, *The Quest of William Hunter*, from *Good Housekeeping* Magazine; Photographed by: Henry Sharp; Operative Cameraman; Warner Cruz; Art Director: Lewis H. Creber; Supervising Editor: William Ziegler; Editor: Stewart S. Frye; Decor: Murray Waite and Emile C. Poter; Wardrobe: Catherine Garabedion; Music Supervisor: David Chudnow; Musical Score: Rudy Schrager; Sound: Ferol Redd; Makeup: Robert Cowan; Hairdresser: Jane Romeyn; Production Supervisor: Sherman A. Harris; Running Time: 64 minutes; Released: February 14, 1948

CAST: Don Castle (Willie Hunter); Audrey Long (Judy Gage); Peggy Knudsen (Pat Ferris); Samuel S. Hinds (Dana Ferris); Gloria Holden (Jenny Ferris); John Miljan (Carter Larkin); Walter Sande (Franklin); Stanley Andrews (Capt. Porter); Cy Kendall (Boss Slade); Gene Garrick (Fred); George Ramsey (Bart); Mike Kilian (Brooks); Julian Rivero (Fisherman)

THE PEARL
a.k.a.: LA Perla
(F.A.M.A.–Aguila Films/RKO-Radio Pictures, Inc.)

John Steinbeck experienced better luck than most other Great American Novelists at seeing his stories transferred to the screen. Even the occasional blatant Hollywoodization, such as MGM's big-budget *Tortilla Flat* (1942), takes nothing away from such triumphs as John Ford's wonderful *The Grapes of Wrath* (1940), one of those rare pictures that capture both the style and the spirit of a source-novel; and Lewis Milestone's to-the-bone *Of Mice and Men* (1939), as well as Gary Sinise's 1992 version; and even *Cannery Row* (1982), a sweet and stylized box-office flop.

By the time *The Pearl* rolled around, Steinbeck was both a big-name writer and a big-time celebrity, although it is fair to say he had sought neither station. Hollywood had discovered his books, though, and it was through such movie-town contacts as producer Milestone that Steinbeck became involved in the development of *The Pearl*, which put the cinematic cart before the literary horse.

Essentially a fable about the deadly perils of wealth and possessions in a community plagued by greed and superstition, *The Pearl* had been kicking around in Steinbeck's head for quite a while, as both inspiration and irritant. He first had written about it in the narrative section of *Sea of Cortez* (1941), an account of a scientific—and philosophical—expedition with his great friend, the biologist Ed Ricketts, who shares co-author credit. The few paragraphs that Steinbeck had devoted to his *Pearl* story in that book would grow into not only a film script, but also into an example of another narrative form with which he worked from time to time, the play-novella.

These play-novellas were intended as short books that could, with a minimum of effort, be transposed into scripts for stage or screen. By far, the best-known of Steinbeck's play-novellas is *Of Mice and Men*; others include his wartime story *The Moon Is Down* (1942), the interesting misfire *Burning Bright* (1950), and *The Pearl*, which was a script before it became a book. (Steinbeck's kindred project of 1941, *The Forgotten Village*, has a chapter in *Forgotten Horrors 2*. Elsewhere, the novelist-turned-producer Val Lewton also

had nurtured such an approach as early as 1942, when he assigned DeWitt Bodeen to write the first scenario for *Cat People* as a 50-page prose story, though not for publication. A later advancer of this method is Ira Levin, notably in the script-concept novel that would become *Rosemary's Baby* in 1968.)

The Pearl features Pédro Armendáriz, eventually a significant character actor in American pictures, as Kíno, an impoverished pearl diver whose baby, Juaníto (María Cuádros), is stung

María Eléna Marqués contemplates the treasure that will signify doom for her household.

by a scorpion during a particularly bad stretch of luck for Kíno's family. Even though Kíno is so broke that the village's doctor (Charles Rooner) refuses to help, Juaníto survives. Kíno goes on to pry a huge and valuable pearl from a great big oyster, instantly earning respect and envy.

Of course, the pearl also attracts—or provokes—trouble. Kíno's wife, Juana (María Eléna Marqués), grows to believe the pearl accursed and begs him to destroy it. Kíno believes the wealth thus promised will bring prosperity and freedom. Instead, the pearl attracts thieves and deceivers and murderous attackers. After a hideous gauntlet of backstabbing, double-dealing, and a nightmarish pursuit through a swamp onto a cliffside, Kíno finds himself bereaved beyond redemption and casts the pearl into the ocean, too late to reverse any misfortunes.

Steinbeck, who loved Mexico and visited there throughout his life, had begun *The Pearl* in earnest after meeting with director Emílio Fernández and cameraman Gábriel Figueroa on an excursion, early in 1945, and telling them the bare-bones story, which he had heard from Mexican fishermen. The filmmakers proved enthusiastic, and Steinbeck returned home to California to begin a script. Three weeks later, he was back in Mexico with a draft. Plans called for Steinbeck's then-wife, Gwyn, to provide the music for *The Pearl*, and although she did a great deal of research into the region's traditional idioms, that idea ultimately dissolved. Antonío Díaz Conde's finished musical score proves largely folkloric, and as such unobtrusive and evocative; here is an early moviemaking use of "La Bamba," long before its assimilation into American rock 'n' roll.

The Pearl began shooting, in both Spanish- and English-language versions, in September of 1945. Production wrapped at last with the completion of the English edition in November of 1947, more than two months after a formal premiere for the Spanish-speaking version, *La Perla*. *The Pearl* became the first Mexican-made English-language film to be distributed in the United States. *The Hollywood Reporter* pegged the budget for both films—which differ in particulars beyond the spoken tongues—at $400,000, owing to the comparative cheapness of shooting in Mexico. Mexican investors had put up half the money, and RKO-Radio Pictures paid the balance, in addition to opening up its lot for additional Stateside filming.

The book version appeared in conjunction with the American opening. It had been serialized a couple of years earlier as *Pearl of the World*, in *Woman's Home Companion* magazine. The telling owes as much to the influence of Guy de Maupassant's famous tale of ravaged lives, *The Necklace*, as it does to Latinate folklore. *The Pearl*, in turn, worked a telling influence upon the comic-book writer Al Feldstein, who would rechannel such intimate, shattering ironies into many of his scripts for artist Graham Ingels in *The Haunt of Fear* and its kindred magazines from the E.C. Comics group. Without due attribution, of course.

Steinbeck shared the screenwriting credit with director Fernández and Jackson Wagner, an old-time pal of Steinbeck's. Steinbeck and Wagner had collaborated on a small-town satirical drama from Paramount Pictures, *A Medal for Benny* (1945), which earned Oscar nominations for the authors as well as for the star player, J. Carrol Naish.

All during production and distribution of *The Pearl*, Steinbeck was going through a tough stretch, with both a new child and a demanding, high-strung wife. The tepid critical and commercial response to *The Pearl*, both book and movie, could not have raised his spirits much. As Jay Parini wrote in *John Steinbeck: A Biography* (1995), "The autobiographical impulses behind *The Pearl* are not hard to discern; this is clearly a story about the price of success, and about the inevitable consequences of trying too hard to rise above one's position in life... One cannot help but see that the origins of the tale are to be found in the author's dismal situation at the time; he felt compromised, disappointed, and terribly alone."

In Mexico, *The Pearl* was a hit, earning five Ariel Awards from the Mexican Motion Picture Academy including Best Picture, Best Director, Best Photography, Best Male Star (Armendáriz), and Best Character Role (Juán García, as a prominent antagonist). And the book itself would survive its sleepy beginnings to become a staple of high school and collegiate curricula, read by generations of students to this day.

CREDITS: Producer: Oscar Dancigers; Director: Emílio Fernández; Assistant Director: Ignácio Villareál; Screenplay: John Steinbeck, Emílio Fernández and Jackson Wagner; Photographed by: Gábriel Figuéroa; Art Director: Javiér Torres Toríja; Editor: Gloria Schoemann; Mu-

The novella-to-movie tie-in edition of John Steinbeck's *The Pearl*

sical Score: Antonío Díaz Conde; Sound Director: James L. Fields; Sound Engineers: Nicholas de la Rosa and Clem Portman; Re-recording Engineer: Calindo R. Samperio; Sound Effects: Victor Lewis; Makeup: Armando Meyer; Unit Manager: Federíco Amérigo; Production Manager: Alberto A. Ferrer; Running Time: 78 minutes; Released: Following New York Premiere of English-Language Version on February 17, 1948; Spanish-Language Premiere, September 12, 1947, in Mexico City

CAST: Pédro Armendáriz (Kíno); María Eléna Marqués (Juana); Charles Rooner (Doctor); Alfonso Bedoya (Godfather); Gilbérto Gonzáles (Gachupin); Juán García (Sápo); María Cuárdos (Juanito); Enedína Díaz de León (Medicine Woman)

MADONNA OF THE DESERT
(Republic Pictures Corp.)

Frank Wisbar, the party most directly responsible for those ambitious PRC entries *Strangler of the Swamp* and *Devil Bat's Daughter* (see *Forgotten Horrors 3*), takes a less prominent hand in Republic's *Madonna of the Desert*, as its primary author. The yarn, though every bit as pious and humble as its title would suggest, recalls the righteous-as-a-fist ferocity of *Strangler* and its source-film, Wisbar's 1936 German masterwork *Fahrmann Maria*, in its tale of a sacred artifact that seems to dispense miracles and murder according to circumstances.

California rancher Joseph Salinas (Don Castle) is the owner of a bejeweled effigy of the Madonna, which attracts the attention of a dealer in antiques, Hank Davenport (Paul E. Burns), and his associate, Nick Julian (Sheldon Leonard). Julian visits the Salinas spread. Caught trespassing, he introduces himself as a collector and pitches an offer to buy the statue. No dice, replies the rancher, innocently provoking Julian to sneakier measures.

Meanwhile, a local lout named Tony French (Donald Barry) returns from a term in prison. French reckons he'll devote his newfound freedom to stealing the Madonna. Julian and Davenport conspire to swap a replica for the genuine article. Julian's sweetheart, Monica Dale (Lynne Roberts, whose top billing might suggest a trace of redemption for her character), follows his orders to infiltrate Salinas' ranch, posing as a stranded motorist.

Salinas proves helpful enough, even after Monica brings up the subject of the Madonna. Salinas has allowed a neighboring family to borrow the statue for a wedding. He suggests that Monica attend the reception with him while her car awaits repair; she accepts the invitation as an opportunity to exchange Madonnas. A candle sets her clothing afire just as she attempts the switch. Salinas extinguishes the flames. The wedding guests attribute the rescue to the statue's intervention. Salinas agrees, declaring that the Madonna had cured him of a wartime combat injury.

The crooks converge. Monica attempts the exchange, but the statues look so nearly alike that she becomes confused as to which is genuine. She buries one of them in Salinas' garden. French arrives and attempts to detain her. French nabs the other Madonna. French is stopped, in turn, by Julian in a roadside struggle. Salinas has retrieved the buried statue—the real Madonna—and confronts Monica. A climactic shoot-out finds French and Julian killing one another.

The leading portrayals are uniformly solid, although the character writing and the casting play Holy Ned with ethnic authenticity, with Don Castle impersonating a Latinate *padrón* and Hispanic actors playing members of various Italian-surnamed households. Castle holds forth admirably, nonetheless, as the tough-but-trusting owner of the sacred object. Lynne Roberts resists every opportunity to Do the Right Thing but seems vaguely rueful at the fade-out. Sheldon Leonard, as the chief conniver, and Donald Barry, as the more conspicuous crook, stir up a pleasing conflict. For such changes-of-pace from his more familiar Western heroism, Barry used his formally christened name as opposed to the marquee moniker Don "Red" Barry; the "Red" had come from a career-defining role in Republic Pictures' *Adventures of Red Ryder* (1940)—prior to which, Barry had dealt largely in bad-guy roles.

Madonna's real scene-snatcher, however, is a backup character, a garrulous ranch-hand played by the wonderful Paul Hurst. A working actor since 1911, Hurst had come decisively to the screen during the 1920s and established himself over the long stretch

MADONNA *of the* DESERT

A Republic Picture

as an indispensable master of comic timing and, occasionally, chilling menace. His great showcase role of the early-talkie years is the dim-witted Detective Grump of 1932's *The Thirteenth Guest,* but many enthusiasts might remember Hurst more vividly as the scavenging Yankee deserter who takes a gunshot to the face from Vivien Leigh in *Gone with the Wind* (1939), or as the most overtly malicious of the lynch-mob agitators in *The Ox-Bow Incident* (1943). *Madonna of the Desert* provided Hurst with something of a homecoming: He had spent his childhood on a California ranch. The late 1940s found Hurst well situated at Republic as a sidekick to cowboy hero Monte Hale. Hurst became a suicide at age 65 in 1953.

CREDITS: Producer: Stephen Auer; Director: George Blair; Assistant Director: Joe Dill; Screenplay: Albert DeMond; Story: Frank Wisbar; Photographed by: John Mac-Burnie; Operative Cameraman: Herb Kirkpatrick; Stills: Don Keyes; Special Effects: Howard Lydecker and Theodore Lydecker; Art Director: Frank Arrigo; Editor: Harry Keller; Decor: John McCarthy, Jr., and George Milo; Costumer: Adele Palmer; Music: Mort Glickman; Sound: Fred Stahl; Makeup: Bob Mark; Hair Stylist: Louise Landmeir; Script Supervisor: Dorothy Yutzil; Grip: Whitey Lawrence; Running Time: 60 minutes; Released: February 23, 1948

CAST: Lynne Roberts (Monica Dale); Donald Barry (Tony French); Don Castle (Joseph Salinas); Sheldon Leonard (Nick Julian); Paul Hurst (Pete Connors); Roy Barcroft (Buck Keaton); Paul E. Burns (Hank Davenport); Betty Blythe (Mrs. Brown); Grazia Narciso (Mama Baravelli); Martin Garralaga (Papa Baravelli); Frank Yaconelli (Beppo); Maria Genardi (Mrs. Pasquale); Renee Donatt (Marie Baravelli); Vernon Cansino (Enrico)

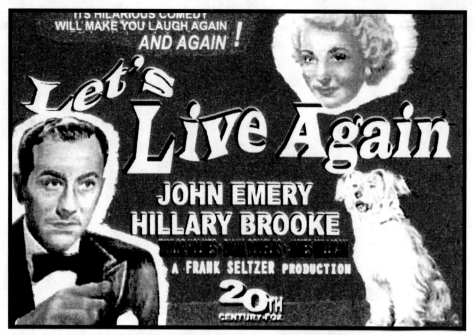

LET'S LIVE AGAIN

(Frank Seltzer Productions, Inc./Twentieth Century-Fox Film Corp.)

A uniquely strange fusion of brotherly rivalries, reincarnation mania and psychiatric dabbling—complete with a nod to postwar America's favorite new obsession, nuclear science—Herbert I. Leeds' *Let's Live Again* seems not to have survived intact despite its supposedly long-term protection as an acquired property of Twentieth Century-Fox.

The independent production dates from a shoot during the closing half of November 1947 at General Service Studios—a business-as-usual low-budget schedule that somehow managed to yield extraordinary results. Too bad for the aficionados of suchlike that the official surviving footage runs scarcely more than three-quarters of an hour; there is bound to be at least a TV-syndicate print that neither our colleagues nor the combined archival resources of Fox and the American Film Institute have turned up.

But notes exist that were taken down during entire showings, and so does a cutting continuity filed with Fox's copyright registration of February 19, 1948. Together with what is known to remain of the actual picture, the archive yields this story:

Larry Blake (played by John Emery), an atomic-energy researcher, considers his brother, explorer George Blake (James Millican), an embarrassing crackpot. Larry already is consulting a head-doctor (Charles D. Brown) in an attempt to sort out his resentments toward George, but a nervous breakdown seems a foregone conclusion—especially after George humiliates Larry by announcing an expedition to investigate reincarnation in Tibet. To make matters worse, Larry's secretary, Terry (Diana Douglas), finds George fascinating.

Word comes of George's death in a plane crash. Larry visits a bar, where a persistent dog (played by Rags the Dog, also of 1948's *Rocky* and *Who Killed Doc Robbin*) appears. The dog's behavior seems so thoroughly George-like—following Larry insistently, seizing objects from him and the like—that Larry accepts George's reincarnation as a matter of demonstrable fact. Larry develops an obsession with the dog, and when it vanishes he launches a search that leads to an antagonistic romance with Sandra Marlowe (Hillary Brooke), who has claimed the animal as her own. Larry's belief in reincarnation comes and goes so erratically that he at last finds himself committed to an asylum. And then released. And then re-committed. During all of which, George turns up alive and okay. Everything turns out for the better. Except for Larry's relapse, which ends the tale on a decidedly bipolar note.

The peculiarly conceived screenplay takes more than a few cues from Mary Chase's celebrated play, *Harvey*, which had arrived in 1944 but would not reach the screen until 1950. John Emery's Larry Blake is by far a less intriguing character than *Harvey*'s Elwood P. Dowd, though similarly tipsy and comparably persuasive with the arguments for an intrusion of supernatural fantasy upon the workaday world. Emery would have made a pretty fair Elwood, for that matter—all due respect to James Stewart and Art Carney—given that he makes far more than is written of the Blake character.

Though a leading man on Broadway since 1925 (and a favorite co-star of the great Katherine Cornell), Emery (1905–1964) gained top billing only twice during his Hollywood career. Once was on *Let's Live Again*, and next was on the same year's *The Gay Intruders*. Emery remained better known for the air of polished menace he could radiate as a supporting player, in such assignments as *Here Comes Mr. Jordan* (1941), *Spellbound* (1946) and *The Woman in White* (1948). On professional terms, he reserved his greater loyalties for Actors Equity over the Screen Actors Guild.

Spirited leading lady Hillary Brooke had recently come into her own as a key player after more than a decade of largely unbilled assignments. Her resume ranges far beyond the intertwined realms of horror-SF-*noir* but of course is generously highlighted by such essential examples as *Strange Impersonation* (1946) and William Cameron Menzies' back-to-back productions of *The Maze* and *Invaders from Mars* (both 1953).

Director Herbert I. Leeds (*né* Levy) had turned to directing in 1937 from a lengthy hitch as a film editor—a background that made him a natural for action pictures, although he also practiced a sharp command of characterizing touches and lifelike conversational dialogue that would distinguish a good many B-unit assignments. A best-of-Leeds roster also would include the wartime-siege drama *Manila Calling* (1943) and the suspenseful *Bunco Squad* (1950).

CREDITS: In Charge of Production: Lewis J. Rachmil; Executive Producer: Edward Lasker; Producer: Frank N. Seltzer; Associate Producer: Hugh King; Director: Herbert I. Leeds; Assistant Director: Harold Godsoe; Screenwriters: Rodney Carlisle and Robert Smiley; Story: John Vlahos and Herman Wohl; Photographed by: Mack Stengler; Operative Cameraman: Fred Kaifer; Musical Score: Raoul Kraushaar (a.k.a. Ralph Stanley); Musical Director: David Chudnow; Editor: Bert Jordan; Art Director: Jerome Pycha, Jr.; Costumer: Helen Ruth; Makeup: Gus Norin; Hair Stylist: Vera Peterson; Production Manager: Lewis J. Rachmil; Script Supervisor: Jack Herzberg; Sound: W.C. Smith; Grip: Burnett Jacques; Stills: Samuel Manatt; Running Time: 69 minutes; Released: February 27, 1948

CAST: John Emery (Larry Blake); Hillary Brooke (Sandra Marlowe); Taylor Holmes (Uncle Jim); James Millican (George Blake); Charles D. Brown (Psychiatrist); Jeff Corey (Bartender); Diana Douglas (Terry); Percy Helton ("Mr. President"); Earle Hodgins (Salesman); John Parrish (Doctor); Ralph Sanford (Cop); and Dewey Robinson, Richard Bond, Rags the Dog

I WOULDN'T BE IN YOUR SHOES
(Monogram Pictures Corp.)

Cornell Woolrich's great inventiveness as an author of crime yarns lies largely in an uncompromisingly bleak attitude and a gift for making despair appear adventurous. His stories convey an obsessive attention to detail of the sort that only can come from an obsessively lonely person. Woolrich also possessed an ability to make awkward coincidences seem persuasive, if not necessarily plausible, and to deploy born-loser characters as prominently as if they were important to the Course of Human Events.

Such a pure-Woolrich character is tap-dancer Tom J. Quinn, as played to harassed near-perfection by Don Castle in William Nigh's *I Wouldn't Be in Your Shoes*. The customary assignment of a film's artistic proprietorship to its director (in this case, the veteran hack Nigh) is entirely a formality. Of all the many films that have presumed to adapt Woolrich,

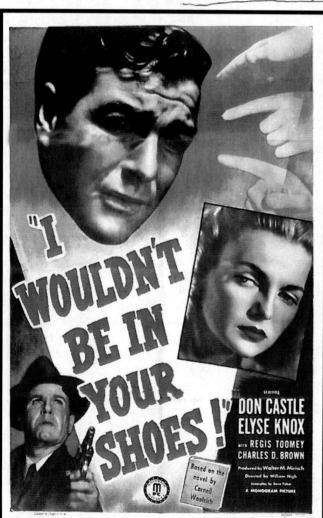

few have managed to usurp his narrative authority or improve upon the material he had provided. (And yes, Alfred Hitchcock's handling of *Rear Window* is an exception—in part because the source-material is a short story.)

Unable to sleep on account of the summertime heat and the yowling of cats in the alley below, Quinn impulsively throws his only pair of tap shoes in the general direction of the noise. When he goes to retrieve his shoes, they are missing. But then Quinn's wife, Ann (Elyse Knox), finds the shoes in a hallway.

Also found nearby, by the police, is the corpse of a wealthy recluse who has been kicked to death. Draw your own conclusions, but take care that you don't falsely incriminate an innocent dancer just because he has big feet and winds up in possession of incriminating objects.

As Fate and Cornell Woolrich would have it, Quinn's misfortune is less that of random happenstance than of opportunistic manipulation by a crooked cop, Clint Judd (a furrowed and impatient Regis Toomey, cast against his breezy and avuncular Irishman nature), who has developed a yen for Mrs. Quinn. Having railroaded Quinn onto Death Row via the footprint evidence, Judd goes so far as to reopen the case and frame up another hapless yutz (Robert Lowell), whom Judd knows will have a seamless alibi—all for the sake of appearing heroic in Ann's eyes. Ann is hardly that dim, though. When Judd finally voices his affections for her, she tricks the lawman into making a confession within earshot of fellow officers.

All of which occurs, of course, right around the time of Quinn's scheduled execution. The absorbed viewer will be too caught up in the urgency of the moment to wonder how much more stretching this particular coincidence can withstand. Break the thrall by over-analyzing it, and the bad guys might as well win.

This immediate period of time finds Don Castle on a modest roll, however diminished his circumstances from a span of attempted stardom during the late 1930s at MGM. A prominent member of the big studio's *Andy Hardy* ensemble, Castle moved laterally from there into generalized character parts, then became more ambitious as a leading man on Poverty Row. Castle gained momentum from a friendship with the actress Bonita Granville and her movie-struck millionaire of a husband, Jack Wrather. In addition to his renewed hopes in the leading-man ranks, Castle also bought into a 16-mm film production laboratory that was among Wrather's holdings. Castle spent the 1950s and early '60s as an associate producer for Wrather's teleseries *Lassie*. He died at 49 in 1966, from an overdose of a painkiller prescribed in the aftermath of an automobile accident.

CREDITS: Produced by: Walter Mirisch; Director: William Nigh; Assistant Directors: William Calihan and Edward Morey, Jr.; Screenplay: Steve Fisher; Based Upon: A 1938 Short Story in *Detective Fiction Weekly* by Cornell Woolrich (a.k.a. William Irish), and upon Woolrich's like-titled novel of 1943; Photographed by: Mack Stengler; Musical Score: Edward J. Kay; Editor: Roy V. Livingston; Art Director: Dave Milton; Decor: Raymond Boltz, Jr.; Hair Stylist: Lela Chambers; Production Manager: Glenn Cook; Sound: Max M. Hutchinson: Stills: Bud Graybill; Grip: Harry Lewis; Supervising Editor: Otho Lovering; Operative Cameraman: William Margulies; Script Supervisor: Ilona Vas; Running Time: 71 minutes; Released: March 23, 1948

CAST: Don Castle (Tom J. Quinn); Elyse Knox (Ann Quinn); Regis Toomey (Inspector Clint Judd); Charles D. Brown (Inspector Stevens); Rory Mallinson and Bill Kennedy (Detectives); Robert Lowell (John L. Kosloff); Steve Darrell (District Attorney); Esther Michelson (Mrs. Finkelstein); Ray Dolciame (Shoeshine Boy); William Ruhl (Police Lieutenant); John Sheehan (Judge); John H. Elliott (Lawyer); Dorothy Vaughan (Mrs. Alvin); Herman Cantor (Jury Foreman); Hugh Charles (Counterman); Laura Treadwell (Mrs. Stevens); Joseph E. Bernard (Janitor); Tito Vuolo (Grocer); Jimmy Aubrey (Tramp); John Shay (Salesman); Donald Kerr (Vaudeville Man); Stanley Blystone (McGee); Matty Fain, John Doucette, Dan White and Bill Walker (Prisoners); Ray Teal and Paul Bryar (Guards); Walden Boyle (Priest); Lou Marcelle (Announcer); Eddie Parker (Policeman); Wally Walker (Clerk)

THE ENCHANTED VALLEY

(Jack Schwarz Productions/Producers Releasing Corp./
Eagle-Lion Films, Inc./Pathé Industries, Inc.)

PRC Pictures had scored in 1945 with *The Enchanted Forest*, a live-action back-to-nature fantasy whose successful run had inspired big-timer Walt Disney to begin thinking more seriously about developing a wildlife-pictures unit. (Disney had contemplated shooting 1942's *Bambi* as a live-actioner, having finagled that story-property away from England's Korda Bros., whose studio had contemplated a live-action *Bambi*. The Kordas retrenched with a live-action *Jungle Book*. Disney, of course, wound up sticking with the animated realm until much later.)

In 1947, PRC and *Forest*'s producer, Jack Schwarz, returned to the concept (and to the hue-saturated Cinecolor process) with *The Enchanted Valley*. This one is not so much a remake or a sequel as it is merely a very similar film—more overtly sentimentalized, perhaps, but still just as deeply concerned with the almost mystical thrall that a spirit-filled patch of nature's own real estate exerts over those who stumble into it.

Frances Kavanaugh's screenplay raises the stakes on intrusive violence, planting a mob of fugitive bandits upon an isolated farm. Here, a crippled youngster named—what else?—Timmy (Donn Gift) and his Grandpa (Charley Grapewin, the scene-stealing Grandpa Joad of 1940's *The Grapes of Wrath*) pass their days in communion with the creatures of the fields and the woodlands. Johnny Nelson, Midge Gray and Bugs Mason (Alan Curtis, Anne Gwynne and Joseph Devlin) seem pretty okay for common hoodlums, and they even find themselves falling under the benevolent spell of the valley. But they have been keeping sorry company in the world outside.

Criminal interlopers are lurking nearby, and good ol' Grandpa isn't likely to go on living forever. The kid really could use that surgery for which Grandpa has been saving up, and there is a bounty on Nelson. Y'know, if Nelson and his moll were to pull light sentences, then maybe Timmy could use a set of slightly shopworn adoptive parents. Meanwhile, a vengeful mobster (John Bleifer) commits such acts of violence against nature as to earn the distinction of being killed by a bear.

The human drama—almost a Disneyfied *Petrified Forest*—is hardly all that gripping though competently played. Director Robert Emmett Tansey had been a matinee-Western specialist since 1930. The trained-animal action supplies the greater charm of *The Enchanted Valley*, conveying an unclassifiably odd dream-reality that transcends the obvious attempt to create something wholesome for the family trade. Jimmy the Crow is altogether more appealing here than in *Bill and Coo*, which is coming right up. An audience of hell-bent-for-sensations kids of the 21st Century would demolish the theater if asked to sit still for a picture so polite and reassuring.

Schwarz would transplant this formula in 1950 to a backlot and stock-footage rain-forest to make *Forbidden Jungle*.

CREDITS: Producer: Jack Schwarz; Director: Robert Emmett Tansey; Screenplay: Frances Kavanaugh; Photographed by: Ernie Miller; Operative Cameraman: Ernest Smith; Stills: John Jenkins; Cinecolor Supervisor: Arthur Phelps; Art Director: Ed Jewell; Editor: George McGuire; Settings: Harry Reif; Musical Score: Lucien Calliet; Musical Supervisor; David Chudnow; Sound: Ben Winkler; Makeup: Dick Johnson; Hair Stylist: Peggy Johnson; Production Manager: Donald Verk; Animal Trainers: Curly Twiford, Earl Johnson and Byron Nelson; Script Supervisor: Jules V. Levy; Grip: Vincent Bratton; Running Time: 77 minutes; Released: March 27, 1948

CAST: Alan Curtis (Johnny Nelson); Anne Gwynne (Midge Gray); Charley Grapewin (Grandpa); Donn Gift (Timmy); Joseph Crehan (Chief Scott); Joseph Devlin (Bugs Mason); Al LaRue (Pretty Boy); John Bleifer (Menelli); Rocky Camron (Constable); Jerry Riggio (Gangster); Curly Twiford's Jimmy the Crow (Himself); Skipper (Dog); Tubby (Bear)

BILL AND COO
(Republic Pictures Corp.)

A character called the Black Menace, handling the villainy in *Bill and Coo*, is nothing more than a big old crow—and at that, the same crow that serves roles more upbeat in this same year's *Miraculous Journey* and *The Enchanted Valley*. Not all that terrifying—until you view the Menace from the perspective of the other players, all birds. To these residents of Chirpendale, U.S.A., the Black Menace is a horrific presence, intimidating them with fly-overs and landing at random or strategic moments to crow-hop through the little town, sowing misery and destruction.

That fine American critic James Agee called *Bill and Coo* "by conservative estimate, the god-damnedest thing ever seen." And while time and rampant exposure to CGI have diminished its effect, *Bill and Coo* is still one of the weirdest features ever to grace a screen. It also is the only bird movie to grace these pages, the *Falcon* pictures (below) notwithstanding.

A promotional card geared to the reissue of *Bill and Coo*, **touting the picture's Special Accomplishment Oscar**

A majority of the cast comes from the trained troupe of George Burton's Love Birds (with, fittingly, the Black Menace contributed by another avian maven, Curly Twiford), although a few other animals—including baby opossums, kittens and guinea pigs, the latter jockeyed by birds—are seen briefly in a set of circus sequences, which take up much of the picture. Crowd scenes are dominated by skittish parakeets, which seem poised to flow into a Hitchcockian swarm at any moment. The main characters are dressed up in little outfits, looking as though they'd rather be just about anywhere else than here.

A prologue features producer Ken Murray, complete with trademark cigar, big-dogging it in his office as the filming gets under way. "We're making a picture with birds," he notes, confidentially, addressing the camera. "*Murder*!" Then he eats some birdseed and watches as George Burton (himself) puts a couple of his winged charges through their paces. Elizabeth Walters also appears in this sequence and turns up later as an off-screen voice.

The story, such as it is, centers upon Bill Singer (the bird, not the ballplayer), a hard-working taxi driver and volunteer fireman; and Bill's girlfriend, Coo, a rich chick from the tony part of Chirpendale. After a circus parade rolls in, Coo almost becomes lovebird *flambé* when the Black Menace strikes. The Menace bullies his way around like Godzilla at large in Tokyo and knocks over a streetcar before he appropriates a match from the matchstick fence of Beatrice Fairfinch, local matchmaker, and sets fire to the hotel where Coo happens to be residing.

The villagers have developed a crow-raid alert (what with the Menace being the only member of the cast that seems capable of flying) and a plan to settle his hash, but so far all they have managed is to get everybody out of the way of an attack. Then, during that long circus sequence featuring some crazy bird tricks, the Menace strikes again. This time, Bill and his pals will take care of the fiend—thanks to a warning from a disturbing character called Johnny Loon, formally referred to by the narrators as the Village Idiot. Bill and Coo touch beaks and peck at one another's outfits during a wedding ceremony. The End.

Ken Murray (1903–1988) was one of those Hollywood-insider types, much more a personality than an actor or a filmmaker, a radio star who achieved his greatest fame during the emerging Television Age by wagging his home movies of big-screen stars around to various talk and variety shows. Like the wily, glad-handing press agent and the fifth-a-day hard-boiled entertainment columnist, Murray was a stereotype-in-the-flesh who could not have existed outside Golden Age Hollywood, a hustler and searcher for ticket-selling gimmickry in a day before such things took on their current tawdry nature. Murray also was a nightclub-act entrepreneur, recycling concepts left over from Vaudeville with a program called *Ken Murray's Blackouts.*

Bill and Coo had its origins in the live-action *Blackouts*—the entire picture, in fact, seems built around the multi-act circus scene, in which such traditional big-top attractions as trapeze and high-wire artists, strongmen and Wild West riders are re-imagined with birds. Those acts probably came directly from the *Blackouts*, along with many of the puns that run through the picture: A tuxedo shop advertises *tails*; a statue memorializes the Wrong Bros., First Birds to Walk; and the character of Beatrice Fairfinch is a nod to the then-famous advice-to-the-lovelorn columnist Beatrice Fairfax.

Bill and Coo's director and co-writer, Dean Reisner, would resurface as an actor in his dad Charles F. Reisner's *The Cobra Strikes*, coming up presently. The film also yielded a phonograph-record spin-off album, from the Mercury label's kid-stuff subsidiary.

Whatever else it may be, *Bill and Coo* is unique among the *Forgotten Horrors* selections as an Academy Award winner (though hardly the only one to garner a candidacy). Granted, the accolade fell outside the Motion Picture Academy's best-in-show categories, acknowledging "Patience and Artistry... novel and entertaining use of the medium," but it was nonetheless a sure-enough Oscar. Of course, one can readily see how that old pro Murray worked the system, calling up friends and calling in favors at the newspapers, the tradesheets and the Academy, laboring hard and long for a line of notice here, and on-the-air mention there—and in the process, helping to create a bit of legend not only for his strange little film, but for himself as well.

CREDITS: Producer: Ken Murray; Director: Dean Reisner; Assistant Director: Don Verk; Screenplay: Royal Foster and Dean Reisner; Photographed by: Jack Marta; Editor: Harold Minter; Sets: Fred Malatesta; Backgrounds: Imagineering; Music: David Buttolph; Musical Director: Lionel Newman; Songs: "Hum a Little Tune" and "Off to the Circus" by David Buttolph, Lionel Newman and Royal Foster, and "Tweet-Tweet," by Buddy DeSylva, Lew Brown and Ray Henderson; Sound: Howard Wilson and T.A. Carman; Running Time: 61 minutes; Released: March 28, 1948

CAST: George Burton's Love Birds (Themselves); Curly Twiford's Jimmy the Crow (the Black Menace); and George Burton, Elizabeth Walters, Ken Murray

IN WHICH THE FALCON KEEPS AN APPOINTMENT ON POVERTY ROW

(Falcon Productions, Inc./Film Classics, Inc.)

RKO-Radio Pictures had shepherded Michael Arlen's highbrow but hard-boiled detective character, the Falcon, through 13 feature-films spanning much of the 1940s, starting out with George Sanders as the (or *a*) Falcon, then shifting gears with the fifth film to introduce Tom Conway—in waking life, Sanders' brother—as a blood-kin Falcon. Two years after the end of the RKO series, an *ad hoc* outfit called Falcon Productions hacked out three films (laundry-listed below) with John Calvert as an entirely different chap known as the Falcon. The series would resume on television (1954–1955) as *Adventures of the Falcon*, with Charles McGraw picking up where Calvert had left off.

• *Devil's Cargo*—The Falcon takes on a client named Delgado (Paul Marion), who readily confesses to murder but may be involved in treacheries even shadier. When the admitted killer turns up dead in a jail cell, the investigation leads the Falcon to a bowling alley locker where Delgado had deposited an ominous package: a bomb that detonates upon opening, killing a thug (Tom Kennedy) who had been trailing Delgado. The deepening conspiracy—involving poisonings, reciprocal double-crosses and infidelity—emerges as a quick-sketch portrait of humankind at its most monstrous. Calvert makes an adequately sophisticated Falcon, but his screen presence isn't a patch on that of either Sanders or Conway. Lapsed big-time leading lady Rochelle Hudson, in the midst of a tentative comeback, has a tough, showy role as Delgado's widow, a shady character in

her own right. An element of magic-trickery showmanship lends a welcome touch of the bizarre, and this Falcon keeps on hand a camera-savvy dog that should have returned for the sequels. Michael Mark's appearance here represents a character unrelated to either of his distinct roles in the next two *Falcon* features, so continuity be damned.

CREDITS: Producer: Philip N. Krasne; Director: John F. Link; Assistant Director: Mack Wright; Screenplay: Don Martin; Scenario: Jason James and Robert Tallman; Based Upon: Michael Arlen's Character; Photographed by: Walter Strenge; Musical Score: Karl Hajos; Musical Director: Paul Dessau; Editor: Asa Boyd Clark; Decor: Tommy Thompson; Makeup: Ted Larsen; Hair Stylist: Gale McGarry; Production Manager: Dick L'Estrange; Sound: Glen Glenn; Special Effects: Ray Mercer; Operative Cameraman: George Clemens; Stills; James Doolittle; Script Supervisor: Mary Gibsone; Grip: Fred Russell; Wardrobe: Donald S. Wakeling; Running Time: 64 minutes; Released: April 1, 1948

CAST: John Calvert (Michael "The Falcon" Waring); Roscoe Karns (Lt. Hardy); Rochelle Hudson (Margo Delgado); Theodore von Eltz (Thomas Mallon); Lyle Talbot (Johnny Morello); Paul Marion (Ramon Delgado); Tom Kennedy (Naga); Paul Regan (Bernie Horton); Eula Guy (Mrs. Murphy); Michael Mark (Salvation Army Captain); Walter Soderling (Coroner); and John Bagni, Fred Coby, Carol Janis, Christine Larsen (a.k.a. Larson), Peter Michael, Dick Rush, Peggy Wynne

• *Appointment with Murder*—Lmx½

The fastest-paced of this lot, *Appointment with Murder* pivots upon an art-thievery plot with an international setting. The big set piece involves an abduction and beating for the Falcon, who turns the tables upon his tormentors with a rousing display of firepower. Peter Brocco stands out as a mastermind whose plan to flood the market with counterfeit canvases is interrupted by his slaying. Jack Reitzen steals the show as a criminal mastermind, and Catherine Craig serves well as a gallery owner who might or might not be in on the scam. The prevailing air is suffused with dread and shadowy menace, with a too-good-for-the-circumstances job of camerawork by Walter Strenge.

CREDITS: Producer and Director: Jack Bernhard; Assistant Director: Frank Fox; Screenplay: Don Martin; Scenario: Joel Malone and Harold Swanton; Based Upon: Michael Arlen's Character; Photographed by: Walter Strenge; Musical Score: Karl Hajos; Editor: Asa Boyd Clark; Decor: Earl Wooden; Costumer: Emanuel Barton; Makeup: Ted Larsen; Production Manager: George Moskov; Sound: Ferol Redd; Operative Cameraman: Wilbur Bradley; Script Supervisor: Mary Gibsone; Grip: Fred Russell; Stills: Al St. Hilaire;

Aside from John Wooley

Claremore, Oklahoma, which lies some 15 miles down Historic Route 66 from my house, is famous as the final resting place of Will Rogers, whose mortal remains lie beneath a first-rate museum called the Will Rogers Memorial. At one time, the town also was famous for its mineral springs and baths, which were said to have curative powers.

Claremore is less well known as the city that spawned Rochelle Hudson, who was well past her big-studio prime when *The Devil's Cargo* came along. In movies (including a first-generation *Forgotten Horrors* entry called *Savage Girl*) since the early '30s, Hudson had achieved a degree of notoriety—at least in her hometown—by proclaiming, "Claremore stinks!" to an interviewer, early in her career. She would make a more decisive comeback (of sorts) during the Old-Gal Horror Craze of the middle 1960s, when she supported Joan Crawford in *Strait-Jacket* and Barbara Stanwyck in *The Night Walker* (both from 1965). Around that time, Hudson proved herself unrepentant by declaring: "Claremore still stinks!"

Although the assertion is not true these days, Hudson had been correct. The mineral springs in the town gave off a pungent and distinctive odor, and everyone who'd ever lived in or near Claremore—Hudson included—was familiar with that ubiquitous smell. A joke whose origins probably stretch back many decades was still around in the Claremore area during the 1960s: The conductor on a passenger train sits down with the notion of catching a couple of winks, but no sooner has he settled into slumber than someone next to him breaks off a powerful burst of flatulence. Automatically, the conductor jumps up, loudly announcing: "Claremore!"

CAST: John Calvert (Michael "The Falcon" Waring); Catherine Craig (Lorraine Brinckley); Jack Reitzen (Norman Benedict); Lyle Talbot (Fred Muller); Peter Brocco (Giuseppe Donatti); Ben Welden (Minecci); Robert Conte (Count Dano); Jay Griffith (Detective); Pat Lane (Customs Official); Michael Mark (Baggage Clerk); Carlos Schipa (Farella); Eric Wilton (Butler); Anna [a.k.a. Ann] Demetrio (Woman); Carole Donne (Miss Connors); Barbara Frcking (Model); Eugene Gericke and Frank Richards (Thugs); Carl Sklover (Guard); Jack Chefe (Clerk); and James Griffith

• *Search for Danger*—The Falcon finds himself trailed while trailing a shady nightclub operator, Larry Andrews (Mauritz Hugo), on orders from Andrews' partners. Andrews and the Falcon's shadow (Peter Brocco), turn up murdered during a search for an embezzled fortune. Sad-eyed Michael Mark—the bereaved father of 1931's *Frankenstein* and the renegade scientist of *The Wasp Woman* (1960)—upstages the formidable likes of Albert Dekker and Ben Welden in the villainy and/or red-herring departments. Mark's big unmasking scene, figuratively speaking, is a marvel of over-acted ferocity and indignation. Leading man John Calvert's career was fast winding down; his last turn on screen, in 1956's *Dark Venture*, would occur under the reverse-spelling name of Trevlac.

CREDITS: Producer and Screenwriter: Don Martin; Associate Producer: George Moskov; Director: Jack Bernhard; Scenario: Jerome Epstein; Based Upon: Michael Arlen's Character; Photographed by: Paul Ivano; Musical Score: Karl Hajos; Editor: Asa Boyd Clark; Art Director: Boris Leven; Makeup: Ted Larsen; Sound: Ferol Redd; Wardrobe: Robert Martien; Running Time: 64 minutes; Released: April 8, 1949

CAST: John Calvert (Michael "The Falcon" Waring); Myrna Dell (Wilma Rogers); Albert Dekker (Kirk); Ben Welden (Gregory); Michael Mark (Mr. Perry); Douglas Fowley (Inspector); James Griffith (Lt. Cooper); Billy Nelson (Gunman); Anna [a.k.a. Ann] Cornell (Elaine Carson); Peter Brocco (Morris Jason); Mauritz Hugo (Larry Andrews); Jack Daly (Drunkard); Peter Michael (Jailer)

THE HUNTED

(Allied Artists Productions, Inc./Monogram
Pictures Corp./Scott R. Dunlap Productions)

Identity crisis time, here, for Monogram Pictures—much as it had been for Producers Releasing Corporation in its irreversible evolution to Eagle-Lion Pictures. Monogram's transformation to Allied Artists was no casual development, but rather a long-in-coming process whose origins dated at least as far back as the King Bros. production company's attempts to raise the little studio's standards. (See the Index of *Forgotten Horrors 3* and spare us all a digression.) By the last-gasp years of the 1940s, such influence had spread companywide, but Monogram was too valuably tenured a crowd-pleasing brand among the working-class and genre-fan audiences for AA to dismiss cavalierly. Said the tradepaper *Variety* of *The Hunted*: "Doesn't rate the Allied Artists releasing label." The greater irony at play here is that Allied Artists never quite made the grade as a classier studio—and soon into the 1950s had reverted to low-budget fare as likeably dreadful and occasionally inspired as anything from the shabbier heyday of Monogram during the '40s.

Convicted bandit Laura Mead (Belita), once a championship ice skater, had threat-ened to kill Los Angeles plainclothes-man Johnny Saxon (Preston Foster), her former fiancé, and lawyer Simon Rand (Pierre Watkin). And so both men have a keen if apprehensive interest in the circumstances of her parole. Inas-much as Belita, a Real World skating star who tended to work that talent into her movie roles, is handling the jailbird part, one might reasonably assume the character's innocence. Belita was hardly the *femme fatale* type, although her looks had by now coarsened somewhat from the slightly earlier *Suspense* and *The Gangster*.

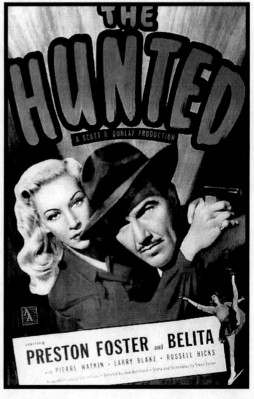

Laura comes looking for Johnny, with anything but murder in mind. She turns angry, however, when he voices an abiding belief in her guilt. She maintains that she had been framed, and he musters enough faith to help Laura resume her career. When Rand turns up slain, the evidence implicates Laura, who turns ferocious when Johnny makes a move to haul her downtown. There follows a cross-country pursuit during which Laura goes incognito as a short-order waitress. Meanwhile, Laura's purported accomplice (Larry Blake) 'fesses up to both pertinent crimes, clearing her. When Johnny finally tracks Laura to a desert-wasteland diner to tell her the good news, she opens fire on him and scrams. After a hitch in a hospital, he hasn't any better sense than to settle down with her.

Jack Bernhard, whose name is all over these pages, was overall a more capable director than much of his work here indicates. *The Hunted* is a pretty sorry example of Bernhard's artistry—if a director's job is to inspire, then Preston Foster must have been beyond the reach of inspiration—but Belita overacts her heart out as if in compensation. Her game show of desperate resentment qualifies merely as a nice try, but her ice-skating sequence is a jim-dandy.

CREDITS: Producer: Scott R. Dunlap; Associate Producer: Glenn Cook; Director: Jack Bernhard; Assistant Director: Frank Fox; Story and Screenplay: Steve Fisher; Photographed by: Harry Neumann; Musical Score: Edward J. Kay; Editor: Richard Heermance; Art Director: F. Paul Sylos; Decor: Raymond Boltz, Jr.; Production Manager: Charles J. Bigelow; Sound: Tom Lambert; Operative Cameraman: Robert "Bob" Gough; Script Supervisor: Moree Herring; Technical Director: Ernest R. Hickson; Grip: Harry Lewis; Stills: Talmadge Morrison; Running Time: 88 minutes; Released: April 7, 1948

CAST: Preston Foster (Johnny Saxon); Belita (Laura Mead); Pierre Watkin (Simon Rand); Edna Holland (Miss Turner); Russell Hicks (Meredith); Frank Ferguson (Harrison); Joseph Crehan (Police Captain); Larry Blake (Hollis Smith); Cathy Carter (Sally); Thomas Jackson, Charles McGraw and Tristram Coffin (Detectives); Ernie Adams (Attendant); George Chandler (Joe); Tom Fadden (Passenger); Rory Mallinson (Highway Patrolman); and Paul Guilfoyle

MONEY MADNESS
(Sigmund Neufeld Pictures, Inc./Film Classics, Inc.)

… limited to the dualers and nabes.—A spot
of "Say *what*?" from the *Variety* review

What the *Variety* critic meant by that rather cavalier dismissal of Sam Newfield's *Money Madness*, translates from archaic show-speak as this: "This picture is worth no more than a double-bill [*dualer*] or neighborhood-theater [*nabe*] engagement." Too bad such colorful lingo hasn't survived the passage of time.

Money Madness survives nicely, however, into an age when the only double-bill showings are those which one programs for oneself on the video-playback carousel and practically every residence on any given street serves as a neighborhood theater. And more power to it, for despite a conspicuous shabbiness—Sigmund Neufeld's production unit was pinching the pennies particularly hard this time out—the little film boasts a redoubtable impersonation of a psychopathic killer from Hugh Beaumont. Yes, *that* Hugh Beaumont. And no, the title is not merely figurative.

Psychopathic killer Hugh Beaumont insinuates his way into the unhappy household of Frances Rafferty, left, and Cecil Weston in Sam Newfield's rough-and-ready *Money Madness*.

Taxi jockey Steve Clark (Beaumont) has hidden $200,000 in ill-gotten currency in anticipation of the day when he can start spending it without arousing suspicions. Seducing a waitress named Julie Saunders (Frances Rafferty) into a tense, secretive marriage, Clark brings about the convenient death of Julie's crotchety aunt (Cecil Watson), then arranges to pass off the hidden loot as Julie's inheritance.

Clark's machinations grow ever more brutal as Julie's misgivings deepen, although she has no better gumption than to submit. Her dawning attraction to lawyer Donald Harper (Harlan Warde), who is unaware of any marriage, only complicates matters after Clark murders a former accomplice (Danny Morton) and enlists Julie's help in disposing of the corpse. A confrontation with Harper looks like curtains for the lawyer and the captive bride, but Clark makes the mistake of cranking the volume on a radio to mask the sound of gunfire. The racket attracts a patrol car, and the cops arrive in time to gun down Clark before he can dispatch Harper and Julie. Julie lands a hitch in prison, with a vague promise that Harper will be awaiting her release.

Top-billed Beaumont plays the vicious role with all due discomfort. Harlan Warde is similarly effective as the unwitting interloper who takes a while to see through Beaumont's scam. Frances Rafferty looks quite the part of a susceptible low-life who deserves better but probably won't get it. Supporting actress Cecil Watson has some show-stopping moments as a kvetching hypochondriac. Newfield allows the extravagant performances to do most of his work.

Dreams That Money Can Buy

CREDITS: Producer: Sigmund Neufeld; Director: Sam Newfield (as Peter Stewart); Assistant Director: Stanley Neufeld; Screenplay: Al Martin; Photographed by: Jack Greenhalgh; Editor: Holbrook N. Todd; Decor: Harry Reif; Makeup: Harry Ross; Production Manager: Bert Sternbach; Props: Eugene C. Stone; Sound: Ben Winkler; Special Effects: Ray Mercer; Musical Director: Leo Erdody; Running Time: 73 minutes; Released: April 15, 1948

CAST: Hugh Beaumont (Steve Clark); Frances Rafferty (Julie Saunders); Harlan Warde (Donald Harper); Cecil Watson (Aunt Cora); Ida Moore (Mrs. Ferguson); Danny Morton (Rogers); Joel Friedkin (Wagner); Lane Chandler (Policeman); Don C. Harvey (Harry); Gladys Blake (Martha); Carol Donne (Photo Clerk)

RUHTLESS

(Producing Artists, Inc./Arthur S. Lyons Productions/
Eagle-Lion Films, Inc./Pathé Industries, Inc.)

Edgar G. Ulmer's *Ruthless* marks an escalating bid for renewed respectability from an artist who had started out in the big time, fumbled his chances by alienating Universal

Pictures (during production of 1934's *The Black Cat*), and then held his breath indefinitely as a mainstay of the lower-echelon studios. His rallying with a powerful *little* picture, 1945's *Detour*, had encouraged Ulmer to aim higher the next time and the next. He came away from a triumphant showing on the musical sudser *Carnegie Hall* (1947) with a determination to establish *Ruthless* as an epic saga of an American life.

His failure to do so—and *Ruthless* is nothing to bear mentioning in the same breath with such similarly concerned films as William Wyler's *Dodsworth* (1936) and Orson Welles' *Citizen Kane* (1941)—is no shame, for the film is at least an interesting misfire, with moments of brilliance. Built around a monstrously effective portrait of rampant megalomania from Zachary Scott, *Ruthless* comes prepared to ride out the crippling shortcomings of a self-important and cliché-ridden screenplay, an overlong running time, and an affected directing style that lacks the straightforward ferocity of prime Ulmer. The secret screenwriter, Alvah Bessie, was among talents blacklisted in the postwar Commie-buster purges; this insight helps to explain the vitriolic bitterness that courses through the film.

Plutocrat Horace Woodruff Vendig (Scott) endows an anti-war foundation to the tune of $25 million. This show of tax-advantage generosity triggers an extended flashback, as related by Vendig's former associate, Vic Lambdin (Louis Hayward). The reflections illustrate Vendig's struggle from poverty to power. He seems to have wrecked one life after another while en route to his present state of contrived benevolence. The suicide of a wronged colleague—a discreetly played shocker, enacted with all due desperation by Charles Evans—fuels a crisis that peaks in an oceanside confrontation between Lambdin and Vendig.

As the fallen-out friends harangue one another, there arrives the mountainous Sydney Greenstreet—playing an industrialist named Mansfield, whose wife and whose company Vendig had stolen—bent upon murder. Mansfield and Vendig topple from a pier and drown without so much as a fare-thee-well.

Scott dominates the proceedings with a performance that reminded *Variety* of Budd Schulberg's famous novel of haywire ambition, *What Makes Sammy Run?* Greenstreet, as a once-powerful, now-broken tycoon, makes a formidable Nemesis. Lucille Bremer, as Greenstreet's wife, captures well the vanity that drives her to Scott and the dawning realization that she has been played for a fool. Raymond Burr has a creepy turn as Scott's flamboyant father. The jolting payoff is worth the wait: The only bad Edgar Ulmer, really, is no Edgar Ulmer.

CREDITS: Producer: Arthur S. Lyons; Associate Producer: Joseph Justman; Director: Edgar G. Ulmer; Assistant Director: Marty Moss; Screenplay: Alvah Bessie (Unacknowledged), S.K. Lauren and Gordon Kahn; Based Upon: Dayton Stoddart's 1945 Novel, *Prelude to Night*; Photographed by: Bert Glennon; Musical Score: Werner Janssen; Musical Director: Paul Dessau; Editor: Francis D. Lyon; Casting Director: Barbara Canterbury; Art Director: Frank Sylos; Decor: Edward Robinson; Costumer: Don Loper; Hair Stylist: Helen Lierley; Makeup: Bob Littlefield; Sound: Max Hutchinson; Special Effects: William Simpson; Operative Cameraman: Wilbur Bradley; Aide to Mr. Ulmer: Hugh MacMullan; Grip: C.O. Morris; Stills: Morrison B. Paul; Script Supervisor: Shirley Ulmer; Running Time: 105 minutes; Released: Following World Premiere in Chicago on April 16, 1948

CAST: Zachary Scott (Horace Woodruff Vendig); Louis Hayward (Vic Lambdin); Diana Lynn (Martha Burnside and Mallory Flagg); Sydney Greenstreet (Buck Mansfield); Lucille Bremer (Christa Mansfield); Martha Vickers (Susan Duane); Edith Barrett (Mrs. Burnside); Dennis Hoey (Burnside); Raymond Burr (Pete Vendig); Joyce Arling (Kate Vendig); Charles Evans (Bruce Endicott McDonald); Robert "Bob" Anderson (Horace Vendig, as a Child); Arthur Stone (Vic Lambdin, as a Child); Ann Carter (Martha Burnside, as a Child); Edna Holland (Libby Sims); Frederic Worlock (J. Norton Sims); John Good (Bradford Duane); Claire Carleton (Bella); Douglas Evans (George); and Harry Cheshire

THE NOOSE HANGS HIGH

(Abbott & Costello Productions, Inc./Eagle-Lion Films, Inc./Pathé Industries, Inc.)

Bud Abbott and Lou Costello, beloved funnymen of the burlesque-into-cinema school, had spent the war years as a Midas-touch act for Universal Pictures. Such hits as *Buck Privates*, *Hold That Ghost*, *Who Done It?* and *Here Come the Co-Eds* (1941–1945) made the partners as popular with a massed audience as Stan Laurel and Oliver Hardy had been during the 1920s and '30s. Backstage tensions and resentments, however, combined with a repetitive team-comedy *shtick* to lessen the ticket-selling appeal of Abbott & Costello (the ampersand implies a public image greater than the sum of its parts) during the post-WWII period.

As the decade waned, the merger-driven re-incorporation of Universal as Universal–International cost the team a great deal of the security to which its players had grown accustomed. Chronic estrangements between Abbott and Costello (and see how the absence of an ampersand diminishes the presence?) came to such a head at times that the occasional picture—1946's *The Time of Their Lives*, for example—found the artists enacting essentially solo roles despite shared star billing. Hit-and-miss successes notwithstanding, they remained popular, awaiting only a restoration of the seemingly magical spell they had cast with *Buck Privates*, their second film. After all, their first big-screen venture, 1940's *One Night in the Tropics*, hardly had been a success, so patience must count for something.

The comics, resilient and resourceful, had better sense than to part ways: Art will see you through times of compromised income better than money will see you through times of lapsed artistry. For *The Noose Hangs High*, an interim picture undertaken independently after Universal–International had balked at Costello's demands for higher pay, they pooled their interests as Abbott & Costello Productions, Inc. This *ad hoc* company provided a number of board positions for members of Costello's family, the less overtly Anglicized

Cristillo clan. In a practical inspiration, Abbott & Costello hired Charles Barton, the boys' director-of-record since 1946, as producer-director. Barton's style is enough by itself to make the film look bigger than its modest origins would indicate; technical values, especially the photography, approach Universal's B-picture standard. By the time *Noose* had wrapped, U–I was ready to begin developing *Bud Abbott & Lou Costello Meet Frankenstein* (1948)—a triumphant resurgence.

The Noose Hangs High was completed during late 1947 and acquired for distribution by Eagle-Lion, the slightly more upscale permutation of Producers Releasing Corporation. Eagle-Lion released the film with a three-month head start on the Barton-directed *A&C Meet Frankenstein*, which had gone before the cameras about six weeks after the completion of *Noose*.

Noose follows the formula of casting Abbott as the arrogant manipulator who fancies himself in charge of Costello's childlike bumbler—with the predictable device of their falling into dangerous company. Window washers Ted Higgins (Abbott) and Homer Hinchcliffe (Costello), mistaken for mob couriers, are ordered to deliver a wad of cash. The payload goes missing, only to turn up in the hands of an innocent (Cathy Downs), who spends most of the loot before Ted and Homer can catch up

Abbott and Costello released *The Noose Hangs High* through Eagle-Lion Films rather than Universal.

with her. There follows a scheme to parlay the remaining stake into a winning racetrack bet before the hoodlums can do away with Ted and Homer.

Joseph Calleia is a suitably menacing small-time mobster, and Leon Errol—who had been a favorite foil of W.C. Fields, as well as a comedy-series star in his own right—strengthens the yarn considerably as a can't-lose (or *can* he?) gambler. Calleia's threats are no sham, and Abbott & Costello seem throughout in mortal peril. Mike Mazurki and Jack Overman lend both intimidation and numbskull humor as Calleia's henchmen. The bad guys' climactic humiliation—mired in a load of wet concrete with which they had intended to do away with Bud & Lou—makes for a nice touch of boneheaded irony. Cathy Downs, a former Fox contractee who had seemed destined for bigger things, is pleasantly spirited as Costello's might-be love interest, who out-foxes the crooks at their own game.

Abbott & Costello's all-important slapstick and surreal wordplay are generously deployed, especially in a high-anxiety window-washing scenario and in a routine called *You Can't Be Here*, a variant upon the famous *Who's on First?* exchange. Abbott told us during the late 1960s that he and Costello had drawn much of their inspiration for the verbal business from Moran & Mack, a white-guy team of the 1920s who performed in blackface and specialized in double-talk disorientation, and from the black artists Flournoy E. Miller and Mantan Moreland—in particular, Miller & Moreland's *Indefinite Talk* routine, in which each would finish the other's sentences in a rapid-fire exchange.

CREDITS: Producer and Director: Charles Barton; Production Supervisor: James T. Vaughn; Associate Producers: Lolly Cristillo and Shirley Feld; Assistant Director: Howard W. Koch; Screenplay: John Grant and Howard Harris; Adapted from a Screenplay by: Charles Grayson & Arthur T. Horman; Story: Daniel Taradash, Julian Blaustein and Bernard Fins; Photographed by: Charles Van Enger; Special Photographic Effects: George J. Teague; Special Art Effects: Jack R. Rabin; Art Director: Edward L. Ilou; Editor: Harry Reynolds; Decor: Armor Marlowe; Costumer: France Ehren; Music: Walter Schumann; Orchestrations: Arthur Morton; Musical Director: Irving Friedman; Sound: Leon S. Becker and Robert Pritchard; Makeup: Ern Westmore and Russell Drake; Hair Stylists: Joan St. Oegger and Gwen Holden; Running Time: 76 minutes; Released: April 17, 1948

Dreams That Money Can Buy

CAST: Bud Abbott (Ted Higgins); Lou Costello (Homer Hinchcliffe); Joseph Calleia (Mike Craig); Leon Errol (J.C. McBride); Cathy Downs (Carol Blair); Mike Mazurki (Chuck); Fritz Feld (Psychiatrist); Jack Overman (Joe); Vera Martin (Elevator Operator); Joe Kirk and Matt Willis (Gangsters); Joan Myles (Secretary); Ben Welden (Stewart); Harry Brown (Upson); Jimmy Dodd and Ben Hall (Messengers); Ellen Corby (Maid); Isabel Randolph (Miss Van Buren); Frank O'Connor (Mailman); Benny Rubin (Chinaman); Bess Flowers (Patient); Murray Leonard (Dentist); Sandra Spence (Dentist's Helper); Pat Flaherty (Roughneck Driver); Alvin Hammer (Tipster); Jerry Marlowe (Cashier); Ralph Montgomery and Fred M. Browne (Waiters); Lois Austin (Woman on Street); Herb Vigran (Man with Coat); James Flavin (Traffic Cop); Lyle Latell (Workman); Paul Maxey (Jeweler); Fred Kelsey (Cop); Minerva Urecal (Husky Woman); James Logan (Valet); Tim Wallace and Chalky Williams (Cabbies); Arno Frey (Headwaiter); Russell Hicks (Manager); Oscar Otis (Racetrack Announcer); and Irmgard Dawson, Elvia Allman

CAMPUS SLEUTH

(Monogram Productions, Inc./Monogram Distributing Corp.)

Stranglers-at-large and carefree American youth make a wholesome combination for any comedy franchise—just ask Frankie Darro and Mantan Moreland, whose wartime starring series had dealt almost entirely in murder mo' foulest—and Will Jason's *Campus Sleuth* is no exception. As a last gasp for Monogram's *Teenagers* series, *Campus Sleuth* takes things out on a note of frantic adventure with a genuinely baffling whodunit angle and a killer who means business. The picture is nonetheless pretty blasted silly.

Homicide Inspector Watson (Donald MacBride), a no-nonsense sort and don't you forget it, cracks down on his collegian son, Lee Watson (Warren Mills), for reading too many murder mysteries and not enough textbooks. All that pulp-literature may be affecting Lee's senses, for after the kid stumbles onto the scene of a slaying and rushes to report the crime to his father, he returns to find no such evidence.

Sounds to us like a setup for the old familiar vanishing-corpse routine, and sure enough: Lee grows ever more determined to prove to his dad that a murder *was, too* committed—he even claims to know the identity of the victim, a magazine photographer named Dunkel (Charles Campbell)—while the inspector begins to wonder whether Lee might bear commitment to a nuthouse.

Lee vindicates himself through sheer stubborn gumption, however, finally turning up the cadaver hidden among the effects of an orchestra that has been hired to entertain on campus. The likeliest culprit, the musicians' road manager (Billy Snyder), proves culpable but merely a pawn in a larger scheme. Finally, Lee and his classmates peg bandleader Bobby Davis (real-life bandleader Bobby Sherwood) as the killer, and the victim as a crook who had merely gotten what was coming

Forgotten Horrors 4

to him. Which amounts to some pretty ferocious going, for a series that is scarcely more than a poor man's *Andy Hardy* franchise.

Producer-director Will Jason was a versatile composer and screenwriter, as well, and his grasp of mortal terror is established beyond question in a little gem from Columbia's B-picture unit called *The Soul of a Monster* (1944). Jason seems more interested in the criminal shenanigans of *Campus Sleuth* than in the imitation-*Archie* business, and his deployment of dance-band music serves both facets of the story. A highlight is an appearance by the great jazz singer Mildred "Little Miss Cornshucks" Gorman. Bobby Sherwood shines as the energetic bandleader and hits the right notes of desperation when unmasked as the killer.

CREDITS: Producer and Director: Will Jason; Associate Producer: Maurice Duke; Assistant Director: William Calihan, Jr.; Screenplay: Hal Collins; Based Upon: a Story by Hal Collins and Max Wilson (a.k.a. Joel Malone); Photographed by: Mack Stengler; Musical Score: Will Jason, Bobby Sherwood and Freddie Stewart; Lyricist: Sid Robbin; Musical Director: Edward J. Kay; Songs: "Sherwood's Forest" and "Jump for Joey" by Bobby Sherwood, and "Jungle Rhumba" by Tony Beaulieu; Editors: Otho Lovering and William Austin; Art Director: Dave Milton; Decor: Raymond Boltz, Jr.; Production Manager: Glenn Cook; Western Electric Sound: John Carter; Grip: George Booker; Operative Cameraman: William Margulies; Stills: Talmadge Morrison; Script Clerk: Bobbie Sierks; Running Time: 58 minutes; Released: April 18, 1948

CAST: Freddie Stewart (Freddie Trimball); June Preisser (Dodie Rogers); Warren Mills (Lee Watson); Noel Neill (Betty Rogers); Donald MacBride (Inspector Watson); Monte Collins (Dean McKinley); Stan Rose (Winkler); Bobby Sherwood (Bobby Davis); Billy Snyder (Ronnie Wallace); William Norton Bailey (Coroner); Charles Campbell (Dunke); Paul Bryar (Houser); George Eldredge (Officer Edwards); Dottye Brown (Telegraph Clerk); Harry Taylor (Husband); Margaret Bert (Wife); Lane Chandler (Cop); Joey Preston (Joey); Mildred "Little Miss Cornshucks" Jorman (Herself); Jimmy Grisson (Boy); George Fields (Roadie); Gerri Galian (Singer)

DREAMS THAT MONEY CAN BUY
(Art of This Century Films, Inc.)

During its opening day at the Fifth Avenue Playhouse in New York, *Dreams That Money Can Buy* frequently wandered off the movie screen and onto the theater's ceiling, prompting audiences to whistle and clap and a *Variety* critic to speculate that "the [projector] operators must have been doping out their next day's horse bets."

Well, maybe. But more likely, it was just some of those wacky Dadaists upping the Surrealist ante—and having a little artistic fun in the bargain. *Dreams That Money Can Buy*, after all, represented nothing less than an attempt by producer-director-writer Hans Richter (1888-1976) to lay a little of the Old School European avant-garde on American audiences by creating a film in which the likes of Man Ray, Marcel Duchamp, Max Ernst and Alexander Calder would have a chance to strut their stuff.

The result—shot in New York during 1944–1946 at a cost variously reported at $15,000 and $25,000—is unlike anything else you're likely to see, with elements of

This scene captures the avant-garde noir essence of *Dreams That Money Can Buy*, which projectionists often showed on walls and ceilings to add to the mystique.

experimental theater and flights of symbolic and metaphorical fancy wedded to a storyline that seems to be trying for both coherent narrative and incongruous dream-logic. The long stretches of narration over silent footage, the strange imagery, and the odd acting by unknown (however readily identified) players gives the feeling of admission into a dark hidden world, rather in the manner of Edward D. Wood, Jr.

The tragic small-time *auteur* Wood and such a brilliant maverick as Orson Welles may not have been all that different from one another; this notion is persuasively suggested, though left largely unexplored, in Tim Burton's 1992 bio-fantasy *Ed Wood*. Likewise, the line between a Wood exploitation film such as *Glen or Glenda* and some artistically justifiable piece of Surrealist cinema is undeniably thin. Perhaps Wood should have thrown in with the Dadaists instead of attempting to crash Hollywood.

Although the opening credits establish that "this is a story of dreams mixed with reality," the picture falls heavily onto the dream-state side from the outset, when we meet a guy named Joe (Jack Bittner), a man with a new apartment but no prospects. However, as the narrator tells us—in rhyming couplets, no less—Joe has discovered the knack of "looking inside himself," and because of that he is "no longer a bum," but rather an artist. By extension, at least via the perception-equals-reality logic of this film, Joe can now look inside others and thus create the dreams they desire. At least, we *think* that's what he does. Richter seems to be trying hard here to tell a story the masses might vaguely grasp, but he cannot resist the grip of Dada, giving his narrator lines like this one: "Even if poets misbehave / They always remember to shave."

Whatever it is that Joe does, he suddenly has plenty of clients, lined up and looking helpless, right outside his door. The first is a mousy bank clerk, Mr. A. (Schmuel "Sam" Cohen), accompanied by his pushy wife (Ethel Beseda). Joe dismisses the missus, then gets into the husband's dream, which involves a woman with a sphere floating above her lips as a female voiceover observes: "What is innocence but a pair of gloves to warm the hands?" Figures crawl from beneath a bed as a man idly casts a pair of dice.

These images seem to satisfy Mr. A., who pays Joe and makes way for the next client, a woman with sheafs of petitions and membership forms for Joe to sign. "He doesn't understand," explains a narrator. "He has to belong to something. Otherwise, how will he know who he is?" Joe diagnoses the client with "organizational neuroses" (a foreshadowing of Obsessive-Compulsive Disorder?) and then launches into the woman's dream. This fantasy involves crudely animated but nonetheless effective mannequins, jerking about in a courtship ritual accompanied by a *biergarten*-style song about "a girl with a prefabricated heart."

Next up is Mr. A.'s wife—once a girl with poetry in her soul, but now a dull harpy. Her dream involves a carefree, artistic existence, including a sequence in which every member of a movie audience mimics the movement of the character on the screen. (This segment was written and directed by Man Ray, and, unlike the rest of the film, boasts mostly synchronized dialogue rather than off-camera narration.)

By this time, the people outside Joe's door are squabbling, and things take a violent turn when a handcuffed thug enters. The subsequent dream features work from a couple of well-known artists: John Cage does the music, and Marcel Duchamp directs, staging live-action riffs upon his famous painting of 1912, *Nude Descending a Staircase* (this element probably is what earned the film its adults-only designation) along with many scenes of whirling discs, an evocation of the silent-era German Expressionist cinema's use of spiral images to convey chaos. The hoodlum beats Joe and shoves him into a closet. Joe is found by a girl and her blind grandfather. This encounter leads to a couple of dreams about mobiles and wire sculptures. (The direction of both sequences is credited to Alexander Calder, well known for such wire-and-string creations.) A circus sequence utilizing the wire sculptures is especially noteworthy, creating a sense of animation without being animated at all, but manipulated by human hands in real time.

Finally Joe ends up playing cards with three other guys; finds that he has turned blue; becomes an outcast; and tries to follow the cable-like "blue thread of hope" back home. But it is a hopeless task: He finds himself forever changed.

You might find yourself changed, too, after seeing this frequently puzzling and self-consciously radical picture, which retains its challenging uniqueness nearly 60 years after its creation. Throughout, in both the wild flights of artistic indulgence and the more comparatively accessible parts, one can sense the earnestness of Richter, a German immigrant and proponent of European Surrealism who since 1941 had been in charge of the Institute of Film Techniques at City College of New York (where he found several of his actors). As the film unfolds, one can almost see Richter working to balance art and commerce by striving to supply enough narrative hooks to hold an audience, but presenting at the same time an array of uncompromising and sometimes difficult visions. The theme of a person's being altered by art, and, specifically, by a commitment to artistic pursuits,

The BFI (British Film Institute) released this DVD of *Dreams That Money Can Buy*.

shines through undimmed. The extensive use of voiceover and narration instead of dialogue, however, does as much as the dream-like content to force and sustain a distance between the movie and its viewers.

Johannes Siegfried "Hans" Richter spent four decades as a spearhead of the cinematic advance guard. Born in Berlin, he joined the emerging Dadaist movement in 1916 after being mustered out of the German army as an invalid. His interest lay at first in painting, but in 1920–1921 he also had turned to moviemaking. His "Rhythmus 25" (1925), part of a series of shorts, appears to hold pride of place as the first abstract film shot in color.

Having fled Germany, Richter spent the 1930s on several abortive feature-film ventures, including a retelling of the exploits of the world-class crackpot fabulist Baron Munchausen. At this latter project, Richter was beaten to the punch by the German Josef von Báky, whose *Münchausen* (long in production and finally issued in 1943) remains unsurpassed in its combination of heroic fantasy and nightmarish ambiguity.

By 1941, Richter had resettled in New York. During more than a decade at City College, Richter became a mentor to such experimental filmmakers as Maya Deren and Jonas Mekas. And he continued with his own films: In addition to the ambitious *Dreams That Money Can Buy*, he completed the short subject "8–by–8" (1957), a study of his favorite game of strategy, chess; "Dadascope: From Dada to Surrealism" (1961); and "Alexander Calder: From the Circus to the Moon" (1963). Richter moved during the middle 1950s to Switzerland, where he continued painting until his death at 88, early in 1976.

One can only guess what contemporary audiences beyond the art-world intelligentsia thought about *Dreams That Money Can Buy*. There is evidence that the film was seen well outside of those circles—a handbill from the Texas-based Interstate Circuit Theatres features a drawing of a woman lying languorously among bedcovers to promote an "exclusive engagement" of the film, suggesting that the more erotic elements of *Dreams That Money Can Buy* were played up to whatever hinterland audiences the film managed to reach. (We are reminded here of a Southwestern drive-in theater's advertisement, from 1966, for Michelangelo Antonioni's high-minded *Blow-Up*: "Girls! *Girls! GIRLS!*" One catches one's audience as one can, with what gimmicks one can muster.)

Which is as it should be. Art and exploitation have long been intertwined in the popular consciousness. And both have been looked upon with a (sometimes) justifiable suspicion by whatever passes for mainstream society. *Dreams That Money Can Buy*, with its relentless and curiously sensual fever-dream quality, not only supports that idea, but also makes a dandy subtitle for a book about films that flew—and continue to fly—below the radar of that very same society.

Incidentally: A pristine copy of the program booklet for *Dreams That Money Can Buy*, containing art and commentaries by the artists involved, was changing hands for hundreds of dollars-at-a-whack among Internet speculators during the earlier years of the present century.

Max Ernst contributed this fanciful self-portrait to the promotional booklet for *Dreams That Money Can Buy*.

CREDITS: Associate Producer: Kenneth MacPherson; Directors: Hans Richter, Man Ray *et al.*; Assistant Directors: Miriam Raeburn and John Stix; Screenwriters: Hans Richter and Man Ray; Photographed by: Arnold Eagle; Camera Operators: George Lubalin, Meyer Rosenblum and Herman Shulman; Musical Director: Louis Applebaum; Contributing Composers: Louis Applebaum ("Narcissus" Sequences), Paul Bowles ("Desire" and "Ballet"), John Cage ("Discs"), David Diamond ("Circus") and Darius Milhaud ("Ruth, Roses, & Revolvers"); Sound: Stanley Kote; Contributing Art Directors and Designers: Alexander Calder; Marcel Duchamp, Man Ray and Fernand Léger; Max Ernst; Lyricist: John Latouche; Running Time: 99 minutes; Released: Following New York Opening on April 23, 1948

CAST: Ethel Beseda (Mrs. A); Jack Bittner (Joe/Narcissus); Schmuel "Sam" Cohen (Mr. A); Max Ernst (President); Jo Fontaine-Maison (Girl); Bernard Friend (Cop); Bernard Graves (Male Voice); Anthony Laterie (Blind Man); John Latouche (Gangster); Julien Levy and Arthur Seymour (Men); Ruth Sobotka and Valerie Tite (Girls); and Dorothy Griffith, Evelyn Hausman, Jo Mitchell, Ray Pippitt, Miriam Raeburn

THE COBRA STRIKES
(Eagle-Lion Films, Inc./Pathé Industries, Inc.)

Snake venom, brain surgery, a deadly invention, a hovering mystery woman and prevailing cruel intentions—these are a few of our favorite things, but they come together as a muddled mess in *The Cobra Strikes*.

Fourth-billed Herbert Heyes dominates the proceedings in a dual role as an inaugural victim, Dr. Damon Cameron, and his twin, Ted Cameron. It develops that an ambush against Damon (who has survived, with brain damage) probably was meant to prevent the scientist from announcing a medical breakthrough.

Colleagues in Ted's orbit begin dying off under peculiar circumstances. Damon's daughter, Dale Cameron (Sheila Ryan), begins to suspect that her father's invention may have been put to use as a murder weapon. The device proves to be a hypodermic

jet, capable of infusing medication via the pores—except that the lurking killer is using the device to dispense venom.

Ted Cameron's fascination with cobras emerges as a giveaway when he invites Dale to view a reel of expeditionary film he had shot while on safari in India. Damon, recovering, mentions that he had confided to Ted the nature of the invention. The murder victims prove to have been Ted's partners in a jewel-smuggling enterprise. A standoff with Dale as hostage ends in a safe-and-sound clinch for her and a newspaperman (Richard Fraser) who has been following the case.

Heyes' accomplished air of dignity and gathering menace upstages the elements of heroism and romance, although stilted dialogue and coincidence-driven plotting can only defeat all concerned. Silents-into-talkies director Charles F. Reisner, in one of his last handful of assignments, devotes altogether too much attention to a (purportedly) Russian adventuress, played by Leslie Brooks. Her presence proves merely a distraction. Silent-era child actor Dean Reisner, son of the director, appears as a detective; Dean also worked as director and co-author of 1948's *Bill and Coo*; he eventually would develop into a top-drawer screenwriter, a favored scribe of Clint Eastwood.

CREDITS: Executive Producer: Ben Stoloff; Producer: David I. Stephenson; Director: Charles F. Reisner; Story and Screenplay: Eugene Conrad; Photographed by: Eugene Conrad; Special Photographic Effects: George J. Teague; Operative Cameraman: Leland Davis; Stills: Ted Weisbarth; Art Director: Frank E. Durlauf; Editor: Louis Sackin; Decor: Armor Marlowe; Costumer: France Ehren; Musical Director: Irving Friedman; Sound: Leon S. Becker and Perc J. Townsend; Makeup: Ern Westmore and Del Armstrong; Hair Stylists: Joan St. Oegger and Gwen Holden; Production Supervisor: James T. Vaughn;

Script Supervisor: Jack Herzberg; Grip: Louis Kusley; Running Time: 62 minutes; Released: April 24, 1948

CAST: Sheila Ryan (Dale Cameron); Richard Fraser (Mike Kent); Leslie Brooks (Olga Kaminoff); Herbert Heyes (Ted Cameron and Dr. Damon Cameron); James Seay (Capt. Monihan); Richard Loo (Hyder Ali); Lyle Latell (Sgt. Harris); Pat Flaherty (Atlas Kilroy); Philip Ahn (Kasim); Fred Nurney (Franz Lang); Leslie Denison (Morton); George Sorel (Victor Devereaux); Selmer Jackson (Dr. Keating); Howard Negley (Doorman); Dean Reisner (Detective); Vic Cutler (Cop); George Chandler (Janitor); Milton Parsons (Mortician); Virginia Farmer (Housekeeper); and James Logan

THE ARGYLE SECRETS

(Eronel Productions, Inc./Film Classics, Inc.)

Based upon a *Suspense* radio-series drama and centering upon a maguffin involving a book of Nazi-conspirator identities, Cyril Endfield's *The Argyle Secrets* is a striking example of artistry-on-a-budget, with a fascinatingly convoluted quest and a fine heroic turn from William Gargan as a journalist-turned-fugitive.

No sooner has Harry Mitchell (Gargan) been entrusted with scraps of guarded information regarding the elusive Argyle Album, than his mentor, investigative reporter Allen Pierce (George Anderson), is slain. Branded a suspect, Mitchell retrenches underground while attempting to beat an international goon squad to the hiding place of the album, which would serve to expose a ring of Nazi diehards. Both the turncoats and a ring of would-be blackmailers believe that Mitchell must possess the document. Chief

Mickey Simpson and John Banner mingle treason with blackmail to menacing effect in *The Argyle Secrets*.

Dreams That Money Can Buy

blackmailer Winter (John Banner) dispatches an accomplice, Marla (Marjorie Lord), to keep tabs on Mitchell.

Marla experiences a change of heart—sort of—after her backup thugs have treated Mitchell to a beating, and she allows him to escape after revealing to him the sensitive nature of the album. Mitchell resumes the hunt while dodging the law, closing in on a shipyard salvage operator (Alex Fraser) who proves by turns helpful and threatening. A mutually lethal showdown between the salvage man and a blackmail-gang member (Jack Reitzen) prompts Harry to turn himself in, but the police already have discounted him as a suspect: Seems that Pierce's stabbing had been arranged as camouflage for a poisoning.

Marla turns against Winter, who proves to be one of the traitors named in the Argyle Album. Winter and a henchman (Mickey Simpson) corner Mitchell, who sets his antagonists against one another. Marla makes a threatening play to nab the album. Mitchell trumps her move, however, and declares he will publish the incriminating materials as a tribute to Allen Pierce's courage.

The newsgathering racket scarcely could have found a public-relations tool more effective than *The Argyle Secrets*, which casts journalism in a light more adventurous and fulfilling than *The Front Page* and *The Adventures of Superman* combined. As a more true-to-life Clark Kent with no powers greater than stubborn determination, William Gargan not only makes good on an urgent professional commitment but also honors the memory of a slain colleague while outwitting the police, a Nazi-holdout contingent, and the criminal underworld. Even Gargan's outlaw phase is consistent with the character's law-abiding nature: If he should allow the cops to nab him too soon, then they might miss the point. Marjorie Lord justifies her co-star billing with an *almost*-sympathetic presence that gives way at length to the film's most persistent show of villainy. Miss Lord would make her most lasting mark as the television-sitcom wife of Danny Thomas, during the 1957–1965 run of *Make Room for Daddy*.

Cyril Endfield performs triple duty, supplying the original yarn (written for CBS-Radio's *Suspense*), opening it up generously as a screenplay, and directing the piece with a brisk ferocity that covers plenty of dangerous ground in just over an hour's running time. Endfield was one of the great practical eccentrics of the industry, a busy director for three decades and a writer so prolific that he found himself compelled to invent a speed-typing system that allowed the use of only one hand. The patent patriotism of his work notwithstanding, Endfield would find himself blacklisted as a Communist sympathizer as the postwar years wore on. He developed such pseudonyms as Hugh Raker and Jonathan Roach and spent much of his remaining career in England.

From a savage beginning with a hospital-ward attack through the twist ending, *The Argyle Secrets* cracks right along with nary a wasted moment. Endfield also pleased his investors by wrapping the picture in just a week and a day at almost 10 percent below the budgeted cost of $125,000.

CREDITS: Producers: Alan H. Posner and Sam X. Abarbanel; Associate Producer: Albert Bildner; Director and Screenwriter: Cyril Endfield, from His Radio Play of 1945; Assistant Director: Clarence Eurist; Photographed by; Mack Stengler; Operative Cameraman: Fred Kaifer; Stills: Buddy Longworth; Art Director: Rudi Feld; Editor: Gregg Tallas; Decor: Joe Kish; Wardrobe: John E. Dowsing; Music Supervisor: David Chudnow; Musical Score: Ralph Stanley; Sound: Max Hutchison; Makeup: Ted Coodley; Hair Stylist: Ann

Walker; Assistant to the Producers: Raymond Rohauer; Script Supervisor: Mary Gibsone; Grip: Karl Reed; Running Time: 64 minutes; Released: May 7, 1948

CAST: William Gargan (Harry Mitchell); Marjorie Lord (Marla); Ralph Byrd (Dr. Samuel Samson); Jack Reitzen (Panama); John Banner (Winter); Barbara Billingsley (Elizabeth Court); Alex Fraser (Jor McBrod); Peter Brocco (Scanlon); George Anderson (Allen Pierce); Mickey Simpson (Gil); Alvin Hammer (Pinky); Carol Donne (Nurse); Mary Tarcai (Mrs. Rubin); Robert Kellard (Melvyn); Kenneth Greenwald (Gerald); Herbert Rawlinson (Dr. Van Selbin)

HITLER'S STRANGE LOVE LIFE

a.k.a.: Love Life of Adolph [sic] Hitler; Conform or Die!
You Conform or Die!; Mussolini Speaks; Will it Happen Again?;
Will it Happen Again? The Personal Life of Hitler;
Uncompleted Re-Edit: Day of the Despot
(American Film Producers/Film Classics, Inc./Navy Club of the U.S.A.)

They may not have saved Hitler's brain, after all (whoever *they* are). But they did

manage to salvage Hitler's Braun — Eva, that is — along with a generous representation of der Fuehrer himself at play amidst the strangeness and charm of his native turf, in banally pernicious home-movie footage retrieved from the wreckage of the Third Reich. This closest possible approximation of identifiable mortal remains impressed the hellbent-for-Cold War Navy Club of the United States of America as sufficiently authentic to merit incorporating into a postwar propaganda manifesto.

But the real brains behind the film belong to that cunning old-time exploitation-film impresario, Dwain Esper.

Amazing, how Esper (1892-1982) kept finding new ways to bait the suckers with the same old hook, line and stinkers, time and again, though more or less retired from active filmmaking by the 1940s and more keenly concerned with his movie-theater and burlesque-show interests. A fundamental presence in the *Forgotten Horrors* canon, Esper is of course responsible for the 1934 *Maniac*, along with *Marihuana, Weed with Roots in Hell*—both of which feigned social responsibility while dispensing anti-social sensationalism—and for that strip-tease primer disguised as a therapeutic marital aid, *How to Undress in Front of Your Husband*. These are prominent among the Esper studios' pageant of ratty delights, many of them considered within this series of books.

The production history of *Hitler's Strange Love Life* is a tangle, starting with Esper's questionable acquisition of footage seized following the collapse of Nazi Germany and progressing through several re-edits, with or without Esper's involvement. Esper had quit the filmmaking-from-scratch game around 1937, but he and his wife, Hildegarde Stadie Esper, continued to assemble patchwork features from found-object footage.

Mrs. Esper's *A Japanese Pipe Dream*, from 1943, is such a cobbled-together job, combining the ticket-selling appeal of drug racketeering with an Axis-buster zeal. A more elusive and doubtless more remarkable entry is the Esper production of *Curse of the Ubangi* (which see), which would seem to have made a rapturously incoherent use of stock footage as a feature-length expansion of a semi-original Esper featurette from the Depression years.

The Esper company thus proved itself an avid practitioner of recycling before re-cycling became the environmentally correct Thing To Do. And never mind that Dwain Esper's approach to recycling fostered its own brand of pollution.

Hitler's Strange Love Life, in its original form, seems not to have been reviewed by the major trade publications, much less by the mainstream press. A more nearly respectable cut, known as *Will It Happen Again? The Personal Life of Hitler*, achieved a higher profile as an anti-Soviet propaganda tract sponsored by the Navy Club of the United States of America—whether with or without Esper's involvement—and released by Film Classics, a near-mainstream distributor. (The Navy Club had been chartered in 1940 under provisions of the U.S. Code as a support group for members past and present of the Navy, the Marine Corps and the Coast Guard. Its manifesto called for its members "to serve as ably as citizens as they have served the Nation under arms.")

Where Esper's chief interest lay in gossip-driven quasi-voyeurism about the trounced Hitler mob, the Navy Club's re-edited version concerned itself more with drawing parallels between Hitler and Josef Stalin. This version closes with a warning that Communist Russia poses a comparable threat.

A prologue to *Will It Happen Again?* states: "This picture, made up almost entirely of film shot by the Germans themselves, ... is presented as a public service ... in the belief that some things should not be forgotten." An off-screen narration track identifies Adolf Hitler and his mistress, Eva Braun, as the parties who shot most of the footage.

In whatever form one might have seen it, the film begins in a ruined Berlin and then cuts to the Bavarian village of Berchtesgarten, where fire has destroyed Hitler's residence, revealing a network of underlying tunnels. (This footage would have come from the Allies' post-invasion expeditions.) One passageway leads to the Eagle's Nest, the hideaway where Hitler and Eva Braun entertained their accomplices with illicit pleasures while the Third Reich-at-large kept busy tormenting the rest of the world. A flashback sequence (mixed newsreel footage) discusses the improbable rise of Hitler, chiefly via his identification of the Jewish populace as a scapegoat for Germany's social and economic miseries. At the height of World War II, Hitler receives a visit from Benito Mussolini's son-in-law, Count Ciano, and is seen frolicking with two children whom the film assumes to be Hitler's offspring. Now targeting Russia, Hitler's forces begin to lose ground following the Allied invasion of North Africa, and a subsequent invasion of Germany brings word that Hitler has killed himself at the Eagle's Nest. The liberation of the Nazis' concentration camps follows in short order, and assorted surviving Nazi bigwigs are tried and convicted at Nuremberg.

Esper's role in the Navy Club re-editing job remains unclear, but his source-film makes a great deal better sense without the forced coda suggesting that the Nazis' spirit endures in Soviet Russia. Although it might seem appropriate that Esper—well known for his piracy of legitimate stock footage for use in illegitimate productions—should have found himself cheated at his own racket, still the earlier cut is the more valid and authentic version. Without the dour narration and the reasonably accurate reconstruction of recent history, the home-movie footage is as numbingly amateurish as any Joe Schmoe's 16-mm account of How We Spent Our Summer Vacation. But of course, authenticity packs its own fascination.

A comparatively more accessible surviving version, which we screened in Hollywood during 1992–1993 as part of a research project for the American Film Institute, bears the proxy title *Will It Happen Again? The Personal Life of Hitler*, with its Navy Club attribution and its epilogue denouncing Russia. Dwain Esper's name does not appear among the opening credits.

A likely identical cut (entitled simply *Will It Happen Again?*) caused a ruckus in 1979 when selected for the International Film Festival at Nyon, Switzerland, during a retrospective marathon of pictures concerned with World War II. Soviet Russia threatened to withdraw its featured selections in light of the American film's glorification of the U.S. military; its perceived slighting of the Red Army's role in defeating the Nazis; and its so-what-else-is-new? tendency to equate Stalin with Hitler. No films were withdrawn, after all, and everybody went away more or less content that every dog had had its day.

But the globally enlightened cineastes at Nyon in 1979 heard not a kind word said on behalf of Dwain Esper, who meanwhile at age 87 was living in prosperous obscurity in San Diego.

The master exploiteer had long since transformed his old-fashioned burlesque theaters into easy-sell porno-picture showcases, like a farmer willing to let his acreage go fallow for the sake of a subsidy. But the moviemaking urge had gripped Esper anew, and though unaware of the Nyon revival he had returned to *Hitler's Strange Love Life* with recharged inspiration. He began recutting the film as a war-atrocities documentary, retaining the basic footage but shifting the emphasis onto the crimes of Hitler and Mussolini. *Day of the Despot* was Esper's intended title for this decades-later edition, but he died before he could complete the project.

CREDITS: Producers: Robert Gross and Lawrence Glesnes; Director: Dwain Esper; Screenwriters: Jean Oser (a.k.a. Osa) and Doris Reichhart; Editor: Jean Oser; Assistant Editor: Doris Reichhart; Music: Edward Craig; Sound: Richard Vorisek; Sound Effects: Leon Levy; Running Time: 61 minutes; Released: Following New York Opening on May 15, 1948

CAST: George Bryan and Phillip Stahl (Narrators); and Adolf Hitler, Eva Braun, Herrmann Goering, Paul Joseph Goebbels *et al.*

BLONDE ICE
(Martin Mooney Productions, Inc./Film Classics, Inc.)

It is not a nice story, and wastes the comely charms of Leslie Brooks…
little for the marquee excepting the title and lurid pictures.—From the
Variety Review

This one is tops—outdoes all my previous roles. I'm no novice at playing wenches and witches, but I've never killed anyone on the screen
before. But I get a real workout in this one—murdering three guys, and
trying to do in a fourth.—Leslie Brooks; from the publicity kit

What was that we had said about No Accounting for Taste? Leslie Brooks
clearly relishes the opportunity to play things nine-below-zero, whether Fahrenheit or
Centigrade, in Martin Mooney's production of *Blonde Ice*, and Mooney's background as
a prominent crime journalist patently informs the adaptation of a Depression-era novel
by Whitman Chambers. It is decidedly "not a nice story," and all the better for that. *Film
noir*? *Film froid* is more like it. Or etymologically speaking, film Freud. In a postwar
Hollywood that had become thoroughly well attuned to the predatory potential of its
prettier leading ladies—witness Joan Fontaine in *Ivy*, Olivia de Havilland in *The Dark
Mirror*, Laraine Day in *Guest in the House* and Jessica Tandy in *A Woman's Vengeance*—
Blonde Ice stands apart by virtue of sheer homicidal ferocity. (The similarly conceived
Daughter of Darkness, with Siobhan McKenna in the taboo-busting role of a homicidal
nymphomaniac, arrived from England's Alliance Studio during the same year.)

Blonde Ice establishes social-climbing greed as motivation enough for San Francisco
newspaper columnist Claire Cummings (Miss Brooks), who launches her campaign by
marrying a wealthy businessman named Carl Hanneman (John Holland). No sooner has
she done so, however, than she reassures her jilted sweetheart, sportswriter Les Burns
(Robert Paige), that he is her one true love. Fat lot of good that does him, except maybe
in the illicit-romance department. Hanneman gets wise to Claire's dalliances with Burns
and makes ready to divorce her. She attends instead to Hanneman's fatal shooting, then
arranges an out-of-town alibi and invites Burns to call upon her; he discovers Hanneman,
who is to all appearances a suicide. The damning catch is that no fingerprints can be
found on the weapon.

Reporter Al Herrick (James Griffith), another of Claire's discards, smells murder
and grows to suspect Burns. Claire goes blithely about her business of hacking out
Social Register drivel and calling it news—a traditional sop-to-the-snobs amenity of
the brothel-economics newspaper industry. Claire trains her wiles next upon an up-and-
coming politico, Stanley Mason (Michael Whalen), intending to wed him in order to
use his imminent election to Congress as a leg up on the high-roller scene. Meanwhile,
the aviator (Russ Vincent) who had piloted Claire's alibi flight pulls a blackmail scam.
Claire kills him.

Mason catches Claire with Burns and calls off the engagement. She sweet-talks
Mason into a farewell tryst, then stabs him to death and arranges a frame-up for Burns.

A friend of Mason's, psychiatrist Geoffrey Klippinger (David Leonard), has been
following Claire's progress with interest, though from a calculated distance. Dr. Klippinger

arranges finally to visit with her in person, explaining that he has devoted his career to the study of distorted minds. He follows through with an outright accusation, and she responds by showing him what she intends as her final column: a confession to the three slayings. She then attacks Klippinger, and during the struggle she guns herself down.

Director Jack Bernhard, who also headed his own separate production company at the time, paces this exercise in escalating madness with all deference to Miss Brooks' immersion in a role that is at once reprehensible and irresistible, and yet so tastefully played as to keep all that *psychopathia sexualis* 'way beyond the grasp of the Production Code censors. This element reflects the influence of Edgar G. Ulmer, as a contributing screenwriter. Miss Brooks' headlong rush

toward oblivion is all the more terrifying for her statuesque beauty. Camera chief George Robinson keeps the star lighted and framed to gorgeous effect, the modest production values notwithstanding. The portrayal owes as much to Krafft-Ebing as it does to stagecraft.

The men in the orbit of this taxing woman are all but incidental, serving chiefly as expendable ciphers—precisely the way the character regards them. Only Robert Paige, as the gullible jock-journalist, is allowed a measure of depth. Even the shrink who cracks the case is a lesser presence, although David Leonard informs the role with a welcome hint of mystery: This Dr. Klippinger (rather like Tom Conway's character in *Cat People*) seems more keenly interested in collecting trophies of derangement than in curtailing any homicidal impulses.

The crucial daily-rag setting is well represented, with toilers in the various departments going about their chores pretty much as working journalists would in those days, fooling themselves into perceiving robust adventure amid wage slavery and drudgery. Most City Room reporters, of course, merely *cover* crime and tend not to get involved in its commission. But we've known a number of journalists over the long haul who might find it a modest leap from acts of treachery to acts of murder. Most of them have been, all the same, nowhere near as pleasing to the eye as Leslie Brooks.

CREDITS: Producer: Martin Mooney; Associate Producer: Robert E. Callahan; Director: Jack Bernhard; Assistant Director: Frank Fox; Adapted Scenario and Screenplay: Kenneth Gamet, Dick Irving Hyland, Raymond Schrock and Edgar G. Ulmer; Based Upon Whitman Chambers' 1938 Novel, *Once Too Often*; Photographed by: George Robinson; Musical Score: Irving Gertz; Editors: Douglas Bagier and Jason Bernie; Art Director: George Van Marter; Decor: Joseph Kish; Hair Stylist: Loretta Bickel; Makeup: Ted Larsen; Production Manager: George Moskov; Sound: Ferol Redd; Special Effects: Ray Mercer; Dialogue Director: Jack Daly; Script Supervisor: Eleanor Donahoe; Stills: James Doolittle; Operative Cameraman: Harvey Gould; Grip: Fred Russell; Assistant to Mr. Mooney: William Stirling; Running Time: 74 minutes; Released: May 20, 1948

CAST: Robert Paige (Les Burns); Leslie Brooks (Claire Cunningham); Russ Vincent (Blackie Talon); Michael Whalen (Stanley Mason); James Griffith (Al Herrick); Emory Parnell (Capt. Bill Murdock); Walter Sande (Hack Doyle); John Holland (Carl Hanneman); Mildred Coles (June Taylor); Julie Gibson (Mimi Doyle); Rory Mallinson (Sgt. Benson); David Leonard (Dr. Geoffrey Klippinger); and Jack Del Rio, Selmer Jackson

RAW DEAL
(Reliance Pictures, Inc./Eagle-Lion Films, Inc./Pathé Industries, Inc.)

Escaped felon Joe Sullivan, as portrayed in *Raw Deal* by the dashing Dennis O'Keefe, emerges as the most fully realized equivalent of a masculine vampire, allegorically speaking, in the *film noir* canon. Vamps (not to say literalized *vampires*) abound, of course, in classic-manner *noir*, but these are female if not thoroughly feminine presences—descended from lethal-seductress stereotypes of the 1920s and defining the *femme fatale* component of *noir* as an essential means of assuring the downfall of any number of susceptible men.

Raw Deal inverts such fundamental elements to a radical extent but remains loyal to the sensibilities of this peculiarly American idiom, achieving a charge of erotic violence without the expected brutality and packing a resonance of romanticism that renders the cruelties at large all the more unnerving.

Director Anthony Mann addresses the collaborative screenplay from a tough-dame vantage, utilizing an off-camera narration by leading lady Claire Trevor—one of the more versatile recurring players in *noir*, as adept at conveying world-weariness as brittle menace—to brace the absorbed viewer for what can only be one of the bleakest endings ever committed to film. (A.D. 1948 also is the year of Miss Trevor's involvement with the major-league production of *Key Largo*.)

Pat Regan's (Miss Trevor) narration makes it patent that she regards O'Keefe's Sullivan with a helplessly fascinated combination of contempt and unquestioning love. The film's inversion-of-type thus renders O'Keefe what several historians have called a *homme fatale*, but his interpretation goes beyond merely pulling a gender-switch on some stock-in-trade lethal-lady character.

Joe Sullivan is more than an appealing scoundrel. His deeper struggle lies not with any forces of Law & Order, but rather with his innate polarities of decency and worthlessness. This war finds itself literalized in the women in Sullivan's orbit, with whom he forms a triangle of inexorably shifting dimensions. Marsha Hunt plays Ann Martin, the upstanding do-gooder who sees redeeming qualities in Sullivan—even after he and Pat

have made her a semi-willing hostage—and at length proves ready to sacrifice her own goodness for Sullivan's sake. Ann stands in stark contrast to Trevor's gang moll Pat, who has waited for Sullivan like some tainted Penelope for Ulysses and doesn't intend to indulge any interlopers. Pat, at least, seems to understand that she has no choice but to stand by her man—such is Sullivan's unwholesome persuasiveness, like a Dracula without the symbolic bloodletting. Farther along in the prior century, the *noir*-savvy songwriter John Hiatt would articulate this concern in a lyrical manifesto: "Your love is just like blood to me."

Threatening throughout to steal the show is the commanding presence of Raymond Burr, whose villainous credential was as decisive at this early stage as his heroic typecasting would become during the next decade. Burr plays ganglord Rick Coyle, a sadistic arsonist-for-the-hell-of-it who also happens to be the party for whom Sullivan had taken a dive into prison. Now, Coyle's objective is to lure Sullivan into a death trap under the ruse of a pay-off, with help from a rat-faced flunky known as Fantail (John Ireland).

The niceties of plotting, Point A to Point B and so forth, are virtually irrelevant to a story that unspools with the snakebit randomness of Real Life. Sullivan's seduction of Ann seems complete when she asserts herself as his protector, even to the extent of a willingness (if not necessarily an ability) to kill. This willingness on her part, in turn, sets Ann up as ready prey for the Coyle mob, which counts upon her to lure Sullivan toward a tailor-made doom. Sullivan's kindlier nature finds him prepared to rescue Ann—and if the cost should be his life, well, then, at least he can anticipate the pleasure of shoving Coyle through a high window and then dying in the arms of the one he has grown to love. The ironic tone of Pat's off-screen narration track (sadder and wiser, but never omniscient) is fulfilled on-screen by her late arrival, with a police escort, in time neither to save neither Sullivan's life nor to reverse her own misfortunes.

Dreams That Money Can Buy

The prevailing emotional turbulence and Sullivan's headlong rush toward a show-down combine to create a picture that will resonate long after the viewing experience has come and gone. This haunting quality stems as much from the lonesome resignation of Claire Trevor's off-camera voice as it does from composer Paul Sawtell's strategic use of a Theremin, that otherworldly electronic instrument, to underscore the monologue. (The Theremin is best known nowadays as a component of the Beach Boys' recording of "Good Vibrations.") Director Mann tracks the ordeal in linear order, but with a dreamlike twist: Trevor's Pat Regan shifts now and again from reflective narration to real-time dialogue. This time-shifting device serves to remove the safe-distance factor of a retrospective account, and to cinch the film's commitment to Pat's embittered and self-aware point of view. Pat seems to dread Sullivan's jailbreak as much as she looks forward to rejoining him.

Mann and cinematographer John Alton create a dimly lighted landscape dominated by the figurative chaos of physical clutter and a sense of decay that renders the air of romantic high adventure as foreboding as it is alluring. None of this design is particularly subtle, and in fact the closing scene is rendered distracting by a prominent sign reading "Corkscrew Alley"—an over-obvious reminder of Sullivan's bad-side-of-town origins. (The film's work-in-progress title had been *Corkscrew Alley*.)

O'Keefe is dominant throughout as a rogue heading for a bad end, even though the dramatic weight falls about equally upon him, Miss Hunt, and Miss Trevor. Raymond Burr, whose mastery of ill-balanced menace proved likewise suited for the soon-to-come *Pitfall*, is just right in the role of O'Keefe's ungrateful Nemesis. Backup menace Whit Bissell would come to the fore during the 1950s as a renegade physician in the likes of *I Was a Teenage Werewolf* and *I Was a Teenage Frankenstein*.

CREDITS: Produced and Presented by: Edward Small; Director: Anthony Mann; Assistant Director: Ridgeway Callow; Screenplay: Leopold Atlas and John C. Higgins; Suggested by a Story by: Audrey Ashley and Arnold B. Armstrong; Photographed by: John Alton; Operative Cameraman: Lester Shorr; Musical Score: Paul Sawtell; Musical Director: Irving Friedman; Theremin Solos: Dr. Samuel Hoffman; Editor: Alfred De-Gaetano; Art Director: Edward L. Ilou; Decor: Armor Marlowe and Clarence Steensen; Makeup: Ted Larsen and Ern Westmore; Hair Stylists: Anna Malin and Joan St. Oegger; Dialogue Director: Leslie Urbach; Production Manager: James T. Vaughn; Sound: Leon Becker; Special Art Design & Effects: Jack Rabin; Special Photographic Effects: George J. Teague; Stuntman: Carey Loftin; Costumer: Frances Ehren; Grip: Lou Kusley; Stills: Donald MacKenzie; Script Supervisor: Richard Walton; Running Time: 78 minutes; Released: May 26, 1948

CAST: Dennis O'Keefe (Joseph Sullivan); Claire Trevor (Pat Regan); Marsha Hunt (Ann Martin); John Ireland (Fantail); Raymond Burr (Rick Coyle); Curt Conway (Spider); Chili Williams (Marcy); Regis Toomey [Billed as Richard Fraser] (Police Capt. Fields); Whit Bissell (Murderer); Cliff Clark (Gates); Gregg Barton (Motorist); Robert Bice (Crewman); John Daheim (Cop); Ray Teal (Commander); Tom Fadden (Grimshaw); Ilka Grüning (Fran); Harry Tyler (Oscar); Robert Williams (Sergeant); Beverly Wills (Girl); and David Clarke, Victor Cutler, Alex Davidoff, Abe Dinovitch, Lloyd Everett, Vincent Graeff, Frank Hyers, Richard Irving, Willard Kennedy, Paul Kruger, Mike Lally, Carey Loftin, James Magill, Joan Myles, Edna Ryan, Arnold Stanford

SECRET SERVICE INVESTIGATOR
(Republic Pictures Corp.)

The presence of a great character actor lies not necessarily in just the time spent before the cameras. There is also that ability to cast a looming shadow that will reach into those places where the artist himself is not necessarily seen. Consider how much more effective Sir Anthony Hopkins is in *The Silence of the Lambs* (1991), where he dominates the proceedings with minimal appearances on screen, than in the sequel, *Hannibal* (2001)—which requires a more nearly constant direct participation. Granted, of course, that Hopkins serves impressively in either moderation or excess.

We might say likewise of George Zucco, even when tested by the lesser likes of *Fog Island* and *The Black Raven*. The present selection, *Secret Service Investigator*, is no more significant a film, but it demonstrates vividly how Zucco could commandeer a picture from almost a sideline vantage.

The outcome of a struggle between veteran bogeyman Zucco and up-and-coming heroic lead Lloyd Bridges is a foregone conclusion. But third-billed Zucco handily prevails in terms of a memorable presence. *Secret Service Investigator* is Zucco's show, start to finish, and he seems to hold the fort before his character appears in person—and even during those segments where the camera's attention is diverted elsewhere.

Bridges is Capt. Steve Mallory, a WWII hero who, typical of neglected returning warriors left to fend for themselves, finds himself struggling to land a decent job. When invited to hire on with an agency that might or might not be the U.S. Secret Service, Mallory learns that his looks are more in demand than his combat record: He is a ringer for a chap named Dan Redfern, who appears crucial to an investigation. Assigned to impersonate Redfern and deliver a set of counterfeiting plates to a mastermind named Otto Dagoff, Mallory is soon mistaken for Redfern by Redfern's wife, Laura (June Storey), and her brother, Benny Norris (John Kellogg). Upon realizing their mistake, Mrs. Redfern and Norris knock Mallory unconscious and steal the plates.

Mallory rallies, only to wind up under suspicion in the murder of Dan Redfern. The men who had hired him, he learns, were impostors. The genuine Secret Service enlists Mallory to help corral the gang. The hunt veers from San Francisco to New York, where Dagoff (Zucco) and his bodyguard, Herman (Jack Overman), receive the plates. Dagoff pronounces them bogus—a counterfeit of a counterfeit. Dagoff and his mob journey to Frisco, where they confront Mallory with a deadline to deliver the bonafides and their engraver, Henry Witzel (Trevor Bardette). A search, using clues supplied by a helpful newspaper clerk named Susan Lane (Lynne Roberts), turns up Witzel at a well-concealed printing shop. Impatient, Herman summons Dagoff, who barges right in and kills the disloyal Witzel. Mallory guns down Dagoff, and the surviving racketeers surrender.

Director R.G. "Bud" Springsteen was just beginning to break away from three years' typecasting as a horse-opera helmer when he tackled *Secret Service Investigator*. The film's plot structure is, really, little different from a stock Western formula. Zucco raises the stakes considerably, however: His vigorous presence, sparingly used to striking effect, makes Dagoff one of the artist's more memorable arch-criminal portrayals. Bridges, in his first leading role following 12 years of dues-paying backup assignments, requires abundantly more screen time to come near the dominant impression Zucco leaves. Top-billed Lynne Roberts (formerly Mary Hart, and billed elsewhere as Lynn Roberts) is very good as the advertising rep who helps crack the case and becomes Bridges' love interest in the process. A charming trouper who had spent 11 years in Hollywood by now, Roberts was as far from name-brand stardom as ever she had been; a handful of additional pictures led her to retirement in 1953.

CREDITS: Associate Producer: Sidney Picker; Director: R.G. Springsteen; Screenplay: John K. Butler; Photographed by: John MacBurnie; Assistant Director: Roy Wade; Camera Operator: Herb Kirkpatrick; Stills: Ira Hoke; Art Director: Frank Arrigo; Editor: Arthur Roberts; Set Decor: John McCarthy, Jr., and Charles Thompson; Costumer: Adele Palmer; Music: Mort Glickman; Sound: Victor B. Appel; Makeup: Bob Mark; Hair Stylist: Lynn Burke; Grip: C.B. Lawrence; Script Supervisor: Joan Eremin; Running Time: 60 minutes; Released: May 31, 1948

CAST: Lynne Roberts (Susan Lane); Lloyd Bridges (Steve Mallory and Dan Redfern); George Zucco (Otto Dagoff); June Storey (Laura Redfern); Trevor Bardette (Henry Witzel); John Kellogg (Benny Norris); Jack Overman (Herman); Roy Barcroft (Al Turk); Douglas Evans (Inspector Crahan); Milton Parsons (Miller); James Flavin (Leadbetter); Tommy Ivo (Teddy Lane); Sam McDaniel (Porter); Billy Benedict (Counterman); Minerva Urecal (Mrs. McGiven); George Douglas (Gregory); Charles Sullivan (Cabbie); Carole Gallagher (Stenographer)

CLOSE-UP
(Marathon Pictures Corp./Eagle-Lion Films, Inc./Pathé Industries, Inc.)

Richard Kollmar, of network radio's *Boston Blackie* detective franchise, found his screen-starring debut in Jack Donohue's *Close-Up*, a talky-but-tight thriller that also owns the distinction of being the first feature-lengther since the 1930s to be shot entirely on Manhattan locations. Gotham provides an automatic boost in the production-values department, providing a range of landmark backdrops that no low-budget production company could otherwise have afforded.

Kollmar anchors things well enough as a fugitive Nazi pursuing an incriminating piece of newsreel film, but the understated role allows him little of a showcase. *Close-Up*

wallows in cruelties to an unnerving extent, from the whipping of a flunky who has failed to retrieve the film, to a triangular shoot-out among Kollmar's Martin Beaumen, Alan Baxter's cameraman-character, and a Nazi thug (Philip Huston) who suspects Beaumen of a double-cross. Most unnerving is the screenplay's tacit argument that Hitler's Reich has defied defeat and lurks yet—all this time after the end of World War II—in America's grandest city.

Virginia Gilmore is particularly effective as a Nazi operative who wises up none too soon to the advantages of American freedom, and Baxter makes a strong showing as a working journalist willing to fight for the principles of his profession. The evocative music marks an early showing by the veteran orchestrator Jerome Moross, who would emerge as a high-profile dramatic composer during the 1950s with scores for the likes of television's *Gunsmoke* and the big screen's *The Big Country*

(1959). Dick Kollmar's intended movie career began and ended with *Close-Up*, leaving the actor to retrench as sleuth Boston Blackie (he stuck with the series into 1949), and later as a game-show personality on television.

CREDITS: Producer: Frank Satenstein; Associate Producer: Robert L. Joseph; Director: Jack Donohue; Assistant Director: James DiGangi; Screenplay: John Bright and Max Wilk; Additional Dialogue: Jack Donohue; Adapted by: Martin Rackin; Based Upon a Story by: James Poe; Photographed by: William Miller; Operative Cameraman: Edward Hyland; Stills: William J. Nallan; Art Director: Furth Ullman; Editor: Robert Klaeger; Women's Styles: Swansdown; Music Composed and Conducted by: Jerome Moross; Sound: Clarence Wall; Makeup: Ira Senz; Business Manager: Leo Rose; Production Manager: Jules Bricken; Script Supervisor: Faith Elliott; Running Time: 72 minutes; Released: June 9, 1948

CAST: Alan Baxter (Phil Sparr); Virginia Gilmore (Peggy Lake); Loring Smith (Avery); Philip Huston (Joe Gibbons); Joey Fayr (Roger); Russell Collins (Beck); Michael Wyler (Fredericks); Sid Melton (Cabbie); Wendell Phillips (Harold); James Sheridan (Jimmy); Marsha Walter (Rita); Erin O'Kelly (Receptionist); Maurice Manson (Lonigan); Lauren Gilbert (Miller); "and Introducing Richard Kollmar" (Martin Beaumen)

STAGE STRUCK
(Monogram Pictures Corp.)

The giddy phenomenon of finding oneself stage-struck, or hellbent-for-footlights to see one's name upon a marquee, is more frequently a career-wrecking delusion than a harbinger of celebrity. Many a hopeful career has collapsed in disappointment, with or without a promise of premature success. In the movie industry alone, the Hollywood Chamber of Commerce once calculated (during the 1920s) that the barest fraction of hopefuls would get so far as even crowd-extra status. In the overpopulated but still stage-struck America of this Grand New Millennium, the odds have grown incalculably disparate. A

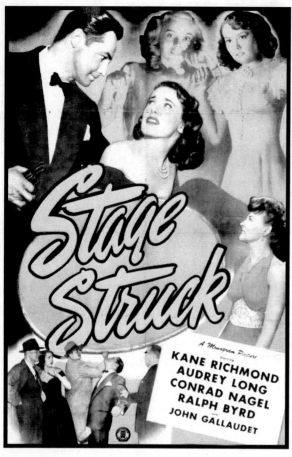

pandering, scandal-prone hack is likelier to Make It Big than an artist with something of substance to offer.

Such daunting prospects figure in William Nigh's career-capping *Stage Struck*, a murder-as-a-way-of-life melodrama that opens with the accidental slaying and callous disposal of Helen Howard (Wanda McKay), a recent high-school graduate from the Heartland, during an ugly scene at a New York nightclub. Yes, and so much for fame and fortune and sending a big Broadway paycheck to the folks left waiting back home.

Helen is identified only as a victim of death-by-misadventure, for slimewads Nick Mantee (Kane Richmond) and Benny Nordick (John Gallaudet), uneasy allies in a white-slavery racket, have covered their tracks too well for the law to trace. Fed up with the tedious progress of investigating officers Williams (Conrad Nagel) and Raney (Ralph Byrd), Helen's older sister, Nancy (Audrey Long), journeys to New York and signs on with the same agency that Helen had employed. Sure enough, the agency is Nordick's camouflaged holding pen for the conscription of naïve young women.

Williams and Raney find Nancy working at Nordick's nightclub and counsel her to leave such matters to the professionals. Nancy forges ever deeper into dangerous territory, trusting too many of the wrong people and almost winding up as an unwilling passenger bound for the stronghold of a high-rolling South American pimp (Anthony Warde). The procurer, fortunately for all concerned except Nordick and Mantee, turns out to be an undercover detective. Everything ends well for the more deserving souls, barring a troubling coda in which Conrad Nagel's Lt. Williams announces he must get cracking on another missing-girl case. They never learn, and their predators never tire of lying in ambush.

Not only director Nigh but also top-billed Kane Richmond allowed *Stage Struck* to mark a decisive exit—Nigh heading off into retirement from an industry he had served since 1914, and Richmond into a long and productive new career as a financier and all-'round captain of industry, with a specialty in women's apparel. The artists' track records, particularly as specialists in a broadly defined and generally low-rent genre, speak well of their accomplishments overall—many desultory assignments notwithstanding.

CREDITS: Producer: Jeffrey Bernerd; Director: William Nigh; Assistant Director: Eddie Davis; Screenplay: Agnes Christine Johnston and George Wallace Sayre, from His Story; Photographed by: Harry Neumann; Operative Cameraman: William Margulies; Musical Director: Edward J. Kay; Stills: Scotty Welbourne; Editor: William Austin; Art Director: Dave Milton; Decor: Raymond Boltz, Jr.; Hair Stylist: Loretta Francel; Production Manager: William A. Calihan, Jr.; Sound: Earl Sitar; Grip: George Booker; Script Supervisor: Ilona Vas; Running Time: 71 minutes; Released: June 13, 1948

CAST: Kane Richmond (Nick Mantee); Audrey Long (Nancy Howard); Conrad Nagel (Lt. Williams); Ralph Byrd (Sgt. Tom Ramey); John Gallaudet (Benny Nordick); Anthony Warde (Mr. Barda); Pamela Blake (Janet Winters); Charles Trowbridge (Capt. Webb); Nana Bryant (Mrs. Howard); Selmer Jackson (Mr. Howard); Evelyn Brent (Miss Lloyd); Wanda McKay (Helen Howard); Lyn Thomas (Ruth Ames); Wilbur Mack (Prof. Corella)

THE BETRAYAL
(Oscar Micheaux Productions/Astor Pictures Corp.)

Oscar Micheaux...fought the odds all his life. Even if he was not always a winner, he was always a contender.—Film archivist G. William Jones

Oscar Micheaux (1884-1951) was nearing the end of a trailblazing career—more successful in retrospect than it can have seemed in its day—when he undertook to tell something of his life story in an (intended) epic of fictionalized aspect. *The Betrayal* brings that career full-circle, in a sense, being an embellishment upon Micheaux's first picture, *The Homesteader* (1919), but it also amplifies the story to such an extent as to stand apart. Micheaux had published a novel along these lines, in the meantime.

Its inclusion here is not meant to categorize *The Betrayal* as anything like a genre-fied horror movie—which would be a stretch, in any event—but rather to point up the Kafkaesque anguish that Micheaux brought to bear upon the story of a black man attempting to beat the prevailing odds against success in this purported Land of the Free.

The horrors implicit are those of bigotry from within and without; of the disoriented confusion that radiates from a culture that has dedicated itself to deciding who can be black and who can be white in a society that pretends not to make such alienating distinctions; and of the violence that such a quandary begets.

Nor was Micheaux without his own prejudices, leaning more toward separatism than toward integration but allowing himself some double-standard indulgences: All that is necessary to qualify oneself as a racist is a belief in the divisive myth of race. Through his main-character mouthpiece, the artist rails interminably against mixed-color marriage, but at length he pronounces such a union acceptable as long as the intended wife is half-black. A few provincial boards of censors deleted much of this impassioned speechifying, objecting in particular to a description of the suicide of an Army conscriptee of mingled ethnicity.

Micheaux' obsessive arguments are hardly as easy to follow as all that, and (chiefly on account of the amateurism that prevails throughout his nearly 50 films) *The Betrayal* requires a certain patience, even if the viewer is automatically interested in the issues

at hand. Unlike a majority of so-called black independent films, which as a rule had white investors and employed white-folks production crews, Micheaux' pictures are resolutely Afrocentric, from underwriting through artistry. They address the inevitable black-to-white culture-clash situations in severe terms that no other artist of color would match until the much later arrival of Melvin Van Peebles and, later yet, Spike Lee.

The unfortunate side of the equation is that Micheaux was essentially a humorless and didactic storyteller, more interested in lecturing than in dispensing entertainment value. *The Betrayal* compounds that quality simply by being an extremely long film—183 minutes in the last-viewed version, which corresponds with the print that premiered on Broadway in 1948 after Micheaux had reduced it from 195 minutes.

Fearing to involve himself in a mixed marriage despite his genuine love for a woman (Myra Stanton) whom be believes white, farmer Martin Eden (Leroy Collins) marries instead into a black family that turns out crooked and causes him all manner of misery. Murder and agonized estrangements result, and the resolution is more hopeful than downright happy. Leroy Collins acquits himself well as a screen presence, but his inexperience is not helped by Micheaux' rambling screenplay, which routinely uses 100 words where 10 would have done the trick. Harris Gaines overacts gloriously as the villain of the piece. As Micheaux' valedictory film, *The Betrayal* was well received among its intended audiences but drew mostly uncharitable reviews from the few mainstream critics who paid notice. Micheaux stands as a maverick among mavericks.

CREDITS: Producer, Director and Screenwriter: Oscar Micheaux; Based Upon: Micheaux' 1944 Novel, *Wind from Nowhere*; Photographed by: N. Spoor; Running Time: 183 minutes; Released: During the Week of June 24, 1948

CAST: William Byrd (Jack Stewart); Leroy Collins (Martin Eden); Verlie Cowan (Linda Lee); Frances DeYoung (Hattie Bowles); Vernon B. Duncan (Duval); Edward Fraction (Nelson Boudreaux); Harris Gaines (Dr. Lee); Jessie Johnson (Preble); Barbara

Lee (Jessie); Yvonne Machen (Terry); Arthur McCoo (Joe Bowles); Vernetties Moore (Eunice); Alice B. Russell (Aunt Mary); Myra Stanton (Deborah Stewart); Lou Vernon (Ned Washington)

MAN-EATER OF KUMAON
(Monty Shaff Productions, Inc./Universal Pictures Co., Inc.)

Jim Corbett's rip-snorting jungle novel *Man-Eaters of Kumaon* had served in 1945 to give the war-ravaged publishing industry an infusion of best-selling vigor. The book also suggested finer possibilities for a moviemaking genre that had grown stale and repetitive. The adaptation to film took a while, for the major studios proved hesitant to tackle such a venture, best-seller or not. This was a climate, after all, where even big-time RKO-Radio Pictures had entrusted its entrenched *Tarzan* franchise to a tenured Poverty Row producer, Sol Lesser—who understood the marketplace for such pictures.

In 1946, *Man-Eaters of Kumaon* would go to an *ad hoc* production company, organized by investor Monty Shaff. Shaff's greater interest was threefold: He would possess a lucrative literary property, adapt it into a film of irresistible exploitability, and then sell the product to a big studio with the resources to promote and distribute it widely. The first two objectives fell readily into line, along with a more-or-less name-brand cast and a director, Byron Haskin, bound for bigger things.

Universal Pictures came aboard as the releasing company, agreeing to provide resources including the services of composer Hans J. Salter, shortly after second-unit camera chief Robert Tansey had brought home a wealth of splendid jungle footage from

an especially commissioned shooting trip to India. Shaff had hoped to capture the entire picture on location, but after a meeting with Jagadash Natarajan, the Indian government's minister of information, the producer chose to dodge the bureaucracy and settled for a built jungle on rented properties in Hollywood. The blending of studio settings with Tansey's location shots is near seamless.

Shaff hedged his bets by registering the copyright in his name, apart from the deal with Universal. The big-time studio, caught up in the complications of a leveraged merger with International Pictures, had become averse to *making* B-unit pictures, but not necessarily to *acquiring* such titles of moneymaking potential.

With a slight change of title to *Man-Eater of Kumaon*, the film went into sound-stage production in December of 1947 and had wrapped by the spring of 1948. Source-author Corbett, though not directly involved in the scripting, provided a prologue explaining the circumstances that can provoke tigers into preying upon humans.

In Northern India, Dr. John Collins (Wendell Corey) triggers a crisis when he wounds a tiger but then abandons the hunt without a clean kill. Thus crippled, the tiger turns man-eater. Collins' response is to leave the district. He is unaware that the tiger is following his trail and anticipating his next move.

Reaching an abandoned village near the base of the Himalayas, Collins finds a boy named Panwah (James Moss) to be the lone survivor of an attack by that same tiger. Collins' sense of duty kicks in belatedly, and he delivers the boy to a better-fortified village, where Narain and Lali (Sabu and Joanne Page), a married couple expecting their first child, agree to look after Panwah. The tiger follows along and attacks Lali. Collins manages to save her life, but she loses her baby and any prospect of further offspring. The loss renders Lali a tribal outcast.

Finally accepting responsibility, Collins undertakes to hunt down the tiger, which in turn begins to stalk him in earnest. Many villagers die in the onslaught. Lali impulsively sets herself up as bait and alerts Collins. Collins arrives in time to distract the tiger, which attacks him. Mortally wounded, he kills the beast. Lali's tribal citizenship is restored, and she and Narain reunite with Panwah as their required heir.

Where many such expeditionary films tend to meander, *Man-Eater of Kumaon* finds an urgent crisis straightaway and sticks with it for the duration. Wendell Corey's John Collins is not so much a Great White Hunter, as he is a soul in torment—driven to a careless act by a personal loss and an attack of malaria, and then menaced by the animal he had intended to kill. Byron Haskin, a seasoned camera operator and special-effects artisan, was just now beginning to restore his credential as a working member of the Directors Guild. Haskin handles *Man-Eater* with a ferocious confidence, treating the tiger as a being of intelligence and wrathful guile while establishing in the foredoomed Dr. Collins a gathering determination and self-sacrificing nobility. (Haskin's next picture, 1949's *Too Late for Tears*, would concern itself with another variety of predator.)

Sabu Dastagir, who in 1942 had become the first Indo-Eastern actor to infiltrate Hollywood's star system, serves less prominent a role than his top billing would suggest. He and Joanne (later billed as Joy) Page make a heroic couple. Sabu, Miss Page and Corey share a particularly touching moment late in the adventure, when Corey explains his realization that he must make amends for a self-centered life. The climax that this revelation triggers is edge-of-the-seat stuff, and so is an interim battle between a tiger and a crocodile.

Universal delivered the goods as to promotion of *Man-Eater*, even to the extent of staging the West Coast premiere aboard a cruise ship bound for Calcutta.

CREDITS: Producer: Monty Shaff; Associate Producer: Frank P. Rosenberg; Director: Byron Haskin; Assistant Director: Robert Agnew; Second Unit Director and Cameraman: Robert Tansey; Screenplay: Jeanne Bartlett and Lewis Meltzer; Adaptation: Richard G. Hubler and Alden Nash; Based Upon: Jim Corbett's 1945 Novel, *Man-Eaters of Kumaon*; Photographed by: William C. Mellor; Musical Score: Hans J. Salter; Editor: George Arthur; Art Director: Arthur Lonergan; Decor: Robert Priestley; Makeup: Robert Cowan; Hair Stylist: Ann Locker; Production Manager: Ben Hersh; Sound: Franklin Hansen; Script Supervisor: Fred Applegate; Operative Cameraman: William Dodds; Dialogue Director: Joan Hathaway; Grip: John Livesley; Stills: William Thomas; Technical Advisor: M.H. Whyte; Running Time: 79 minutes; Released: Following New York and San Francisco Openings on July 1, 1948

CAST: Sabu (Narain); Wendell Corey (Dr. John Collins); Joanne Page (Lali); Morris Carnovsky (Ganga Ram); James Moss (Panwah); Argentina Brunetti (Sita); Eddie Das (Cart Driver); Estelle Dodge (Mother); Ted Hecht (Tribal Doctor); John Mansfield (Bearer); Lal Chand Mehra, Phiroze Nazir and Virginia Wave (Farmers); Charles Wagenheim (Panwah's Father); Jerry Riggio, Alan Foster, Frank Lackteen, Ralph Moody and Neyle Morrow (Villagers)

CAÑON CITY
(Eagle-Lion Films, Inc./Pathé Industries, Inc.)

This is a true story of a prison break and the reign of terror that followed it. The events depicted… are the actual events that transpired at the Colorado State Prison in Cañon City… The convicts you will see are the actual convicts. Roy Best, who appears as the warden, is actually the warden of the prison. The details of the break are portrayed exactly as they occurred and were photographed where they happened. —From the prologue

Better to file that bit, above, under Yeah, Right, Whatever You Say, Boss, and just accept this entry as a harrowing 82 minutes of fictional, or fictionalized, jailbreak horrors. Whatever the finer accuracies that Crane Wilbur's *Cañon City* may harbor, just one misleading promise is all that is required to render all else suspect. And those "actual convicts" thus promised are confined to a prologue. The story itself unfolds via professional actors, holding forth on nonetheless authentic locations. And yes, it's only a movie.

But quite an effective movie, nonetheless. John Alton, a master of naturalistic cinematography and a recurring figure within these pages, shoots *Cañon City* as though addressing a documentary narrative, and Scott Brady renders credible the plight of an inmate who might prefer to serve his time and rejoin society on friendly terms. Reed Hadley's narration track is a debit, hammering a law-and-order message that the film conveys ably enough without such redundant assistance.

Spanish poster for *Cañon City*

Brady's Jimmy Sherbondy finds himself conscripted into a break-out conspiracy. Sherbondy creates an escape hatch from Solitary into a common area. The hardtimers' attempt to mingle with the rank-and-file inmates is noticed by an alert guard (the *Dick Tracy* films' Ralph Byrd), who endures a hellacious beating before he is taken hostage.

Most of the escapees scatter through the nearby town of Cañon City, Colorado, but Carl Schwartzmiller (Jeff Corey), the mastermind, leads an invasion of one household—establishing a base from which to spread the rampage. Finally, a police siege closes in on Sherbondy, who takes refuge with a family (John Doucette and Eve March) facing a medical crisis. Sherbondy yields to a compassionate impulse, then surrenders to resume his career as a jailbird.

Director Wilbur had become a crime melodrama specialist during the 1930s, then contributed to the postwar *noir* cycle such essential work as 1950's *Outside the Wall* and the story for *He Walked by Night*. Wilbur's work on *Cañon City*, though perfectly capable of finding characterization in what is essentially an extended mob scene, is secondary to the cinematography of John Alton. Alton, in turn, is vibrantly attuned to the suffocating prison setting and the forbidding snowscapes. Alton's book *Painting with Light* remains a standard reference and a practical textbook, its relevance having survived even the technological transition from real-film photography to the digital realm.

CREDITS: Producers: Bryan Foy and Robert T. Kane; Director and Screenwriter: Crane Wilbur; Assistant Directors: Ridgeway Callow and Allen K. Wood; Second Unit Director: James Leicester; Photographed by: John Alton; Musical Director: Irving Friedman; Editor: Louis H. Sackin; Art Director: Frank Durlauf; Decor: Armor Marlowe and Clarence Steensen; Costumer: Frances Ehren; Hair Stylists: Beth Langston and Joan St. Oegger; Makeup: Ern Westmore and Frank Westmore; Production Manager: James T. Vaughn; Sound: Leon S. Becker and Hugh McDowell; Special Effects: George J. Teague; Second Unit Cinematographer: Walter Strenge; Dialogue Director: Burk Symon; Stills: Milton Gold; Script Supervisor: Arnold Laven; Grip: Charlie Rose; Operative Cameraman: Lester Shorr; Stills: Ted Weisbarth; Running Time: 82 minutes; Released: July 6, 1948

CAST: Scott Brady (Jim Sherbondy); Jeff Corey (Carl Schwartzmiller); Whit Bissell (Richard Heilman); Stanley Clements (Billy New); Charles Russell (Tolley); DeForest Kelley (Smalley); Ralph Byrd (Officer Joe Gray); Warden Roy Best (Himself); Henry Brandon (Freeman); Alfred Linder (Lavergne); Robert Bice (Morgan); Ray Bennett (Klinger); Robert Kellard (Officer Winston Williams); Richard Irving (Trujillo); Bud Wolfe (Officer Clark); Mabel Paige (Ethel Oliver); Reed Hadley (Narrator); Bob Reeves and Brick Sullivan (Guards); Donald Kerr (Convict Waiter); Victor Cutler (Convict Photographer); Lynn Millan (May); James Ames (Mug); Ruth Warren (Mug's Wife); Henry Hall (Guard Captain); Cay Forrester (Mrs. Wilson); Bill Walker (Prisoner); Officer McLean (Himself); Paul Scardon (Joe Bondy); Ralph Dunn (Convict Blacksmith); Capt. Kenny (Himself); Alvin Hammer (Convict Tailor); John Shay and Paul Kruger (Officers); Raymond Bond (Lawrence Oliver); Mack Williams (Lon Higgins); Capt. Gentry (Himself); Howard Negley (Richard Smith); Virginia Mullen (Mrs. Smith); Bill Clauson (Joel); Shirley Martin (Judith); Elysabeth Goetten (Barbara); Margaret Kerry (Maxine); Eve March (Mrs. Bauer); John Doucette (George Bauer); Phyllis Callow (Myrna); Anthony Sydes (Jerry Bauer); Jack Ellis (Man at Roadblock); John Wald (Radio Announcer); James Magill (Hathaway); Esther Somers (Minnie Higgins)

THE SPIRITUALIST

a.k.a.: The Amazing Mr. X
(Eagle-Lion Films, Inc./Pathé Industries, Inc.)

More than merely a jewel of its kind, Bernard Vorhaus' *The Spiritualist*, with its top-flight production values and its provocative and intelligent handling of a topic more often sacrificed to sensationalism, could have pointed toward major-league status for Eagle-Lion Films. Here is one extreme of the little studio's uneven output—a borderline art film of impeccable packaging and big-studio pretensions. Of course, it is the other extreme of exploitation-minded schlock, stabilized by a saner middle ground of naturalistic *noir*s and B-movie potboilers, that makes Eagle-Lion such a fascinating study in contradictions.

Eagle-Lion's open-secret standing as a haven for organized crime also figured in its fundamental self-contradictions. By late 1947, Eagle-Lion had become a home base for Johnny Roselli, recently paroled from prison in

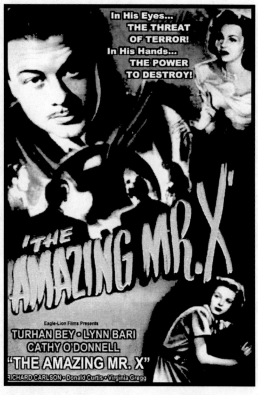

connection with a corporate extortion scandal. Roselli lost no time in reasserting himself as the Chicago Mob's chief loan shark in Hollywood, among duties more unsavory. At Eagle-Lion, Roselli became a purchasing agent reporting to former Vaudevillian Bryan Foy, vice president for production, and gradually attained in-house producer status. Though never formally accredited as a filmmaker, Roselli nonetheless held a position of say-so during the period in which Eagle-Lion excelled as a crime-thriller factory. At around this same time, Roselli had installed himself as the DuPont Film Corp.'s representative to the studios, responsible for peddling raw 35-mm stock. This small but significant power play—and never mind Roselli's patent lack of any specialized knowledge—was in keeping with DuPont's bid to compete against Eastman Kodak, whether via salesmanship or coercion.

Where Eagle-Lion's better known crime dramas tend to concentrate upon *dis*-organized crime (the aberrant rampages, for example, of *He Walked by Night* and *Cañon City*), *The Spiritualist* concerns itself with a conspiratorial scam of a sort that would have been dear to Johnny Roselli's crooked heart.

Fancying herself haunted by the spirit of a husband long dead, wealthy widow Christine Faber (Lynn Bari) consults a crystal-gazing crackpot named Alexis (Turhan Bey), who knows so much of her troubled history that he must be either a clairvoyant or an accomplished snoop. Christine errs on the side of trust and begins patronizing Alexis' racket in an attempt to communicate with her husband, Paul Faber. Christine's sister, Janet Burke (Cathy O'Donnell), and Christine's fiancé, lawyer Martin Abbott (Richard Carlson), enlist a detective named Hoffman (Harry Mendoza), who specializes in spook-show debunkery.

Sure enough, Alexis has a swindle in the works. During a rehearsed séance, he materializes a convincing replica of Paul. Challenged to repeat the stunt, Alexis finds Paul (played by Donald Curtis) materializing without any trickery—the genuine article, having faked his death with a proxy victim—and demanding the quack's assistance in an estate-grabbing plot. Ordered to lure Janet into marriage while Paul does away with Christine, Alexis finds himself beginning to fall for the sister in earnest. Alexis and Janet manage to foil Paul's attempt at murder. At length, Alexis is mortally wounded while protecting Janet from Paul. Paul dies in a stand-off with the police.

Turhan Bey (Austrian-born in 1922, of Turkish-Czech ancestry), whose presence suggests a more boyish, less expressive Bela Lugosi, faced a life sentence of typecasting from the moment he set foot in Hollywood. On occasion, an assignment such as *The Spiritualist* would allow Bey to modulate the exotic essence of his popular image with a better-rounded character. Bey makes Alexis so much more than an elusive mystery man as to upstage principal villain Donald Curtis, the leading ladies, and the mild-mannered and ostensibly heroic lead, Richard Carlson.

"Bey chips in with probably his top performance," raved the *Variety* review, and amen to that. Lynn Bari makes a convincingly anguished target of all that scheming, and Cathy O'Donnell takes charge of the investigation at all the right moments. Carlson's role is under-written by comparison with those of the women, and he does little to beef it up. Harry Mendoza is terrific as a sleuth with a Houdini-like background in stage magic and spiritualistic racket busting.

John Alton's photography captures well the ominous settings—notably a lonely seacoast manor house—and the special effects camerawork of Leon S. Becker creates an otherworldly ambiance, assisted by an ethereal score of music from Alexander Laszlo. The closing sequence, in which Cathy O'Donnell releases the charlatan's trained raven in a symbolic memorial gesture, is particularly haunting.

CREDITS: Producer: Ben Stoloff; Director: Bernard Vorhaus; Assistant Director: Ridgeway Callow; Screenplay: Muriel Roy Bolton and Ian McLellan Hunter; Based Upon: Crane Wilbur's Story; Photographed by: John Alton; Musical Score: Alexander Laszlo; Musical Director: Irving Friedman; Editor: Norman Colbert; Art Director: Frank Durlauf; Decor: Armor Marlowe and Clarence Steensen; Costumer: Frances Ehren; Hair Stylists: Joan St. Oegger and Gwen Van Upp; Makeup: Bud Westmore, Frank Westmore and Ern Westmore; Production Manager: James T. Vaughn; Sound: Leon S. Becker; Special Effects: George J. Teague; Special Art Effects: Jack Rabin; Dialogue Director: Stewart Stern; Stills: George Hommel; Grip: E. Truman Joiner; Script Supervisor: Arnold Laven; Operative Cameraman: Lester Shorr; Running Time: 78 minutes; Released: July 7, 1948

CAST: Turhan Bey (Alexis); Lynn Bari (Christine Burke Faber); Cathy O'Donnell (Janet Burke); Richard Carlson (Martin Abbott); Donald Curtis (Paul Faber); Virginia Gregg (Emily); Harry Mendoza (Hoffman); and Norma Varden

EYES OF TEXAS
(Republic Pictures Corp.)

Here we have a selection that has eluded even the near-infallible radar of the genre-conscious American Film Institute—except for its narrow formal classification as a conventional Western. Which *Eyes of Texas* is, of course, in the sense of star player Roy Rogers' stock-in-trade sense of wholesome adventure and heroic justice. But the film also pits Rogers against a particularly cunning madwoman, played by Nana Bryant, who masquerades as a trustworthy lawyer while pursuing a conspiracy of murderous proportions.

Eyes of Texas confronts the audience early on with the death of a lovable rancher (Francis Ford, the crusty character-actor brother of the great director John Ford) in a siege by wolf-like creatures. As the truer nature of the attack becomes evident, Bryant's portrayal grows ever more obsessive and flamboyant. She plays attorney-at-law Hattie Waters, who is enforcing a land-grab scam with a well-hidden pack of wolf-dog creatures trained to kill upon command. Director William Witney plays the attacks for full measure of nightmarish impact, setting the rampages against sunny, bucolic backdrops of a type usually reserved for romance or robust adventure.

The lawyer's comeuppance is surprising by the conventional measures of the sagebrush genre. Where the absorbed

viewer reasonably expects Hattie Waters to fall prey to her own animals, Miss Bryant deepens the character by giving Hattie a nervous demeanor that will complicate her (inevitable) demise. Rogers suffers more cruel indignities here than he usually allowed himself, including a perilous scrape that requires the intervention of his magnificent Palomino, Trigger. One of the attack dogs turns out to be an okay sort, after all—and even helps to hoist the villainess upon her own petard, as it were. Lovable Andy Devine plays a physician who may be harboring a grim secret or two.

CREDITS: Associate Producer: Edward J. White; Director: William Witney; Assistant Director: Jack Lacey; Screenplay: A. Sloan Nibley; Photographed by: Jack Marta; Musical Score: Dale Butts; Musical Director: Morton

Scott; Songs: "Texas Trails," "Padre of Old San Antone" and "Graveyard Filler of the West" by Tim Spencer; Editor: Tony Martinelli; Art Director: Frank Hotaling; Decor: John McCarthy, Jr., and George Milo; Costumer: Adele Palmer; Makeup: Bob Mark; Production Manager: Johnny Grubbs; Sound: Herbert Norsch; Special Effects: Howard Lydecker and Theodore Lydecker; Script Supervisor: Joan Ercmin; Grip: Gerry Lambrecht; Stills: Mickey Marigold; Operative Cameraman: Joe Novak; Running Time: 71 minutes; Released: July 15, 1948

CAST: Roy Rogers (Marshal Roy Rogers); Trigger, the Smartest Horse in the Movies (Himself); Lynne Roberts (Fanny Thatcher); Andy Devine (Dr. Cookie Bullfincher); Nana Bryant (Hattie Waters); Roy Barcroft (Vic Rabin); Danny Morton (Frank Dennis); Francis Ford (Thad Cameron); Pascale Perry (Pete); Stanley Blystone (Sheriff); Bob Nolan and the Sons of the Pioneers (Themselves); Pat Brady (Pat); Bob Reeves (Cowboy)

16 FATHOMS DEEP

(Monogram Productions, Inc./Arthur Lake Productions/Monogram Distributing Corp.)

Fathom this: Creighton Chaney, reluctantly attempting to honor the great-actor legacy of his father, Lon Chaney, takes the second-billed heroic lead in a 1934 Monogrammer called *Sixteen Fathoms Deep*, as an honest fisherman struggling against the treacheries of a rival. Little acclaim greets the artist, who might fare a great deal better if only he would start billing himself as Lon, Jr. Or so the industry would have him believe.

Fourteen years later, as Lon Chaney, Jr., the actor has climbed a long way and fallen just as far—a lapsed star of Universal Pictures' monster-movie machine, but a better actor by far as a consequence of all that experience. Disappointments both personal and professional, complicated by an appetite for carousing, have aged Chaney prematurely. His career, now gone almost fallow to catch-as-can free-agentry, finds Chaney back in harness as a Monogram player, and once again starring in a version of *16 Fathoms Deep*. (A.D. 1948 would prove a hopeful year of mixed blessings for Chaney, who saw, among other opportunities and setbacks, a tentative resurgence at Universal–International in *Bud Abbott & Lou Costello Meet Frankenstein*.)

The changes imposed on *Fathoms* run deeper by far, however, than just the abridgment within the title of *Sixteen* to *16*. Chaney now commands top billing, but his role becomes that of the treacherous plotter, scheming to undo the sponge-fishing ambitions of Lloyd Bridges, as the proverbial deep-sea diver with a stroke that can't go wrong.

The greater historical interest lies in the pride-of-place of this version of *16* (not *Sixteen*) *Fathoms Deep* as the first feature-length film to sport a new Ansco color process, which combined low-budget affordability with a warm-toned naturalness. The overall eye-appeal of the photography cannot compensate for a stodgy pace, which drones on for about an hour before any thrilling momentum kicks in.

Chaney is very good, of course, as the crook who seeks to discourage Bridges' upstart venture. Murder is a foregone conclusion, with the perils

ranging from severed air-supply lines to conveniently deployed sharks and gigantic clams. The antagonisms peak in a confrontation between Chaney and the bereaved father (John Qualen) of a sponge-harvesting clan. A climactic chase and slug-fest pitting Chaney against Bridges, John Gonatos and Eric Feldary ends with the payoff of Chaney's being impaled upon a sponge-gathering hook.

Bridges' eventual television stardom would hinge upon the Don Quixote-meets-Davy Jones exploits of *Sea Hunt* (1958–1961). At the stage documented in *16 Fathoms Deep*, Bridges has not quite achieved much screen presence beyond the requisite hearty aspect, and his off-screen narration becomes tiresome. Feldary is an abler heroic type, serving also as a romantic figure opposite the lovely Tanis Chandler. Dickie Moore, an *alumnus* of the *Our Gang* comedies, plays a diver done in by the grip of a giant clam. Arthur Lake, whose production company supervised the shoot, lends a forced comedy relief as a snapshot-happy tourist—Dagwood Bumstead, gone semi-tropical.

Director Irving Allen was a producer-director of several fine short subjects, including the Oscar champs "Forty Boys and a Song" (1942) and "Climbing the Matterhorn" (1947). Allen's few features as a director show little grasp of dramatic momentum. By 1951, he had switched over entirely to producing. His business partner in Warwick Films of Great Britain was Albert R. Broccoli.

CREDITS: Producers: James S. Burkett and Irving Allen; Director: Irving Allen; Assistant Director: Charles S. Gould; Screenplay: Max Trell; Adaptation: Forrest Judd; Based Upon: Eustace L. Adams' 1932 Story "Sixteen Fathoms Under"; Photographed by Jack Greenhalgh; Operative Cameraman: Paul Burress; Stills: Charles O'Rourke; Special Effects: Ray Mercer; Ansco Process Color Director: M. Peter Keane; Editor: Charles Craft; Musical Director: Lud Gluskin; Musical Score: Lucien Maroweck and René Garriguene; Sound: Josh Westmoreland; Production Manager: Belmont S. Gottleib; Script Supervisor: Mary Gibsone; Grip: Grant Tucker; Stand-in: John Gonatos; Running Time: 78 minutes; Released: July 25, 1948

CAST: Lon Chaney, Jr. (Dimitri); Arthur Lake (Pete); Lloyd Bridges (Lloyd Douglas); Eric Feldary (Alex); Tanis Chandler (Simi); John Qualen (Athos); Ian MacDonald (Nick); Dickie Moore (George); Harry Cheshire (Mike); John Bleifer (Capt. Briacos); Grant Means (Joe); John Gonatos (Johnny); Allen Matthews (Bus Driver)

Aside from Mike Price: I once left a newsroom flunky, I mean assistant, to her own best devices in an assignment to catalogue every last movie-information kit in my office. A big and perilous job, fraught with tedium and papercuts. I went looking for the file pertaining to this very film, 16 Fathoms Deep, some time later—only to find it missing from the New and Improved Order. Turned out my resourceful helper, unable to decide whether 16 belonged under O for "one-six" or S as in sixteen, had created a separate system for numerical titles. By which time, she also had progressed about halfway through the task of placing all titles beginning with the article-adjective "the" under the letter T.

This specimen later became a pop-culture expert, self-appointed, who soon proved incapable of distinguishing Bonnie Raitt from Bonnie Bramlett and fretted herself into a frenzy while attempting to fathom the difference between an electric guitar and an acoustic guitar. One of those horrors better left forgotten.

MARSHAL OF AMARILLO
(Republic Pictures Corp.)

Substantially more than just a spooky-hotel melodrama with a frontier setting, Philip Ford's *Marshal of Amarillo* is in fact a takeoff—unadmitted, of course—on one of the Depression-era pictures basic to all this *Forgotten Horrors* business. The patent source is Spencer Gordon Bennet's *The Midnight Warning* (1932), which had taken its cue from a baffling urban legend dating from 1893, and from a magazine piece called "The Most Maddening Story in the World," by Alexander Woollcott. Just a year before *Marshal of Amarillo* took shape, Anthony Thorne had reworked that same legend—involving a baffling disappearance and an elaborate cover-up—into a novel that would be filmed in England in 1950 as *So Long at the Fair*.

The present version finds businessman James Underwood (Tom Chatterton) checking into an ominous hotel, along with prospector Nugget Clark (Eddy Waller) and salesman Hiram Short (Charles Williams). Underwood goes missing, and so does a small fortune in currency that he had carried. Short turns up croaked. Nugget steals a stagecoach and hightails it. The coach veers out of control, and Nugget's shouts for help attract Marshal Rocky Lane (Allan Lane), who finds Short's body in the passenger cabin.

A return trip finds the lodge looking altogether less creepy. The proprietor (Trevor Bardette) asserts that Nugget has never set foot in the place. When Nugget attempts to show Marshal Lane to Underwood's room, the space proves to be a closet. The coach-

man (Roy Barcroft) who had deposited the travelers proves connected with a kidnapping scheme. A re-enactment of the prior evening turns up Underwood's missing money, then Underwood himself, and finally exposes the innkeeper and an overzealous border agent (Clayton Moore, in anti-Lone Ranger mode) as the perpetrators.

Mayhem is at a minimum, but the prevailing eeriness is adequate. Denver Pyle and Minerva Urecal contribute the right ghoulish grace-notes as incidental characters, and Eddy Waller's portrayal of the nervous grubstaker is by turns amusing and heroic. Western series star Allan Lane, a lesser Henry Fonda type, tends more to react to the mystery than to take control of things, barring the rousing stunt-action business. The most winning set-piece is the runaway-coach routine, with Waller dangling from the chassis and Lane charging to the rescue.

CREDITS: Associate Producer: Gordon Kay; Director: Philip Ford; Assistant Director: Joe Dill; Screenplay: Robert Creighton "Bob" Williams; Photographed by: John Mac-Burnie; Editor: Harold Minter; Art Director: Frank Arrigo; Decor: John McCarthy, Jr., and Charles Thompson; Hair Stylist: Della Barnes; Makeup: Bob Mark; Sound: Victor Appel; Special Effects: Howard Lydecker and Theodore Lydecker; Stills: Ira Hoke; Grip: C.B. "Whitey" Lawrence; Operative Cameraman: Enzo Martinelli; Musical Director: Morton Scott; Script Supervisor: Robert "Bob" Walker; Running Time: 60 minutes; Released: July 25, 1948

CAST: Allan "Rocky" Lane (Rocky Lane); Blackjack (Himself); Eddy Waller (Nugget Clark); Mildred Coles (Marjorie Underwood); Clayton Moore (Art Crandall); Roy Barcroft (Ben); Trevor Bardette (Frank Welch); Minerva Urecal (Mrs. Pettigrew); Denver

Pyle (Clerk); Charles Williams (Hiram Short); Tom Chatterton (James Underwood); Peter Perkins (Sam); Tom London (Snodgrass); Lynn Castile (Mathilda Snodgrass)

JUNGLE GODDESS
(Crestwood Pictures, Inc./Lippert Productions, Inc./William Stephens Productions/ Screen Guild Productions, Inc.)

An early misfire from Robert L. Lippert's grasping little company is Lewis D. Collins' *Jungle Goddess*, which comes up so dry that it should have been called *Desert Goddess*. Even George Reeves, not far from his blessing-or-curse plunge into *The Adventures of Superman*, turns in an uncharacteristically flat performance. Of course, the hackneyed circumstances of Jo Pagano's screenplay—adventurer chums experience a lethal falling-out while trying to bring home a missing heiress—carry no motivation greater than the paycheck waiting at the end of the shoot.

Almost 10 years after her plane had crashed in a backlot jungle, Greta Vanderhorn (Wanda McKay) has become the white goddess of a human-sacrificing tribe. Aviators Mike Patton (Reeves) and Bob Simpson (Ralph Byrd) locate the tribe easily enough, but Simpson's violent response to the natives' approach makes him a candidate for ritual slaughter. Greta, having ordered Bob's discombobulation as a ruse, plots with Patton to escape her kingdom, such as it is. Bob, meanwhile, has a more sinister conspiracy in the works, involving the usual issues of greed and lust. We cut herewith to a showdown on the point of takeoff, a decisive spear-impalement for Simpson, and a slick-as-a-whistle exit for Patton and Greta.

Ralph Byrd, Hollywood's once-and-future Dick Tracy, manages a credible show of villainy as Bob Simpson degenerates into a jungle-fever strain of madness. Byrd does not sustain the routine sufficiently, but he nonetheless registers an occasional immersion in character. Reeves, usually a more energetic player, neither enacts nor reacts. Wanda McKay looks sufficiently imperious, but radiates no conviction. Devotees of

VCI released a George Reeves double feature including *Jungle Goddess.*

the Poverty Row chillers will get a kick out of spotting Zack Williams (mis-billed here as Zach), the lanky and spastic gorilla-man of 1940's *Son of Ingagi*, as *Jungle Goddess'* chief-in-residence.

Robert L. Lippert (1909–1976) will come more decisively into his own in subsequent volumes of *Forgotten Horrors*. Suffice for now to acknowledge that Lippert delivered more than one small-time producer's share of entertaining schlock—along with some pretty respectable films, here and there—en route to a prolonged involvement with various major-league studios. Returning during the 1960s to his origins as a picture-show operator, Lippert left his most lasting mark upon film going as the originator of the low-overhead multiplex-theater concept. For better or for worse, and certainly for the cheaper.

CREDITS: Presented by: Robert L. Lippert; Producer and Basic Scenarist: William Stephens; Director: Lewis D. Collins; Assistant Director: Melville Shyer; Screenplay: Jo Pagano; Photographed by: Carl Berger; Musical Director: Irving Gertz; Song: "There's No One in My Heart but You" by Irving Bibo; Editor: Norman Cerf; Art Director: Martin Obzina; Decor: Alfred E. Spencer; Makeup: Paul Stanhope; Sound: Glen Glenn; Script Supervisor: Mary Chaffee; Grip: Bill Johnson; Stills: Fred Parrish; Operative Cameraman: Vaughn Wilkins; Running Time: 62 minutes; Released: August 13, 1948

CAST: George Reeves (Mike Patton); Wanda McKay (Greta Vanderhorn); Armida Vendrell (Wanama); Ralph Byrd (Bob Simpson); Smoki Whitfield (Oolonga); Dolores Castle (Yvonne); Rudy Robles (Nugara); Linda Johnson (Helen); Helena Grant (Mrs. Fitzhugh); Fred Coby (Pilot); Jack Carroll (Accompanist); Onest Conley (Drummer); Zack Williams (M'benga)

LADY AT MIDNIGHT

(John Sutherland Productions, Inc./Eagle-Lion Films, Inc./Pathé Industries, Inc.)

This one looked like such a classy item-in-the-making that the too-prolific director Sam Newfield trotted out his less frequently used pseudonym of Sherman Scott for the occasion. The story boasted prestigious origins in *Good Housekeeping* magazine, with author Richard Sale attached to adapt his yarn to the screen. (Sale was a refugee from the pulps, also working by now as a screen director—as on 1947's *Spoilers of the North*.) Composer Leo Erdody matched the menacing tone of the piece with a portentous musical score, designed to convey the striking of clocks as time runs out for a young family. The crucial role of a child in peril went to seven-year-old Lora Lee Michel, a fresh discovery who had registered impressively as Olivia de Havilland's younger self in *The Snake Pit* (1948).

Such a concentration of higher intentions should have meant a greater success for *Lady at Midnight*, but a lack of marquee-value names and the bland leading work of Richard Denning and Frances Rafferty left the picture ill prepared to compete beyond its bottom-of-the-bill double-feature engagements. Sale's source-story is a respectable stab at

bringing a pulp-magazine sensibility to the higher-paying realm of the middlebrow slicks, but his idea of hard-boiled dialogue runs to such hackery as "Open *up* in there!" and "You can say *that* again!" Newfield-as-Scott indulges Sale at every turn, including treacly sentimental detours, and the director allows Denning and Miss Rafferty to get by on agreeable looks and stilted earnestness.

The setup is fearsome, all the same, and the bad-guy players—their machinations are but gradually revealed—pose a menace with which to reckon, given the million-dollar stakes of the motivating crime. Miss Michel is a wonder, ad-libbing some of her lines like a natural kid and delivering one lengthy take of formal dialogue with a grasp that puts the grown-up players in the shade.

One midnight, Pete and Ellen Wiggins (Denning and Miss Rafferty) wake to the sound of

THE CLOCK TICKED OFF MURDER AT MIDNIGHT!

LADY AT MIDNIGHT

A JOHN SUTHERLAND PRODUCTION · AN EAGLE-LION FILMS RELEASE

an intruder. Daughter Tina (Miss Michel) tells her parents that "a pretty lady" has visited. (This information is affirmed for the audience in a dreamlike tracking shot, over a minute in length, of a woman's legs as she descends a staircase and exits. The child's parents are denied such explicit knowledge.) Only the emotional state of the household seems to have been disturbed.

The next day, Pete, a Los Angeles radio announcer, receives a newsbreak: An heiress named Amanda Forsythe was shot to death the night before along the street where the Wigginses live. Meanwhile, Tina reveals something more: The "pretty lady" had spoken of Tina's adoption as an infant. Tina has long known that fact, but her account of the encounter makes the intrusion all the more troubling.

A challenge to the Wigginses' parental rights arises from an anonymous party. Pete's lawyer, Ross Atherton (Harlan Warde), seems helpful enough in a bumbling way—but Atherton also is working for the Forsythe family. Pete wonders whether the victim's brother, Freddy Forsythe (former child star Jackie Searle, still playing to type as a google-eyed sneak), might have a connection with the adoption suit. Showgirl Carolyn Sugar (Claudia Drake), purported to be Tina's natural mother, lams out for the East Coast after receiving a cash-money windfall—only to change her mind and turn up murdered before she can reveal much of anything.

Pete and a determined cuss of a private eye (Ralph Dunn) have learned enough, however, to pin suspicion upon the weasly-looking Freddy. Freddy has not only learned that his sister was the plaintiff in the adoption case but also grows to suspect that she was Tina's birth-mother. Freddy presses the lawsuit. His aunt, Lydia Forsythe (Nana Bryant), plays cagey with Pete but finally comes clean with the entire dirty lowdown. Not only is Tina Amanda's offspring, but Amanda had recently made out a will leaving her fortune to the child. Hence Freddy's murderous interest.

Except that Freddy doesn't seem quite bright enough to have engineered such a campaign. The mastermind proves to be Atherton, who guns down Freddy as a turncoat and gives Pete a roughing-up before the police can arrive. All turns out well, and also lucrative, for the restored Wiggins family.

Lady at Midnight earns its ominous title, evocative of that *noir*-master Cornell Woolrich, with a splendidly well-built opening sequence. (The title player, though seen only from the knees down in that foreboding staircase scene, is Jean Bain.) Erdody's musical score is melodramatically effective as a conventional symphonic work, but it is rendered distinctive by the use of 35 clock-sounds, from the tolling of Big Ben and the melodious chimes of Swiss-made antiques to the clanging and buzzing of modern-day timepieces. These tones were achieved via a combination of pre-recorded sound effects and real-time ringings, with many of the clocks placed among the members of the orchestra and cued like instruments.

The principal players are a mixed lot. Richard Denning was on the rise as a B-movie action-and-thrills star, with a nearer-the-mainstream sideline in network television. (Denning's best-remembered big-screen turn, in 1955's *Creature with the Atom Brain*, would find him playing yet another distressed middle-class family man.) Frances Rafferty was on her way out as a movie star of modest acclaim, having left a long-standing ingénue berth at MGM to try freelancing with the smaller studios. Miss Rafferty would fare better in the realm of television, with steady work on a hit situation comedy, *December Bride*, and its spin-off, *Pete & Gladys*, during 1954–1962.

Lora Lee Michel carried on as a scene-stealer in films large and small, from Ernest B. Schoedsack's *Mighty Joe Young* (1949) to William Castle's disturbing outsider melodrama *It's a Small World* (1950). A re-christening to Laura Lee Michel did little to bolster her prospects for the longer term.

Jackie Searle was in the midst of a busy but short-lived comeback that he had launched in 1947 with the big-band bio-picture *The Fabulous Dorseys*, ending a five-year hiatus. "I feel comfortable playing the villain," Searle said in a prefabricated interview from Eagle-Lion's publicity department. "After all, I *did* get a good start at it as a kid." Searle had served memorably as a bratty annoyance to Jackie Coogan and Junior Durkin in the matched set of *Tom Sawyer* and *Huckleberry Finn* (1930–1931), and to Jackie Cooper in *Peck's Bad Boy* (1934).

The spring-of-1948 filming of *Lady at Midnight* yielded one of the niftier blooper anecdotes of postwar Hollywood. One scene called for Denning and Miss Rafferty to react in close-up to the discovery of a crucial document in the adoption case. Properties chief George Bahr provided the slip of paper, and Newfield and camera chief Jack Greenhalgh nailed the shot in a take. The screening of the rushes the next day, however, found the document legible on screen: It was an invoice to Eagle-Lion Films from a florist's shop. The scene was re-shot with a less conspicuous page.

Newfield, whose mastery of quick-and-cheap production tactics was a simultaneous blessing-and-curse for him as a Hollywood workhorse, also claimed to have given *Lady at Midnight* the shortest location-shooting trip on record. Requiring an air-terminal exterior for one transition, Newfield noticed that St. Anne's Maternity Hospital in Los Angeles had an appropriate look about its façade. So he herded the cast and crew over to St. Anne's and ordered everybody to make believe the hospital was an airport. The facility was located just across from Eagle-Lion's studios.

Daylight Saving Time kicked in during the two-week shoot, prompting this memorandum from producer John Sutherland: "Despite the start of D.S.T., the title of this picture will positively not be changed to *Lady at 1 a.m.*"

CREDITS: Producer: John Sutherland; Director: Sam Newfield (as Sherman Scott); Assistant Director: Stanley Neufeld; Screenplay: Richard Sale, from His Story, "Lady at Midnight," in the February-March 1945 Issue of *Good Housekeeping*; Photographed by: Jack Greenhalgh; Operative Cameraman: Ernest Smith; Stills: Harry Ross; Special Effects: Ray Mercer; Supervisor of Process Photography: Ray Smallwood; Art Director: Edward Jewell; Editor: Martin Cohn; Decor: Elias Reif; Properties: George Bahr; Music: Leo Erdody; Sound: Ben Winkler; Makeup: Harry Ross; Production Manager: Bert Sternbach; Script Supervisor: Emily Ehrlich; Grip: Walter Culp; Running Time: 60 minutes; Released: August 15, 1948

CAST: Richard Denning (Pete Wiggins); Frances Rafferty (Ellen Wiggins); Lora Lee Michel (Tina Wiggins); Ralph Dunn (Al Garrity); Nana Bryant (Lydia Forsythe); Jack [Jackie] Searle (Freddy Forsythe); Harlan Warde (Ross Atherton); Claudia Drake (Carolyn Sugar); Jean Bain (Amanda Forsythe); Ben Welden (Willie Gold); Pierre Watkin (John Featherstone); Sid Melton (Benny Muscle)

PITFALL

(Regal Films, Inc./United Artists Corp.)

The old-time Poverty Row producer Samuel Bischoff (1890-1975) is a fundamental presence in the realm of *Forgotten Horrors*, what with his involvement in such cornerstone titles as *Tombstone Canyon* (1932) and *A Study in Scarlet, The Lone Avenger* and *Deluge* (all from 1933). Bischoff was the *B* in KBS Productions, an ambitious and artistically inclined independent outfit with a major-league attitude. KBS' communion with the bigger studios was such that, for example, *Deluge* wound up with an RKO-Radio Pictures release and Bischoff himself landed producer credentials on such pictures as Warners' *Return of the Terror* (1934) and *Earthworm Tractors* (1936).

Bischoff's momentum would continue apace all through the 1950s, meeting the 1960s with a dwindling output that capped itself off with *The Strangler* in 1964. More than merely a Status Quo bankroller and supervisor, Bischoff followed closely and occasionally even paced the tastes and trends of whatever generation of customers he happened to be courting. Such a timely and socially wide-awake picture is Bischoff's production of Andre de Toth's *Pitfall*, a boldly moralistic fusion of the *film noir* style with a melodrama of the middle-class American Dream gone haywire.

Jay Dratler's 1947 novel *The Pitfall* is the source, a tale that punctures the postwar era's prevalent notion of bourgeois security. Dick Powell stars as John Forbes, a suburbanite family man and insurance adjuster whose stable existence only bores him. Married too soon to his school-days sweetheart Sue (played by Jane Wyatt, the archetypal American Mom-to-be of network television's *Father Knows Best*), Forbes has grown at once complacent and resentful of his complacency and takes out his frustrations on his household.

An overbearing private detective named J.B. "Mack" MacDonald (Raymond Burr) draws Forbes into the sordid aftermath of an embezzlement case involving a crook, Bill Smiley (Byron Barr), whom Forbes' agency had bonded. The trail of the stolen loot leads to fashion model Mona Stevens (husky-voiced Lizabeth Scott), whose extravagant tastes would suggest she has benefited most directly from the theft.

Forbes' approach to Mona is strictly business, but MacDonald—who makes no secret of his lust for Mona—also presses Forbes to plead Mack's case with the sultry dame, who considers the detective repellent. Mona finds herself attracted to Forbes, who allows himself a spot of adulterous indulgence.

The upshot is a precipitous downfall. Mack learns of the affair and administers

A MAN CAN BE STRONG AS STEEL ...but somewhere there's a woman who'll break him!...

Regal Films presents

DICK POWELL
LIZABETH SCOTT in "PITFALL"

with
JANE WYATT and Raymond Burr
Byron Barr · John Litel · Ann Doran · Jimmy Hunt · Selmer Jackson
Based on the Novel "The Pitfall" by Jay Dratler · Screenplay by Karl Kamb
Directed by ANDRE De TOTH · Produced by SAMUEL BISCHOFF · Released thru UNITED ARTISTS

a beating to Forbes, threatening to inform Mrs. Forbes of her husband's lapse. Forbes leaves his wife guessing about his all-too-obvious injuries and declines to summon the police. The surprising turn here is Mona's appeal to Forbes upon learning of his marital status: "Why... mess up something that you have that's so good?"

Mack escalates from thuggish annoyance to outright menace, provoking Forbes to retaliate in defense of Mona and at length informing jailbird Smiley of Mona's involvement with Forbes. Released early on a clemency bid, Smiley becomes a ready pawn in Mack's campaign to put Forbes out of commission. Even when warned that the jealous Smiley has him in the cross-hairs, Forbes cannot muster the gumption to call the police: His family might get wise.

Forbes lies in ambush for Smiley, who winds up croaked and explained away as a common prowler. Meanwhile, Mack barges in on Mona with an agenda of abduction and ravishment, but she guns him down.

Forbes, cornered at last in his own web of lies, 'fesses up and finds both the law and his wife forgiving. In a cruel twist that amounts to the film's cold-comfort indictment of double-standard gender discrimination, Mona must face charges in the slaying of Mack MacDonald.

The picture reserves its greater indictments for smug middle-class materialism, and for the cranky nature of one who blames his comfortable surroundings for his innate shortcomings. Raymond Burr—an imposing presence who seems gaunt and unhealthy despite his bulk—may be more obviously the monster of the piece, but it is Powell who motivates the mayhem through sheer ingratitude for the generous hand that he has dealt himself. Burr renders MacDonald terrifying through sheer oafishness and single-minded determination to Do the Wrong Thing at every opportunity, apart from his character's law-abiding interest in recovering a stolen bankroll. Powell's John Forbes is more the backbone-of-society type with a few slipped discs, and he'd sooner lash out at his loved ones than try to figure out what makes him so blasted irritable. The prescience of *Pitfall* is such that it plays out today as almost a more robust prototype for Sam Mendes' overrated Oscar-bait picture of 1999, *American Beauty*—with a greater life-or-death urgency, of course, and without the *Lolita* angle.

The finer surprise of *Pitfall* is its employment of kid actor Jimmy Hunt in the role of Powell and Jane Wyatt's overanxious and nightmare-prone son, who senses but cannot comprehend the tensions warping his family circle. Tommy Forbes' account of his latest such bad dream inspires no fatherly comforting from Powell's John Forbes—just a snide observation that the child would be a great deal better off if he'd stop reading those blasted comic books. In a stroke, *Pitfall* crystallizes the Real World's herd-mentality intolerance that soon would put the entire comics-magazine industry on trial for its existence before the U.S. Senate's witch-hunting Subcommittee on Juvenile Delinquency.

As for Jimmy Hunt, this gemlike small performance anticipates explicitly his crucial role in 1953's *Invaders from Mars*—in which Hunt carries the show as a nightmare-prone schoolboy with an appetite for comic books.

CREDITS: Producer: Samuel Bischoff; Director: André de Toth; Assistant Directors: Joseph Depew and Dick Dixon; Screenplay: Karl Kamb, From Jay Dratler's 1947 Novel, *The Pitfall*; Photographed by: Harry J. Wild; Operative Cameraman: Charles Straumer; Stills: Frank Tanner; Editor: Walter Thompson; Decor: Robert Priestley; Musical Director: Lou Forbes; Sound: Frank Webster; Makeup: Robert Cowan and Kiva Hoffman; Hair Stylist: Hedvig Mjorud; Production Supervisor: Ben Hersh; Running Time: 85 minutes; Released: August 19, 1948

CAST: Dick Powell (John Forbes); Jane Wyatt (Sue Forbes); Lizabeth Scott (Mona Stevens); Raymond Burr (J.B. "Mack" MacDonald); John Litel (District Attorney); Byron Barr (Bill Smiley); Ann Doran (Maggie); Jimmy Hunt (Tommy Forbes); Selmar Jackson (Ed Brawley); Margaret Wells (Terry); Dick Wessel (Desk Sergeant)

SONS OF ADVENTURE
(Republic Pictures Corp.)

Yakima Canutt, the most innovative daredevil among Old Hollywood's stuntmen, had turned director on occasion since 1935, taking the craft ever more seriously during the mid-to-late 1940s. Canutt tackled *Sons of Adventure* as a project of particularly personalized interest. The yarn sends a Western-movies stuntman to play detective, the better to trap a killer at large—the Phantom of the Horse Opera, you should pardon the expression.

Andy Baldwin (Gordon Jones), fresh out of uniform and in need of a job, finds a wartime pal, Steve Malone (Russell "Lucky" Hayden), working as a Hollywood stunts ace. Steve arranges similar work for Andy, who lands in a heap of trouble after a scene in which he must open fire on the star player, an arrogant cuss named Paul Kenyon (John Holland), with a gun containing blanks. The blanks turn out to be live ammunition, and Andy becomes a candidate for a murder frame.

The resemblance to Edwin L. Marin's *The Death Kiss*, a sound-stage sleuther from 1932, is unmistakable, not only in the inaugural crime but also in the revelation of the victim's *persona non grata* standing with any number of people. Steve Malone undertakes to solve things, undaunted by a rash of hairy scrapes as he comes nearer to smoking out the killer. In a standoff atop a scaffolding rig, an assistant director (George Chandler) is revealed as the slayer as a prelude to a fatal plunge. Seems Kenyon had driven the chap's sister to suicide.

The stress upon all that stunting tends to obscure the slightness of the story—the path is nowhere near as cruelly twisted as that which makes *The Death Kiss* so unpredictable—but Canutt's homage to his meat-and-potatoes profession is its own reward. Veteran oater star Hayden handles the leading role with dash and vigor—clearly supplying some of his own stunt work—and Gordon Jones makes an effectively determined sidekick. Lynne Roberts is particularly pleasing as a stunt artist engaged to marry Hayden. George Chan-

DRAMA OF HOLLYWOOD STUNT MEN

SONS OF ADVENTURE

LYNNE ROBERTS
RUSS HAYDEN
GORDON JONES
GRANT WITHERS
JOHN NEWLAND
STEPHANIE BACHELOR

Directed by YAKIMA CANUTT
ORIGINAL SCREEN PLAY BY FRANKLIN ADREON AND SOL SHOR

A REPUBLIC PICTURE

dler renders credible the motivations of the killer, keeping his presence subdued until the high-anxiety finale. The behind-the-scenes hustle-and-bustle provides a fascinating look at the operations of Republic Pictures' Western-movie unit. Cost-cutting measures are evident only in the brief running time and the use of canned music from Republic's library of original works—which lends a cliffhanger atmosphere. The working title was *The Thrill Man*.

CREDITS: Associate Producer: Franklin Adreon; Director: Yakima Canutt; Assistant Director: Robert G. "Bob" Shannon; Screenplay: Franklin Adreon and Sol Shor; Photographed by: John MacBurnie; Musical Director: Morton Scott; Stock Music Composed by: R. Dale Butts; Joseph Dubin; Mort Glickman; Charles Maxwell; Heinz Roemheld; Walter Scharf; Nathan Scott; Editor: Harold Minter; Art Director: James W. Sullivan; Decor: John McCarthy, Jr., and James Redd; Hair Stylist: Peggy Gray; Makeup: Bob Mark; Production Manager: Joe Dill; Sound: Earl Crain, Sr.; Special Effects: Howard Lydecker and Theodore Lydecker; Stills: Ira Hoke; Grip: C.B. "Whitey" Lawrence; Operative Cameraman: Joe Novak; Script Supervisor: Robert "Bob" Walker; Running Time: 60 minutes; Released: August 27, 1948

Dreams That Money Can Buy

CAST: Lynne Roberts (Jean Taylor); Russell "Lucky" Hayden (Steve Malone); Gordon Jones (Andy Baldwin); Grant Withers (J.L. Sterling); George Chandler (Billy Wilkes); Roy Barcroft (Leslie Bennett); John Newland (Peter Winslow); Stephanie Bachelor (Laura Gifford); John Holland (Paul Kenyon); Gilbert Frye (Sam Hodges); Richard Irving (Eddie); Joan Blair (Glenda); John Crawford (Norton); Keith Richards (Harry); James Dale (Whitey); George Douglas (Guard); Bud Wolfe (Leader); Sailor Vincent (Baldy); Louis R. Faust (Bearer); Steve Dunhill (Actor)

THE CREEPER
(Reliance Pictures, Inc./Twentieth Century Fox Film Corp.)

A horror-movie fan coming cold to *The Creeper* might be forgiven for expecting a Rondo Hatton vehicle from Universal Pictures and/or PRC. After all, Hatton — Universal's last horror-movie personality and a Real World victim of acromegaly, the glandular malfunction that distorts the face and extremities — had played a character called the Creeper in three pictures: the 1944 Sherlock Holmes entry *The Pearl of Death* (as the Hoxton Creeper, the better to establish a certain English-ness about the menace) and two from 1946, *House of Horrors* and *The Brute Man*. Not only that, but the 1946 entries also had boasted the contributions of *The Creeper*'s executive producer and director, respectively Ben Pivar and Jean Yarbrough.

But this present film bears no narrative kinship to Universal's *Creeper* series, being a self-contained fantasia upon mad-doctor and serial-murder themes with undercurrents of Third World superstition. Two developments in 1946 had made a new *Creeper* series entry from Universal very improbable: First, Hatton died. Second, Universal merged with International Pictures Corp., and in an effort to class up the newly minted Universal–International product, the company cut loose most of its B-unit producers — including Pivar, who had been around the lot since the late 1930s.

This sudden putting-on of airs goes a long way toward explaining why the emerging Universal–International chose not to issue *The Brute Man*, selling it instead to Producers Releasing Corporation.

The Creeper met with a comparable fate. Edward Small's hardy little Reliance Pictures — which had been around since the Depression-era glory days of *I Cover the Waterfront* and *Let 'Em Have It* — produced *The Creeper* with Universal–International resources and technical talents in expectation of a U–I release. Shot on an efficient two-week schedule during March of 1948, *The Creeper* sat idle until the late summer of that year, when Twentieth Century-Fox acquired it (nailing the copyright in the process) for a September release. This tactic is called a negative pick-up. The expression has rather a scrofulous ring to it — sounding a bit like the title of a Mickey Gilley song — but in fact it refers literally to the *picking-up* of a film's *negative* by an otherwise unaffiliated company. Hence the term.

And so why, then, was this picture called *The Creeper*? Maybe because its original working title, *The Cat Man*, had come under challenge from Republic Pictures, whose *The Catman of Paris* dated from just a few years earlier. Maybe there is no one left who knows, but there assuredly is a story there. And maybe the Powers That Did Be simply knew that *The Creeper* was a marketable title, with or without Rondo Hatton. *Cat Man* or *Creeper*, the film promptly became fair game for the Infringement Police: A radio

scenarist named Joseph Ruscoll filed suit early in 1949 on grounds that a program he had scripted, called *The Creeper*, took prior claim. Fox paid Ruscoll a settlement, sum undisclosed, to scram. By which time, *The Creeper*—the movie—had enjoyed its day in the enlivening glare of the carbon-arc projector lamp and gone on to become a soon-forgotten picture.

At any rate, the titular creature this time around is not a deformed man, but a black cat that hangs out in the lab of heroic allergist John Reade (John Baragrey), a research scientist working with his archly creepy associate, Dr. Van Glock (Eduardo Ciannelli). (Veterinary allergy research makes for some weird movies: Witness 2001's *Cats and Dogs*, which boasts Jeff Goldblum as a purely benevolent but nonetheless off-kilter doctor.)

Meanwhile, Dr. Lester Cavigny (Ralph Morgan) and one Dr. Borden (Onslow Stevens) return from a long residency in the West Indies and move back in next door to the allergy lab, bringing along a strange-looking handyman named André Dussaud (David Hoffman), ice-queen researcher Gwen (June Vincent) and Cavigny's daughter, Nora (Janis Wilson). Both women crave the dashing Reade, but each is so neurotic that you could scarcely blame the guy for bailing and setting up shop in another time zone, leaving no forwarding address. Nora, in fact, seems hopelessly nutty; she is given to crazy dreams in which a giant cat's paw comes flailing through a window or snaking out from underneath her bed. She also is prone to sleepwalking with a loaded gun, and she goes absolutely buggy every time she sees a cat. Of course, since young Dr. Reade loves having felines around, and Nora's pop and Dr. Borden are performing the bulk of their research on cats, Nora does a lot of screaming, eye rolling, and fainting over the course of the picture.

As it develops, Dr. Borden's experiments with injecting phosphorescence into living tissue—the better to illuminate the organs during surgery—probably had led to the death of Andre's wife. In fact, on the night poor Mrs. Dussaud had croaked over there in the godforsaken West Indies, a fever-ridden Nora experienced her first *felis domesticus giganticus* nightmare, and since the natives believe that the souls of the dead enter the bodies of cats, well...

The whole thing comes to a resolution at Dr. Cavigny's house—with Nora, who makes curious choices throughout, at home alone—but not before three deaths and a good deal of eeriness. One scene in particular stays in the mind: a corpse, face-down on the floor, with cats sniffing about.

The plot does not stand up under scrutiny. Veteran scripter Maurice Tombragel gives a slight indication that the ordeal may have taken place in Nora Cavigny's somewhat askew head, which makes more sense than anything else. (Tombragel had worked with Pivar at Universal on the 1940 Richard Arlen starrer *Hot Steel*, which trades upon murder and infidelity in a steel-mill setting—or a steel *milieu*, as it were.)

But even with its loopy plotting, *The Creeper* ends up looking and feeling pretty much like a later Universal spooker—as it should, since it was intended as such. It neither looks nor moves like a Fox B-unit picture, if measured against the glossier standard of such little Foxes of the '40s as *Dr. Renault's Secret*, *The Undying Monster* and *The Man Who Wouldn't Die*. (The backstage kinships run deep: Set decorator Fay Babcock was the wife of writer Dwight V. Babcock, the detective-pulp specialist and B-picture scripter who also had worked for the Pivar unit at Universal.)

While there are no major marquee names, the three top-billed old-timers—Eduardo Ciannelli, Onslow Stevens and Ralph Morgan—are familiar faces to lovers of genre pictures, if not of quite the same stature as a Lionel Atwill or a George Zucco. The three had, in fact, been featured in some of the classic-manner Universal horrors: the cadaverous Ciannelli as the High Priest in *The Mummy's Hand* (1940); Stevens as the memorable Dr. Edelmann in 1945's *House of Dracula* (and, earlier, the Universal-reject oddity *Life Returns*, from 1934); and the avuncular Morgan in *Night Monster* (1942) and *Weird Woman* (1944). All concerned do fine work, as does the rest of the cast, although a little of June Vincent's spacey histrionics goes a long way. Miss Wilson, sporting a compellingly strange two-tone hair color, goes nicely bipolar at unexpected moments, and Philip Ahn makes memorably much of a bit role as the cheerfully capitalistic owner of an Oriental eatery.

In an interesting outcropping of Small World Syndrome, Ralph Morgan also starred in the PRC chiller *The Monster Maker* (1944)—in which he is injected with a serum that causes acromegaly! Rondo Hatton's elongated visage may not have been on display in this particular *Creeper*, but his ghost must certainly have been hovering about.

CREDITS: Executive Producer: Ben Pivar; Producer: Bernard Small; Director: Jean Yarbrough; Assistant Director: Eddie Stein; Screenplay: Maurice Tombragel; Photographed by: George Robinson; Operative Cameraman: Edward Coleman; Musical Score: Milton Rosen; Editor: Saul A. Goodkind; Art Director: Walter Koessler; Decor: Fay Babcock; Makeup: Ted Larsen; Hair Stylist: Betty Pedretti; Production Manager: James Dent; Sound: Frank McWhorter; Grip: Walter Dalton; Stills: C. Ken Lobben; Script Supervisor: Bobbie Sierks; Running Time: 64 minutes; Released: During September of 1948

CAST: Eduardo Ciannelli (Dr. Van Glock); Onslow Stevens (Dr. Jim Bordon); June Vincent (Nora Cavigny); Ralph Morgan (Dr. Lester Cavigny); Janis Wilson (Gwenn

Ronstrum); John Baragrey (Dr. John Reade); Richard Lane (Inspector Fenwick); Philip Ahn (Wong); Lotte Stein (Nurse Halpern); Ralph Peters (Laborer); David Hoffman (Andre Dousseau); Stuart Holmes (Medical Examiner); and Julie Morgan

MIRACULOUS JOURNEY

(Sigmund Neufeld Pictures, Inc./Film Classics, Inc.)

It is difficult not to like any picture that puts Rory Calhoun in charge of a jungle rescue, but Sam Newfield's *Miraculous Journey* comes up wanting, at least upon this occasion of rediscovery. Perhaps the ambitious and conflicted little film suffers from on-the-spot comparison with this same year's *Angel on the Amazon* and *Man-Eater of Kumaon*, films that steepen the curve.

Miraculous Journey is nonetheless a handsomely packaged adventure, and one of the better-looking jobs of Cinecolor photography, as handled by Jack Greenhalgh. The scenery looks as lush as it is forbidding, and this quality goes a long way toward rendering Calhoun's trek urgent.

An airborne hijacking over Africa leaves stranded an oddly matched set of passengers. Mary (Audrey Long) had been traveling to meet a surgeon who might cure her blindness. Patricia (Virginia Grey) is a spoiled-brat heiress. Kendricks (Thurston Hall) is a pompous industrialist. René La Cour (June Storey) is an entertainer. Racketeer Nick Travelli (Jim Bannon, playing against his usual heroic type) might have refrained from scuttling the flight, if only stewardess Jane Mason (Carole Donne) had not recognized him as a fugitive and sounded an alarm. Pilot Larry Burke (Calhoun) arms himself with Travelli's gun after the gangster is knocked unconscious in the crash.

A hermit (George Cleveland) shows up in time to show the survivors how to subsist in what he calls "the biggest swamp in the world," which also contains a diamond field that proves damnably tempting to Kendricks and Travelli. The scenario calls for the ranks to be depleted and humbled by such plot-device menaces as a gorilla, a crocodile, a storm and a quicksand bog. The crisis has a peculiar socializing effect upon the castaways, whose survivors probably will come away changed for the better. Assuming, of course, that Calhoun can finagle a rescue.

Calhoun is squarely within his heroic element. Thurston Hall, as the big shot reduced to menial chores, and Audrey Long, as the sightless traveler who finds herself attracted to Calhoun, deliver performances worthy of a bigger, or at least a more self-confident, picture. Most of the players do far less with their under-written, quick-sketch roles. The most memorable enactment belongs to a trained dog named Flame, who appears as George Cleveland's fierce protector.

Newfield leans toward tough action while Fred Myton's screenplay tries too hard to validate itself as a redemption fable. The struggle between imperatives is a terrible distraction.

That said, we also should acknowledge Myton here and now as a grand presence in the greater perspective of cinema. The guy's career dates all the way back to 1916, when at 31 (no greenhorn kid trying to grow up with the industry) he became a scenarist on such early-times features as *The Social Buccaneer* and *Some Medicine Man*. He would continue to write for the movies — and for television's *The Gene Autry Show* — until three years before his death in 1955.

More pointedly, Myton is responsible for such *Forgotten Horrors* standards as *Nabonga*, *The Mad Monster*, *The Black Raven* and *Dead Men Walk*. He even wrote *The Terror of Tiny Town* and one of Herbert Jeffries' trailblazing all-Negro Westerns, *Harlem on the Prairie*. Myton was really something—an unsung hero of the genre and beyond.

CREDITS: Producer: Sigmund Neufeld; Director: Sam Newfield (as Peter Stewart); Assistant Director: Stanley Neufeld (a.k.a. Newfield); Story and Screenplay: Fred Myton; Photographed by: Jack Greenhalgh; Music: Leo Erdody and Lew Porter; Editor: Holbrook N. Todd; Decor: Harry Reif; Makeup: Harry Ross; Production Manager: Bert Sternbach; Sound: Ben Winkler; Grip: Walter Culp; Script Supervisor: Emily Erlich; Stills: Milton Gold; Running Time: 76 minutes; Released: September 1, 1948

CAST: Rory Calhoun (Larry Burke); Audrey Long (Mary); Virginia Grey (Patricia); George Cleveland (Hermit); Jim Bannon (Nick Travelli); June Storey (René La Cour); Thurston Hall (Kendricks); Carole Donne (Jane Mason); Tom Lane (Co-Pilot); Flame (Himself); Curly Twiford's Jimmy the Crow (Himself); Charlie (Chimpanzee); and William Bakewell

BEHIND LOCKED DOORS
a.k.a.: The Human Gorilla
(ARC Films/Eagle-Lion Films, Inc./Pathé Industries, Inc.)

Filmed in eight days on a tiny budget, *Behind Locked Doors* is a minor gem with plenty of sparkle. Oscar "Budd" Boetticher's hard-hitting direction, persuasive performances by a cast of thoroughgoing professionals, and the know-how of a veteran production crew make for a compact, satisfying chiller. A nicely modulated backup performance from the mountainous Tor Johnson is a crowning touch.

The script wastes little time in establishing star player Richard Carlson within the walls of a mental hospital—a sufficiently grim setting even on a legitimate basis, but in this case one overseen by a crooked doctor and a sadistic attendant. From here to the last, the suspense never lags. There is no evidence of budget cutting, and of course no spectacular settings are required for an adequate telling. Clever use of lighting imparts a claustrophobic milieu, enfolding both sympathetic characters and menaces.

"I took the picture because it looked like fun—and it was!" Boetticher told us during the early 1990s. "How could I pass up a chance to work with Dick Carlson, my old Navy pal? And lovely Lucille Bremer—I loved every day of it. Carlson was just as good an actor as I knew he would be."

Cathy (Bremer), a San Francisco newspaper reporter, tells private eye Ross Stewart (Carlson) that she knows where the disgraced Judge Drake (Herbert Heyes), a fugitive from justice, is hiding. She proposes that Ross have himself admitted to La Siesta Sanitarium and get evidence. Ross refuses until Cathy mentions a large reward.

Posing as Cathy's mentally disturbed husband, Ross is admitted after an interview with Dr. Porter (Tom Browne Henry). Ross meets two attendants: the mild-mannered Hobbs (Ralf Harolde) and the unpleasant Larsen (Douglas Fowley). Ross soon ascertains that somebody is living in luxury within the asylum.

Another room contains Champ (Tor Johnson), a crazed brute. A grouchy patient, Purvis (Trevor Bardette), angers Larsen, who takes the man from his room and subjects

he lied... cheated... KILLED!..

This Pit... WAS MEANT FOR HER!

HIDEOUT for HORROR

PLUS

The HUMAN GORILLA

IN A HOUSE OF MADMEN!

There is MURDER

There is HORROR!

There is TERROR!

him to a beating from Champ. A youth known only as the Kid (Dickie Moore) also endures Larsen's abuses.

Ross spots Madge Bennett (Gwen Donovan), the judge's lover, stealing into a private suite. Ross sneaks matches to Coppard (Morgan Farley), a pyromaniac entrusted with cleaning up the hideout. Coppard sets a fire that routs the judge long enough for Ross to identify him. Hobbs, who proves to be the father of the Kid, fears that Larsen plans to kill Ross.

Meanwhile, Cathy is rebuffed when she seeks help from the state medical authorities. Larsen sets Ross up for a beating from Champ. Cathy waylays Madge at gunpoint

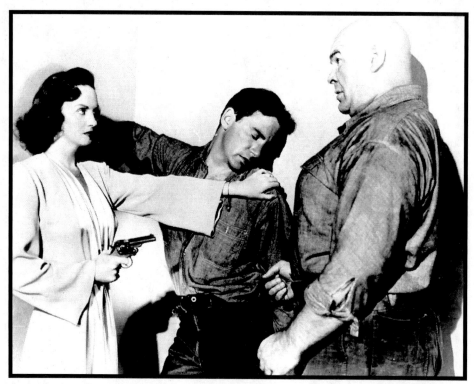

An unbilled Tor Johnson flirts with typecasting-for-life as a crazed pugilist in Budd Boetticher's
Behind Locked Doors.

and forces her to exchange clothes. Disguised as Madge, Cathy gains entrance to the judge's suite and forces him to free Ross. Champ runs amok. Dr. Porter shoots Champ to death. It appears that Cathy and Ross will be next, but none too soon the police arrive, summoned by Hobbs.

Lucille Bremer, an actress and dancer who had been a favored leading lady of Fred Astaire at MGM; and Richard Carlson, whose intellectual aspect spared his youthful good looks from shallow typecasting, give the central roles a cultured quality unusual in the low-budget sector. Among the backup players, Douglas Fowley excels as the cruel keeper, and Tom Browne Henry, Ralf Harolde, Morgan Farley, Trevor Bardette and *Our Gang* series survivor Dickie Moore contribute strong characterizations. Henry would, as Thomas B. Henry, go on to become familiar as a doctor or military-man standby of many B-movie chillers of the 1950s.

An unbilled (and, at the time, unfamiliar) Tor Johnson is terrifyingly effective as an inarticulate homicidal maniac, his first and most arresting appearance in a role so often repeated as to muffle the impact of the actor's imposing presence. This characterization, powerful only in moderation, was so abused in the likes of *Bride of the Monster* (1956) and *Plan 9 From Outer Space* (1959) that it transformed Johnson from a formidable presence to a clownish stereotype. Johnson was an exhibition wrestler from Sweden—a personable sort whose imposing bulk contributed to a distinguished appearance in civilian life.

And speaking of Tor Johnson, this can only be the place to mention that John Wooley has retold the actor's story in a fact-meets-fantasy comic book called *Tor Johnson, Hollywood Star* (Fantagraphics Books/Monster Comics; 1990). Both John and Mike Price have pursued lengthy subordinate (or insubordinate) careers in comics, infusing their stories with a fondness for B-movies and pulp-magazine narrative style. Such an approach hardly has made for hot-selling funnybooks in a marketplace dominated by glamorized superhero shenanigans. And so much for attempting to bring the peculiar brilliance of Tor Johnson to a readership that could not imagine a comics magazine without an ensemble cast of alienated teenage mutant world-beaters.

CREDITS: Producer: Eugene Ling; Director: Oscar "Budd" Boetticher; Screenplay: Malvin Wald (from His Story) and Eugene Ling; Photographed by: Guy Roe; Special Effects: George I. Teague; Art Director: Edward L. Ilou; Decor: Armor Marlowe and Alexander Ohrenbach; Music: Irving Friedman; Editor: Norman Colbert; Sound: Leon S. Becker and Robert Pritchard; Production Manager: James T. Vaughan; Assistant Director: Emmett Emerson; Operative Cameraman: Lee Davis; Script Supervisor: Richard Walton; Hair Stylists: Joan St. Oegger and Helen Turpin; Makeup: Ern Westmore and Del Armstrong; Costumer: Frances Ehren; Grip: Charles Rose; Stills: Milt Gold; Running Time: 61 minutes; Released: Following Los Angeles Opening on September 3, 1948

CAST: Lucille Bremer (Cathy); Richard Carlson (Ross Stewart); Douglas Fowley (Larsen); Tom Browne Henry (Dr. Porter); Herbert Heyes (Judge Drake); Ralf Harolde (Hobbs); Gwen Donovan (Madge Bennett); Morgan Farley (Coppard); Trevor Bardette (Purvis); Dickie Moore (Kid); Tor Johnson (Champ); John Holland (Dr. Ball); Wally Vernon (Sign Painter); Kathleen Freeman (Nurse); Tony Horton (Sheriff)

Aside from John Wooley

I suspect most of us stayed around comics fandom long after we knew it was over, after fun had transmogrified into commerce and love into cynicism. I knew I was done with it somewhere around 1990. I'd been doing all right as a part-time comics writer for a few years. Then, I wrote what I figured must be my masterpiece, *Tor Johnson, Hollywood Star*, for Fantagraphics Books.

Just about the time Tor arrived, I went to Dallas as a guest for one of Larry Lankford's Fantasy Fair events—one of those long weekends combining a comics-biz trade show with a gathering of the fans. Larry put his guests to work on panels that offered, say, an alternative for those who didn't want to hear Todd McFarland hype his latest line of action-figure toys. It was on one of those panels—hosted by Michael Price—that I finally realized I was through with fandom.

Michael and I always drew a few show goers who were genuinely interested in what one or the other of us was doing. So we were going along, about 10 minutes into the thing, when in walked these two fellows, shaped like the Liberty Bell but with more crack showing, exhibiting that peculiar swagger of freed geeks on a weekend rampage. They began asking questions that had nothing to do with the panel discussion—one went something like, "Wouldn't you just love to hold Dr. Smith [of the teleseries *Lost in Space*, that is] down and stick needles in his eyes?" Michael was polite and attentive, but even he began to get a little sore as all this went on.

Finally, one of these guys walked up to the table, where we had our new books out on display. He snatched up a copy of *Tor Johnson* and held it as though he were examining a pack of wieners at an IGA meat counter.

"What's this?" he asked.

I explained the nature of the book, choking back the impulse to plant the toe of a Jack Purcell Blue Tip between the guy's ample buttocks. He tossed the book down with a haughty flourish.

"I like mutants," he said, and walked away.

SOFIA

(ARPI Productions, Inc./Film Classics, Inc.)

With Soviet captives hopping out of consulate windows and testimony of derring-do unfolding in Washington as the current [Real World] headliners, *Sofia* is promoted from the implausible to a strictly exploitable film. —From the *Variety* review

John Reinhardt's interest in hot-topic assignments led him in short order from the ethnic-hatred mayhem of *Open Secret* to the atom-spy shenanigans of *Sofia*. The title refers not to a character, but to the Bulgarian city of Sofia. Here, O.S.S. veteran Steve Roark (Gene Raymond) re-encounters a lost love, Linda Carlson (Sigrid Gurie), whom he had believed slain by the Nazis.

The reunion is rendered more tense than tender by Steve's discovery that Linda and a fellow concentration-camp survivor, Dr. Eric Viertel (Fernando Wagner), are at work on an atom-bomb project for the Soviets. Steve, who has handled the occasional bit of double-agentry for Russia, is nonetheless appalled, but he is heartened to learn that Linda and Viertel intend to escape to America. He is less heartened to learn that Linda and Viertel have married.

Hope and treachery spring eternal, however. Frederick Stephani's screenplay proves a tangle of plot-convenience complications that nonetheless stir up quite a bit of suspense, with welcome outbursts of terror. Mischa Auer is by turns droll and deadly as a Turkish agent. The *Casablanca*-like romantic triangle among Gene Raymond, Fernando Wagner and Sigrid Gurie accounts for its share of tension, although the top billing of Raymond and Miss Gurie is sufficient to telegraph the outcome in that department. Much of the super-spy business is suitably secretive, but Raymond's Steve Roark makes himself altogether too conspicuous while supposedly working undercover behind the Iron Curtain. Raymond nonetheless would have made a good James Bond, had that franchise taken shape earlier. (Raymond landed *Sofia*'s lead after Helmut Dantine and Milburn Stone had passed it up.)

Reinhardt directs with a style-over-substance relentlessness that keeps the implausibilities for the most part at bay. The editing is inconsistent, working against Reinhardt's straightforward approach with some distracting glitches in continuity. A set of musical numbers from Patricia Morison, playing a bistro warbler leading a double life in the spy game, is keenly well integrated into the action. William Clothier's camerawork takes strategic advantage of the hue-saturated Cinecolor process. The large complement of Latinate talents, before and behind the cameras, reflects the site of principal photography, Mexico City's Churubusco Studios.

CREDITS: Producers: Robert R. Presnell, Sr., and John Reinhardt; Director: John Reinhardt; Assistant Director: William McGarry; Screenplay: Frederick Stephani; Photographed by: William Clothier; Musical Score: Raúl Lavista; Songs: "Lucky Star," "Wake Up, It's Love" and "My Beloved" by Karen Walter and Sergé Walter; Editor: Charles L. Kimball; Art Directors: Jorge Fernández and Alfred Ybarra; Decor: Pablo Galván; Costumers: Don Loper and Beverly Devon; Makeup: Ana Guerrero; Hair Stylist: Mari Lepe; Production Manager: Frank Parmenter; Sound: James L. Fields, Hamil Petroff,

Rafael Ruiz Esparza and Galdino R. Samperio; Assistant to the Producers: Mischa Auer; Cinecolor Consultant: Gar Gilbert; Production Advisor: Luis Sánchez; Operative Camera- man: Enrique "Henry" Wallace; Running Time: 82 minutes; Released: Following World Premiere in New York on September 3, 1948

CAST: Gene Raymond (Steve Roark); Sigrid Gurie (Linda Carlson); Patricia Morison (Magda Onescu); John Wengraf (Peter Goltzen); Mischa Auer (Ali Imagu); George Bax- ter (James Braden); Charles Rooner (Dr. Stoyan); Luz Alba (Ana Sokolova); Fernando Wagner (Dr. Eric Viertel); Hamil Petroff (Dmitri); José Torvay (Sergeant); Chel López (Ivan Chodorov); John Kelly (Lt. Cmdr. Stark); Peter O'Crotty (Brother Johannes); Egon Zappert (Marow); José Torvay (Warden)

URUBU

a.k.a.: Urubu—The Vulture People; Urubu—The Story of the Vulture People
(World Adventures/United Artists Corp.)

Explorers George Breakston and Yorke Coplen hire friendly natives to search the Matto Grosso region of Brazil for a long-vanished British expeditioner. They encoun-

ter all manner of exotic wildlife, dodging such perils as a siege by piranhas, until they reach the land of the Urubu. This predatory tribe has captured a white schoolteacher. Breakston and Coplen rescue the captive, find evidence of the earlier explorer's slaying, and hightail it.

Former child actor Breakston broke ranks with the Hollywood establishment during the early 1940s—no doubt having enjoyed all he could tolerate of playing Beezy the Milkman in MGM's *Andy Hardy* pictures—and began indulging a passion for Third World globetrotting. During 1946–1948, Breakston reconciled this interest with a certain expertise at filmmak- ing, starting with *Urubu.* Though largely dramatized, the picture boasts sufficient authenticity to ex- cuse its advertising slogan: "Twice as Thrilling Because It's True!"

Urubu comes rather late in the game for this sort of nature-in- the-raw thriller, which proliferated during the Depression years—see

NSS-URUBU

Ingagi and *Savage Gold*, among others, in the original *Forgotten Horrors*—but finally wore thin as a consequence of its repetitive nature. Today, the genre's intrinsic conceit of the White Man's Burden poses additional obstacles against popular acceptance.

Urubu, an independent production granted the curious dignity of a major-studio release, is scarcely more than a rehash of time-tested hokum in the script department, but it benefits from authentic documentary photography, which overwhelms the fabricated yarn. Portions of the trek, however, have the look and feel of a sound-stage jungle. The camerawork is excellent, and the variety of wildlife thus captured is astonishing. Yorke Coplen's narration, typical of the so-called goona-goona pictures, is overenthusiastic and topheavy with adjectives—quite a contrast with the low-key portrayals that he and George Breakston convey. Tribal nudity abounds. The only non-native players other than the filmmakers themselves are Mike Roginsky and an uncredited young woman who impersonates the purportedly abducted settler.

Breakston is most popularly known today as the writer-director of an audacious horror picture of Japanese-American origin, *The Manster* (1962).

CREDITS: Producers, Directors and Photographers: George Breakston and Yorke Coplen; Associate Producer and Editor: Holbrook N. Todd; Story: George Breakston; Narration: Yorke Coplen; Narrative Script by: Patrick White; Musical Score; Albert Glasser; Running Time: 66 minutes; Released: September 24, 1948

CAST: George Breakston, Yorke Coplen (Themselves, More or Less); Mike Roginsky (Doctor); and Native Players

MACBETH

(Mercury Theatre/Republic Pictures Corp.)

> Curiosity factor is strong regarding how Welles interprets Shakespeare,
> but results are not likely to please.—From the *Variety* review

Throughout most of his life, the great American *auteur* Orson Welles seemed obsessed with reinventing Shakespeare and bringing the Bard to the masses by means unconventional. He came up with such vehicles as a black-ensemble *Macbeth* (a.k.a. *Voodoo Macbeth*), staged in 1936 to tremendous popular acclaim at Harlem's Lafayette Theatre; a chaotically assembled filming of *Othello*, from 1952; and the 1966 Spanish-Swiss feature *Chimes at Midnight*, in which Welles as writer-actor-director would re-interpret Sir John Falstaff via material cherry-picked from five of Shakespeare's plays.

The 1948 *Macbeth* is an effectively disquieting version starring Welles and several players from his groundbreaking *Citizen Kane*, which had come seven years earlier. *Macbeth* represented a bid for autonomy with a smaller U.S. studio that would grant Welles creative leeway while basking, presumably, in the finer artistry that his name had come to represent. He accepted the Republic berth over a more promising offer from Great Britain's preeminent film producer, Sir Alexander Korda, who had assured Welles of a blank-check arrangement if *Macbeth* would come to England.

Republic Pictures proved a godsend, at least, in the found-object department: Welles modified sets and locations familiar to fans of the studio's serials and B-Westerns. If you don't look too hard during a few scenes of horsemen galloping through mountain

Dreams That Money Can Buy

passes, that could just as easily be Allan "Rocky" Lane or Don "Red" Barry escaping an ambush or thundering down to halt a runaway stagecoach. Welles even utilized the talents of the Lydecker brothers, Howard and Theodore, creators of all those wondrous special-effects dummies and miniatures for Republic's many chapter-a-week adventure serials.

Almost everybody knows at least a little bit about *Macbeth*, which has been filmed a good many times since its first arrival on-screen as a one-reel Vitagraph condensation of 1908. The play remains durable enough to be taught even yet as a staple of high-school English and staged in any variety of ways by legions of amateur and professional theater groups. For those who don't know a *lot* about *Macbeth*, however, it's the story of an Eleventh Century warrior (Welles, in this version) who, goaded by his overly ambitious wife (here, Jeanette Nolan), uses treachery and murder to become King of Scots. But the ghosts of his past return to haunt him—literally so in one case, when the slain Banquo (Edgar Barrier) shows up to ruin a late-night banquet. Accumulated remorse and guilt finally do the Macbeths in, with help from the exiled Macduff (Dan O'Herlihy), young Malcolm (Roddy McDowall) and a bunch of soldiers who disguise themselves with tree branches to become a mobilized forest, creeping up on the fortress of the increasingly nutty king.

The scene of the regiment's advance under a leafy cover is one of the most effective uses of cinematic technique in Welles' entire body of work, and something that scarcely could be duplicated on-stage. There are other nice touches, too, from the craggy, stylized settings (often, those semi-disguised B-Western locations) to the frightening depiction of the play's famous prognosticating witches (Peggy Webber, Lurene Tuttle and Brainerd Duffield, each of whom takes an additional role elsewhere), whose features are barely glimpsed, their aspect conveyed via eerie shadowplay. The witches, of course, provide a strong element of horror, as does the banquet scene, even though the latter is done *sans* special effects.

Jeanette Nolan makes her film debut here as Lady Macbeth. Prior to *Macbeth*, Miss Nolan had been known as a radio player, working with Welles several times on his *Mer-*

cury Theatre of the Air broadcasts. Later, of course, she would become a well-known character actress, especially on television. Her "Out, damned spot!" speech near the end of the picture is a masterpiece of unrestrained emotionalism.

The cast also includes William Alland—the reporter obsessed with deciphering the mysteries of "Rosebud" in *Citizen Kane*—as an unscrupulous ally of Macbeth. Alland, who also was the dialogue coach on the picture, would go on to become a staff producer at Universal–International, overseeing such fondly remembered pictures as *It Came from Outer Space* (1953), *Creature from the Black Lagoon* (1954), *Tarantula* (1955) and *The Deadly Mantis* (1957). In 1958, Alland would work again with a *Macbeth* player: Peggy Webber, who had been Lady Macduff in Welles' picture, starred in Alland's production of *The Space Children*.

Although Welles variously whacked and rearranged much of *Macbeth* for the movie, he re-created the speech of the place and the time with an unerring ethnic accuracy. This indulgence leads us to wonder how the feature might have been received by the few who saw it in 1948. A hint comes from *Variety*—whose assigned critic responded with a dumbfounded bluff of a review, leading off with this facile dismissal: "William Shakespeare's *Macbeth* will survive its latest interpretation." Which can only fall under the heading of So What Else Is New?

The tradepaper seemed conflicted, however, as to the worth of Welles' reinterpretation. "Crammed with scenery-chewing theatrics in the best Shakespearean manner with Welles dominating…," it said at one point, then: "Only a few of the Bard's best lines are audible. The rest are lost in strained, dialectic gibbering that is only sound, not prose." And furthermore: "There are similar bits of Wellesian license taken throughout, with which there would have been no quarrel had there been an improvement."

The *Variety* reviewer, anonymous except for a pseudonym of the sort once customary at that paper, would seem to speak for a consensus. Following previews during early October, many critics complained that the dense Scots accents rendered the dialogue unintelligible (hence *Variety's* "gibbering"). *The Hollywood Reporter*, fully aware of Welles' experimental imperative, nonetheless assailed *Macbeth* as "one of the most disastrous of all motion-picture enterprises." (It helps to remember the box-office bias of the tradepapers, of course—but the mass-market critics were just as intolerant.)

Daily Variety reported in 1949 that Republic had acknowledged "a problem" and had decided to pull all prints from circulation. So much for Welles' assumption of creative autonomy, for in his absence—he had left for England and Continental Europe shortly after the close of production—studio boss Herbert J. Yates ordered the associate producer, Richard Wilson, to re-record the dialogue in a Kinglier English and re-edit the film for brevity. Nine months of transformation led to a reissue in September of 1950. *Macbeth* had been shorn from 107 minutes to 86 minutes.

The paring can only have been a vain and spiteful exercise, for in either form Welles' *Macbeth* was never given much of a chance to catch on with the artist's sought-after adventurous audience. *Macbeth* remained a little-seen curiosity until 1979–1980—five years before Welles' death at age 70—when the UCLA Film Archive and the Folger Shakespeare Library of Washington, D.C., reclaimed the original elements and completed a restoration that closely resembles Welles' original construction. Also restored were an eight-minute soundtrack overture, showcasing the dire compositions of Jacques Ibert, and a three-and-a-half-minute program of exit music. (This project seems almost a prototype for the rebuilding during the1990s of a similarly butchered Welles film, 1958's *Touch of*

Evil.) A company descended from Republic mounted a digital-video reissue of *Macbeth* during the early 1990s with selective theatrical playdates, but the project proved more prestigious than lucrative.

CREDITS: Presented by: Charles K. Feldman; Producer and Director: Orson Welles; Associate Producer: Richard Wilson; Dialogue Director: William Alland; Assistant Director: Jack Lacey; Adapted by: Orson Welles, from *The Tragedy of Macbeth* (1623) by William Shakespeare; Photographed by: John L. Russell; Second Unit Photography: William Bradford; Special Effects: Howard Lydecker and Theodore Lydecker; Optical Effects: Consolidated Film Industries; Art Director: Fred Ritter; Editor: Louis Lindsay; Decor: John McCarthy, Jr., and James Redd; Set Designer: Robert Shapiro; Costumers: Adele Palmer and Ricki Grisman; Music: Jacques Ibert; Conductor: Efrem Kurtz; Sound: John Stransky, Jr., and Garry Harris; Makeup: Bob Mark; Hair Stylist: Peggy Gray; Technical Adviser: The Rev. John J. Devlin; Running Time: 107 minutes; Released: Following Previews during October 1948, Then Recalled for Re-Recording and Trimming; Reissued: During September of 1950 in an 86-minute cut

CAST: Orson Welles (Macbeth); Jeanette Nolan (Lady Macbeth); Dan O'Herlihy (Macduff); Roddy McDowall (Malcolm); Edgar Barrier (Banquo); Alan Napier (Holy Father); Erskine Sanford (Duncan); John Dierkes (Ross); Keene Curtis (Lennox); Peggy Webber (Lady Macduff and Witch); Lionel Braham (Siward); Archie Heugly (Young Siward); Jerry Farber (Fleance); Christopher Welles (Macduff Child); Morgan Farley (Doctor); Lurene Tuttle (Gentlewoman and Witch); Brainerd Duffield (First Murderer and Witch); William Alland (Second Murderer); George Chirello (Seyton); Gus Schilling (Porter)

MOONRISE

(Charles K. Feldman Group Prodcutions, Inc./Marshall Grant Pictures/
Republic Pictures Corp.)

Frank Borzage, who had directed Spencer Tracy to an early semblance of greatness in *Man's Castle* (1933), might have made *Moonrise* a centerpiece of that Depression-era movement toward poetic naturalism in cinema. But *Moonrise*, the source-novel, had not existed until 1946. For that matter, the *film noir* movement of which *Moonrise* is a tangent would not come into its fullest maturity until the late-wartime and postwar years. All things in good time, and Borzage—a prolific artist since the silent-screen age—was nothing if not a patient man.

The conventional wisdom holds that *Moonrise* is Borzage's

only outstanding picture of the 1940s. It is handily his best of a three-year association with Republic Pictures, where Borzage also delivered the impressive likes of *I've Always Loved You* and *That's My Man* (speaking of poetic naturalism) as a prelude to this career-capper. Borzage would direct again, but not until 1955, when he tried his hand at network-television drama as a prelude to a brief string of comeback assignments including 1959's *The Big Fisherman*.

Which might qualify *Moonrise* as a grand finale, and the later work as an extended curtain call. A shining moment that demonstrates the independent studios' finer worth as a class, *Moonrise* finds Borzage bringing into play a boldly expressionistic technique. His vehicle is a story that combines the desperate urgency of the *noir* movement with the mingled beauty and squalor that had provided the soul of such acknowledged classics as *Man's Castle* and *Little Man, What Now?* (1934). More a romantic melodrama than a typically cynical *noir*, *Moonrise* juggles reproach and redemption in a dizzying spiral. Charles Laughton once acknowledged *Moonrise* as an influence upon his handling of *The Night of the Hunter* (1955), but that masterpiece of seething terror seems more a reduction of Borzage than an amplification.

Danny Hawkins (Dane Clark, a tough-guy player of Byronic intensity) has grown up as a tormented outcast in a Southern village; his father had been hanged for a murder committed during an onslaught of grief. After one such taunt too many, Danny accidentally kills one of his persecutors, Jerry Sykes (Lloyd Bridges). Living now in fear of being branded a second-generation murderer, Danny finds himself haunted by hallucinations. A romantic attraction to Sykes' fiancée (Gail Russell) helps matters none at all. When finally Sykes' body is discovered, Danny flees into a nearby swamp, where a moment's reflection leaves him ready to turn himself over to the law. His reception by the local sheriff (Allyn Joslyn) suggests a hope of clemency—after all, Clem is the sheriff's christened name.

From such simple fabric, comes one of the most haunting and emotionally complex movies of the postwar years. The novel, as first presented in *Hearst's International-Cosmopolitan* magazine, had conveyed such a texture before any screenplay treatment had taken shape, but the combination of a loyally adapted script, Borzage's grim-but-humane approach, and Dane Clark's vivid show of tenderness and torment achieves an impact that honors and exceeds the prose version.

Novelist Theodore Strauss had sold the rights before publication to Paramount Pictures, which then sold them to independent producer Marshall Grant. The early casting process considered Alan Ladd, Burt Lancaster and James Stewart for the role of Danny Hawkins, with such prospective directors as William A. Wellman and Stewart himself. Grant then sold the property to Charles K. Feldman as part of a deal with Republic. Feldman insisted upon Borzage's attachment as director. The combination of talents proved ideal.

Gail Russell matches Clark in terms of intensity, as a schoolteacher torn between a genuine affection for Danny and a perfectly reasonable fear of his turbulent state of mind. Allyn Joslyn is a sympathetic lawman, and the lordly Rex Ingram stands out as a swamp-dweller who has a philosophical observation for every occasion. Ethel Barrymore makes much of an extended cameo as Danny's grandmother; her role had initially been designated for Lillian Gish.

CREDITS: Executive Producer: Marshall Grant; Producer: Charles F. Haas; Director: Frank Borzage; Assistant Director: Lee Lukather; Screenwriter: Charles F. Haas; Based Upon the 1946 Novel by: Theodore Strauss; Photographed by: John L. Russell; Musical Score: William Lava; Songs: "Lonesome" by Theodore Strauss and William Lava, and "It Just Dawned on Me," a.k.a. "The Moonrise Song," by Harry Tobias and William Lava, and "Work, For the Night Is Coming," by Al Coghill and Lowell Mason; Editor: Harry Keller; Production Designer: Lionel Banks; Decor: John McCarthy, Jr., and George Sawley; Costumer: Adele Palmer; Makeup: Bob Mark; Hair Stylist: Peggy Gray; Production Manager: Virgil Hart; Sound: Earl Crain, Sr., and Howard Wilson; Special Visual Effects: Howard Lydecker and Theodore Lydecker; Grip: Ben Bishop; Stills: Don Keyes; Operative Cameraman: John F. Warren; Script Supervisor: Dorothy Yutzi; Running Time: 90 minutes; Released: October 1, 1948

CAST: Dane Clark (Danny Hawkins); Gail Russell (Gilly Johnson); Ethel Barrymore (Grandma); Allyn Joslyn (Clem Otis); Rex Ingram (Mose); Harry [as Henry] Morgan (Billy Scripture); David Street (Ken Williams); Selena Royle (Aunt Jessie); Harry Carey, Jr. (Jimmy Biff); Irving Bacon (Judd Jenkins); Lloyd Bridges (Jerry Sykes); Houseley Stevenson (Uncle Joe Jingle); Phil Brown (Elmer); Harry V. Cheshire (J.B. Sykes); Lila Leeds (Julie); Virginia Mullen (Miss Simpkins); Oliver Blake (Ed Conlon); Tom Fadden (Homer Blackstone); Charles Lane (Man in Black); Clem Bevans (Jake); Helen Wallace (Martha Otis); Archie Twitchell, Bill Borzage, Jimmie Kelly, Ed Rees and Casey MacGregor (Barkers); John Harmon (Baseball Attendant); Monte Lowell (Man); Jimmy Hawkins, Gary Armstrong, Robert "Buzz" Henry, Jimmy Crane, Harry Lauter, Bob Hoffman and Joel McGinnis (Boys); Timmy Hawkins (Alfie); Doreen McCann and Candy Toxton (Girl); Steven Peck (Danny at 7); Johnny Calkins (Danny at 13); Tommy Ivo (Jerry at 7); Michael Dill (Jerry at 13); Linda Lombard and Stelita Ravel (Dancers); Renee Donatt (Ticket Agent); Monte Montague and George Backus (Hunters)

 # HOLLOW TRIUMPH
a.k.a.: The Scar
(Hollow Triumph Inc./Eagle-Lion Films, Inc.)

Paul Henreid pulls off a dual role to gripping effect in *Hollow Triumph*, which ranks among Eagle-Lion's better forays into film noir. The picture is at least the most formidable and atmospheric of director Steve Sekely's output as a self-exile on Poverty Row.

Viennese-born Henreid, well established in mainstream Hollywood as the very image of the Continental Romantic, was trying a new approach with *Hollow Triumph*. The little film marks a radical departure from Henreid's previous assignment, impersonating the troubled maestro Robert Schumann in 1947's *Song of Love*. Not only does Paul

Henreid serve *Hollow Triumph* as its producer while defying a near-indelible typecasting as both leading man and supporting player; he also asserts a greater versatility that he would continue to develop on into the 1950s, gradually adding to his resume a gift for incisive directing.

Hollow Triumph finds Henreid, at 40, playing a born loser named Johnny Muller, a once-promising medical student, long since turned to crime. Newly released from jail and safely fixed up with a hospital-supply job, Muller yields to temptation long enough to engineer a bungled heist, barely escaping with his life and a small fortune in filthy lucre.

Returning to honest toil, Muller discovers that he has a big-shot double, practicing psychiatry nearby. Dr. Victor Bartok (Henreid) pursues a way of life that Muller can only covet, and their resemblance to one another suggests to Muller a stolen-identity ploy. Muller puts the moves on Evelyn Hahn (Joan Bennett), Bartok's now-contemptuous, now-trusting receptionist, and begins learning all he can about the doctor's comings and goings.

One catch: A scar on Bartok's face. Maneuvering closer, Muller obtains a photograph of the doctor and mutilates himself with a look-alike blemish. The time comes to kill Bartok and assume his routine. Muller notices belatedly that he has scarred the wrong side of his mug. To Muller's relief, nobody seems to notice, and Bartok's patients marvel at the improvements in the shrink's techniques.

Evelyn finally sees through the impersonation. Having persuaded her to leave the country with him, Muller goes rushing to meet Evelyn aboard an ocean liner. He is detained by thugs who intend to confront Bartok about a gambling debt. The impersonation, already successful, proves fatally so.

Dreams That Money Can Buy

Sekely was nearing the end of his stay in Hollywood as a fugitive from the Third Reich. He had committed hackwork as an artist in America, and he had delivered some splendid rot—anybody out there remember *Revenge of the Zombies*?—but even Sekely's least picture bespeaks an intelligence that should have found a berth in the major leagues. Or maybe not. The culture would be much the poorer without the caustic hatred of Hitlerism that eats through the veneer of triviality of *Revenge of the Zombies*. And such a gem as *Hollow Triumph*, with its essence of cynicism ("The older you get, the worse things get," says Joan Bennett's Evelyn Hahn) and its contempt for-plus-acceptance of a stultifying Status Quo, could never have been made at Warner Bros. Not with Steve Sekely at the helm, and not even with Paul Henreid in the lead.

CREDITS: Executive Producer: Bryan Foy; Producer: Paul Henreid; Director: Steve Sekely; Assistant Director: Emmett Emerson; Screenplay: Daniel Fuchs; Based Upon the Novel by: Murray Forbes; Photographed by: John Alton; Musical Score: Sol Kaplan; Musical Director: Irving Friedman; Conductor: Charles Previn; Editor: Fred Allen; Art Directors: Frank Durlauf and Edward Ilou; Decor: Armor Marlowe and Clarence Steensen; Customer: Kay Nelson; Hair Stylists: Merle Reeves and Joan St. Oegger; Makeup: Ern Westmore and Frank Westmore; Production Supervisor: James T. Vaughn; Sound: Leon S. Becker and Hugh McDowell, Jr.; Special Effects: George J. Teague; Dialogue Director: Stewart Stern; Grip: E. Truman Joiner; Script Supervisor: Arnold Laven; Operative Cameraman: Lester Shorr; Stills: Ted Weisbarth; Running Time: 82 minutes; Released: October 3, 1948

CAST: Paul Henreid (John Muller and Dr. Victor Emil Bartok); Joan Bennett (Evelyn Hahn); Eduard Franz (Frederick Muller); Leslie Brooks (Virginia Taylor); John Qualen (Swangron); Mabel Paige (Cleaning Lady); Herbert Rudley (Marcy); Charles Arnt (Coblenz); George Chandler (Aubrey); Sid Tomack (Artell); Alvin Hammer (Jerry); Ann Staunton (Blonde); Paul Burns (Prison Clerk); Charles Trowbridge (Deputy Warden); Morgan Farley (Howard Anderson); Robert Ben Ali (Rosie); Ray Bennett and Lyle Latell (Ship's Officials); Robert Bice and Dave Shilling (Hoodlums); Jeanne Blackford, Felice Ingersoll, Vera Marshe, Joan Myles and Dulcie Day (Women); Lulu Mae Bohrman (Guest); Henry Brandon (Big Boy); Steve Carruthers, Eddie Dunn and Sayre Dearing (Men); Cliff Clark (Motorist); Catherine Doucet (Mrs. Nielson); Joaquin Elizondo (Housekeeper); Franklyn Farnum (Jackpot Winner); Sam Finn and Tony Horton (Patrons); Cay Forrester (Nurse); Joel Friedkin (William); Thomas Browne Henry (Rocky Stansyck); Carmencita Johnson (Elevator Pilot); Victor Jones (Bellhop); Nolan Leary (Newcomer); Lucien Littlefield (Davis); Babe London (Lady with Orchid); Jerry Marlowe (Hiker); Renny McEvoy (Clerk); Philip Morris (Doorman); Constance Purdy (Mrs. Neyhmer); Cyril Ring (Croupier); Benny Rubin (Cabman); Tom Stevenson (Thompson); Norma Varden (Mrs. Gerry); Jack Webb (Bullseye); Dick Wessel (Bullseye's Sidekick); Mack Williams (Cashier); Florence Wix (Guest); Bud Wolfe (Al)

THE STRANGE MRS. CRANE

(John Sutherland Productions, Inc./Eagle-Lion Films, Inc./
Pathé Industries, Inc.)

A killer lurks with impunity behind the social-climbing guise of Gina Crane, new wife of a wealthy candidate for high office, in Sam Newfield's *The Strange Mrs. Crane*. Mrs. Crane (played by Marjorie Lord) hardly even seems all that strange until a former associate — who had known her under another name — shows up and decides to subject her to a spot of blackmail. Floyd Durant (Robert Shayne) proposes to turn an incriminating photo over to Gina's lawyer husband (Pierre Watkin) unless she meets a few demands. Whereupon Gina stabs Durant to death and sets up his sweetheart, Barbara Arnold (Ruthe Brady), to take the rap.

Where *The Strange Mrs. Crane* begins to live up to its title, is in the Kafkaesque coincidence that lands Gina Crane on the jury that will try Barbara Arnold's case. The jury tends to consider Barbara innocent, but Gina, as foreman, hasn't any better sense than to press for a conviction. Seems Barbara's lawyer (James Seay), a colleague of Gina's husband, has been attempting to trace the whereabouts of a certain woman from Durant's past, and an acquittal for Barbara can only mean a reopening of the investigation. Gina prevails in her insistence upon a declaration of guilt, but when pressed to deliver the verdict she retrieves the wrong slip of paper. The court clerk winds up receiving the blackmail note that Durant had sent to Gina.

Sam Newfield, billed here as Sherman Scott, cranks the tension for more than so slight a yarn is worth. The ordeal builds so relentlessly to a forced-irony climax as to obscure its essence as a shaggy-dog story, plain and simple. Marjorie Lord looks almost too elegant to be a blackmailer-turned-killer, but she plays the role with conviction. Robert Shayne is a study in slimy opportunism as Lord's deserving victim.

CREDITS: Producer: John Sutherland; Director: Sam Newfield (as Sherman Scott); Assistant Director: Stanley Neufeld; Screenplay: Al Martin; Based Upon a Story by: Frank Burt and Robert Libott; Photographed by: Jack Greenhalgh; Editor: Martin

Cohn; Art Director: Edward Jewell; Decor: Harry Reif; Makeup: Harry Ross; Production Manager: Bert Sternbach; Props: Gene Stone; RCA Sound: Ben Winkler; Special Effects: Ray C. Smallwood; Stills: Milton Gold; Grip: William Johnson; Script Supervisor: Marie Messinger; Operative Cameraman: Ernest Smith; Musical Director: Paul J. Smith; Running Time: 60 minutes; Released: Following Los Angeles Opening on October 7, 1948

CAST: Marjorie Lord (Gina Crane); Robert Shayne (Floyd Durant); Pierre Watkin (Clinton Crane); James Seay (Mark Emery); Ruthe Brady (Barbara Arnold); Claire Whitney (Edna Emmerson); Dorothy Granger (Jeanette Woods); Mary Gordon (Nora); Chester Clute (Fred Marlow); Charles Williams (McLean); Stanley Blystone (Bailiff); Minerva Urecal (Juror)

SMUGGLERS COVE
(Monogram Productions, Inc./Jan Grippo Productions/
Monogram Distributing Corp.)

> ...a juve screech-arouser of sliding doors, secret passageways and dungeons...—From the *Variety* review

All films in the *Bowery Boys* series are murder pictures, if one regards the English language as the recurring victim. William Beaudine's *Smugglers Cove* is not so much a literalized murder yarn, as it is an Old Dark House melodrama with more implied menace than outright mayhem. Beaudine and the Bowery Boys' ensemble had become old pals by now, and their cordial working relationship imparts to the loyal and accustomed audience the sense of slipping into a favorite pair of loafers—threadbare and down-at-the-heels, perhaps, but invested with too much sentimental value to toss.

Terence "Slip" Mahoney (Leo Gorcey) receives notice of an inheritance and hastens to claim the property, a cliffside manor on Long Island (pronounced *Lon Guyland*, if one hails from those parts). Elsewhere and meanwhile, another, more distinguished Terence Mahoney, Esq. (Paul Harvey), awaits the letter that Slip had received. Slip and his gang are greeted by gunfire, which daunts them not in the least. The caretaker, Digger (Eddie Gribbon), ushers the boys to their quarters while Digger's boss, diamond smuggler Boris Petrov (Martin Kosleck), sets out to scare the newcomers into scramming. No such luck; the fellows seem to like the place.

The genuine heir arrives. Petrov has better luck

at throwing a scare into Mahoney, Esq., and his daughter (Amelita Ward). Slip's pal, news reporter Gabe Moreno (Gabriel Dell), stumbles onto an act of jewel-thievery and finds Slip, Sach (Huntz Hall) *et al.* in a state of captivity. Terence Mahoney, Esq., and Terence "Slip" Mahoney become allies after a spot of hostilities, and the gang puts the kibosh on Petrov's racket. The rightful heir, fed up with countryside living, deeds the cliffhouse to Slip. So there.

Smugglers Cove — the absence of a correct apostrophe seems appropriate for a *Bowery Boys* film — ranks right up there with *Master Minds* and *Boys of the City* (a proto-*Bowery* vehicle, from the *East Side Kids* series) in terms of cream o' the crop. Leo Gorcey, Huntz Hall, Billy Benedict and Gabriel Dell are in peak form as both goofballs and battlers.

The perpetually busy character man Paul Harvey, who graced films galore from 1928 until his death in 1955, makes a classy namesake for that lovable lowbrow Leo Gorcey. Eddie Gribbon is likewise good as the caretaker in cahoots with the now-scary, now-silly racketeer, Martin Kosleck. Kosleck's very presence blurs the line between meanness and madness. He is as effective here as in his best showcases for reptilian villainy, as a kvetching lackey to Basil Rathbone in *The Mad Doctor* (1940–1941) and as a put-upon sculptor using Rondo Hatton to dispatch unappreciative critics in *House of Horrors* (1946).

CREDITS: Producer: Jan Grippo; Director: William Beaudine; Assistant Director: Wesley Barry; Screenplay: Tim Ryan and Edmond Seward; Based Upon: Talbert Josselyn's 1933 Story, "Smuggler's Cove," from *Blue Book* Magazine; Photographed by: Marcel Le Picard; Musical Director: Edward J. Kay; Editors: Otho Lovering and William Austin; Art Director: Dave Milton; Decor: Raymond Boltz, Jr.; Production Manager: William Calihan, Jr.; Sound: Earl Sitar and Don Raubiere; Running Time: 66 minutes; Released: October 10, 1948

CAST: Leo Gorcey (Terence "Slip" Mahoney); Huntz Hall (Sach); Gabriel Dell (Gabe Moreno); Martin Kosleck (Count Boris Petrov); Paul Harvey (Terence Mahoney, Esq.); Amelita Ward (Teresa Mahoney); William "Billy" Benedict (Whitey); David Gorcey (Chuck); Jacqueline Dalya (Sandra Hasso); Benny Bartlett (Butch); Eddie Gribbon (Digger); Hans Schumm (Karl); Gene Roth (Capt. Drum); Emmett Vogan (Williams); Buddy Gorman (Messenger); John Bleifer (Dr. Franz Lieber); William Ruhl (Ryan); George Meader (Manager); Leonid Snegoff (Dr. Latka)

INNER SANCTUM
(M.R.S. Pictures, Inc./Film Classics, Inc.)

A little history, here, to bring things up to the moment: In January of 1941, a radio show called *The Squeaking Door* arrived over NBC's Blue Network. *The Squeaking Door* dealt in creepy crime stories, occasionally filigreed with supernatural elements. The ear-catching gimmicks included not only a very noisy door but also a ghoulishly wisecracking host. This series found great fame after its re-christening to *Inner Sanctum*. And the *Inner Sanctum* franchise also launched a successful series of mystery thrillers, published under that imprint by Simon & Schuster.

In 1943, Universal Pictures delivered the first of a half-dozen *Inner Sanctum* features, which like the radio program worked the area between murder and the supernatural. That run of adequately mounted pictures starred Lon Chaney, Jr., as hero, here, and villain, there.

Then—like the *Charlie Chan* pictures' slippage from Twentieth Century-Fox to Monogram, but with less staying power—a smaller outfit came along to pick up a lapsed movie-biz trademark, hoping to squeeze out a few more bucks.

And so we have this particular *Inner Sanctum,* a threadbare production when compared with the Universal features (and lacking Chaney, even though he was freelancing by now). But the film possesses weird charms all its own.

Directed by old pro Lew Landers (*né* Louis Friedlander), *Inner Sanctum* fits squarely into the postwar *film noir* mold, with a decidedly unheroic-looking Charles Russell playing a fellow named Harold Dunlap, ultimately ground down by Fate after stabbing to death an insistent girlfriend and dumping her body onto the baggage car of a moving train. Unfortunately for Dunlap, the body-loading part of his crime is witnessed (but not quite comprehended) by a gangly, beanie-wearing kid named Mike Bennett (Dale Belding), who almost becomes a victim. After the kid splits, Dunlap attempts to do likewise, but rampant flooding—the story takes place in the Pacific Northwest during the spring thaws—hems him in. The best Dunlap can manage is to obtain a lift from a glad-handing newspaperman (Billy House) to the local boarding house, run by Mrs. Mitchell (*Eyes of Texas'* Nana Bryant). Here, Dunlap meets the landlady's hot-to-trot niece, Jean (Mary Beth Hughes), a classic *noir* dame who has been living in the place for a couple of years because she's too lazy to work. Of course, Dunlap and Jean hit it off—after a fashion.

"Every man I ever met was ruined before I met him," she muses to him over shared dishwashing chores. "I don't have any luck at all."

"You're very pretty," he returns, "when your lips aren't moving."

On the downside, as though the attraction to Jean were not downer enough, Dunlap also re-encounters Mike, who just happens to be lodging there with his mother (the veteran actress Lee Patrick, easing neatly into matronhood). Much of the suspense thereafter involves the question of whether Dunlap will find it necessary to chill Mike—especially after news of the railyard killing reaches the boarding house and the kid starts putting two and two together. This element would be much more compelling if Mike, who appears post-pubescent but behaves like some grammar schooler, weren't such an annoying and whiny little jerk, constantly running off to climb trees and hang out by the railroad tracks. Even given the changing standards of child rearing in the years since *Inner Sanctum*, freckle-faced Dale Belding's portrayal simply does not engender in the viewer much response greater than a desire to be rid of him.

Both Mike's mom and Jean size up Dunlap as a potential mate, what with Mrs. Bennett on the lookout for a daddy for her feisty offspring and Jean grasping for a ticket out of town. Dunlap wants out even more urgently: His number is almost up. The inevitable showdown with Mike sets into motion a series of events that will involve everyone in the place — followed by a strangely quiet, but believable, ending.

In addition to the murderous chills, *Inner Sanctum* nods to the supernatural in its framing sequences. Aboard a streamliner's lounge car, a restless traveler named Marie Kembar (Eve Miller) strikes up a conversation with the prescient Dr. Valonius (Fritz Leiber). Marie complains that her fiancé is traveling with her but prefers not to leave their compartment. Valonius responds with a tale involving a woman in circumstances that might resemble Marie's. Thus does Valonius introduce the crime that will leave Harold Dunlap a fugitive with nowhere to run.

Then, after Dunlap's misadventure has run its course, the film comes full-circle to the encounter between Marie and Valonius. He cautions her to stay aboard at the next stop. Marie sees her fiancé — Russell, again, looking a whole lot like Valonius' description of Harold Dunlap — exit the train and runs after him. He stabs her during a struggle and hefts her body onto the train as it pulls away. The Valonius character was intended as a recurring presence in a destiny-conscious series destined never to progress, a clairvoyant who warns of danger ahead but then sits back and allows the other characters to stumble headlong into those very pitfalls. (The device of a fortune-telling narrator would work to sharper effect in an English-made portmanteau film of 1965, *Dr. Terror's House* of *Horrors*, among others from the Amicus Pictures partnership.)

That element distinguishes *Inner Sanctum* from the usual *noir*, as do a couple of sequences of pure comic relief. Such funny business is well entrusted to garrulous Billy House, as a newsman who understands too well the kinship between gossip and provincial journalism, and to tenants Eddie Parks and stammer-prone Roscoe Ates, as a b-b-boarder with an appetite for b-b-b-booze. Ates had been wowing 'em with that crowd-pleasing speech impediment since 'way back before his show-stopping turn in *Freaks* (1932),

and why tamper with an effective gimmick?

Charles Russell, with his high forehead and pained Everyman looks, is a perfect-pitch protagonist for a *noir*. Russell lets his voice do most of his acting—he was the title player on network radio's popular crime show, *Yours Truly, Johnny Dollar*, during the waning 1940s—but manages a persuasive portrayal throughout, as if inviting the absorbed viewer to accept Dunlap as a victim of circumstance. Russell's low-profile movie career spans 1943–1949.

Mary Beth Hughes is so good in her quasi-*femme fatale* part that it is surprising, except perhaps to the devotee who remembers Miss Hughes' murder-by-manipulation portrayal in 1945's *The Great Flamarion*. Even though Miss Hughes' days as a faithful Gal Friday to Lloyd Nolan's Michael Shayne were a few years past, many filmgoers of 1948 still knew her best from that handsomely mounted series from Twentieth Century-Fox. There, she had been a resourceful, all-American ingénue; in *Inner Sanctum*, however, she is a full-grown and not altogether wholesome woman, whose smoldering passivity seems a forerunner of Lola Albright's classic portrayal of singer Edie Hart on Blake Edwards' *Peter Gunn* teleseries.

Dale Belding, as the nosy but none-too-bright kid, seems almost a refugee from *Our Gang*—and in fact had appeared in Hal Roach's ill-advised attempt at an *Our Gang* revival, with the *Curley* pictures of 1947–1948 (which see). Belding would find a more prominent niche as part of a hillbilly family in two of Universal–International's *Ma & Pa Kettle* comedies of 1949–1950, but his acting career was kaput by the end of 1950.

Inner Sanctum seems in the debt of such superior backwater *noirs* as George Blair's *Whispering Footsteps* (1943) and Edgar G. Ulmer's *Detour* (1945), echoing both the no-exit desperation of Tom Neal's portrayal in *Detour* and the busybody rooming-house setting of *Footsteps*. Director Landers, a recurring talent within the realm of *Forgotten Horrors*, finds little coherence in Jerome Todd Gollard's coincidence-laden screenplay but concentrates to rewarding effect upon the folksy backup players.

More a curiosity than a compelling entry, *Inner Sanctum* nonetheless deserves better than oblivion. The film went unacknowledged when MCA/Universal Home Video issued an otherwise complete shelf of the *Sanctum*s during the late 1990s. Some television-syndicate prints are missing the prologue and the beginning of Valonius' tale: The picture, thus diminished, begins after Harold Dunlap has committed murder, leaving raveled threads throughout and rendering Fritz Leiber's reappearance puzzling for lack of precedent. So there's what's missing, for anybody who has been wondering. (The versions offered in the catalogues of Life Is A Movie and Alpha Video are intact from start-to-finish.)

Except for a brief stab at a teleseries during the middle 1950s, and the resurrection of its radio installments on audiocassette and compact disk by Radio Spirits and other such companies, the *Inner Sanctum* brand has remained buried deep within the popular dream-stream since this picture came and went. The identity has been resurrected only once for a new product: The direct-to-video impresario Fred Olen Ray used *Inner Sanctum* as the title of a 1991 sex-and-murder feature starring Joseph Bottoms, Tanya Roberts and Margaux Hemingway. (The exploitation-film artist Herschell Gordon Lewis once informed us that his 1970 shocker *The Wizard of Gore* "nearly ended up bearing the title of *Innard Sanctum*." Rimshot sound-effect here, please.)

The Universal *Inner Sanctum* pictures, for the record, are *Calling Dr. Death* (1943); *Weird Woman* and *Dead Man's Eyes* (both from 1944); and *Strange Confession*, *The Frozen Ghost* and *Pillow of Death* (all from 1945). A concordance to these films can be found in the *Lon Chaney, Jr.* volume of Midnight Marquee Press' *Actors Series*.

CREDITS: Chairman of M.R.S. Pictures, Inc.: Irving M. Levin; Executive Producer: Richard B. Morros; Producers: Samuel Rheiner and Walter Shenson; Director: Lew Landers (Louis Friedlander); Dialogue Director: Irvin Berwick; Assistant Directors: Louis Germonprez and B.F. McVeedy; Screenwriter: Jerome Todd Gollard; Photographed by: Allen G. Siegler; Operative Cameraman: Sam Rosen; Stills: Stax (as Stacks) Graves; Musical Score: Leo (as Leon) Klatzkin; Musical Director: Emil Newman; Editor: Fred R. Feitshans, Jr.; Art Director: William Ferrari; Makeup: Paul Stanhope; Hair Stylist: Loretta Bickel; Production Manager: Bernard F. McEveety; Western Electric Sound: Elmer Raguse and William Randall; Script Supervisor: Mary Chaffee; Running Time: 62 minutes; Released: October 15, 1948

CAST: Charles Russell (Harold Dunlap); Mary Beth Hughes (Jean Maxwell); Dale Belding (Mike Bennett); Billy House (McFee); Nana Bryant (Thelma Mitchell); Lee Patrick (Ruth Bennett); Roscoe Ates (Willy); Eddie Parks (Barney); Eve Miller (Marie Kembar); Fritz Leiber (Dr. Valonius)

THE ANGRY GOD

(Carlyle Productions, Inc./United Artists Corp.)

Every culture has its version of Genesis, and one such ancient legend yields the story behind Van Campen Heilner's *The Angry God*, a film that takes its narrative cue as much from a recent geological phenomenon as from ancient lore. The formal source is a 1927 short story, but the more direct inspiration—and the actual shooting site—dates from 1943 and the emergence and eruption of the volcano Paricutín in Central Mexico.

Photographed in 16-mm Kodachrome and blown up to theatrical 35-mm in an unnatural-looking, reddish-tan process called Fullcolor, *The Angry God* purports to relate the origins of Life as Some of Us Know It at the hands of a godlike being named Colíma (played by Casimíro Ortéga). Colíma develops an all-too-human fixation with a beauty named Mápoli (Alicia Parla) and resorts to stalking her after one rejection too many. The obsession turns to treachery against Mápoli's sweetheart (Mario Forastieri), but finally Colíma says to hell with it and decides to kill everybody within shouting distance with a volcanic eruption. Whereupon Zatéco, the boss-god, intervenes and sentences Colíma to life imprisonment in his own volcano—the smoking gun, writ large.

United Artists splurged big-time on promotion, supplying an elaborate lobby display for participating theaters and an advertising campaign of epic proportions. The modest film came ill prepared to live up to such a come-on, however. It leaves instead the overriding impression of a school-auditorium travelogue, jazzed up with an infusion of mythology.

It helped none at all that director Heilner—a respected documentarian with the American Museum of Natural History—had shot the works without synchronized sound. A dubbed-in dialogue track provides voices ill-matched to the players. What passes for acting is mere pageantry.

The discovery of Paricutín is credited to the family of a Tarascan Indian farmer named Dominic Pulído, who thus became the first denizens of the Twentieth century to witness the birth of a volcano and live to tell about it. During its nine years of erratic activity (it went dormant in 1952), Paricutín developed a 1,400-foot cinder cone in the highlands southwest of Mexico City. Its earliest outpourings had forced the evacuation of two villages in the path of the lava, in addition to smothering the surrounding landscape with ash. Volcanologists cite Paricutín as part of a vast field containing almost 1,000 such volatile formations in the Mexican states of Guanajuáto and Michoacoán.

CREDITS: Producer: Edward J. Peskay; Director: Van Campen Heilner; Assistant Director: Mario Martini; Dialogue Director, Writer and Scenarist: Lester Crocker; Screenplay: Harold McCracken; Based Upon: Emma-Lindsay Squier's 1927 Short Story, "The Angry God and the People of Corn," Published in *Good Housekeeping* magazine; Photographed by: Luís Orsóno Baróna; Operative Cameraman: António Martínez Ortís; Editor: Robert Matthews; Costumer: Marissa; Music Director: Harley Dainger; Musical Score: Vernon Duke; Song, "Songs of Our Love," by Vernon Duke and Harold Rome; Orchestrations: Robert Stringer; Makeup: Rosíta Guerréro; Running Time: 57 minutes; Released: October 19, 1948

CAST: Alicia Parla (Mápoli); Casimíro Ortéga (Colíma); Mario Forastieri (Nezatl); and a Native Backup Ensemble

HARPOON
(Danches Bros. Productions/Screen Guild Productions, Inc.)

A compact generational saga of hatred-unto-death fuels a better-than-average screenplay for *Harpoon*, which finds itself undone by Ewing Scott's hyperactive style of directing and an all-but-cartoonish show of macho posturing from John Bromfield and Frank Hagney. The film seethes, nonetheless, and enough of the writing (a collaboration between Paul Girard Smith and Scott) shines through to make a rediscovery worthwhile.

Dreams That Money Can Buy

Shanghaied whaler Kurt Shand (Edgar "Ed" Hinton) develops a grudge-for-life against Capt. Red Dorsett (Frank Hagney) during the 1880s after a series of beatings and bullyraggings en route from San Francisco to coastal Alaska. Escape from this enslavement is not enough for Shand, who raises a son, Michael Shand (Bromfield), to nurture the same hatred against the House of Dorsett. Early on in the new century, Michael has grown up peaceable despite his old man's vile tutoring. In a playful bout of fisticuffs with his father, Mike deals a lethal blow by accident and swears out a guilt-driven oath on the spot to honor his dad's vengeful longings.

The campaign from there takes on a tone of gathering derangement as Mike seeks out Dorsett's surviving son, Red, Jr. (James Cardwell), beats the holy bojeffries out of him, commandeers his ship, and winds up entangled in a harpoon line and thus presumed drowned. Junior eventually finds Mike alive but sets him adrift with scarcely a hope of survival. Mike is rescued and sheltered by a missionary, the Rev. Mr. McFee (Jack George), and his daughter, Christine (Patricia Garrison). The two-party grudge match expands to a triangular affair when Kitty Canon (Alyce Lewis), a saloon singer whom Junior had seduced and abandoned, takes over Mike's ship upon the assumption of his death. The preacher's daughter complicates the quadrangle to a triangle as she presses Mike back into service for the sake of a starving tribe of Eskimo Indians. A showdown over whaling rights forces Mike and Junior back into direct conflict, and Junior winds up hanged by a tow-rope. Whew.

Scott is capable enough at handling the requisite action sequences, but the episodic construction—more a fault of the editing, perhaps—allows little in the way of character growth or explicable motivation. Dialogue is seldom uttered, much less interpreted, so much as it is snarled and shouted. Bromfield's transformation from a pacifist bookworm into a petty avenger comes too abruptly to convey much conviction. Cardwell appears more persuasively vicious. Both Alyce Lewis and Patricia Garrison show plenty of gumption. Even at a fairly lengthy 83 minutes, *Harpoon* cracks right along, heedless of its unsteady foundation.

CREDITS: Producer and Director: Ewing Scott; Associate Producer: George Danches; Assistant Director: Maurice M. "Maurie" Suess; Screenwriters: Ewing Scott and Paul Girard Smith, From Smith's Story; Photographed by: Frederick Gately; Musical Director: David Chudnow; Musical Score: Lucien Cailliet; Song: "This Is Real" by Doc Mason and Dok Stanford; Editor: Robert O. Crandall; Production Manager: Ben A. Bradley; Sound: William H. Lynch; Special Effects: Ray Mercer; Technical Advisor: Capt. Jack Benson; Stills: Ken Lobben; Operative Cameraman: Andy McIntyre; Grip: Earl Nickerel; Script Supervisor: Mildred Scott; Running Time: 83 minutes; Released: Following World Premiere in New Bedford, Massachusetts, on October 20, 1948

CAST: John Bromfield (Michael Shand); Alyce Lewis (Kitty Canon); James Cardwell (Red Dorsett, Jr.); Holly Bane (Kodiak); Grant Means (Swede); Steve Dunhill, a.k.a. Williard Jielson (Lockerby); James Martin (Fuzzy); Jack George (the Rev. Mr. McFee); Patricia Garrison (Christine McFee); Ed Hinton (Kurt Shand); Frank Hagney (Red Dorsett); Ruth Castle (Patsy Shand); Gary Garrett (Galloway); Sally Davis (Sally); Lee Elson, Lee Roberts and Alex Sharp (Whalers)

UNKNOWN ISLAND

(Albert Jay Cohen Productions, Inc./Film Classics, Inc.)

A dysfunctional engaged couple, a sadistic sea captain and a recovering drunkard vie for screen time with animated models, guys in dinosaur suits and Ray "Crash" Corrigan (inside a modification of one of his famed gorilla outfits) in *Unknown Island*, a well-received box-office attraction in its day that still, in a curious way, holds up. Shot in Cinecolor, a bargain-basement process that sometimes makes a picture look as if viewed through a glycerin filter, the film combines hard-boiled dialogue and unusual human relationships with a plot that lurches around like one of its Ceratosauruses, eventually staggering to a reasonably satisfying conclusion.

Much of the interest lies in the performance of veteran screen heavy Barton MacLane, soaring over the top as a kind of low-rent Capt. Bligh named Tarnowski, given to bursts of nutty laughter and mean-spirited goading of crewmen and passengers alike. We first meet Tarnowski in a seedy Singapore bar called the Port of All Nations, throwing down whisky, neat, with his first mate, Sanderson (Dick Wessel). Along come photographer Ted Osborne (Philip Reed) and his fiancée, Carol Lane (Virginia Grey), looking to find a boat to take them to an uncharted island where Ted wants to photograph the wildlife. It develops that these animals are dinosaurs, which Ted could swear he had spotted on an unscheduled flight over the island during World War II.

Ted shows a snapshot he had taken from the sky, and—in one of the film's funnier scenes—Tarnowski suddenly appears to be right up there with Roy Chapman Andrews as a paleontology expert.

By pure serendipity, a chronic boozer named John Fairbanks (Richard Denning) also happens to be in the bar that same night. The only one of a group of Marines to have survived an accidental landing on the island, Fairbanks apparently has stayed plastered ever since. Of course, he has no interest in joining the expedition, but when the ship sails, he's on it, courtesy of a Tarnowski Mickey Finn. Fairbanks is hardly happy about the voyage, and neither is the Lascar crew, whose members begin a muttering that peaks in a quickly quelled mutiny.

A long-necked prehistoric giant of the Brontosaurus (okay, Apatosaurus) class is spotted from the steamer, and the en-

SEE KING TYRANT LIZARDS IN DEADLY COMBAT!

Color By CINECOLOR

UNKNOWN ISLAND

Dreams That Money Can Buy

Barton MacLane finds himself treading upon Richard Denning's last nerve.

counters get much closer once the passengers and crew disembark onto the island. As Ceratosauruses, Dimetrodons and the most aggressive giant sloth in screen history (played by Corrigan) menace the encamped humans, Ted becomes more interested in his photos than in Carol. Tarnowski guns down an imperiled crewman in lieu of a rescue attempt. The captain also treats a case of jungle fever by gulping whisky. Fairbanks, that Mickey Finn still fresh in his mind, climbs on the wagon, celebrating his alcohol-free existence by shooting up whisky bottles. (Fairbanks' recovery would seem to vindicate a forced binge as a cure-all for alcoholism, but don't try this at home.) Eventually, Tarnowski attacks Carol, accidentally sets fire to their camp, and decides he will not be leaving until he captures a Ceratosaurus to bring back home with him.

Well, the captain is right about one thing: He doesn't leave the island. However, after a money-shot montage in which the gorilla-like sloth and a Ceratosaurus fight (a weirdly staged battle, done mostly in quick-cut close-ups), Ted and Carol and John find themselves back on board ship for an almost offhanded resolution of their romantic triangle.

In a time when even a syndicated television program such as *Sir Arthur Conan Doyle's The Lost World* boasts computer-generated creatures undreamt of by the filmmakers of prior generations, the variously stop-motion, mechanical and stuntmen-in-suits beasts of *Unknown Island* seem quaint and unconvincing. And yet, when the first monster is glimpsed from the ship, the combination of murky Cinecolor and the weird, slick body of the dinosaur model gives the little scene an otherworldly feeling that rings somehow truer than all the roaring raptors of *Jurassic Park* (1993) and its ilk. Of course, once the adventurers get to the Unknown Island, the wonder level drops considerably, but the first sighting nonetheless stands out as a creepy approximation of the way it might really feel to get a sudden glimpse of a prehistoric creature from afar.

Scripters Robert T. Shannon—a veteran of B-pictures for Republic and other studios during the 1930s and '40s—and Jack Harvey (co-author of the 1936 novel *The Phantom of 42nd Street*, upon which the 1945 PRC movie was based) put a lot of hard-boiled dialogue in the mouths of their characters, including Grey's Carol; this tactic helps the proceedings considerably. So does the casting, full of faces that were already, or would become, familiar to genre fans. (Philip Reed, on the other hand, was a stage veteran who had become a movie actor during the Depression years, starring opposite Mae West in 1936's *Klondike Annie*. Much later, he would show up in several episodes of the network television series *Alfred Hitchcock Presents*.) Director Jack Bernhard (of 1946's *Decoy*) appears to have let his actors, especially MacLane, improvise a bit, to good effect. A throwaway scene in which Tarnowski sneaks up on Sanderson, grabbing him by the bicep with a set of Lascar tongs, has all the wicked, spur-of-the-moment élan of a wet-towel whack in some high-school locker room.

Richard Denning, in a turnabout from his rather starchy work in *Lady at Midnight*, serves a respectably heroic function, looking every bit the two-fisted man of action and yet acquitting himself as well in the early drunk-scene business. It bears noting that the former Ludwig Albert Heindrich Denninger, who by now had spent over a decade in Hollywood, had borne the nickname of "Fatty" as a schoolboy in Poughkeepsie, New York.

"I was a shy, painfully shy, 250-pounder, back home in the neighborhood," Denning once told us. "But I finally endured enough taunts and practical jokes to want to turn off that noise. The torments became my incentive. So just before I graduated high school, I put myself on a rabbit-food diet and started working out, taking manual-labor jobs—anything to shed that blubber.

"Broke a leg digging a cesspool, one time, I did, but the experiences overall honed me down to 180 pounds and gave me the confidence I needed to come out of the shadows and try living a fuller life. Got into a dramatics club while attending business college—and the rest is histrionics," said Denning, relishing the pun.

Denning had at first joined his father in the garment-manufacturing business with apparent executive-class ambitions, but a successful appearance on a radio-broadcast acting contest led to a screen test at Paramount and a run of acting assignments as a result. He appeared in approximately 50 films between 1937 and his enlistment in the Navy in 1942. His professed favorite of these was 1942's *Beyond the Blue Horizon*, which cast Denning as a Tarzan type opposite Dorothy Lamour. From the late 1940s into the '50s, Denning starred with Lucille Ball in the CBS Radio Network's *My Favorite Husband*, an ominous warning, ill-heeded, of the shrieking horror that would come to television in the form of *I Love Lucy*. Denning's television credits include *Mr. and Mrs. North*, *Flying Doctor*, *Michael Shayne*, and *Karen*—all leading to his final role, a 12-years-running portrayal of the governor of Hawaii on *Hawaii Five-O*.

Denning was never actually "one of the most sought-after young romantic leads in Hollywood," as one wishful-thinking small-studio publicist had called him, but his longevity speaks agreeably well for itself. Denning and genre-picture favorite Evelyn Ankers had one of the most enduring of Hollywood marriages, from 1942 until Ankers' death in 1985. Denning died at 84 in 1998.

Filmed with, variously, *The Unknown Continent* and *The Unbelievable* as its working titles, *Unknown Island* was a runaway hit for Film Classics—an outfit more widely noted, as its name indicates, for resurrecting major-studio pictures and giving them another theatrical go-'round. Five months after its release, the film was still drawing, prompting this from *The Hollywood Reporter*: "… highest grosser in Film Classics' history… Brought in at around $150,000…, the film is expected to bring… $850,000, more than five times its cost"—which is to say, one of the highest proportionate returns within the industry at large.

Producer Albert Jay Cohen, however, boasted to the *New York Times* of a $450,000 budget, with a little more than a third of that going to creating and photographing the prehistoric monsters. The creature effects cannot have been particularly costly or time-consuming. The Palmdale, California, location work, with its predominant ordinary shrubbery standing in effectively enough for deep-jungle undergrowth, saved Cohen a bundle in the travel and scenic-design department. (The found-object settings illustrate a complaint registered by the big-league effects artisan Marcel Delgado, who had come to prominence as a key talent on 1933's *King Kong*: Most dimensional-animation producers, Delgado told us, "never take any pains with the sets. They just use a few trees and rocks. In *Kong*, the sets have depth. You can see into them for miles, it seems.")

And speaking of *King Kong*: *Unknown Island* might bear rediscovering more for the opportunistic circumstances of its making. It had come along as a blatant attempt, with the ticket-selling trump cards of dinosaurs and garish color, to undercut a black-and-white and dinosaur-free production from the more highly pedigreed *King Kong* family of film-makers—the Argosy/RKO-Radio production of *Mighty Joe Young*.

Mighty Joe Young, which is essentially a streamlined reworking of *King Kong* with improved special effects but little of the tragic ferocity of the 1933 original, was in production during 1947–1948; extensive post-production polishing delayed *Joe*'s release until midsummer of 1949. In May of 1948, two months after principal photography had wrapped on *Joe Young*, Cohen launched *Unknown Island* as a hurry-up ambush. Filming was completed the following month, and *Unknown Island* beat *Mighty Joe Young* to market by half a year. *Island* seems more a superficial swipe from the Merian C. Cooper–Ernest B. Schoedsack production of *King Kong* (1933) and its near-ancestor, *The Lost World* (1925), with a great deal of borrowing from Jack London's "The Sea Wolf."

There is no clear-cut answer as to whether *Island*'s success compromised the commercial prospects of *Joe Young*—which, after all, was a disappointment at the box office in its first release. But this raggedy little upstart may well have sated the popular appetite for brand-new big-ape movies over the short haul. *Joe*'s director, Ernest B. Schoedsack, once told us he believed that to have been the case.

CREDITS: Producer: Albert J. Cohen; Director: Jack Bernhard; Assistant Director: Clarence Eurist; Screenplay: Robert T. Shannon and Jack Harvey; Original Story: Robert T. Shannon; Photographed in Cinecolor by: Fred Jackman, Jr.; Operative Cameraman: Robert Gough; Stills: Milton Gold; Special Effects Created and Photographed by Howard A. Anderson and Ellis Burman; Color Supervisor: Henry J. Staudigl; Art Director: Jerome Pycha, Jr.; Editor: Harry Gerstad; Decor: Robert Priestley; Music: Raoul Kraushaar; Sound: Max Hutchinson; Makeup: Harry Ross; Production Manager: R.F. Abel; Script Supervisor: Mary Gibsone; Running Time: 75 minutes; Released: During November of 1948

CAST: Virginia Grey (Carol Lane); Philip Reed (Ted Osborne); Richard Denning (John Fairbanks), Barton MacLane (Capt. Tarnowski); Dick Wessel (Sanderson); Daniel White (Edwards); Philip Nazir (Golab); and Ray Corrigan

HE WALKED BY NIGHT

(Eagle-Lion Films, Inc./Pathé Industries, Inc.)

He Walked by Night takes its cue from the forensic-procedural orientation of Chester Gould's long-running comic strip *Dick Tracy*, and from such documentary-styled lawmen-at-work movies as *Let 'Em Have It* and *"G" Men* (both from 1935) and Anthony Mann's *T-Men* (1947). Though hardly unique as a fusion of a *noir* attitude with the you-are-there narrative approach, *He Walked by Night* may well be the most influential film of its kind: In its turn, the film inspired one of its supporting players, Jack Webb, to create a star vehicle for himself in the broadcast series *Dragnet*—which itself wound up spawning a big-screen feature, also called *Dragnet*, in 1954. For that matter, practically all the police shows of early-day commercial television, from *Highway Patrol* to *Racket Squad*, owe their prevailing tone of dry, stern understatement to *He Walked by Night*.

He Walked by Night is a brooding tale of a hunt for a brilliantly dangerous loner who knows the storm-control drains and sewers underlying Los Angeles the way most born-and-bred Angelenos know the main thoroughfares. Richard Basehart plays Morgan, a former police-lab technician and amateur inventor-turned-thief, whose rampage begins with the slaying of a police officer. Descriptions of Morgan vary wildly, for he is as adept at disguising himself as he is at staying aloof. Finally, the police cobble together a composite portrait. This allows them to trace Morgan to an electronics merchant (Whit Bissell) who has innocently purchased Morgan's illicit rewirings of stolen equipment. Eluding the law in a chase through the city's drainage channels, Morgan is tracked to an unassuming bungalow. He slips out and escapes into the sewer system, only to find his exit blocked by an automobile parked atop a manhole cover. The killer is shot to death on sight.

Underground maps hold the key to capture.

Dreams That Money Can Buy

Richard Basehart conveys Morgan's alienation to commanding effect, to the extent of seeming oblivious to the consequences that must follow his increasingly antisocial deeds. Morgan steals an expensive, one-of-a-kind television projector, then sells it to a shop where it cannot help but be noticed. The slaying of the cop, a witness to a burglary, is likewise performed as though Morgan cannot foresee its repercussions. "The epitome of the 'underground man,'" as the *noir* scholar Robert Porfirio has described the character, Basehart's Morgan possesses enough scientific and ballistic savvy to pose a threat to the entire Los Angeles Police Department—and yet he hasn't the common sense to seek even outlaw medical help when wounded. Basehart's self-surgery scene, removing a bullet, is more than merely a cringe-inducer, although it has that effect, too: It is a concise declaration, not far removed from the deliberately outlandish fugues-into-madness of *The Devil Bat* and *The Ape* and *Invisible Ghost*, of the *alone*-ness that can drive a higher intellect to the ragged edge. The sewer-dwelling aspect pronounces Morgan a spiritual descendant of the predatory self-exile of Gaston Leroux' *The Phantom of the Opera*. A film similar in setting and tone to *He Walked by Night*, Gregory Gieras' *Dark Asylum*, arrived in 2001 from Lion's Gate Films—no kin to Eagle-Lion.

Where Basehart's Morgan emerges as a vividly defined individual, the citizenry-at-large and the assembled might of the L.A.P.D. come across more as a massed uproar against a finely focused menace to society. Scott Brady is effective as the case's most resourceful investigator, whose impersonation of a milkman at one crucial point dates the film most poignantly as a relic of a more neighborly society, long lost beyond recovery. Jack Webb plays a forensics expert. George Chan, Bernie Suss and George Goodman stand out as incidental suspects. Reed Hadley narrates in a monotone of somber authority, declaring the tale to have derived from "a true story" in which "only the names" have been altered. (The factual basis lay in the slaying of a Pasadena police officer by an employee of the force's fingerprinting division.) Eagle-Lion Films hired L.A.P.D. Sgt. Marty Wynn as a technical advisor.

The resemblance of *He Walked by Night* to Eagle-Lion's slightly earlier *T-Men* has obviously a great deal to do with the projects' having a camera chief and a director in common. John Alton had photographed *T-Men* in a similarly semi-documentary style. Alfred Werker launched *He Walked by Night* as its director-of-record, but he was replaced amidships during the month-long shoot by *T-Men*'s Anthony Mann. Mann completed the film without screen credit.

The key triumph of *He Walked by Night* is that it achieves such an alarming degree of emotional tension without itself succumbing to emotionalism. The final chase is one of the most gripping jobs of unrelieved tension in postwar American cinema, making a suffocatingly fine use of the "700 miles of hidden highways," as the *New York Times*' review put it, that constitute the tunnels so perilously well hidden beneath the City of Los Angeles.

CREDITS: Producer: Robert T. Kane; Directors: Alfred Werker and Anthony Mann; Dialogue Director: Stewart Stern; Screenplay: Crane Wilbur (from His Story) and John C. Higgins; Additional Dialogue: Harry Essex; Additional Contributions to Screenplay: Bert Murray; Photographed by: John Alton; Assistant Director: Howard W. Koch; Camera Operator: Lester Short; Stills: George Hommell; Photographic Effects: George J. Teague; Special Art Effects: Jack R. Rabin; Art Director: Edward Ilou; Editor: Alfred De Gaetano; Decor: Armor Marlowe and Clarence Steensen; Musical Director: Irving Friedman; Musical Score: Leonid Raab; Sound: Leon S. Becker and Hugh McDowell; Makeup: Ern Westmore and Joe Stinton; Technical Adviser: Sgt. Marty Wynn; Production Supervisor: James T. Vaughn; Script Supervisor: Arnold Laven; Grip: Truman Joiner; Running Time: 79 minutes; Released: Following Los Angeles Opening on November 24, 1948

CAST: Richard Basehart (Morgan); Scott Brady (Marty Brennan); Roy Roberts (Capt. Breen); Whit Bissell (Paul Reeves); James Cardwell (Chuck Jones); Jack Webb (Lee); Robert Bice (Detective Steno); Reed Hadley (Narrator); Police Chief Bradley (Himself); John McGuire (Rawlins); Lyle Latell (Sergeant); Jack Bailey (Pajama Top); Michael Dugan and Garrett Craig (Patrolmen)

ANGEL IN EXILE
a.k.a.: Dark Violence
(Republic Pictures Corp.)

The emergence of a cycle of spiritually themed pictures during 1948 saw the prestigious likes of William Dieterle's *Portrait of Jennie* as well as such more explicitly *religioso* melodramas as *Madonna of the Desert* and *Angel in Exile*. Neither of these immediate selections was calculated to proselytize, so much as to introduce an earnestly pious element of redemption to a conventional crime-melodrama context.

The redemption of *Angel in Exile* belongs to John Carroll, playing an ex-convict named Charlie Dakin, who hooks up with a paroled jailbird pal (Art Smith) in a scheme to salt an abandoned mine with stolen gold dust.

The sudden reappearance of wealth from the claim prompts the neighboring villagers to believe that a legendary spirit is responsible. Meanwhile, the renewed mining activity has tainted the water table, causing an outbreak of disease.

Interlopers—including career tough guys Barton MacLane and Paul Fix, and a conniving bureaucrat played by Howland Chamberlain—begin swarming about. The townspeople begin to shake off the epidemic as if

JOHN CARROLL and ADELE MARA
with
THOMAS GOMEZ • BARTON MacLANE
ALFONSO BEDOYA • GRANT WITHERS

A REPUBLIC PICTURE

Directed by ALLAN DWAN and PHILIP FORD

Dreams That Money Can Buy

miraculously cured. Mutual distrust among the crooks leads to a mutually lethal show-down, and the town finds itself restored to prosperity by a combination of gold dust and reward money, if not necessarily by divine intervention. Dakin believes the latter, of course, and his eventual arrest carries the promise of a short jail term and his return as a responsible citizen.

Carroll is likably desperate as the crook-turned-hero, and Adele Mara provides a winning romantic interest as the daughter of a dedicated physician (Thomas Gomez). Nathan Scott's musical score hits the right emotional notes without turning manipulative, and the conflict among the more genuinely bad guys generates adequate suspense. The team-directing job by Allan Dwan and Philip Ford is brisk and efficient, allowing plenty of space for characterizing touches.

The proxy title, *Dark Violence*, dates from a 1954 reissue.

CREDITS: Associate Producer: Allan Dwan; Directors: Allan Dwan and Philip Ford; Assistant Director: Dick Moder; Screenplay: Charles Larson; Photographed by: Reggie Lanning; Operative Cameraman: Herb Kirkpatrick; Stills: Don Keyes; Special Effects: Howard Lydecker and Theodore Lydecker; Optical Effects: Consolidated Film Industries; Art Director: Frank Arrigo; Editor: Arthur Roberts; Decor: John McCarthy, Jr., and Charles Thompson; Costumer: Adele Palmer; Musical Score: Nathan Scott; Musical Director: Morton Scott; Song: "Yo Me Alegro" (Trad.); Sound: Victor B. Appel; Makeup: Bob Mark; Hair Stylist: Peggy Gray; Production Manager: Virgil Hart; Script Supervisor: Dorothy Yutzi; Grip: Nela Mathias; Running Time: 91 minutes; Released: November 1, 1948

CAST: John Carroll (Charlie Dakin); Adele Mara (Ráquel Chávez); Thomas Gomez (Dr. Estabán Chávez); Barton MacLane (Max Giorgio); Alfonso Bedoya (Ysidro Alvarez); Grant Withers (Sheriff); Paul Fix (Carl Spitz); Art Smith (Emie Coons); Tom Powers (Warden); Ian Wolfe (Public Health Officer); Howland Chamberlain (J.H. Higgins); Elsa Lorraine Zepeda (Carmencita); Mary Currier (Nurse); and Abdullah Abbas, Roy Barcroft, Don Haggerty

PAROLE, INC.
(Equity Pictures, Inc./Oribt Productions, Inc./Eagle-Lion Films, Inc./
Pathé Industires, Inc.)

If the concept of a B-movie represented some schoolmarmish system of quality grading instead of a literal *B-as-in-budget*, then Alfred Zeisler's *Parole, Inc.* would be a solid B-minus. We don't calibrate our interests that way, though, and we reserve a contemptuous pity for those moviegoers who must know "what grade the critics gave it" before they will settle in to watch a picture.

For those who must know what the horrific quotient is, however, we are willing to cut some slack. That quality kicks in at the very beginning of *Parole, Inc.*, with the jarring image of a hospitalized man—his face ominously swathed in bandages—who launches into the wobbly dictation that will serve as a narration. The injured party turns out to be Federal Operative Richard Hendricks (Michael O'Shea). He has been on the receiving end of a torturous beating.

The villainy at large here is a corrupt system of official authority, headed from deep cover by an aloof parasite named Barney Rodescu (Turhan Bey) and clawing its way from a game-of-chance racket into the sanctum of a state parole board. The board has a history of granting freedom to unregenerate criminals, who then become Rodescu's indentured servants. The latest such parolee is a violent soul named Harry Palmer (Charles Bradstreet).

No sooner has Palmer come due for favorable consideration, than Hendricks goes undercover as a parole violator to infiltrate

Beatings are a specialty of the house in *Parole, Inc.*

the spidery mob. Accepted into the gang despite the misgivings of fraudster Jojo Dumont (a cast-against-type Evelyn Ankers), Hendricks stirs things up sufficiently that Rodescu starts ordering hits on his own kind out of sheer paranoia. His distrustful nature will be Rodescu's undoing, and soon enough Hendricks has traced the mob to a farm where murder is a cash commodity. The jig is almost up when a new parolee pegs Hendricks as the lawman who had nabbed him, but the police arrive at Hendricks' summons before he can be beaten to death. As things stand, Hendricks has been sufficiently trounced that he has found it necessary to relate the entire story — as an eventful flashback — from a hospital ward.

Peril lurks throughout *Parole, Inc.*, which pivots on Turhan Bey's late-arriving but commanding portrayal of a suave manipulator who orders murder the way some guys order a shave-and-a-haircut (which, incidentally, still cost six bits in 1948). Bey shows up at around the halfway mark but casts a looming shadow before and behind himself, suffusing the entire picture with oily menace. Bey's larger identification with horror movies and exotic adventure pictures lends an eerie subtext to a film that is too much of a rip-snorting underworld thriller to qualify as a *noir*. Michael O'Shea makes a winning hero, and he seems persuasively in danger throughout. The absorbed viewer cannot help but spend much of the film wondering and worrying about when and how the lawman will come to suffer such ghastly abuse as his bandages indicate. The picture dangles that violent payoff, like bait, until late.

Evelyn Ankers, given a richer opportunity than *Parole, Inc.* allows her, could have made as effective a *femme fatale* as those whom Barbara Stanwyck had defined in such bigger pictures as *Double Indemnity* and *The Strange Love of Martha Ivers* (1944–1946). Under Zeisler's pace-over-characterization style of directing, Miss Ankers seems just too doggoned wholesome to render convincing her role as Bey's callous consort. The secondary female lead, Virginia Lee, plays a bartender in the employ of Miss Ankers' Jojo Dumont; Miss Lee is perfect as a decent sort who becomes entangled with the mob. The backup cast includes career milquetoast Charles Williams, playing (slightly) against type as a member of the parole board, and *Forgotten Horrors* standby Lyle Talbot—whose supporting role as a police commissioner requires him to deliver such hard-boiled lines as this one: "We found one of 'em with enough lead in him to start a pipe factory."

Parole, Inc. also features what may be the first cinematic use of the voice-activated audio recorder, which is used in an undercover manner despite its being about the size of a dorm-room refrigerator.

CREDITS: Producer: Constantin J. David; Associate Producer: Anthony Z. Landi; Director: Alfred Zeisler; Assistant Director: Mack V. Wright; Screenplay: Sherman L. Lowe; Based Upon: a Story by: Royal K. Cole and Sherman L. Lowe; Photographed by: Gilbert Warrenton; Musical Score: Alexander Laszlo; Editor: John D. Faure; Art Director: Rudi Feld; Decor: Jacques Mapes; Makeup: Jack Casey; Hair Stylist: Jane Gorton; Production Manager: Bartlett Carre; Sound: Ben Winkler; Dialogue Director: Marshall Edson; Costumer: Lucille Sothern; Stills: Bill Crosby; Operative Cameraman: Fred Kaifer; Grip: Charles Morris; Script Supervisor: Terry Wright; Running Time: 71 minutes; Released: Following Los Angeles Opening on November 24, 1948

CAST: Michael O'Shea (Richard Hendricks); Turhan Bey (Barney Rodescu); Evelyn Ankers (Jojo Dumont); Virginia Lee (Glenda Palmer); Charles Bradstreet (Harry Palmer); Lyle Talbot (Commissioner Hughes); Michael Whalen (Kid Redmond); Charles Williams (Titus Jones); Marshall Bradford (Governor); Paul Bryar (Charley Newton); James Cardwell (Duke Vigili); Noel Cravat (Blackie Olson); Edgar Dearing (Whitmore); Bess Flowers (Mary); Charles Jordan (Monty Cooper); Harry Lauter (Donald Perkins); and John Merton

KIDNAPPED

(Monogram Productions, Inc./Lindsley Parsons Productions/
Monogram Distributing Corp.)

William Beaudine's take on Robert Louis Stevenson's *Kidnapped* is a pleasurable, lavish-for-its-circumstances foreshadowing of the tenured director's later work as a helmer for the Disney company's live-action adventures. The pacing is a tad too leisurely to take full advantage of the yarn's possibilities for virile adventure—and of course the film is no pretender to the robust qualities achieved by Alfred Werker's 1938 version for Twentieth Century-Fox. But at least the Monogram production is not saddled with the annoying Freddie Bartholomew.

Roddy McDowall stars, and also hedges his bets for longevity in the picture-making racket by doubling as an associate producer. McDowall loses himself in the role of an Eighteenth century Scot named David Balfour, who runs afoul of his evil Uncle Ebenezer (Houseley Stevenson). Having failed in an initial attempt to kill the youngster, Ebenezer proposes a truce and feigns acceptance of a long-ago agreement regarding David's inheritance. Ebenezer intends no such courtesy, of course, and conspires instead with a sea captain named Hoseason (Roland Winters, on sabbatical from Monogram's *Charlie Chan* pictures) to have David shanghaied and sold into slavery. Rescued by Alan Breck (Dan O'Herlihy), a fellow Scot in revolt against the English Throne, David sets aside his family's traditional loyalties and joins Alan in a cross-country series of swashbuckling exploits. Hoseason follows right along with murderous intentions, and the rebellious chums fall into the helpful company of an innkeeper's daughter (Sue England) who proves comparably heroic. A full-circle confrontation with David's uncle leads to a swordfight between Ebenezer and Hoseason, who take a fatal plunge from a staircase. Some romantic plot threads will be tied off in a touching epilogue.

The element of villainy is rabidly well served by Roland Winters and Houseley Stevenson, who start off mean and grow ever meaner as the chase progresses. Beaudine directs with a keener-than-usual understanding of his characters, although he sacrifices momentum for such welcome personalizing touches. The mal-

Roddy McDowall, pictured with Sue England, gained producer credentials on William Beaudine's *Kidnapped*.

ice radiated by both schemers recalls the predatory vibe given off by Gustav von Seyffertitz in Beaudine's masterful *Sparrows* (1926). Production values are sufficient to suggest a million-dollar production (a whopping sum, believe it or not, in those days), but McDowall told us that chief producer Lindsley Parsons brought the film in for "under a quarter of a million, and in less than a month's principal photography." (Monogram Pictures had cracked the million-dollar ceiling on 1946's *Suspense*.) Of course, Monogram justified its occasional big-picture extravagances with its cheap ($40,000 to $50,000) and extremely popular thrillers and Westerns.

Much of the cost of this *Kidnapped* involved the leasing and full-canvas operation of James Cagney's historic-looking three-masted schooner, *The Swift*. The seascapes, as photographed by William Sickner, are breathtaking. Houseley's lair, an imposing but decayed manor house, supplies the opening moments with a palpable sense of dread.

CREDITS: Producer: Lindsley Parsons; Associate Producers: Ace Herman and Roddy McDowall; Director: William Beaudine; Assistant Director: Wesley Barry; Screenplay: W. Scott Darling; Based Upon: Robert Louis Stevenson's Novel of 1886; Photographed by: William Sickner; Musical Score: Edward J. Kay and Dave Torbett; Editor: Ace Herman; Art Director: Dave Milton; Decor: Raymond Boltz, Jr.; Sound: Tom Lambert; Stills: Bud Graybill; Operative Cameraman: John J. Martin; Grip: Grant Tucker; Script Supervisor: Ilona Vas; Running Time: 81 minutes; Released: November 28, 1948

CAST: Roddy McDowall (David Balfour); Sue England (Aileen Fairlie); Dan O'Herlihy (Alan Breck); Roland Winters (Capt. Hoseason); Jeff Corey (Shuan); Houseley Stevenson (Ebenezer Balfour); Erskine Sanford (Rankeillor); Alex Frazer (Fairlie); Winifriede McDowall (Innkeeper's Wife); Robert Anderson (Ransome); Janet Murdoch (Janet Clouston); Olaf Hytten (Red Fox); Erville Alderson (Mungo); Jimmie Dodd (Sailor); Hugh O'Brian (Sailor)

MIRACLE IN HARLEM
(Herald Pictures, Inc./Screen Guild Productions, Inc.)

Sequences which were intended to impart a warm glow were actually laughed at, and the gauche acting, directing and production were never taken seriously at any point.

Particularly appalling is the story line which drags religious themes into a routine murder yarn. — From the *Variety* report on opening night at Harlem's Apollo Theatre

Some hot combination: brimstone and treacle. An extended rehearsal for death, punctuated by a phantom-killer attack and a chain of treacheries vicious enough to send nearly everybody involved straight to Hades and/or Death Row, distinguishes Jack Kemp's *Miracle in Harlem* as the most morbid and unsettling example of black independent cinema in a segregated America. Even the dour and forbidding Oscar Micheaux (see *The Betrayal*) would be hard-pressed to out-do *Miracle in Harlem* in terms of a maudlin outlook, which Kemp sustains for an hour-and-change of anguished incoherence. There lies in store an unnaturally happy ending. Go figure.

Hilda Offley Thompson, in her third and final film, makes a headlong rush toward oblivion as a small-time candy manufacturer known as Aunt Hattie. Hattie looks forward to the return of her adopted son, Bert Hallam (William Greaves), a soldier who intends to become a student of divinity, and we don't mean fudge. Bert also is sweet on Hattie's niece, Julie Weston (Sheila Guyse), who stands to inherit the confectionary shop.

Meanwhile, a manhunt spreads to Harlem in search of a murderous confidence artist named Phillip Manley (Jack Carter), who is known to have been involved in a swindling

racket in Chicago with Jim Marshall (Kenneth Freeman), son of big-time candy manufacturer Albert Marshall (Laurence Criner). Learning that Jim intends to set up a rival company, Albert conspires to cheat Hattie out of her shop and puts Jim in charge. An out-of-nowhere twist finds Albert Marshall poisoned and Julie accused of his murder. Jim Marshall tries to do away with Julie, but a shadowy intruder kills Jim instead. The slayers turn out, respectively, to be Albert's secretary (Sybyl Lewis) and Phillip

Manley, and you can't tell a player without a scorecard. Vincent Valentini's screenplay is a muddle of implausibilities.

At least Laurence Criner, who had done some impressive small-parts work at Monogram Pictures, registers strongly as the crooked big-shot businessman. Miss Offley Thompson seems lovably vulnerable as a victim of Criner's scheming, but her obsessive fascination with death—early on, she experiences a vision that orders her to begin preparing for her funeral—casts a pall that renders the film at once queasy and laughable. An ill-fitting veneer of comedy relief is supplied by lapsed big-timer Lincoln "Stepin Fetchit" Perry, with his customary impersonation of a slow-as-molasses handyman. Various musical sequences, ranging from amen-corner gospel to bawdy-house blues, are more pleasing but just as ill-fitted.

The one-shot director, Jack Kemp, was a Yiddish filmmaker who ordinarily worked as an editor of other artists' movies. Kemp

had been associated with the great director Edgar G. Ulmer on a string of pictures spanning 1937–1939 and including the Yiddish-language *Gruene Felder*, *Yankl der Schmid*, *Cossacks in Exile* and *Fishke der Krumer* and the black-ensemble drama *Moon over Harlem*.

CREDITS: Producers: Jakob "Jack" Goldberg and David Goldberg; Director: Jack Kemp; Dialogue Director: James Light; Story and Screenplay: Vincent Valentini; Photographed by: Don Malkames (a.k.a. Melkalmes); Musical Score: John Glusken (a.k.a. Gluskin) and Juanita Hall; Musical Director: Jack Shaindlin; Songs: "I Want To Be Loved (But Only by You)" by Savannah Churchill, "Patience and Fortitude" by Blackie Warren and Billy Moore, Jr., the traditional "Swing Low, Sweet Chariot" Arranged by Henry Thacker Burleigh, and "John Saw the Number," "Chocolate Candy Blues" and "Watch Out," Composers Undocumented; Editor: Don Drucker; Art Director: Frank Namaczy; Makeup: Rudolph G. "Doc" Liszt; Sound: Nelson Minnerly; Wardrobe: Ann Blazier; Technical Advisor: J.M. Lehrfeld; Running Time: 72 minutes; Released: November 29, 1948

CAST: Hilda Offley Thompson (Aunt Hattie); Sheila Guyse (Julie Weston); Kenneth Freeman (Jim Marshall); William Greaves (Bert Hallam); Sybyl [a.k.a. Sybil] Lewis (Alice Adams); Creighton Thompson (Rev. Mr. Jackson); Laurence [a.k.a. Lawrence] Criner (Albert Marshall); Jack Carter (Philip Manley); Milton Williams (Wilkinson); Monte Hawley (Lt. Renard); Ruble Blakey (Foley); Alfred "Slick" Chester (Detective Tracy); Savannah Churchill (Herself); Lavada Carter (Himself); Norma Shepherd (Herself); Juanita Hall (Herself); Stepin Fetchit [Lincoln Perry] (Swifty); and Hilda Geeley

HOMICIDE FOR THREE

(Republic Pictures Corp.)

This one comes off as a lightweight variation upon MGM's famous *Thin Man* recipe for mingling criminal horrors with breezy banter, to achieve a sophisticated equation of romance with life-or-death adventure. George Blair's *Homicide for Three* neither makes nor breaks any molds, but it follows a comfortable formula with style and wit and a fair measure of grisly business.

Overdue for a honeymoon getaway, Peter and Iris Duluth (Warren Douglas and Audrey Long) celebrate their first wedding anniversary during his 36-hour pass from Naval duty. While Peter visits a Turkish bathhouse in their hotel, Iris receives a peculiar telephone call from somebody who has mistaken her for her look-alike cousin, Mona Crawford. Peter returns in the company of a private detective (Grant Withers), whom he had met at the steam-bath suites. Peter's uniform has been stolen.

At the hotel's bar, a drunken patron (Lloyd Corrigan) raves about "blood and roses" and informs Iris that he has seen her likeness in a newspaper. The photograph proves to be that of Mona Crawford. The Duluths rush to Mona's apartment, where a concierge (Dick Elliott) welcomes Peter as if in recognition—a shred of a clue as to the missing uniform. Mona turns up defunct, alongside a bouquet of roses.

And so it goes, with the drunkard reappearing to name a next victim and a next. (The homicides thus promised, per the title, come out more like two-and-counting.) Captured and imprisoned while attempting to deliver a warning, Iris and Peter find their boozehound friend to be a criminologist who has been sending roses to the victims as an ill-heeded warning. Seems that two no-account brothers named Rose are conducting a campaign of murder-

Death has the last laugh in... *Homicide FOR THREE* A Republic Picture

ous revenge. Once rescued, Peter and Iris end their adventure on a symbolic note of anticlimax: The police have nabbed the bad brothers, who had been masquerading as Peter's detective acquaintance and a partner. And so much for the movies' presumption of effectiveness on the part of the amateur sleuth.

The odd conceit of Bradbury Foote's screenplay is to attach a keener urgency to the couple's limited span of time together than to the clear-and-present danger. Audrey Long's grimly coincidental resemblance to a close-kin victim is a memorable touch; such a device would figure again, many years later, in the teleseries *Twin Peaks*. Warren Douglas and Miss Long give generously of themselves to try preventing further killings — but not without a load of kvetching about his dwindling shore leave. The ominous title raises expectations that the film's breezy tone neglects to address, but the killers are a formidable pair nonetheless. The lovely Tala Birell makes plenty of an unnerving scene as a victim who, upon mistaking Douglas for an assailant, thwarts his attempt to protect her.

CREDITS: Producer: Stephen Auer; Director: George Blair; Assistant Director: Roy Wade; Screenplay: Bradbury Foote; Additional Dialogue: Albert DeMond; Based Upon: Hugh Wheeler's 1941 Story, "Murder with Flowers," as Published in *The American Magazine*, and His 1944 Novel, *Puzzle for Puppets*, Published under the Name of Patrick Quentin; Photographed by: John MacBurnie; Musical Director: Morton Scott; Editor: Harry Keller; Art Director: Frank Hotaling; Decor: John McCarthy, Jr., and George Milo; Makeup: Steve Drumm; Sound: Earl Crain, Sr.; Script Supervisor: Joan Eremin; Stills: Ira Hoke; Grip: C.B. "Whitey" Lawrence; Operative Cameraman: Enzo Martinelli; Running Time: 60 minutes; Released: December 8, 1948

CAST: Warren Douglas (Lt. Peter Duluth); Audrey Long (Iris Duluth); Grant Withers (Bruno Rose, a.k.a. Joe Hatch); Lloyd Corrigan (Emmanuel Catt); George Lynn (Bill Daggett, a.k.a. Ludwig Rose); Stephanie Bachelor (Collette Rose); Tala Birell (Rita Brown); John Newland (Desk Clerk); Patsy Moran (Maid); Benny Baker (Timothy); Joseph Crehan (Capt. Webb); Billy Curtis (Dwarf); Eddie Dunn (Circus Doorman); Dick Elliott (Doorman); Sid Tomack (Cab Driver); Carole Gallagher (Drunkard); Craig Lawrence (Barman); Bob Wilke (Cop); David Perry and Charles Sullivan (Laborers); Patricia Knox (Blonde); Earle S. Dewey (Desperate Man)

IN WHICH
JOHNNY WEISSMULLER BECOMES
JUNGLE JIM—AND VICE VERSA
(The Sam Katzman Corp./Columbia Pictures Corp.)

The Austro-Hungarian athlete Johnny Weissmuller, most memorable of the talkie-era Tarzans, relinquished that born-to-play role in 1948 at age 44 after the ordeal of filming *Tarzan and the Mermaids* on location in Mexico for producer Sol Lesser and RKO-Radio Pictures. Here was the costliest *Tarzan* entry yet produced, accounting not only for a million-dollar production tab (as opposed to Lesser's usual budget ceiling of $800,000) but also for the death of Weissmuller's stunt double, Angel Garcia, during a high-dive sequence. Lex Barker took over the title role for *Tarzan's Magic Fountain* (1949) while Weissmuller retrenched promptly into the *Jungle Jim* series for Sam Katzman, Lesser's fellow pioneering *alumnus* of Poverty Row. (Columbia Pictures allowed Katzman a limit of $500,000 per *Jungle Jim* entry, but the producer preferred to hold costs below $100,000—and even that lowball figure was a fortune by comparison with the under-$50,000 budgets on Katzman's Monogram productions of the WWII years.)

"The *Tarzans* had lost their charm for me," Weissmuller told us during the 1960s, "and I for them, if the truth be known. Mr. Lesser was good enough to keep on believing in me, but *Mermaids* took a toll on the ol' human spirit, I'll tell you. Sam Katzman was, no doubt about it, a step downwards, but he came along at the right time with the right character for me. And it was some relief, to trade in Tarzan's loincloth for Jungle Jim's khakis! I came aboard as both the star player and a shareholder, too, so it was a winning situation all 'round."

Although Katzman had by now successfully infiltrated the name-brand major leagues via a secure alliance with Columbia Pictures, he remained as great a cheapskate-and-proud-of-it as he had been while running his more raggedy studios and package-deal companies during the Depression and wartime years. These *Jungle Jim*s are almost uniformly afflicted with the convenient overuse of stock footage; pageantry in lieu of concerted storytelling; a disdain for natural authenticity; and a condescension (at best) toward tribal folkways as a class.

And yet the films also exert a weirdly lethargic magnetism that can be addictive and even enjoyable. *Jungle Jim* fan clubs persisted into the 1960s, when numerous regional television stations built week after week of Saturday-afternoon presentations around the 16 features. Weissmuller is amiable and authoritative, even in slow decline, and he packs an air of serene control that occasionally erupts into welcome violent reminders of his 16 years as Edgar Rice Burroughs' jungle man. An eventual television spinoff, starring Weissmuller as the head of a soundstage jungle household, proved so insipidly wholesome and moralistic as to suggest a *Father Knows Best*-gone-native. But certain of the feature-length *Jim*s are out-and-out horror movies, with grotesque monsters-at-large, rampant bad-hoodoo sorcery and daunting body counts.

Jungle Jim, the series' pop-literary source, is the least known of Alex Raymond's splendidly illustrated newspaper comic strips for the Hearst-controlled King Features Syndicate. Raymond's *Flash Gordon* and *Secret Agent X–9* had become crowd-pleasing chapter-a-week serials for Universal Pictures during the 1930s. Universal mounted a *Jungle Jim* cliffhanger as well, during 1936–1937, starring Grant Withers. A long-running *Jungle Jim* radio series had taken shape in 1935, featuring Matt Crowley and, then, Gerald Mohr in the role of Jungle Jim Bradley. Such efforts remained the last such word on the character until Katzman stepped in to befriend and exploit the still-bankable Weissmuller. (It is a hallmark of the Poverty Row style to make renewed use of stars cast adrift by the larger production companies.)

After a tentative start, popular demand for additional *Jim*s kicked in during 1949–1950, goosing the output considerably. The franchise earned Katzman the moniker of "Jungle Sam," which some contemporaries invoked snidely but which Katzman appropriated as a badge of honor, even to the extent of signing autographs as "Jungle Sam Katzman." He liked the identity especially because the *Jim*s became Katzman's biggest moneymakers during his tenure with Columbia. The pool house at Katzman's residence was adorned with large paintings of his movie characters, Jungle Jim prominent among them. (A Southern theaterman wrote in 1952 to *The Motion Picture Herald*: "These *Jungle Jim* films have never failed me yet. They bring in just as much business as any *Tarzan* picture I have ever played.") It can scarcely be reckoned a coincidence that a manufactured playground fixture called the Jungle Gym proliferated during these same years in schoolyards and neighborhood parks.

Then in 1954, Columbia relinquished the *Jungle Jim* trademark to its television-syndicate subsidiary; for the last three features, Weissmuller simply played himself, more or less, under his actual name. *Devil Goddess*, the finale, also marked Weissmuller's exit from moviemaking stardom—even though his iconic cultural standing would keep him a household name. In a sideline evocation of his pre-Hollywood fame as a competitive swimmer, he became an executive of the Johnny Weissmuller Pool Co., among other image-conscious business ventures, and he delivered a well-received autobiography, *Water, World & Weissmuller*, in 1967. In 1970, he reprised his Tarzan character for an *Esquire* magazine cover and graced the big screen one last time with a cameo in *The Phynx*. Weissmuller died in 1984.

The Katzman-Weissmuller *Jungle Jim*s are inventoried and dissected herewith:

• *Jungle Jim* (**1948**)—Jim's discovery of a strange golden vial prompts a colonial commissioner (Holmes Herbert) to order a search for the lost Temple of Zimbalu, where a society of devil-doctors means no good to nobody. Government scientist Hilary Parker

(Virginia Grey) determines that the poisonous contents of the vial hold the promise of a cure for poliomyelitis. Closely following the safari is a treacherous photographer, Bruce Edwards (George Reeves), who gains the trust of the vain hoodoo-men by snapping their portraits. Jim retrains the sorcerers' fury upon Edwards by disabling his camera, and Jim and his friends escape amid the resulting riot. Edwards topples into a pit of fire while attempting to flee with a cache of gold.

A promising start, *Jungle Jim* boasts an oily job of opportunistic villainy from Superman-to-be George Reeves. Weissmuller exhibits an unusual show of gunplay and struggles with a prop-department monster whose fishy-reptilian aspect suggests a prehistoric survival: Such a creature, in fact, was the Jurassic marine crocodile, which redeveloped its tail for swimming and evolved paddles in place of feet. Backup player Lita Baron, *née* Isabel Beth Castro, plays a seductive native girl, effectively stealing the thunder of leading lady Virginia Grey. (Miss Baron's role had been intended for the voluptuous Acquanetta Davenport, who declined—lest she become identified with a recurring-character franchise so few years after she had jumped ship on Universal Pictures' *Captive Wild Woman* franchise.) Weissmuller makes a point of inviting Miss Grey to accompany him on his next adventure, but she is nowhere to be found in the follow-up picture, *The Lost Tribe*.

CREDITS: Producer: Sam Katzman; Director: William Berk; Story and Screenplay: Carroll Young; Based Upon: Alex Raymond's Comic Strip; Photographed by: Lester White; Operative Cameraman: Irving Klein; Assistant Director: Wilbur McGaugh; Stills: Ted Allen; Art Director: Paul Palmentola; Editor: Aaron Stell; Decor: Sidney Clifford; Music: Mischa Bakaleinikoff; Sound: George Cooper; Script Supervisor: Arlene Cooper; Hair Stylist: Sherry Banks; Grip: Al Becker; Running Time: 73 minutes; Released: Following Los Angeles Opening on December 16, 1948

CAST: Johnny Weissmuller (Jungle Jim); Virginia Grey (Hilary Parker); George Reeves (Bruce Edwards); Lita Baron (Zia); Rick Vallin (Kolu); Holmes Herbert (Godfrey Marsden); Tex Mooney (Chief Devil Doctor); Paul Stader (Diving Double for Johnny Weissmuller); Damoo Dhotre and His Trained Leopard, Sonia; and Neyle Morrow, Helen Crlenkovich, Al Kikume, Max Reid

• *The Lost Tribe* (1949)—Thuggish white-guy interlopers stalk native woman Li Wanna (Elena Verdugo, actually of Spanish ancestry) after killing her traveling companions, in hopes that she will lead them to the lost African city of Dzamm. The fortune-hunters are slain in turn by a lion, but Jim rescues Li Wanna. Which is convenient, because she had been traveling to seek his help, in any event. Li Wanna's peaceful tribe, back home in Dzamm, is under siege by hunters who want to steal the city's sacred diamonds.

The greater point here is to engage Weissmuller in battles with crocodiles, lions and a shark. He also saves the life of a gorilla, which returns the kindness in the best tradition of Aesop by leading a massed animal attack upon Jim's antagonists. Myrna Dell plays a gold-digging adventuress who is slain by her no-good uncle (Joseph Vitale) after she attempts to defect to the heroic side. The intrigues, with murderous disloyalties on every hand and an alarming mortality rate, provide a redeeming

grace. The action comes in fits and starts, with frequent stock-footage interruptions. Except for the consistency of Weissmuller's performance, *The Lost Tribe* establishes early on a general disregard for character continuity or sequel-sense.

Sam Katzman had noticed Elena Verdugo on duty with Gene Autry at Columbia and found her ideally suited to his Latinate vision of a mock-African populace. Miss Verdugo, descended from California's original land-grant elite, found her casting opposite Weissmuller something of a homecoming. As Weissmuller related, "Back when I was married to Lupe Velez [during 1933–1938], Elena was a frequent visitor—as a child, y'know—to our home. Elena was the daughter of Lupe's secretary. What a small world it is, and Hollywood is an even smaller world. And what a delightful reunion that picture was!"

A prominent fixture in *The Lost Tribe* is the lost city of Dzamm, whose imposing walls are in fact a set of Corsican-styled properties left over from Howard Hughes' 1946 production of *Vendetta* (delayed in release until 1950). The set was situated at Ray Corrigan's famous movie-location ranch, Corriganville, which would preserve such special construction jobs for long-term use by other movies and television productions. The *Vendetta* site would remain in use until Bob Hope acquired Corriganville during the 1960s.

CREDITS: Producer: Sam Katzman; Director: William Berke; Screenplay: Arthur Hoerl and Don Martin; Based Upon: Alex Raymond's Comic Strip; Photographed by: Ira H. Morgan; Assistant Director: Wilbur McGaugh; Art Director: Paul Palmentola; Editor: Aaron Stell; Decor: Sidney Clifford; Music: Mischa Bakaleinikoff; Sound: Russell Malmgren; Running Time: 72 minutes; Released: Following Los Angeles opening on May 3, 1949

CAST: Johnny Weissmuller (Jungle Jim); Myrna Dell (Norina); Elena Verdugo (Li Wanna); Joseph Vitale (Calhoun); Ralph Dunn (Capt. Rawling); Paul Marion (Chot); Nelson Leigh (Zoron); George J. Lewis (Whip Wilson); Gil Perkins (Dojek); George DeNormand (Cullen); Wally West (Eckle); Rube Schaffer (Lerch); John Merton (Kesler); Jody Gilbert (Zulta); Paul Stader (Diving Double for Weissmuller); and Mike Mazurki, Jack Ingram, Ray Corrigan, Billy Jones, Charles Gemora

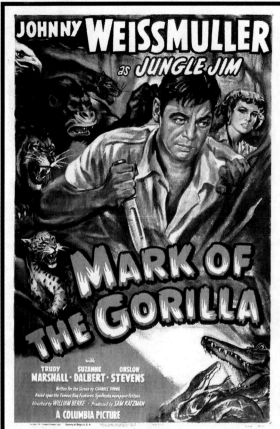

• *Mark of the Gorilla* (1950) — Jim's pet crow witnesses a gorilla's lethal attack on a game-preserve ranger. The bird summons Jim, who registers astonishment: Gorillas are not known hereabouts. (But what better excuse to recycle the gorilla costumes left over from *The Lost Tribe*?)

Jim rescues a young woman (Suzanne Dalbert) from another such attack; she will prove to be a princess of a gold-rich tribe under siege by looters. The rampaging gorillas turn out to be costumed thugs in the service of one Dr. Brandt (Onslow Stevens), who seeks gold stolen by Nazi raiders during the last war.

Weissmuller seems particularly stout-hearted and energetic here; his antagonists include an eagle and a huge eel.

"Sam Katzman kept me on a strict diet," Weissmuller told us, "and he made it almost a ceremonial deal for me to weigh in at the start of each new picture. Weight has always been a problem with me, and playing Jungle Jim was a good incentive for me to keep battling that middle-aged spread."

The opening footage is illuminated with a narration about the grislier realities of the balance of nature. One of the men-as-apes can be seen fondling Suzanne Dalbert during an abduction scene; astonishing, what one can get away with when the producer is a past-master at avoiding the expense of retakes and nobody else is paying particularly close attention.

Mark of the Gorilla serves additionally to signal a crucial changing-of-the-guard among Old Hollywood's community of ape-impersonators. Ray Corrigan, who had long pursued a lucrative gorilla-suit sideline, sold his distinctive costumes to bit player Steve Calvert and coached Calvert in the finer points of ape mimicry. Calvert picked up the Corrigan legacy with *Mark of the Gorilla* and carried on with it in such films as the *Jungle Jim* entries *Pygmy Island* and *Devil Goddess*, as well as *My Friend Irma Goes West* (1950), *Bride of the Gorilla* (1951), *Bela Lugosi Meets a Brooklyn Gorilla* (1952), *Road to Bali* (1952) and *The Bowery Boys Meet the Monsters* (1954).

Another of the mock-gorillas in *Mark of the Gorilla* is Pierce Lyden, a veteran tough-guy player. Lyden once told our late colleague George E. Turner of an awkward episode during the shoot: "My gorilla suit was so cumbersome that I had to be lifted by a cranehoister apparatus into a tree. So [director William] Berke calls lunch and pretends to forget that I need to be hoisted back down—just leaves me stranded there. Now, you can't wear a gorilla suit like that for long without it getting pretty stuffy inside that headpiece, so I decide I'll just try and get down myself—get out of that costume and grab some chow. Well, so I just got free the easy way. Fell straight down! Only thing that kept me from being hurt was that my gorilla suit was so heavily padded!"

CREDITS: Producer: Sam Katzman; Director: William Berke; Screenplay: Carroll Young; Based Upon: Alex Raymond's Comic Strip; Photographed by: Ira Morgan; Assistant Director: Paul Donnelly; Art Director: Paul Palmentola; Editor: Henry Batista; Decor: George Montgomery; Music: Mischa Bakaleinikoff; Sound: Josh Westmoreland; Unit Manager: Herbert Leonard; Running Time: 68 minutes; Released: Following Los Angeles Opening on January 12, 1950

CAST: Johnny Weissmuller (Jungle Jim); Trudy Marshall (Barbara Bentley); Suzanne Dalbert (Nyobi); Onslow Stevens (Dr. Brandt); Robert Purcell (Kramer); Pierce Lyden (Gibbs); Steve Calvert (Evans); Neyle Morrow (Ranger); Selmer Jackson (Warden Frank R. Bentley); Holmes Herbert (Narrator); and Paul Stader, Jack Ingram

• *Captive Girl* (1950)—African chieftain Mahala (white guy Rick Vallin) asks Jim to track down a mysterious white goddess, who commands a tiger. The woman just might be the long-lost daughter of an expeditionary couple who had died years ago while searching for the legendary Lake of the Dead. The search is compromised by a vengeful witch doctor, Hakim (John Dehner), and an indignant crocodile, but Jim finally determines

the elusive beauty is indeed the missing Joan Martindale (championship swimmer Anita Lhoest)—whose parents were not merely killed but murdered, and by Hakim, yet. Hakim closes in for a fresh slaying, but Jim rallies the jungle animals to make short work of the sorcerer and a near-incidental bad guy played by Buster Crabbe.

Crabbe, himself a former Tarzan, lends vigor despite the afterthought nature of his role, which Katzman had ordered written in when the actor unexpectedly became available. Crabbe is clearly delighted to be involved, relishing the latitude allowed him by director William Berke.

"Berke was of the traffic-cop school of directing," Crabbe told us in 1971. "My kind of director—among the good, or at least competent, directors I worked with. I never worked for any of the really first-rate directors, although I'd read for parts for John Ford, whom I'd really have liked to've done a picture or two with. But that traffic-cop style, just blocking out the shot and showing the cameraman where to shoot, then letting the actors do their stuff—that's *my* kind of director."

His *Flash Gordon–Buck Rogers* image aside, Crabbe said, "I always preferred to be the bad guy. I always fared better when I didn't have to play nice. The hero is locked into a certain attitude while the villain gets to slice it thick—the ham, y'know. Besides, the bad-guy roles allowed me to be more myself, let me indulge my secret mean streak without actually doing anybody any harm." (Crabbe, with a grin, left that cryptic last remark hanging.)

The pageant-like aspect of the *Jungle Jim* series is at its most pronounced in *Captive Girl*, which moves at a tedious pace with more padding than substance or style. Perhaps the tedium *is* the style. And never mind what business an Eastern Hemisphere tiger might have in Africa. Much of the padding comes from Wilhelm Thiele's *The Jungle Princess* (1936).

Anita Lhoest, whose attempted movie career began and ended with *Captive Girl*, landed the jungle-woman role via an acquaintance with Weissmuller through the Los Angeles Athletic Club. Miss Lhoest also was an accomplished cellist and pianist.

Notable among the lesser players is the Turkish Frank Lackteen, who had launched his acting career during the silent-screen era, specializing in a near-cadaverous appearance and a menacing voice. As a villager in *Captive Girl*, Lackteen manages a more nearly sympathetic presence. Lackteen would serve the *Jungle Jim* series again in *Devil Goddess*.

CREDITS: Producer: Sam Katzman; Director: William Berke; Screenplay: Carroll Young; Based Upon: Alex Raymond's Comic Strip; Photographed by: Ira H. Morgan; Assistant Director: Paul Donnelly; Art Director: Paul Palmentola; Editor: Henry Batista; Decor: James Crowe; Music: Mischa Bakaleinikoff; Sound: Josh Westmoreland; Unit Manager: Herbert Leonard; Running Time: 74 minutes; Released: During July 1950

CAST: Johnny Weissmuller (Jungle Jim); Buster Crabbe (Barton); Anita Lhoest (Joan Martindale); Rick Vallin (Mahala); John Dehner (Hakim); Rusty Wescoatt (Silva); Nelson Leigh (Missionary E.R. Holcom); Frank Lackteen (Villager); Stanley Price (Drummer)

• *Pygmy Island* (1950)—A *Who's Who* of Old Hollywood's midgets (to use the since-outmoded parlance of the day) was enlisted to handle the collective title role in this entry, which posits the outlandish notion of ofay Pygmies, and *The National Geographic* be damned. Call it *The Terror of Tiny Tribe*.

Jim finds the credentials of a missing WAC captain (*Detour*'s Ann Savage) among the belongings of a slain Pygmy. The Army sends backup. The dwarf ensemble must rescue Jim from a squad of Communist agents as the search expands to discover the source of an exotic plant that yields a fiber impervious to flames.

A few of the tribesmen are famous Hollywood character actors with credentials far bigger than any *Jungle Jim* adventure: Billy Barty and Angelo Rossitto have noticeable roles, and veteran dwarf actor Billy Curtis plays the tribal chief. The three were among the founders of Little People of America, which would exert a greater influence upon the insurance industry and the medical profession than upon Hollywood.

Johnny Weissmuller's *Aquacade* show went on the road during the spring of 1950, serving incidentally to promote the *Jungle Jim* pictures with a beauty contest whose winner supposedly would become the leading lady in *Pygmy Island*. This bit of hype was a sham, of course, inasmuch as Sam Katzman had already chosen the accomplished B-picture actress Ann Savage.

Four-foot-two Billy Curtis was a veteran of Vaudeville and the midget-wrestling circuit by the time he weighed in as a screen player in a 1936 comedy short called "Neighborhood House." Curtis starred in Sam Newfield's dwarf-ensemble gimmick Western *The Terror of Tiny Town* (1938), then cracked the bigger leagues of feature-filmmaking as a Munchkin potentate in 1939's *The Wizard of Oz*. As the chieftain of *Pygmy Island*, Curtis packed sufficient name value to command a $750-a-week salary, with the added luxury of a midget stunt double for his action sequences. Most of the other dwarf players on deck settled for far less.

CREDITS: Producer: Sam Katzman; Director: William Berke; Screenplay: Carroll Young; Based Upon: Alex Raymond's Comic Strip; Photographed by: Ira H. Morgan; Assistant

Dreams That Money Can Buy

HERE COME THE AMAZONS... BEAUTIFUL! BARBARIC! WILD!

COLUMBIA PICTURES presents

JOHNNY WEISSMULLER as JUNGLE JIM

FURY OF THE CONGO

Sherry Moreland · William Henry · Lyle Talbot

Written for the screen by Carroll Young
Based upon the famous Jungle Jim King Features Syndicate newspaper feature
PRODUCED BY SAM KATZMAN DIRECTED BY WILLIAM BERKE

Director: Roger M. Andrews; Art Director: Paul Palmentola; Editor: Jerome Thoms; Decor: Sidney Clifford; Music: Mischa Bakaleinikoff; Unit Manager: Herbert Leonard; Running Time: 69 minutes; Released: During November 1950

CAST: Johnny Weissmuller (Jungle Jim); Ann Savage (Capt. Ann R. Kingsley); David Bruce (Maj. Bolton); Steven Geray (Leon Marko); William Tannen (Kruger); Tristram Coffin (Novak); Billy Curtis (Makuba); Tommy Farrell (Captain); Pierce Lyden (Lucas); Rusty Wescoatt (Anders); Billy Barty (Kimba [or Tembo, per Press Materials]); Selmer Jackson (Colonel/Narrator); Harry Wilson (Henchman); Marion Nichols, John George, Angelo Rossitto, Buster Resmondo, Hazel Resmondo, Waine Johnson, Lillie Johnson, Mary Brown, Jeanette Fern and Jerry Maren (Pygmies); and Larry Steers, Jack Ingram, Charles Horvath

• *Fury of the Congo* (1951)—The venom of a huge spider yields a narcotic that keeps the local tribesmen in a state of addiction. Jungle Jim aids the abandoned women of the tribe in a plot (which can only have been appropriated from Aristophanes) to get their absentee menfolk unhooked from the arachno-dope and restored to normalcy.

William Henry, playing a supposed lawman, maneuvers Jim into the ordeal. There also is a hunt involving a herd of sacred zebra-like animals, called the Okongo—actually horses, crudely striped. This animal, unknown outside the peculiar orbit of Jungle Jim, is the source of a potent glandular secretion that a dope-trafficking gang proposes to exploit. Jim's obstacles, courtesy of the stock-footage department and the properties dock, include a leopard and the gigantic spider.

While *Pygmy Island* was still in production, Sam Katzman had leaked a hint of the nature of *Fury of the Congo* to *The Hollywood Reporter*: "I've put in a call for two

Forgotten Horrors 4

dozen Amazon dames." His key such discovery was Sherry Moreland, a low-profile import from the New York stage, who plays the leader-by-default of the men-deficient tribe. Miss Moreland had handled a small-but-showy role in 1950's *Rocketship X-M*, and would graduate from *Fury of the Congo*—hardly a starmaker assignment, however impressive—to lesser work in the Abbott & Costello starrer *Lost in Alaska* (1952) and in *Mesa of Lost Women* (1953).

Fury of the Congo shared a first-run double-bill with *The Man from Planet X*.

CREDITS: Producer: Sam Katzman; Director: William Berke; Assistant Director: Wilbur McGaugh; Story and Screenplay: Carroll Young; Based Upon: Alex Raymond's Comic Strip; Photographed by: Ira H. Morgan; Editor: Richard Fantl; Art Director: Paul Palmentola: Decor: Sidney Clifford; Production Manager: Herbert Leonard; Musical Director: Mischa Bakaleinikoff; Sound: Josh Westmoreland; Running Time: 69 minutes; Released: During April 1951

CAST: Johnny Weissmuller (Jungle Jim); Sherry Moreland (Leta); Lyle Talbot (Grant); William Henry (Ronald Cameron); Joel Friedkin (Prof. Dunham); Paul Marion (Raadi); George Eldredge (Barnes); Rusty Wescoatt (Magruder); Pierce Lyden (Allen); Blanca Vischer (Mahara); John Hart (Emmett); Lynn Copeland (Native Girl); James Seay (Narrator)

• *Jungle Manhunt* (1951)—Mock-dinosaur footage from 1940's *One Million B.C.* provides the bulk of the thrills here. The tale is less a manhunt—which would imply a pursuit—than a rescue mission for an athlete and war hero, played by Bob "The Bomb" Waterfield, in waking life a championship quarterback with the Los Angeles Rams.

Dreams That Money Can Buy

"I'm a big-time football fan," Sam Katzman told us during the 1960s, "and 'specially a fan of the U.C.L.A. players and the Rams. The pro-ball boys, now, they've always been pretty eager to pick up movie work—stunt doubling and stand-in assignments, like that—and I always used to help 'em connect with the pictures, including mine, during off-season for the Rams. Once in a while, one of the jocks would show some promise, and Bob Waterfield impressed me well enough that I put him up alongside Johnny Weissmuller. And Bob had a kind of Hollywood pedigree, thanks to his marriage to Jane Russell, although he never asked her to open any doors to Hollywood for him. Acting ability? Forget it. Since when did anybody cast a *Jungle Jim* picture for acting ability?"

In a 1951 interview with the *Los Angeles Mirror*, Waterfield described his screen duties: "It's easy… mostly action, and that's not difficult."

Jungle Manhunt complicates itself surprisingly well by revealing that the missing athlete enjoys being lost, having assumed leadership of a tribe. Then there is the more problematical matter of an atom-age mad scientist (Lyle Talbot) who has enslaved and imperiled the natives as a crew in search of a radioactive source of synthetic diamonds. Bob Miller (Waterfield) turns up to rescue his would-be rescuers from an uprising. Miller's gimmick is an arsenal of explosive coconuts, which he lobs as though they were pigskins.

Waterfield had played himself, more or less, in 1948's *Triple Threat*. He went over so well in *Jungle Manhunt* that Katzman began envisioning a separate starring series for the champ. The producer announced as much to the movie-biz newspapers in 1952, the year of Waterfield's retirement from football. Waterfield, however, made no additional pictures as an actor, although he would appear as himself in the football picture *Crazylegs* (1953).

Waterfield had been married since 1943 to the actress Jane Russell—his school-days sweetheart from Van Nuys, California—and she had been influential in the moving of his first pro-football team, the Cleveland Rams, to L.A. In 1955, Waterfield and Miss Russell organized Russ-Field Productions, which generated four major-league pictures: *Gentlemen Marry Brunettes*, *A King and Four Queens*, *Run for the Sun* and *The Fuzzy Pink Nightgown*. Waterfield wound up back with the Rams, as head coach.

CREDITS: Producer: Sam Katzman; Director: Lew Landers (Louis Friedlander); Story and Screenplay: Samuel Newman; Based Upon: Alex Raymond's Comic Strip; Assistant Director: Jack Corrick; Art Director: Paul Palmentola; Decor: Sidney Clifford; Musical Director: Mischa Bakaleinikoff; Stock Compositions by: Mischa Bakaleinikoff, Gerard Carbonara; Mario Castelnuovo-Tedesco, Joseph Dubin, Hugo Friedhofer, Louis Gruenberg, Lucien Moraweck, Paul Sawtell, Ernst Toch and Clarence Wheeler; Photographed by: William Whitley; Editor: Henry Batista; Sound: Josh Westmoreland; Unit Manager: Herbert Leonard; Special Effects: Roy Seawright; Running Time: 66 minutes; Released: During October 1951

CAST: Johnny Weissmuller (Jungle Jim); Sheila Ryan (Anne Lawrence); Bob Waterfield (Bob Miller); Rick Vallin (Chief Bono); Lyle Talbot (Dr. Mitchell Heller); William P. "Billy" Wilkerson (Maklee Chief); Peggy (Tamba); Jerry Groves (Sutker Chief); Rusty Wescoatt (Native); and Max Reid

COLUMBIA PICTURES
presents

JOHNNY **WEISSMULLER**
as **JUNGLE JIM**
IN
THE **FORBIDDEN LAND**

with Angela   Jean   Lester   and **TAMBA**
GREENE · **WILLES** · **MATTHEWS** (The Talented Chimp)
Written for the Screen by SAMUEL NEWMAN
Based upon the famous Jungle Jim King Features Syndicate newspaper feature
Produced by SAM KATZMAN · Directed by LEW LANDERS

• *Jungle Jim in the Forbidden Land* (1952)—Jungle Jim is framed for murder in a case involving a race of hairy giants and an ivory-poaching racket. Forced to lead an anthropo-illogical expedition into *terra incognita*, Jim squares off against ivory pirates, resentful natives and the customary stock-footage perils. Here is the briefest entry of the series, crammed nonetheless with a triple-whammy set of subplots centering upon the subhuman tribe.

In addition to Peggy the Chimp's usual appearance as Tamba the Chimp, *Forbidden Land* makes effective use of one of trainer Mel Koontz' big cats, a panther named Dynamite. Additional jungle perils are supplied by stock footage, including scenes from 1932's *Tarzan, the Ape Man* and 1942's *Beyond the Blue Horizon*.

Tex Erickson and Irmgard Raschke convey well the primitive nature of the gi-ants—evidently, a married couple—although their appearance is nowhere near as unnerving as that of Max Palmer in the following year's *Killer Ape*. The makeup artist in both instances is Clay Campbell.

CREDITS: Producer: Sam Katzman; Director: Lew Landers; Assistant Directors: Jack Corrick and Leonard Katzman; Screenplay: Samuel Newman; Based Upon: Alex Raymond's Comic Strip; Photographed by: Fayte Browne, A.S.C.; Art Director: Paul Palmentola; Film Editor: Henry Batista; Set Decorator: Sidney Clifford; Musical Director: Mischa Bakaleinikoff; Unit Manager: Herbert Leonard; Sound Engineer: Josh Westmoreland; Running Time: 64 minutes; Released: During March 1952

CAST: Johnny Weissmuller (Jungle Jim); Angela Greene (Dr. Linda Roberts); Jean Willes (Denise); Lester Matthews (Commissioner Kingston); William Tannen (Doc Edwards); George Eldredge (Fred Lewis); Frederic Berest (Zulu); Clem "Tex" Erickson (Giant Man); Irmgard Helen Raschke (Giant Woman); William Fawcett (Old One); Frank Jacquet (Quigley); John Hart (Commissioner's Aide)

• *Voodoo Tiger* (1952)—The U.S. Army is searching for a stolen art collection, with a Nazi war criminal as the chief suspect. A plane crash strands the fugitive Nazi, along with an exotic dancer (Jeanne Dean) and her trained tiger. Jungle Jim saves the day with no little help from the big cat, which the locals have pegged as a godly creature. The relative absence of fantasy notwithstanding, *Voodoo Tiger* scarcely makes any more sense than the others in the series.

The remarkable presence here belongs to Jeanne Dean, who as a teenage model had become *Esquire* magazine's first genuinely iconic pin-up, as painted by Alberto Vargas. Miss Dean graces *Voodoo Tiger* with a sizzling ticket-seller of a dance sequence. In Scan-

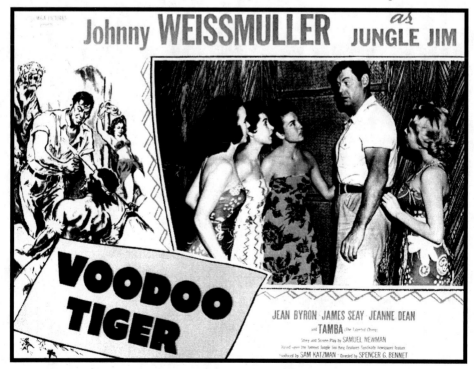

dinavian-market release, the film was known as *Woodoo Tiger*; the term *tiger* in Swedish also translates to "keep quiet." Just in case anybody had been wondering, y'know.

CREDITS: Producer: Sam Katzman; Director: Spencer Gordon Bennet; Screenplay: Samuel Newman; Based Upon: Alex Raymond's Comic Strip; Assistant Director: Charles S. Gould; Camera: William Whitley; Art Director: Paul Palmentola; Film Editor: Gene Havlick; Decor: Sidney Clifford; Musical Director: Mischa Bakaleinikoff; Unit Manager: Herbert Leonard; Sound Engineer: Josh Westmoreland; Running Time: 67 minutes; Released: During November 1952

CAST: Johnny Weissmuller (Jungle Jim); Jean Byron (Phyllis Bruce); James Seay (Abel Peterson); Jeanne Dean (Shalimar); Charles Horvath (Wombulu); Robert Bray (Maj. Bill Green); Michael Fox (Karl Werner); Rick Vallin (Sgt. Bono); John Cason (Jerry Masters); Paul Hoffman (Michael Kovacs); Richard Kipling (Commissioner Kingston); Frederic Berest (Native Chief); Alex Montoya (Native Leader); William R. Klein (Co-Pilot); Josephine Parra, Jeanne Rice and Diane Garrett (Showgirls); and William P. Wilkerson

• *Savage Mutiny* (1953)—Foreign agent Carl Kroman (Gregory Gaye) plots to sabotage a Free World A-bomb test on the populated island of Tulonga. Jungle Jim is on deck to persuade the Tulongans to leave the region, but Kroman convinces the tribe that Jim seeks to mislead them.

    This Cold War fantasia betrays screenwriter Sol Shor's incomplete grasp of the Way the World Works—consider the long-term inhabitability of the island after such a test—but substitutes its own brand of moderately thrilling anti-logic. That the series' purported Africans fall more along a Latinate-Polynesian gene axis allowed Katzman to patch in an array of stock footage from the South Pacific, without anthropological qualms.

Angela Stevens lends a strong presence as a World Health Organization emissary, and Gregory Gaye's villainy is memorable for its energetic arrogance and underhanded treachery. The Apache actor Charles Stevens—grandson of the war chief Geronimo and a favored character actor of John Ford—makes a formidable tribesman. Veteran serial director Spencer Gordon Bennet sustains an adequately suspenseful gait.

CREDITS: Producer: Sam Katzman; Director: Spencer Gordon Bennet; Screenplay: Sol Shor; Based Upon: Alex Raymond's Comic Strip; Assistant Director: Carter De Haven, Jr.; Photographed by: William Whitley; Art Director: Paul Palmentola; Editor: Henry Batista; Decor: Sidney Clifford; Musical Director: Mischa Bakaleinikoff; Production Manager: Herbert Leonard; Sound: Josh Westmoreland; Animal Trainer: Mel Koontz; Scenery and Property Master: Carl Schmaus; Running Time: 73 minutes; Released: During March 1953

CAST: Johnny Weissmuller (Jungle Jim); Angela Stevens (Joan Harris); Lester Matthews (Maj. Walsh); Nelson Leigh (Dr. Parker); Charles Stevens (Chief Wamai); Paul Marion (Lutembi); Gregory Gaye (Carl Kroman); Leonard Penn (Emil Bruno); Ted Thorpe (Paul Benek); George Robotham (Johnson)

• *Valley of Head Hunters* (1953)—A welcome deployment of African-descended actors lends this oil-piracy yarn a bit more quasi-authenticity than usual. But the heightened interest in ethnicity was purely pragmatic: Sam Katzman had acquired the stock-footage rights to Zoltan Korda's superior *Sanders of the River* (England; 1935), a Nigerian tribal adventure taken from a series of novels by Edgar Wallace. This picture as a consequence required backup players who would more nearly match the black Africans on view in the found footage.

Valley of Head Hunters finds Jungle Jim helping to negotiate a mineral-rights agreement. The criminal element (Robert Foulk and Joseph Allen, Jr.) bamboozles a renegade tribal leader (Vince M. Townsend, Jr.) into putting on a head-hunter act, the better to scare away the legitimate interests.

Peggy-as-Tamba, the series' recurring ape, steals the show with an extended drunk scene involving a snootful of ether. (And just in case any agents of P.E.T.A. should be snooping about, no such intoxication was actually involved; cinematographer William Witley achieved the wobbly slow-motion illusion with an over-cranked camera.) Peggy would win a Patsy Award—the trained-animal equivalent of an Oscar—the following year for her work in the *Jim*s, among other appearances.

An unobtrusive element of romance figures between Christine Larson and Steve Ritch, an under-utilized actor of rare intelligence and intensity. Ritch is best known for his anguished title portrayal, 'way better than the material, in another Katzman production, 1956's *The Werewolf*.

CREDITS: Producer: Sam Katzman; Director: William Berke; Assistant Director: Carter DeHaven, Jr.; Screenplay: Samuel Newman; Based Upon: Alex Raymond's Comic Strip; Photographed by: William Whitley; Art Director: Paul Palmentola; Editor: Gene Havlick; Decor: Sidney Clifford; Musical Director: Mischa Bakaleinikoff; Production Manager: Herbert Leonard; Sound: Lambert Day; Running Time: 67 minutes; Released: During August of 1953

CAST: Johnny Weissmuller (Jungle Jim); Christine Larson (Ellen Shaw); Robert C. Foulk (Arco); Steven Ritch (Lt. Jeff Barry); Nelson Leigh (Bradley); Joseph Allen, Jr. (Pico Church); George Eldredge (Commissioner Kingston); Neyle Morrow (Bono); Vince M. Townsend, Jr. (M'Gono); Don Blackman (Chief Bagava); Paul Thompson (Chief Gitzhak); and Elzie Emanuel

• *Killer Ape* (1953)—Max Palmer's title-role portrayal is sufficient to render *Killer Ape* the most memorable of the *Jim*s, even though it takes Palmer a while to get thoroughly into character: During the main body of the picture, the seven-foot-plus wrestler-turned-actor assumes a lurching, rump-sprung gait that emphasizes the subhuman nature of the character—but a main-title sequence catches Palmer ambling blithely about as if bound for the studio commissary after a morning's shooting. A formidable headpiece by makeup artist Clay Campbell places Palmer's ape-man on a par with Glenn Strange's Frankenstein Monster of the 1940s and Ralph Morgan's distorted countenance in *The Monster Maker* (1944).

Jungle Jim finds a disturbance in the natural order of the jungle. An investigation

finds a renegade scientist (Nestor Paiva) headquartered in a canyon reputed to be the stomping grounds of a loathsome crossbreed between human and ape—another son of Ingagi, perhaps, or at least a nephew. The expedition is experimenting upon wildlife to perfect a poison that will render its victims incapable of exerting free will, rather like these films' returning customers. Jim finds himself framed for murder in the slaying of a tribal leader.

The monster-in-residence abducts the chief's surviving sister (Carol Thurston). The doctor enslaves the tribespeople in a further test of the serum. Mutual hostilities escalate between the scientist and the man-ape. Jim discombobulates both the evil campaign and the man-ape with an inspired act of arson in the name of justice.

Variety's assigned critic found *Killer Ape* "no worse, but certainly no better, than predecessors in the series."

CREDITS: Producer: Sam Katzman; Director: Spencer Gordon Bennet; Screenplay: Carroll Young and Arthur Hoerl; Based Upon: Alex Raymond's Comic Strip; Assistant Directors: Carter DeHaven, Jr., and Leonard Katzman; Photographed by: William Whitley; Art Director: Paul Palmentola; Editor: Gene Havlick; Decor: Sidney Clifford; Musical Director: Mischa Bakaleinikoff; Production Manager: Herbert Leonard; Sound: Josh Westmoreland; Special Makeup: Clay Campbell; Running Time: 68 minutes; Released: During December 1953

CAST: Johnny Weissmuller (Jungle Jim); Carol Thurston (Shari); Max Palmer (Man-Ape); Burt Wenland (Ramada); Nestor Paiva (Andrews); Paul Marion (Mahara); Eddie Foster (Achmed); Rory Mallinson (Perry); Ray Corrigan (Norley); Nick Stuart (Maron); Michael Fox (Medical Officer); Peggy (Tamba); Tusko (Elephant); Harry Wilson (Henchman)

• *Jungle Man-Eaters* (**1954**)—Generations before the notion of Celebrating Diversity caught on with a massed populace, Sam Katzman was doing precisely that by cheapskate default in his *Jungle Jim* pictures. *Jungle Man-Eaters* is the most extreme such example, confronting Johnny Weissmuller *et al.* with a veritable Third World clearinghouse of ethnicities. Stock footage of black Africans traversing a river segues to a boatload of Central American types, and elsewhere an African tribal celebration is underscored with an American Indian ritual rhythm. An African village conflagration is juxtaposed, as if to offer a closer view of the carnage, with prefabricated footage of flames engulfing a Mideastern enclave. With such straight-faced absurdities as these as the main attraction, any semblance of a story is just gravy-on-the-side.

Jungle Jim joins forces with Scotland Yard to locate a diamond miner reported missing. Meanwhile, a stock-in-trade outbreak of tribal unrest dovetails with a campaign to hijack a lode of natural diamonds.

The Hollywood Reporter's Jack Moffitt, who usually was tolerant of the low-budget sector, wrote: "It is not our business... to pile up witticisms at the expense of the industry's product. The temptation is vast in this instance, but it will be avoided. However, *Jungle Man-Eaters* contains nothing to inspire the praise of any critic who wishes to mean anything to exhibitors." In other words, *The Hollywood Reporter* felt that it owed a greater debt of responsibility to the theaters that might consider playing such a picture, than to the studio that had made such a picture.

Recycled scenes become conspicuously internalized here, with lifts even from earlier *Jungle Jim* pictures, as well as such more customary sources as *One Million B.C.* (1940)

and *King of the Jungle* (1933). More interesting than the stock-footage spotting game is the opportunity to notice such players as Bernie Hamilton and Woody Strode, long before their brushes with mass recognition.

CREDITS: Producer: Sam Katzman; Director: Lee Sholem; Assistant Director: Charles S. Gould; Screenplay: Samuel Newman; Based Upon: Alex Raymond's Comic Strip; Photographed by: Henry Freulich; Art Director: Paul Palmentola; Film Editor: Gene Havlick; Special Effects: Jack Erickson; Decor: Sidney Clifford; Musical Director: Mischa Bakaleinikoff; Production Manager: Herbert Leonard; Sound: Josh Westmoreland; Running Time: 67 minutes; Released: During June of 1954

CAST: Johnny Weissmuller (Jungle Jim); Karin Booth (Bonnie Crandall); Richard [Stapley] Wyler (Inspector Geoffrey Bernard); Bernie Hamilton (Zuwaba); Gregory Gaye (Leroux); Lester Matthews (Commissioner Kingston); Paul Thompson (Zulu); Vince M. Townsend, Jr. (Chief Boganda); Louise Franklin (N'Gala); Rowe Wallerstein (Diamond Miner); Woody Strode (Morro Native); and John Merton, Gil Perkins

• *Cannibal Attack* (1955)—Sometimes the Katzman company played it straight with the titles, as in the what-you-see-is-what-you-get *Killer Ape*. Other such christenings are pure bait-and-switch, as in the sensational but misleading *Valley of Head Hunters* and *Jungle Man-Eaters*. *Cannibal Attack* is worse yet, a humbug title referring to a tribe that is neither cannibalistic nor predisposed to attacking. A line of dialogue explains that these jungle-dwellers *used to be cannibals* but have overcome their appetite for human flesh. So phooey, already.

Dreams That Money Can Buy

Here is where Weissmuller drops the Jungle Jim act (although he would carry on as Jungle Jim throughout the 1955 teleseries) to play just-plain Johnny Weissmuller, tackling a mob of cobalt pirates disguised as crocodiles—another crock.

Columbia stock player and former glamour model Judy Walsh makes a persuasive jungle vamp. Miss Walsh's handling of the required violent action compensates for her awkward and amateurish line readings.

CREDITS: Producer: Sam Katzman; Director: Lee Sholem; Assistant Director: Abner Singer; Screenplay: Carroll Young; Photographed by: Henry Freulich; Art Director: Paul Palmentola; Film Editor: Edwin Bryant; Decor: Sidney Clifford; Special Effects: Jack Erickson; Musical Director: Mischa Bakaleinikoff; Production Manager: Leon Chooluck; Sound: John Livadary and Harry Mills; Running Time: 69 minutes; Released: During November of 1954

CAST: Johnny Weissmuller (Johnny Weissmuller); Judy Walsh (Luora); David Bruce (Arnold King); Bruce Cowling (Rovak); Charles Evans (Commissioner); Steven Darrell (King); Joseph Allen, Jr. (Jason); Michael Granger (Narrator)

• *Jungle Moon Men* (1955)—Sir H. Rider Haggard revolves in the crypt while Sam Katzman plagiarizes the famous (and often-filmed) Haggard novel *She*. A tribal prince (Ben Chapman) is abducted by Pygmies and installed as consort to a goddess-priestess named Oma (Helene Stanton), who seems immortal.

Meanwhile, Jungle Jim-turned-Johnny Weissmuller guides Egyptologist Ellen Marston (Jean Byron) on a research trek. Complicating the itinerary are an

BATTLING THE POISON DART MEN!

COLUMBIA PICTURES presents

JOHNNY WEISSMULLER

JUNGLE MOON MEN

with JEAN BYRON · HELENE STANTON
BILL HENRY
and KIMBA

Screen Play by DWIGHT V. BABCOCK and JO PAGANO
Produced by SAM KATZMAN
Directed by CHARLES S. GOULD

entourage of shifty-looking white-guy interlopers, the now-escaped prince and his mock-Pygmy pursuers, and various indignant tribespeople. A climactic confrontation with Oma proves her immortality to have been conditional: She turns to dust upon exposure to sunlight.

Helene Stanton came from an operatic background, with an interlude in jazz-pop vocalizing. Miss Stanton's performance in *Jungle Moon Men* is perfectly acceptable, with the right aristocratic attitude. Also of note is the presence of the Tahitian Ben Chapman, better known as a title player of Universal–International's *Creature from the Black Lagoon* (1954).

CREDITS: Producer: Sam Katzman; Director: Charles S. Gould; Assistant Director: Eddie Saeta; Screenplay: Dwight V. Babcock and Jo Pagano; Photographed by: Henry Freulich; Art Director: Paul Palmentola; Editor: Henry Batista; Decor: Sidney Clifford; Musical Director: Mischa Bakaleinikoff; Production Manager: Leon Chooluck; Sound: Josh Westmoreland; Running Time: 70 minutes; Released: During April 1955

CAST: Johnny Weissmuller (Johnny Weissmuller); Jean Byron (Ellen Marston); Helene Stanton (Oma); Bill Henry (Bob Prentice); Myron Healey (Mark Santo); Billy Curtis (Damu); Michael Granger (Nolimo); Frank Sully (Max); Benjamin F. Chapman, Jr. [Ben Chapman] (Marro); Kenneth L. Smith (Link); Ed Hinton (Regan); Rory Mallinson (Jones); and Angelo Rossitto

• *Devil Goddess* (1955)—Angela Stevens, from *Savage Mutiny*, returns as somebody else entirely for this series-capper—enabling the company to recycle several minutes of

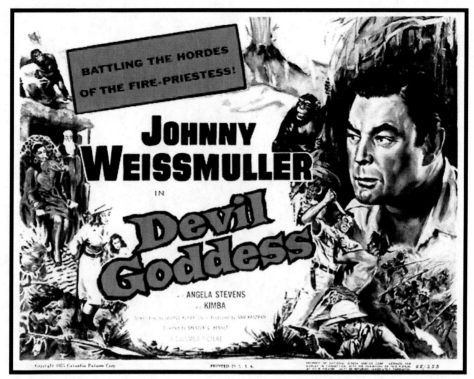

BATTLING THE HORDES OF THE FIRE-PRIESTESS!

JOHNNY WEISSMULLER

IN

Devil Goddess

with ANGELA STEVENS and KIMBA

Copyright 1955 Columbia Pictures Corp.   PRINTED IN U. S. A.   65/353

Mutiny footage. The yarn involves a search for a missing scientist who may have aligned himself with a fire-worshipping cult. Also recycled are moments from *Mark of the Gorilla*, *Captive Girl*, *Pygmy Island*, *Jungle Manhunt*, *Voodoo Tiger* and *Killer Ape*, in addition to outside-source stock footage. Also recycled are the usual Samoans-as-Africans. No one expected the series to continue beyond this point—Weissmuller already had announced his retirement—and thus *Devil Goddess*, however desultory in execution, takes on the tone of a valedictory film.

Even *The Motion Picture Herald* proved tolerant, calling Weissmuller's performance "characteristically convincing" and "ever-resourceful," praising the film's attitude as "a tongue-in-cheek adventure, in the best old-fashioned traditional classification," and asserting that "the younger elements in any audience—as well as the young in heart—will find much to hold dear." And so today do many old-timers and new discoverers alike find a redeeming charm in this raggedy series of unlikely exploits.

CREDITS: Producer: Sam Katzman; Director: Spencer Gordon Bennet; Assistant Director: Leonard Katzman; Screenplay: George Plympton; Based Upon a Story by: Dwight V. Babcock; Photographed by: Henry Freulich; Art Director: Paul Palmentola; Editor: Henry Batista; Special Effects: Jack Erickson; Decor: Sidney Clifford; Musical Director: Mischa Bakaleinikoff; Production Manager: Leon Chooluck; Sound: Harry R. Smith; Running Time: 70 minutes; Released: During October of 1955

CAST: Johnny Weissmuller (Johnny Weissmuller); Angela Stevens (Nora Blakely); Selmer Jackson (Prof. Carl Blakely); William Tannen (Nels Comstock); Ed Hinton (Joseph Leopold); William M. Griffith (Ralph Dixon); Abel Fernandez (Teinusi); Frank Lackteen

(Nkruma); Vera M. Francis (Sarabna); Max Reid (Kirundi Chief); Paul Marion (Matua Chief); John Cason, George Berkely, Lynton Brent (Henchmen); and Sue England

• **The *Jungle Jim* Teleseries (1955)**—And to keep the *Jim*s in perspective, here is a laundry-list rundown of Johnny Weissmuller's television installments in character as the intrepid jungle-dweller. The players also include Martin Huston as Skipper, a sort of Jungle Jim, Jr., and Norman Frederic as a tribal chum named Kaseem:

The Avenger—Jungle Jim hires out to lead a panther hunt.

Blood Money—Jungle Jim undertakes a dangerous mission for charitable purposes.

Code of the Jungle—An envious Tamba the Chimp abandons a pet dog to the mercies of the jungle.

The Deadly Idol—An intruder attempts to bilk a native tribe out of its sacred totem.

The Eyes of Manobo—Manobo is a sacred idol; its eyes are precious jewels. Hence the title, and hence a state of war over possession of the treasure.

A Fortune in Ivory—Skipper and an old-maid schoolteacher tangle with ivory thieves.

Gift of Evil—Skipper becomes a guide for a bad-medicine man.

Golden Parasol—Tamba the Chimp is accused of stealing a royal umbrella, a hanging crime in this particular backwater.

Jungle Justice—A friend of Kaseem is charged with theft from a tribal benevolent fund.

The King's Ghost—Jungle Jim finds himself at large in New Guinea.

The Lagoon of Death—Jim is at the mercy of crooks intent upon stealing the sacred treasure, if not the secret recipes, of a cannibalistic tribe.

Land of Terror—Jim stumbles onto a last outpost of prehistoric beasts.

The Leopard's Paw—An ooga-booga Bar Mitzvah awaits a tribal youth who must kill a leopard in order to be pronounced a *mensch*.

Man Killer—A playboy dilettante explorer wounds a lion but allows it to escape. As usual, Jim must clean up somebody else's mess lest a tribal uprising result.

The Power of Darkness—Jungle Jim, Skipper, Kaseem and Tamba join a Himalayan expedition, intent upon witnessing a solar eclipse from higher ground. Captured by the surviving thugs of a lost civilization, the party must rely upon Jim's quick-thinking ability to plagiarize the legacy of H. Rider Haggard.

Weissmuller and Martin Huston in the *Jungle Jim* teleseries

Precious Cargo—Jim finds an abandoned baby and tries to locate the parents lest the kid grow up to become another Tarzan.

Return of the Tauregs—Jungle Jim tracks down a slave trader who has abducted a safari guide. With Byron Foulger, a key character actor in the *Forgotten Horrors* canon.

Sacred Scarab—Gangsters posing as Interpol agents snooker Jungle Jim into guiding them to the scene of a mysterious plane crash.

Safari Into Danger—Jungle Jim hires out to a safari intending to capture animals for a circus. The expeditioners run afoul of a warlike Pygmy tribe.

The Silver Locket—Jim finds evidence that might solve a long-ago case of a vanished child.

Striped Fury—Jim, Skipper and their circle tangle with terrorism and a rampaging tiger while visiting India.

Treasure of the Amazon—Jungle Jim and Skipper set out for the Lower Americas in search of a lost Incan city. The consequent perils keep Jim busier than a one-legged Mayan in an Aztec-kicking contest.

Voodoo Drums—Jungle Jim, having secured an armistice with a pugnacious tribe, is appalled to hear the beat of war drums issuing from the village.

White Magic—A youthful native whom Jim had sent to medical school returns as a full-fledged doctor. The tribal witch doctor revolts against this outside influence.

Wild Man of the Jungle –Jim is summoned to put down the threat of a predatory man-like creature.

ANGEL ON THE AMAZON

a.k.a.: Drums Along the Amazon; The Jungle Wilderness
(Republic Pictures Corp.)

A one-woman Shangri-La situation and a persuasive jungle-adventure setting lend a mournful weirdness and an air of doomed romance to John H. Auer's *Angel on the Amazon*. The lovely but dramatically limited Vera Hruba Ralston plays an unlikely jungle-dweller whose rescue of a group of plane-crash survivors precipitates a strange crisis.

In the Amazon region near Manáos, Christine Ridgeway (Miss Ralston) is leading a motorized hunting party in search of a panther when one of her vehicles breaks down. She radios for service, and the responding plane cracks up in the jungle. The passengers, including pilot Jim Warburton (George Brent) and Dr. Karen Adams (Constance Bennett), are threatened by a hostile tribe, but Christine and her guide, Paulo (Alfonso Bedoya), intervene. Warburton's fascination with Christine becomes obsessive after she departs without so much as a by-your-leave.

Reconnecting with Christine in Rio, Warburton invites her to dine. She becomes agitated after a middle-aged man presents her with an affectionate note. The man reappears later, as Christine is visiting with Warburton and Dr. Adams over breakfast at a restaurant, and Christine collapses. Warburton catches up with the man, who identifies himself as one

Don Sebastian Ortega (Fortunio Bonanova), who had been a friend of Christine's jungle-explorer parents. Ortega seems amazed to notice how closely Christine resembles her mother.

Long ago, Ortega explains, Anthony Ridgeway and his bride were attacked by a panther while on safari, and the wife had found herself forced to knife the animal to death in order to save her husband. Intrigued by this story, Warburton journeys to California and looks up Anthony Ridgeway (Brian Aherne), who explains with weary candor that Christine is not his daughter, but his wife. Her natural aging processes, so Anthony reckons, had been halted by the shock of killing the panther. The couple had a daughter, Anthony reveals further, but the girl had committed suicide at age 20 upon learning that her fiancé had developed an infatuation with her ever-youthful mother.

French-Belgian release of *Angel on the Amazon*

Christine, meanwhile, has been so jolted by seeing Don Sebastian after all these years that she requires hospitalization. Finally in a semblance of recovery and now looking quite her age, Christine is reunited with Anthony at their daughter's gravesite.

The pervasive haunting qualities of *Angel on the Amazon* go a long way toward inviting suspension of disbelief. Producer-director Auer's belief in the outlandish notion is sufficiently infectious to spread readily to the players, and to the absorbed viewer. Maybe Poncé de Léon should have tangled with a panther or two, rather than tramping all over the Southeastern not-yet-United States in search of that Fountain of Youth.

A vividly applied background, ranging from the primitive settings to the more sophisticated realms of civilization, helps to put across the story, and Miss Ralston conveys adequately the loss of orientation that an ageless existence might inflict upon anybody. George Brent seems suitably confused as the would-be romancer. Brian Aherne registers touchingly as the abandoned husband who has aged normally while his wife has remained stranded in the bloom of youth. Aherne, like Brent and backup leading lady Constance Bennett, had seen better days with the larger studios.

Budapest-born John Auer, an all-round filmmaking talent whose career ranged well into the 1950s and the rise of network television, is responsible for an essential film within the *Forgotten Horrors* collection, 1935's *The Crime of Dr. Crespi*.

The working title of *Angel on the Amazon* was *Drums Along the Amazon*, which became the film's release title in the United Kingdom. A slightly trimmed reissue of 1954 would bear the name of *The Jungle Wilderness*.

CREDITS: Producer and Director: John H. Auer; Assistant Director: Lee Lukather; Screenplay: Lawrence Kimble; Based Upon a Story by: Earl Felton; Photographed by: Reggie Lanning; Musical Score: Nathan Scott; Musical Director: Morton Scott; Editor: Richard L. Van Enger; Art Director: James Sullivan; Decor: John McCarthy, Jr., and George Milo; Hair Stylist: Peggy Gray; Makeup: Bob Mark; Production Manager: Lewis "Lew" Ross; Sound: Victor B. Appel and Howard Wilson; Special Effects: Howard Lydecker and Theodore Lydecker; Stills: Don Keyes; Operative Cameraman: Herb Kirkpatrick; Grip: Nels Mathias; Script Supervisor: Dorothy Yutzi; Running Time: 86 minutes; Released: Following New York Opening on December 27, 1948

CAST: George Brent (Jim Warburton); Vera Ralston (Christine Ridgeway); Brian Aherne (Anthony Ridgeway); Constance Bennett (Dr. Karen Lawrence); Fortunio Bonanova (Don Sebastian Ortega); Alfonso Bedoya (Paulo); Gus Schilling (Dean Hartley); Richard Crane (Johnny MacMahon); Walter Reed (Jerry Adams); Ross Elliott (Frank Lane); Konstantin Shayne (Dr. Jungmeyer); Charles La Torre (Waiter); John Trebach (Waiter); Elizabeth Dunne (Housekeeper); Alberto Morin (Radio Operator); Dickie Jones (George); Alfredo DeSa (Reporter); Tony Martinez (Bell); Gerardo Sei Groves (Native); Manuel París (Clerk)

THE BOY WITH GREEN HAIR
(Dore Schary Productions/RKO-Radio Pictures, Inc.)

Dore Schary had risen impressively within the Hollywood studio ranks since his Depression-era days as a $250-a-script potboiler scenarist. He became a producer wielding considerable influence from a left-of-center political stance. Schary's independent moorings were more firmly anchored (at RKO-Radio) than those of the typical such studio boss.

But to regard the indie/corporate scene in a larger perspective: Even the budget-bound independent producer Sam Katzman had found the industry's postwar turmoil to provide a boost into a major-studio berth for the long haul. The Columbia Pictures Corp. that would have given Katzman the bum's rush during the earlier 1940s—when he was aligned with that stepchild-of-the-racket, Monogram Pictures—had become a welcoming environment, thanks largely to Katzman's lucrative *Superman* serials and his new cash-cow franchise with *Jungle Jim*.

Schary, though a kindred soul to Katzman in the sense that both sought sensational and exploitable gimmicks, was nonetheless the classier maverick: The gulf between Katzman's apolitical *schlock* and Schary's politicized *kitsch* runs wide. Deep, too.

Schary had become an in-house/independent producer, then overall chief of production, at RKO-Radio Pictures before Howard Hughes seized control of the studio. Schary mounted *The Boy with Green Hair* during February-March of 1948 as a rather preachy tolerance/anti-war fable, holding to a moderate budget that director Joseph Losey pegged at $850,000-plus. The figure would have been substantially more, had producer Stephen Ames not been a shareholder in the Technicolor company and thus entitled to a markdown. One can't have a green-haired boy cavorting about in black-and-white.

Schary also subscribed to RKO's established cost-cutting practice of re-using sets and properties from bigger pictures—in this instance, chiefly, 1948's *I Remember Mama*. A costly indulgence was a $10,000 fee for the use of Eben Ahbez' oddly melodic song "Nature Boy," which had provided a hit for Nat "King" Cole the year previous. The song—charming to some, annoying to others, but haunting in any event—nearly was removed during a failed attempt at post-production revisions; it survives as a main-title theme.

Peter Frye (Dean Stockwell), a war orphan who believes himself merely separated from his

Dreams That Money Can Buy

Please Don't Tell Why
His Hair Turned Green!
... after you've seen

A DORE SCHARY PRESENTATION

THE BOY WITH
GREEN HAIR

Color by TECHNICOLOR

PAT   ROBERT   BARBARA   DEAN
O'BRIEN · RYAN · HALE · STOCKWELL
as THE BOY

RICHARD LYON   Produced by STEPHEN AMES   Directed by JOSEPH LOSEY

parents, is booted about from relative to relative until at last he finds a home with a family elder, Gramp Frye (Pat O'Brien). Having learned via cruel gossip of his folks' death, Peter wakes one morning to find that his hair has turned green. (Neither the screenplay nor its source-story literalizes an explanation for this phenomenon, but guesswork ranges from the child's suggestible nature to a batch of tainted milk.) Rendered an outcast on account of the transformation, Peter experiences a dreamlike encounter that leads him to believe his altered aspect carries a responsibility to speak out against warfare. Which renders him still more an outcast. Finally, he consents to have his head shaved—then runs away in the belief that even Gramp has betrayed him.

Having explained his ordeal, now, while in custody of the police, Peter finds Gramp waiting to bring him home.

Schary, as executive producer, had attached producer Adrian Scott (of the social-issue thriller *Crossfire*) to *The Boy with Green Hair*, only to find Scott sacked by RKO, along with director Edward Dmytryk, in view of their hostile dealings with the House Un-American Activities Committee. Stephen Ames stepped in as producer while Joseph Losey—himself due for a HUAC blacklisting, come 1951—filled the directing job that likelier would have gone to Dmytryk, or so Dmytryk once informed us. Losey's breakthrough as a feature-film helmer would cause him no end of hassles down the line: *The Boy with Green Hair* was cited often by HUAC's Red-baiters as proof positive that Losey must be a Communist subversive.

The film bends leftward, certainly—but it is too over-obvious in its naïve arguments to qualify as any act of subterfuge. Where intellect fails, the yarn resorts to emotional manipulation as its means of persuasion. The script took so long in development—Betsy Beaton's story had been acquired fresh off the presses, in 1946—that it should have turned out less heavy-handed. But Schary and Losey and Scott (for as long as he could last at RKO) and screenwriters Ben Barzman and Alfred Lewis Levitt hammered so stubbornly at the script that its more coherent discrimination allegory became subordinate to an awkward plea for pacifism. Even so, the film never turns too treacly or maudlin and plays out almost like something from the Disney machine.

Dean Stockwell, on loan from MGM, handles the title role with innocence and gumption, matching the natural-kid air of Bobby Driscoll in *The Window* (1949) or Jimmy Hunt in *Invaders from Mars* (1953). Stockwell's dome shaving is real, but the green hair is a set of wigs. This amenity enabled the use of one wig for shooting while the others were being dressed and repaired. This is a practical method that RKO-Radio Pictures had developed during 1932–1933, in the preparation of backup animation models for *King Kong*.

"We didn't want Dean being laughed at in real life with a color job," Losey would recall in times more recent. "Having his head shaved slick was hassle enough. So we fixed him up with the green-hair wigs for the shoot and a natural-color wig for when he was off duty."

Pat O'Brien makes a blessedly Irish Gramp Frye, working Vaudeville routines and Gaelic folk-songs into his performance to winning effect. Memorable supporting work comes from Walter Catlett, who shares a delightful musical sequence with O'Brien; and from Samuel S. Hinds, Regis Toomey and Barbara Dale. Stars-in-waiting Russ (Rusty) Tamblyn and Dale (Dayle) Robertson can be spotted in their debut assignments.

The Boy with Green Hair had been all but completed when Howard Hughes came lurching into ownership of RKO during the spring of 1948. Categorically opposed to message-driven movies, Hughes singled out *The Boy with Green Hair* as a special whipping-post. Studio chairman Floyd Odlum, playing a more compliant Charlie McCarthy to Hughes' thuggish Edgar Bergen, amplified that order with a call that the film should preach preparedness for war.

No such alterations could occur, of course, without an outright scalping. Hughes settled for a little bit off the top and sides. Having caught the picture at a trade-show screening in November, *Variety* couldn't quite fathom why all the fuss: "[I]t's reported to be toned down somewhat, [but] none of this intramural stuff is evident."

By now, Dore Schary had quit RKO in disgust. He would remain a part-indie/part-corporate player, however, and by 1951 he had pulled off a power play all his own, usurping the throne of Louis B. Mayer at MGM. Even the most pacifistic producers accept Hollywood as a perpetual war zone, and Schary picked his occasional fights strategically and saw them through.

CREDITS: Executive Producer: Dore Schary; Producer: Stephen Ames; Director: Joseph Losey; Assistant Director: James Lane; Screenplay: Ben Barzman and Alfred Lewis Levitt; Based Upon: Betsy Beaton's 1946 Story, as Published in *This Week* Magazine; Photographed by: George Barnes; Musical Score: Leigh Harline; Musical Director: Constantin Bakaleinikoff; Orchestrations: Gil Grau; Songs: "Nature Boy," by Eben Ahbez, and the Traditional "Tail o' Me Coat" and "Gyp, Gyp, My Little Horse"; Editor: Frank Doyle; Art Directors: Ralph Berger and Albert S. D'Agostino; Decor: Darrell Silvera and William Stevens; Costumer: Adele Balkan; Makeup: Gordon Bau; Hair Stylist: Hazel Rogers; Production Manager: Ruby Rosenberg; Sound: Clem Portman and Earl Wolcott; Color Process Director: Natalie Kalmus; Associate Color Process Director: Morgan Padelford; Script Supervisor: Richard Kinon; Operative Cameraman: Eddie Pyle; Stills: Rod Tolmie; Grip: Ralph Wildman; Running Time: 82 minutes; Released: December 27, 1948

CAST: Pat O'Brien (Gramp Frye); Robert Ryan (Dr. Evans); Barbara Hale (Miss Brand); Dean Stockwell (Peter Frye); Richard Lyon (Michael); Walter Catlett (the King); Samuel S. Hinds (Dr. Knudson); Regis Toomey (Davis); Charles Meredith (Piper); David Clarke (Barber); Billy Sheffield (Red); John Calkins (Danny); Teddy Infuhr (Timmy); Dwayne Hickman (Joey); Eilene Janssen (Peggy); Curtis Jackson (Classmate); Charles Arnt

And no, they (whoever they are) sure enough don't make 'em like they used to—the movies or the showplaces. A first run engagement of *The Boy with Green Hair* at Baltimore's Senator Theatre, one of the few major film palaces still going strong today and now on the National Register of Historic Places.

(Hammond); Don Pietro (Newsboy); Patricia Byrnes, Carol Coombs, Cynthia Robichaux, Georgette Crooks and Donna Jo Gribble (Girls); Billy White, Rusty [Russ] Tamblyn, Baron White, Speer Martin and Michael Losey (Boys); Al Murphy (Janitor); Anna Q. Nilsson and Lynn Whitney (Women); Eula Guy (Mrs. Fisher); Kenneth Patterson, Brick Sullivan and Dayle [Dale] Robertson (Cops); Carl Saxe (Plainclothesman); Sharon Mc-Manus (Crying Girl); Ann Carter (Eva); Howard Brody (Eva's Brother); Ray Burkett and Warren Shannon (Old-Timers); Dianna Graeff (Tiny Girl); Roger Perry (Small Boy); Wendy Oser (Frail Girl); Charles Lane (Passer-by); Max Rose (Man); and Peter Brocco, William Smith

RECOMMENDED VIDEO SOURCES

The purpose of such books as the *Forgotten Horrors* volumes is less to array a pageant of under-the-radar movies, than to help redirect the reader's radar to the purpose of discovery. Spare us the reactionary nostalgia of *Auld Lang Sayonara*, and where's the fun if we're the only ones watching these titles? Many of the pertinent films—some impertinent ones, too—can be found via such helpful sources as these:

Life Is a Movie—The Web catalogue of www.lifeisamovie.com is an enriching source, run by movie buffs for movie buffs, that has yielded fresh screenings of many of the deep-cuts obscurities in the past-present-future realms of *Forgotten Horrors*. Life Is a Movie's perfectly navigable Net site will have undergone a thorough refinement by the time these words appear in print.

Alpha Video—Web-based at www.oldies.com, Alpha Video has become a progressive voice in the popular rediscovery of Old Hollywood as a wellhead of B-movie treasures, with direct-order access and generalized storefront retail distribution. Alpha's distinctive sleeve designs are among the best-looking DVD jackets on the market.

Hollywood's Attic—A tenured presence in the home-video realm, helpfully allied with Life Is a Movie (above) and known for titles of great scarcity—such as *The Black Book*, which will be a key entry in *Forgotten Horrors*' No. 5 collection. URL: www.hollywoodsattick.com

VCI Entertainment—VCI/Liberty Home Video is the oldest independent home-video outfit in the United States—the first, for example, to place such essential titles as *The Dark Eyes of London* and *Chamber of Horrors* before a new massed audience, as early as 1980. VCI's momentum continues apace, with a library of more than 2,500 titles. URL: www.vcientertainment.com

ArtHouse, Inc.—Finely remastered *avant-garde* rarities, in pricey but projection-caliber video transfers—the obliging source of our reference copy of this volume's pivotal selection, *Dreams That Money Can Buy*. Seewww.arthouseinc.com

Sinister Cinema—A pioneering source, dating from Back in the Day when scarcely anybody else was unearthing the Poverty Row rarities for popular consumption—and the first video label to introduce a *Forgotten Horrors* department. Web site:www.sinistercinema.com

ABOUT THE AUTHORS

Michael H. Price first began mining the *Forgotten Horrors* lode in 1975, in collaboration with the film historian-turned-filmmaker George E. Turner. The first such book, published in 1979, has become a perennial and influential collection, casting an unprecedented light onto ill-explored corners of film history. *Forgotten Horrors* yielded a sequel in 2001, then a third volume in 2003. This fourth book expands the overall sweep to a period spanning 1929–1948. Price, a veteran newspaperman and founder of Texas' Fort Worth Film Festival, has recently completed the collaborative graphic novel *Fishhead*, a horrific Southern Gothic; *Mantan the Funnyman*, a biography of the pioneering black comedian Mantan Moreland; and *Daynce of the Peckerwoods*, a study of Texas' indigenous music-making traditions. Price & Turner's graphic novella, *The Ancient Southwest & Other Dispatches from a Cruel Frontier*, has recently arrived from Texas Christian University Press. Price's weekly film commentaries for *The Business Press* of Fort Worth can be found, both fresh and preserved, on the Web at www.fortworthbusinesspress.com.

John Wooley, a prolific novelist, journalist and scriptwriter, joined Price as co-author of the *Forgotten Horrors* books following the death of George Turner in 1999. The Price & Wooley projects also include *The Big Book of Biker Flicks* (2004), *Forgotten Horrors 3: Dr. Turner's House of Horrors* (2003), and a recurring *Forgotten Horrors* column for *Fangoria* magazine. Wooley's recent solo books include *Ghost Band*, *From the Blue Devils to Red Dirt: The Colors of Oklahoma Music*, *Awash in the Blood* and *Dark Within*, in addition to a well-received reissue of his breakthrough collaborative novel of 1982, *Old Fears*. Wooley's radio program, *Swing on This*, airs weekly over Tulsa's KWGS–FM (www.kwgs.org) as a showcase for Western swing and other South-by-Southwestern musical forms. Updates: www.johnwooley.com.

INDEX

Dreams That Money Can Buy

Dreams That Money Can Buy